T0289958

PORTFOLIO SELECTION
AND
ASSET PRICING

PORTFOLIO SELECTION

AND

ASSET PRICING

MODELS OF FINANCIAL ECONOMICS AND THEIR APPLICATIONS IN INVESTING

JAMIL BAZ
HELEN GUO
EROL HAKANOGLU

New York   Chicago   San Francisco   Athens   London
Madrid   Mexico City   Milan   New Delhi
Singapore   Sydney   Toronto

1 2 3 4 5 6 7 8 9   LCR   27 26 25 24 23 22

ISBN   978-1-264-27015-6
MHID   1-264-27015-1

e-ISBN   978-1-264-27016-3
e-MHID   1-264-27016-X

This publication is designed to provide accurate and authoritative information in regard to the subject matter covered. It is sold with the understanding that neither the author nor the publisher is engaged in rendering legal, accounting, securities trading, or other professional services. If legal advice or other expert assistance is required, the services of a competent professional person should be sought.
> —*From a Declaration of Principles Jointly Adopted by a Committee of the American Bar Association and a Committee of Publishers and Associations*

Library of Congress Cataloging-in-Publication Data
Names: Baz, Jamil, author. | Guo, Helen, author. | Hakanoglu, Erol, author.
   Title: Portfolio selection and asset pricing / [by Jamil Baz, Helen Guo, Erol Hakanoglu]
Description: New York : McGraw Hill Education, [2022] | Includes bibliographical references and index.
Identifiers: LCCN 2021052846 (print) | LCCN 2021052847 (ebook) | ISBN 9781264270156 (hardback) | ISBN 9781264270163 (ebook)
Subjects: LCSH: Derivative securities. | Capital assets pricing model.
Classification: LCC HG6024.A3 B397 2022 (print) | LCC HG6024.A3 (ebook) | DDC 332.63/2—dc23/eng/20211103
LC record available at https://lccn.loc.gov/2021052846
LC ebook record available at https://lccn.loc.gov/2021052847

To Zeina, Maurice, Elena, and Alexandra,
with love and admiration.
J.B.

To Yazhen and Zhijun who gave me life
and Adam and Daniel who gave my life new meaning.
H.G.

To Silvia, Aviva, and Orli, with all my love.
E.H.

Contents

PART I
Mathematical Foundations

PART II
Portfolio Models

PART III
Asset Pricing

PART IV
Asset Allocation in Practice

Introduction

Portfolio selection and asset pricing are the centerpieces of finance. If there is any hope to have fundamental theorems in financial economics, these two topics arguably provide the best opportunity. Yet, because financial markets constantly involve complex feedback between actors and models, the size of the gap between the fundamental results of mathematics and physics and those of finance is humbling.

How do we solve quantitative problems? In the realm of mathematics, we formulate rigorous theorems and prove their validity with little left to approximation. Chemistry and physics are built on fundamental laws and theorems that are amenable to rigorous experimental verification, such as Newton's laws of motion and thermodynamics, Maxwell's equations of electricity and magnetism, and Einstein's general relativity theory.

When we move away from pure mathematics, in order to formulate and verify our understanding of nature, we rely on models of reality, built either physically or as thought experiments. If mathematics lies at one end of the spectrum of sciences, economics and finance belong at the other end. In the latter, the models need to account for quirky human behavior, which at times does not even obey basic building blocks of logic such as transitivity.

Compared with mathematics or the physical sciences, the fundamental laws of financial economics are just a valiant attempt to make sense of messy data and behaviors. We try hard to do the best we can. After all, instead of universal constants such as π, Avogadro's number N, gravitational constant g, speed of light c, and Planck's constant h, we must deal with the short-term interest rate set by a subordinate deity who runs the Federal Reserve.

Jorge Luis Borges, a brilliant and sometimes delirious writer of the twentieth century, imagined a realm where the science of map making becomes so precise that only a one-to-one scale is acceptable—acceptable but wholly impractical, even if possible.[1] In this book, we will settle for less than perfect models of portfolios and assets and their interconnections.

Asset Pricing

Asset pricing is about connecting payoffs in future states of the world with the right discount rate. Most interesting pricing problems involve uncertainty around these states of the world and a stochastic discount rate.

In pricing assets, general equilibrium models and consumption-based models help us determine prices for assets based on fundamental risk factors in the economy, such as the capital asset pricing model and the family of models derived from it. Financial markets abound with observable prices for a plethora of assets. Some assets are more easily valued relative to their observably priced reference assets. The Black–Scholes–Merton option pricing model exemplifies these type of valuation methodologies.

Portfolio Selection

From the management of pension funds to personal finances, from corporate capital structure management to sovereign asset-liability management, from insurance company asset portfolio management to endowment and sovereign wealth fund management, literally billions of people around the globe directly or indirectly depend on portfolio selection. We will attempt to present the fundamentals of portfolio selection that evolved into an impressive body of work over the past seven decades.

Once the groundwork is laid, we will discuss portfolio selection theories in depth, studying their interconnections and differences. The efficacy of any model hinges on its theoretical construct and on the realism and accuracy of its inputs. We focus on statistical approaches that help us attain that realism and accuracy, such as robust estimation. In discussing implementation issues, we

---

1 J. L. Borges, "On Exactitude in Science," in *A Universal History of Infamy*. New York: Penguin, 1975.

will describe the leading methodologies in the field and differentiate between them critically.

. . .

The finance literature is home to a vast number of texts on asset pricing and portfolio selection. The focus of these texts is mostly on only one of the two; in only a few cases are both considered together. Our aim is to take the latter approach while demonstrating pathways from one to the other and vice versa and while treating theory and applications holistically.

You should be familiar with the language of mathematics to get the best out of this book. We assume competence in the fundamentals of multivariate calculus, differential equations, linear algebra, probability, and statistics. Having said that, Part I of this text is dedicated to a review and extension of these fundamentals. If you are familiar with relevant topics, you can skim through Part I and jump to Part II without missing the essence of this book.

The intended audience of this text includes advanced undergraduates in mathematics, economics, finance, and engineering; MBA students with a quantitative bent; students in financial engineering master's programs; doctoral students in mathematical economics, finance, and financial engineering; and practitioners in the financial industry interested in quantitative finance and economics.

This book is divided in four parts. Even though they could be appreciated independently, we believe that going through each individually is most beneficial. We have written the chapters so that they are as self-contained as practically possible. In this spirit, each chapter has a summary of contents up front. We outline the four parts as follows:

In Part I, we lay out the mathematical foundations of the theories and practical applications that make up the rest of the text. The idea is to provide a compact introduction to many concepts of mathematical analysis that lurk in the background, sometimes hardly visible yet fundamental to the development of modern finance. We rely on well-known texts in summarizing definitions, theorems, and their proofs, which we believe promote a thorough understanding of what follows.

In Part II, we cover portfolio selection models. The fundamental concepts and theories are laid out in detail in single-period and continuous-time settings. In what we believe is an interestingly novel treatment, the last section of Chapter 7 is dedicated to analogies and correspondences between the concepts and theories discussed in earlier chapters.

In Part III, we describe the fundamental theories and concepts behind asset pricing, starting with equilibrium models and moving on to factor models before delving into derivatives pricing from the simple to the exotic. In this part, we also focus on interest-rate models and derivatives pricing associated with fixed-income markets. The part concludes with the intricate concept of risk premia.

Part IV is where we move to the practice of portfolio selection. Despite the intuitive appeal of many quantitative models, over the years we have observed that practitioners are often reluctant to apply them in practice. In this part, we analyze the key issues methodically and offer solutions that have had a good track record in practice.

It's important in any book to appeal to readers. Italo Calvino, a true Italian master of literature who embodied the word *simpatico*, was asked to deliver the 1985 Norton Lectures at Harvard. The honor led to the writing of his ultimate book, *Six Memos for the Next Millennium*, a compendium of six lectures, each addressing a quintessential quality for a writer to impart on a text: lightness, quickness, exactitude, visibility, multiplicity, and consistency.[2] We tried to abide by all six, yet it is the first lecture from the sextet that we took to heart as we tried to lighten the weight from the narrative as much as we could.

---

2 I. Calvino, *Six Memos for the New Millennium*. Boston: Harvard University Press, 1988. Italo Calvino passed away just before completing the final "memo" and could not actually deliver the much-anticipated lectures in September 1985.

Acknowledgments

We start by extending special thanks to Emmanuel Roman for his friendship. The coauthors would not have met without his intercession, and this project owes much to his encouragement and intelligent guidance.

Robert Merton had a profound influence on the authors and hence on this manuscript. His work was foundational in every aspect of asset pricing, derivatives, and portfolio theory. We are, as ever, in his debt.

We are beholden to many people who have helped us in our intellectual formation, our professional growth, and our life journey. We thank them from our hearts and minds.

First are our teachers, some of whom have left us: Takeshi Amemiya, Kenneth Arrow, Fischer Black, Michael Boskin, Roger Brockett, Robert Dorfman, Robert Ferrandier, Harry Gregor, Yu-Chi Ho, Lawrence Lau, John Lintner, Andrew Lo, Franco Modigliani, Peter Rogers, and Jean-Luc Vila.

Then there are our colleagues past and present: Ramasastry Ambarish, Armen Avanessians, Driss Ben Brahim, Jonathan Berk, Thomas Brennan, Eric Briys, Terry Burnham, Jean-Paul Calamaro, George Chacko, Josh Davis, Sanjiv Das, François Degeorge, Ludovic Feuillet, Normane Gillmann, Nick Granger, Mahmoud Hajo, Campbell Harvey, Lloyd Han, Dan Ivascyn, Soraya Kazziha, Sean Klein, Vincent Koen, Sudi Mariappa, René Martel, Ravi Mattu, Scott McDermott, Nikola Miljkovic, Ben Mills, Arun Muralidhar, Vasant Naik, Michael Pascutti, Brian Pinto, Vlad Putyatin, Scott Pinkus, German Ramirez, Steve Sapra, Lester Seigel, Nassim Taleb, Jason Tilroe, Jerry Tsai, Emmin Shung, Sadek Wahba, Larry Wieseneck, Richard Witten, Francis Yared, Ziqi Zhang, and Wentao Zhao.

We cannot stop thanking our colleague Zhifeng Wang for an incredible amount of excellent work that went into this book throughout the process, improving its quality significantly. Our colleague Tarek Nassar pored through the manuscript with diligence and provided us with excellent suggestions. As such, they both have to take responsibility for all remaining mistakes.

We also thank our colleague Tony Crescenzi for introducing us to McGraw Hill and Stephen Isaacs and Judith Newlin for being the best editors any author could ever hope to have on their side. Our thanks also go to Patricia Wallenburg from TypeWriting who has done a terrific job in the many aspects of the production of this book.

We are immensely thankful to our families for all the love and support they have given us throughout our lives and during this project in particular.

This book came together in a most difficult year. The pandemic took a lot from all of us. We consider ourselves lucky to have worked together so harmoniously while getting to know each other more throughout the process. We acknowledge the tremendous support we found in each other throughout our adventure. In particular, we shared movies as a means of sustenance. Films by Robert Bresson, Carl Dreyer, Krzysztof Kieślowski, Yasujirō Ozu, Andrei Tarkovsky, and Béla Tarr gave us ample food for thought, and discussing them helped keep our spirits up. Also, we owe film directors Ernst Lubitsch and Billy Wilder many gifts of laughter. We marveled at the wit and lightness of these emigrants from central Europe who understood so much about their time and society.

PORTFOLIO SELECTION
AND
ASSET PRICING

PART I

Mathematical Foundations

1

Functional Analysis in Real Vector Spaces

Summary

The primary mathematical idea behind portfolio selection theory and practice is optimization. Functional analysis, which is the study of vector spaces in finite and infinite dimensions using concepts and insights from linear algebra, analysis, and geometry, serves as the mathematical basis for theories and optimization models of portfolio selection.[1] Representation, projection, duality, extension, and separating-hyperplane theorems form the analytic basis for a significant portion of resource and asset allocation, planning, optimal control, approximation, and estimation problems in financial economics. Optimization theory could be developed in finite-dimensional Euclidean space using elementary geometric concepts and intuitions. As the complexity of the underlying problems increases, extension to infinite-dimensional spaces becomes indispensable.

---

1 The following are standard symbolic abbreviations used throughout this part: $\forall$ is "for all"; $\in$ is "in"; $\ni$ is "such that"; $\exists$ is "there exists"; $\equiv$ is "defined as"; $\neq$ is "not equal to"; $\nexists$ is "there does not exist"; $\varnothing$ is "empty set"; $\cap$ is "intersection"; $\cup$ is "union"; $\subset$ is "subset"; $\Longrightarrow$ is "implies"; $\leftrightarrow$ is "if and only if"; and $\blacksquare$ is "quod erat demonstrandum" or "QED," which means "that which has been proven."

Such underlying complexity is the reason for going through the trouble of introducing Hilbert spaces, for example. In the projection theorem, the simple geometric concept in our three-dimensional Euclidean space—that the shortest distance from a point to a plane is the perpendicular—is extended to spaces of higher and infinite dimensions by moving the concept to Hilbert space. There are numerous applications of these extensions to financial economics problems such as least squares and other estimation problems. The same is true of the separation theorems that are fundamental to capital asset pricing.

If you are familiar with basic functional analysis or are not interested in a more mathematical treatment, you could skim through this chapter or skip it without loss of generality. We draw heavily from excellent textbooks on these topics, including Bartle (1966), Bartle and Sherbert (2010), Lang (1969), Lasdon (1970), Luenberger (1969), and Rudin (1987, 1991).

1.1 Vector Spaces

1.1.1 Basic Properties and Definitions

A vector space V is a set of elements called *vectors* together with the operations of addition and scalar multiplication. If x, y, z are vectors in V and a, b are scalars, the following axioms would be satisfied by the set V and the two operations:

Commutative law:	$x + y = y + x$
Associative law:	$(x + y) + z = x + (y + z)$
Null vector $\overline{0}$ (addition)[2]:	$x + \overline{0} = x$, where $\overline{0} \in V$
Scalar multiplications 0 and 1:	$0x = \overline{0}$, $1x = x$
Distributive law I:	$a(x + y) = ax + ay$
Distributive law II:	$(a + b)x = ax + bx$
Associative law:	$(ab)x = a(bx)$

For every $x \in V$, there exists an element $-x \in V$ called the *additive inverse* of x such that $x + (-x) = \overline{0}$.

---

2 We will suppress the vector notation $\overline{0}$ to describe the null vector when the context is clear.

In any vector space, the following properties hold:

$$x + y = x + z \Rightarrow y = z$$
$$ax = ay, a \neq 0 \Rightarrow x = y$$
$$ax = bx, x \neq 0 \Rightarrow a = b$$
$$(a - b)x = ax - bx$$
$$a(x - y) = ax - ay$$
$$a\overline{0} = \overline{0}$$

1.1.2 Simple Examples of Vector Spaces

Example 1: Given the set of real numbers $\Re$ and the applicability of the standard definition of addition, as well as that of multiplication by a scalar number, and the null vector equaling the real number zero, the set of real numbers (also known as the *real line*) is a one-dimensional vector space.

Example 2: We extend the first example into n-dimensional space by letting $V = \Re^n$ be the set of sequences or n-tuples of real numbers. With $x = (x_1, x_2, x_3, ...,$ $x_n)$ and $y = (y_1, y_2, y_3, ..., y_n)$ being n-tuples, we define $x + y = (x_1 + y_1, x_2 + y_2, ..., x_n + y_n)$. Let $a \in \Re$ and $aX = (ax_1, ax_2, ..., ax_n)$. We can see that the axioms for a vector space are satisfied.

Example 3: If we let V be the nonempty set of all real-valued functions and let f and g be such functions, we may define $f + g$ and af in the standard way to see that V is a vector space.

Example 4: Let us take the closed interval $[a,b] \subseteq \Re$. The collection of all real-valued functions forms a vector space. Let $x = y$ if $x(t) = y(t)$ for all $t \in [a,b]$. The null vector $\overline{0}$ is a function that is identically zero in the closed interval. If x, y are vectors in the space and c is a real scalar, $(x + y)(t) = x(t) + y(t)$ and $(cx)(t) = cx(t)$. It can easily be seen that these are continuous functions. This space is the vector space of real-valued continuous functions in the closed interval $[a, b]$.

1.1.3 Cartesian Products, Subspaces, and Combinations of Vector Spaces

A set of vector spaces could be combined to form a larger one. If V, W are vector spaces, the Cartesian product of V and W, $V \times W$, consists of ordered pairs

(v, w) with $v \in V$ and $w \in W$. The following addition and scalar multiplication properties hold in $V \times W$:

$$(v_1, w_1) + (v_2, w_2) = (v_1 + v_2, w_1 + w_2)$$
$$a(v,w) = (av, aw)$$

Clearly this can be extended to the product of n vector spaces $V_1, V_2, V_3, ..., V_n$. Further we denote the product of a vector space with itself n times as V^n.

A subset of vector space V that is not empty is called a *subspace S* of V if every vector $x, y \in S \Rightarrow ax + by \in S$ for any scalars a, b. The sum of two subsets S_1 and S_2 is $S_1 + S_2$ and consists of all vectors $s_1 + s_2$, $s_1 \in S_1$, $s_2 \in S_2$.

It can be easily proved that if S_1, S_2 are subspaces of vector space V, their intersection $S_1 \cap S_2$ is a subspace of V, as well as that their sum $S_1 + S_2$ is a subspace of V.[3] In a vector space, a linear combination of the vectors $x_1, x_2, x_3, ..., x_n$ with scalars $a_1, a_2, a_3, ..., a_n$ can be written as $\sum_{i=1}^{n} a_i x_i$. If S is a subspace of a vector space V, the set $\{S\}$ is called the *subspace generated by S* consisting of all vectors in V that are linear combinations of vectors in S. A simple way to think of subspaces is the notion of a plane or line through the origin. The *translation* of a subspace is the generalization of a plane or line and is referred to as a *linear variety* (or a *linear manifold* or an *affine subspace*). For a subspace S, a linear variety can be written as $S' = x_0 + S$, where $x_0 \in S$. The subspace S is unique, yet any vector in S' could be taken as x_0. The linear variety generated by a nonempty subspace S of vector space V could be defined as the intersection of all linear varieties in V contained in S.

1.1.4 Convexity

A set C in a linear vector space is *convex* if given $x_1, x_2 \in C$, all points $ax_1 + (1 - a)x_2 \in C$, where $0 \leq a \leq 1$. If C_1, C_2 are convex sets in a vector space, then

$$aC = \{x : x = ac, c \in C\}$$

3 $S_1 \cap S_2$ contains the null vector because it is contained in both spaces themselves; hence the intersection is not empty. If $v_1, v_2 \in S_1 \cap S_2$, they are both in S_1, S_2. For any scalars a,b, the vector $av_1 + bv_2$ is contained in both S_1 and S_2 because they are subspaces of V. Therefore, $av_1 + bv_2 \in S_1 \cap S_2$.

is convex for any scalar a, and

$$C_1 + C_2$$

is convex. For an arbitrary collection of convex sets, their intersection is also convex.[4]

1.1.5 Linear Independence

It is trivial to show that the necessary and sufficient condition for the set of vectors x_i, $i = 1, 2, ..., n$ to be linearly independent is that $\sum_{i=1}^{n} a_i x_i = 0 \Rightarrow a_i = 0$ for all $i = 1, 2, ..., n$. This implies that a vector expressed as a linear combination of linearly independent vectors can be expressed uniquely so. In other words, if vectors $x_i \ \forall i$ are linearly independent, and if $\sum_{i=1}^{n} a_i x_i = \sum_{i=1}^{n} b_i x_i$, then $a_i = b_i \ \forall i$.[5]

1.2 Metric Spaces

A *metric* is a function that defines the distance between any two members or points of a set called a *metric space*. Formally, a *metric* on a set X is a function $d: X \times X \rightarrow \Re$ with the following properties:

Positivity:	$d(x, y) \geq 0, \ \forall \ x, y \in X$
Definiteness:	$d(x, y) = 0 \Longleftrightarrow x = y$
Symmetry:	$d(x, y) = d(y, x), \ \forall \ x, y \in X$
Triangle inequality:	$d(x, y) \leq d(x, z) + d(z, y), \ \forall \ x, y, z \in X$

A *metric space* (X, d) is a set X together with a metric d on X.

Example 1: Normal Metric

$$d(x, y) \equiv |x - y|, \ \forall \ x, y \in \Re$$

---

4 The proof is trivial and left as an exercise for the reader.
5 The reader is encouraged to prove these simple propositions as an exercise.

Example 2: Euclidean Metric

If points $x \equiv (x_1, x_2)$ and $y \equiv (y_1, y_2) \in \mathcal{R}^2$, then $d(x, y) = \sqrt{(x_1 - y_1)^2 + (x_2 - y_2)^2}$.

Example 3: Maximum Metric

For the points x, y in Example 2, $d(x, y) \equiv \max(|x_1 - y_1|, |x_2 - y_2|)$.

Example 4: Discrete Metric

If X is a nonempty set and $x, y \in X$, then

$$d(x, y) = 0, \text{ if } x = y, \text{ and } d(x, y) = 1, \text{ if } x \neq y$$

Let us show that $d(x, y)$ is a metric. Again, the first three properties being trivially satisfied, we show how the fourth, the triangle inequality, holds:

When $x = y$, $d(x, y) = 0 \leq d(x, z) + d(z, y)$.
When $x \neq y$, $d(x, y) = 1 = \{d(x, z) \text{ or } d(z, y)\} \leq d(x, z) + d(z, y)$.

1.3 Open and Closed Sets

For the metric space (X, d), we define an *open ϵ-ball* of radius $\epsilon > 0$ centered at x as

$$B_\epsilon(x) = \{y \in X \mid d(x, y) < \epsilon\}$$

A point $w \in A \subseteq X$ is called an *interior point* of A if $\exists$ an $\epsilon > 0$ such that all points x satisfying $d(x, w) < \epsilon$ are in A. The collection of all interior points of A is the *interior* of A.

Set $A \subseteq X$ is called an *open set* if $\forall x \in A$, $\exists$ an open ϵ-ball with $B_\epsilon(x) \subseteq A$. $x \in X$ is called a *boundary or closure point* of A if $\forall \epsilon > 0$, $B_\epsilon(x) \cap A \neq \varnothing$ and $B_\epsilon(x) \cap A^c \neq \varnothing$, where $A^c \equiv$ *complement* of set $A \subseteq X$. The union of A and the collection of all boundary points of A is called the *closure* of A and is denoted by $\overline{A}$. Set A is called a *closed set* if A^c is open. A is open $\Longleftrightarrow A \cap$ (*all boundary points of A*) $= \varnothing$.

Proposition 1: The complement of an open set is closed; the complement of a closed set is open.

1.4 Convergence and Cauchy Sequences

An infinite *sequence* is an ordered set of points inside the metric space (X, d) denoted as $\{x_1, x_2, \ldots\} \equiv \{x_n\}_{n \in N}$. It is called *convergent* if there is a limit point

$\tilde{x} \in X$ such that for an *index* $K \in N \equiv$ set of natural numbers and $\epsilon > 0$, we can write for every $n > K$:

$$d(x_n, \tilde{x}) < \epsilon$$

If a sequence converges, its limit is unique. A set is closed if and only if every convergent sequence with elements in it has its limits in it.[6]

Let (X, d) be a metric space. A sequence $\{x_n\}_{n \in N} \subseteq X$ is called a *Cauchy sequence* if

$$\forall \epsilon > 0, \exists K \in N \text{ such that } \forall m,n \geq K, d(x_n, x_m) < \epsilon$$

A Cauchy sequence is a generalization of a convergent sequence. Every convergent sequence is a Cauchy sequence, but the reverse is not true.

A metric space (X, d) is *complete* if all Cauchy sequences in it converge. A Cauchy sequence $\{x_n\}_{n \in N}$ is *bounded* in a metric space.

1.5 Normed Linear Spaces

Let X be a real vector space. A function $\|\cdot\|: X \to \mathfrak{R}_+$ is called a *norm* on X if all of the following hold:

1. $\| x \| \geq 0, \forall x \in X$
2. $\| x \| = 0 \Longleftrightarrow x = \overline{0}$
3. $\| ax \| = |a| \, \| x \|, a \in \mathfrak{R}, x \in X$
4. $\| x + y \| \leq \| x \| + \| y \|, \forall x, y \in X$

Example 1: Max or Sup Norm

For $x, y \in \mathfrak{R}^n$, define $\| x \|_\infty \equiv \max\{|x_1|, |x_2|, ..., |x_n|\}$ and $d(x, y) = \| x - y \|_\infty = \max\{|x_1 - y_1|, |x_2 - y_2|, ..., |x_n - y_n|\}$.

Example 2: Manhattan or Taxicab Norm

For $x, y \in \mathfrak{R}^n$, define $\| x \|_1 \equiv \sum_{i=1}^{n} |x_i|$ and $d(x, y) \equiv \| x - y \|_1 \equiv \sum_{i=1}^{n} |x_i - y_i|$.

---

6 Proof of either statement is left as an exercise to the reader.

A vector space together with a norm is called a *normed vector space*. A normed vector space is a special case of a metric space. All the definitions for metric spaces are valid for normed vector spaces. If $\|\cdot\|$ is a norm on vector space V, then the (distance) function $d\colon V \times V \to \mathfrak{R}_+$ defined by $d(x, y) \equiv \|(x - y)\|$ is a metric on V.

A metric space may have no algebraic structure; that is, it may not be a vector space. The concept of a metric space is a generalization of the concept of a normed vector space.

1.5.1 Banach Space

If $(X, d_{\|\cdot\|})$ is a complete metric space where all Cauchy sequences converge, then the normed space $(X, \|\cdot\|)$ is called a *Banach space*. The norm $\|\cdot\|$ is what connects the *analytic* complete metric space and the *algebraic* real vector space.

In solving optimization problems, the advantage of formulating them in Banach spaces as opposed to incomplete spaces should be intuitive. When we are seeking an optimal vector that maximizes the objective we choose, we construct a sequence of vectors where each member is superior to the preceding member, so the optimal vector is the limit of the sequence.

We proceed by giving some examples of Banach spaces.

Example 1: $\mathfrak{R}$ is a one-dimensional real vector space. $\|\cdot\|\colon \mathfrak{R} \to [0, \infty)$ is a norm. $d_{\|\cdot\|}(x, y) \equiv |x - y|$ is a metric. $(\mathfrak{R}, \|\cdot\|)$ is a Banach space if all Cauchy sequences converge in $\mathfrak{R}$.

Example 2: $X = \{0\}$, a zero-dimensional real vector space with just one element in it, has all sequences converge in it. $\|\cdot\|\colon X \to [0, \infty)$, defined by $\|0\| \equiv 0 \Rightarrow$ $(X, \|\cdot\|)$ is a Banach space.

1.5.2 l_p and L_p Spaces

Let l_p with $p \in [1, \infty)$ be defined as all sequences of scalars x_i such that $\sum_{i=1}^{\infty} |x_i|^p < \infty$. Then $\|\cdot\|_p\colon l_p \to [0, \infty)$ with $\|x\|_p \equiv (\sum_{i=1}^{\infty} |x_1|^p)^{1/p}$ is a norm.

l_∞ consists of bounded sequences. The norm for x is defined as $\|x\|_\infty \equiv \sup_n |x_n|$.

The norm of l_p trivially satisfies conditions 1.5: (1)–(3) above. Condition 1.5: (4), the triangle inequality, is satisfied using the following two well-known theorems due to Hölder and Minkowski:

Theorem 1 (Hölder's Inequality):[7] If $1 \leq p$ and $q \leq \infty$ such that $\dfrac{1}{p} + \dfrac{1}{q} = 1$ and if $x = \{x_i\}_{i \in N} \in l_p$ and $y = \{y_i\}_{i \in N} \in l_q$, then

$$\sum_{i=1}^{\infty} |x_i y_i| \leq \| x \|_p \| y \|_q$$

Equality holds if and only if $(|x_i|/\| x \|_p)^p = (|y_i|/\| y \|_q)^q, \forall i.$

Theorem 2 (Minkowski's Inequality):[8] If $x, y \in l_p$, $1 \leq p \leq \infty \Rightarrow x + y \in l_p$ and $\| x + y \|_p \leq \| x \|_p + \| y \|_p$. For $1 < p < \infty$, equality holds $\iff a_1 x = a_2 y$ for some positive constants a_1, a_2.

L_p spaces are defined analogously to l_p spaces, and they consist of real-valued measurable functions x on an interval $[a,b]$ for which $|x(t)|^p$ is integrable.[9] The norm[10] is defined as

$$\| x \|_p = [\int_a^b |x(t)|^p dt]^{1/p}$$

Both Theorems 1 and 2 have their counterparts in L_p space.[11] The norm of a function in L_∞ is given as $\| x \| = $ essential $\sup |x(t)|$.[12]

Theorem 3: The l_p space and its norm $(l_p, \| \cdot \|)$ is a Banach space.[13]

A subset is complete if every Cauchy sequence from the subset converges to a limit in the subset. That is, completeness and closure are equivalent in a Banach space. Before we formalize this in Theorem 4, let us note that this

---

7 Please see Luenberger (1969) and Hardy, Littlewood, and Polya (1952).

8 Please see Luenberger (1969).

9 Strictly speaking Lebesgue integrable. See, for example, Bartle (1966).

10 In L_p space, $\| x \|_p = \overline{0}$ does not necessarily imply $x = \overline{0}$ because of complications involving measure theoretic arguments. We bypass those by not distinguishing between functions that are equal almost everywhere; that is, they differ on a set of measure zero.

11 Hölder's inequality would be as follows: if $x \in L_p [a, b]$, $y \in L_p [a,b]$, $\dfrac{1}{p} + \dfrac{1}{q} = 1$, and $p, q > 1 \Rightarrow$
$\int_a^b |x(t)y(t)| dt \leq \| x \|_p \| y \|_q$, equality holds: $[|x(t)|/\| x \|_p]^p = [|y(t)|/\| y \|_q]^q$. Minkowski's inequality would be as follows: if $x, y \in L_p [a, b]$, then so is $x + y$ and $\| x + y \|_p \leq \| x \|_p \| y \|_p$.

12 As in the case of l_∞, we assume the almost-everywhere interpretation in defining the supremum. For the function $x(t) = 1 - t^2$ for $t \in [-1,1]$; $t \neq 0$, and $x(t) = 3$ for $t = 0$, the supremum or maximum of this function is 3, but the essential supremum is 1.

13 Please see Luenberger (1969).

equivalence is not true for normed spaces in general, which could be closed but not complete.

Theorem 4: A subset in a Banach space is complete if and only if it is closed.[14]

Theorem 5: In a normed linear space, any finite-dimensional subspace is complete.[15]

1.5.3 Transformations, Linear Operators, Functionals, and Their Extreme Values

For linear vector spaces X, Y with a subset $D \subseteq X$ known as the *domain* of X, a *transformation* $T(x)$ from X to Y with a domain D is a rule that maps $\forall x \in D$ to an element $y \in Y$. If $\forall y \in Y$, there exists at most one $x \in D$ for which $y = T(x)$, then the transformation is *one to one*, and if $\forall y \in Y$, there exists at least one $x \in D$ for which $y = T(x)$, T is said to map D onto Y. The collection of vectors $y \in Y$ for which there is an $x \in D$ with $y = T(x)$ is called the *range* of T.

If $T: X \rightarrow Y$ and V is a given set in X, $T(V)$ is the *image* of V in Y, defined as the subset of Y consisting of points of the form $y = T(v)$ for $v \in V$. Given any set $W \subseteq Y$, $T^{-1}(W)$ is the *inverse image* of W consisting of all points $x \in X$ satisfying $T(x) \in W$.

If a transformation is linear, it is referred to as a *linear operator*. For the linear operator $A: X \rightarrow Y$, the *range* is $R(A) \subseteq Y$. The set $\{x: A(x) = \bar{0}\}$ is called the *null space* $N(A)$ of the operator. A is *bounded* if there is a constant $K \ni \|A(x)\| \leq K \|x\|$, $\forall x \in X$. The smallest such constant is called the *norm* of A and is denoted as $\|A\|$. We shorten $A(x)$ to Ax in most of what follows.

A transformation from a vector space X into a space of scalars in real or complex space is defined as a *functional* on X. Optimization involves the maximization or minimization of the value of an objective function, which is usually a functional over a given subset. Obviously, the first question to answer relates to the existence of such a maximum or minimum on a given set. The Weierstrass theorem, which we will state shortly, is a key tool in answering this question.

---

14 The proof is trivial because a complete subset is closed given that all convergent Cauchy sequences have a limit in the subset. A Cauchy sequence from a closed subset has a limit in the Banach space; hence, by closure, this limit is in the subset.

15 The proof is left as an exercise for the reader.

Let us start by noting that in a finite-dimensional space, a continuous function defined on a closed and bounded set has a maximum and a minimum.

A real-valued functional f defined on a normed space X is *upper-semicontinuous* at x_c if given $\epsilon > 0$, $\exists\, \omega > 0$ such that $f(x) - f(x_c) < \epsilon$ if $\| x - x_c \| < \omega$. The functional would be defined as *lower-semicontinuous* at x_c if $-f$ is upper-semicontinuous at x_c.

If C is a set in the normed space X, it is *compact* if given a sequence $\{x_i\} \in C$, there is a subsequence $\{x_{i_n}\} \in C$ converging to an element $x \in C$.

In finite-dimensional spaces, closed and bounded sets are compact. Compact sets are complete because, by definition, any Cauchy sequence in C must have a limit in it.

Theorem 6 (Weierstrass):[16] An upper-semicontinuous functional on a compact subset C of a normed vector space X achieves a maximum on C.

The Weierstrass theorem will mostly be sufficient to establish the existence of a solution to all the optimization problems we will encounter in finite-dimensional normed spaces.

1.6 Inner Products and Hilbert Spaces[17]

We have seen that a *metric* refers to measuring distances and a *norm* refers to measuring distances and lengths. An *inner product* $<x, y>$ is a scalar with $x, y \in X \subseteq \Re^n$ that measures distances, lengths, and angles.

Example (Figure 1.1): $<x, y> \equiv \| x \| \| y \| \cos A$

A *Hilbert space* generalizes the notion of a Euclidean space of two and three dimensions to any finite and infinite number of dimensions. A Hilbert space is a complete linear vector space together with an inner product $<\cdot, \cdot>: X \times X \to \Re$.[18] Being complete, the space accommodates most physics, engineering,

---

16 *Proof:* Please see Luenberger (1969) and Rudin (1976).

17 We will focus on real vector spaces. When complex vector spaces are also allowed, the definitions and axioms need to be modified to include complex conjugates. We refer the interested reader to standard analysis and functional analysis texts Lang (1969), Rudin (1991).

18 We simplify the narrative here. Technically, a *pre-Hilbert* space that satisfies axioms 1–5 is a normed linear space with the concepts defined earlier such as convergence, closure, and completeness holding. A complete *pre-Hilbert* space satisfying axiom 6 above is called a *Hilbert space*. As such, it is a Banach space with an inner product defining the norm.

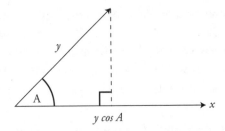

FIGURE 1.1 Inner product of two vectors

economics and finance problems amenable to multivariate calculus and optimization theory.

The inner product satisfies the following axioms:

1. $< x, x > \geq 0, \forall x \in X$
2. $< x, x > = 0 \Longleftrightarrow x = \bar{0}$
3. $< x, y > = < y, x >$
4. $< x, y_1 + y_2 > = < x, y_1 > + < x, y_2 >, \forall x, y_1, y_2 \in X$
5. $< x, ay > = a <x, y>, \forall x,y \in X, a \in \Re$
6. If a sequence $\{x_n\}_{n \in N} \in X$ and if $\lim\limits_{n, m \to \infty} < x_n - x_m, x_n - x_m > = 0$, there exists
   an $x \in X$ such that $\lim\limits_{n \to \infty} < x - x_n, x - x_n > = 0$. $x \in X$ is called the *limit of
   the sequence.*

The following propositions will be helpful in many applications of Hilbert space.

Proposition 2 (Cauchy–Schwarz Inequality): $\forall x, y$ in an inner product space,
$|< x, y >| \leq \| x \| \| y \|$. Equality holds $\Longleftrightarrow x = ay$ for some scalar a or $y = \bar{0}$.[19]

Proposition 3: In a pre-Hilbert space X, the function $\| x \| = \sqrt{<x,x>}$ is a
norm.[20]

---

19 *Proof:* Because the case where $y = \bar{0}$ holds trivially, in the nonzero case for some scalar a, we can write
$0 \leq (<x - ay, x - ay> = <x, x> - a<y, x> - a<x, y> + |a|^2<y, y>$. Setting $a = \dfrac{<x,y>}{<y,y>}$, we
obtain $<x, x> - \dfrac{|<x,y>|^2}{<y,y>} \geq 0$, and therefore, $| <x, y> | \leq \sqrt{<x,x><y,y>} = \| x \| \| y \|$ ∎

20 The proof only requires the triangle inequality to be checked. $\| x + y \|^2 = <x + y, x + y> = <x,
x> + <x, y> + <y, x> + <y, y> = \| x \|^2 + 2 <x, y> + \| y \|^2$. And applying Proposition 2 gives
us $\| x + y \|^2 \leq \| x \|^2 + 2 \| x \| \| y \| + \| y \|^2 = (\| x \|+ \| y \|)^2$. Taking the square root of both sides
proves the proposition. ∎

Proposition 4 (Parallelogram Law): In a pre-Hilbert space, $\| x + y \|^2 + \| x - y \|^2 = 2 \| x \|^2 + 2 \| y \|^2$.[21]

A pre-Hilbert space therefore is a normed linear space with the concepts defined earlier such as convergence, closure, and completeness holding. Some examples of pre-Hilbert spaces follow.

Example 1: $x, y \in \Re^n$ with $<x, y> = \sum_{i=1}^{n} x_i y_i$. The norm $\| x \| = \sqrt{\sum_{i=1}^{n} |x_i|^2}$, which we have seen is the l_2 norm.

Example 2: L_2 space in the real closed interval $[0, T]$ with inner product

$$<x, y> = \int_0^T x(t)y(t)dt$$

with Hölder inequality guaranteeing the finiteness of the inner product.

Proposition 5 (Continuity): If $x_n \to x, y_n \to y$ in a pre-Hilbert space, then $<x_n, y_n> \to <x, y>$.[22]

Pre-Hilbert spaces as infinite-dimensional vector spaces are natural extensions of finite-dimensional vector spaces such as the Euclidean space. As such, concepts from ordinary geometry such as orthogonality have their counterparts here. Two vectors $x, y \in X$ are said to be *orthogonal* $x \perp y$ if $<x, y> = 0$. Two linear spaces $S_1, S_2 \in X$ are orthogonal $S_1 \perp S_2$, if each element in S_1 is orthogonal to each element in S_2. A collection of vectors $\{x_1, x_2, ..., x_n\}$ in a pre-Hilbert space is an *orthogonal system* if $x_i \perp x_j$ for $i \neq j$. The collection is called an *orthonormal system* if in addition the norms of its elements $\| x_i \| = 1$. An orthonormal system is an *orthonormal basis* for its linear span, which is defined as the smallest linear subset that contains it.

Theorem 7: If $\{x_1, x_2, ..., x_n\}$ is an orthogonal system in a pre-Hilbert space, it follows that $\| \sum_{i=1}^{n} x_i \|^2 = \sum_{i=1}^{n} \| x_i \|^2$. Any orthogonal system of nonzero vectors is linearly independent.[23]

---

21 *Proof:* Trivially expand the norms in inner-product terms.
22 *Proof:* The sequences are convergent, and they are bounded, so $\| x_n \| \leq M$. Thus, $| <x_n, y_n> - <x, y> | = | <x_n, y_n> - <x_n, y> + <x_n, y> - <x, y> | \leq | <x_n, y_n - y> | + | <x_n - x, y> |$. With Cauchy–Schwarz inequality $|<x_n, y_n> - <x, y>| \leq \| x_n \| \| y_n - y \| + \| x_n - x \| \| y \|$, given that $\| x_n \|$ is bounded, $| <x_n, y_n> - <x, y> | \leq M \| y_n - y \| + \| x_n - x \| \| y \| \to 0.$ ∎
23 The proof is left as an exercise for the reader.

The first part of the theorem, expressed as if $x \perp y$, then $\| x + y \|^2 = \| x \|^2 + \| y \|^2$, is of course the Pythagorean theorem.

We are now ready to state and prove a key theorem that is important in solving the optimization and estimation problems we will encounter throughout this text. The problems could be stated as: given a vector $x \in X$ and a subspace S of X, find a vector s in the subspace S that is closest to the vector x in the larger space X such that $\| x - s \|$ is minimized. Leaving the obvious case where $x \in S \subseteq X$, we need to show the *existence* of an $s^* \in S$ minimizing $\| x - s \|$, the *uniqueness* of s^*, and what s^* actually is.

Theorem 8 (Projection): Let X be a Hilbert space and S a closed subspace of X. Corresponding to any $x \in X$, there exists a unique vector $s^* \in S$ such that $\| x - s^* \| \leq \| x - s \|, \forall s \in S$. Furthermore, $x - s^* \perp s, \forall s \in S$, and conversely, if $s^* \in X$ is a vector such that $x - s^* \perp s, \forall s \in S$, then $\| x - s^* \| \leq \| x - s \|, \forall s \in S$. A necessary and sufficient condition for the uniqueness of s^* as the minimizing vector is that the so-called error vector $(x - s^*) \perp S.$[24]

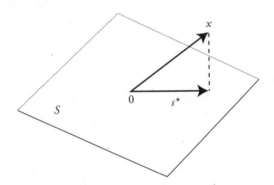

FIGURE 1.2 Projection theorem

We now try to show that given any closed subspace of a Hilbert space, any vector in it can be written as the sum of two vectors in a way that one is in the subspace and the other is in a subspace orthogonal to it. The set of all vectors orthogonal to S is called the *orthogonal complement* $S^{\perp}$. It is trivial to prove that the complement is a closed subspace of the Hilbert space, that $S \subset (S^{\perp})^{\perp}$, and that if $S \subset T$, then $T^{\perp} \subset S^{\perp}$.

---

24 *Proof:* Please see Luenberger (1969).

A vector space X is the *direct* sum of two subspaces S_1 and S_2 if every vector $x \in X$ has a *unique* representation of the form $x = x_1 + x_2$, where $x_1 \in S_1$, $x_2 \in S_2$, notated as $X = S_1 \oplus S_2$. This applies to cases where the sum is unique.

Theorem 9 (Projection Splitting): Let X be a Hilbert space and S_1, $S_2 \subseteq X$, and let them be mutually orthogonal. Then the orthogonal projection of $x \in X$ onto the subspace $S_1 \oplus S_2$ is $s_1^o + s_2^o$, where s_1^o, s_2^o are the projections of x onto S_1 and S_2, respectively.

Proof:

$$<x - s_1^o - s_2^o, s_1> = <x - s_1^o, s_1> - <s_2^o, s_1> = 0,$$
$$\forall s_1 \in S_1, \text{ and } <x - s_1^o - s_2^o, s_2> = 0, \forall s_2 \in S_2$$

Therefore, $x - s_1^o - s_2^o$ is orthogonal to all elements of $S_1 \oplus S_2$. Theorem 8 implies that $s_1^o + s_2^o$ is the projection of x onto $S_1 \oplus S_2$.

Theorem 10: If S is a closed linear subspace of the Hilbert space H, $H = S \oplus S^\perp$ and $S = (S^\perp)^\perp$.[25]

Given a vector x and a closed subspace S in a Hilbert space H, the vector $s^* \in S$ such that $(x - s^*) \in S^\perp$ is called the *orthogonal projection* of x onto S. A set of vectors is said to be an *orthogonal set* if $x_i \perp x_j$ for each x_i, x_j and $i \neq j$. The set is called *orthonormal* if additionally each vector in the set has a norm equal to 1. An orthogonal set of nonzero vectors is a linearly independent set.[26]

1.6.1 Approximation by Normal Equations and Gram Matrices

An application of the projection theorem and minimum norms is readily seen in approximation problems, which are ubiquitous in financial econometrics. An approximation problem can be stated as follows: for an arbitrary set of vectors $x \in H$, what is the vector $\hat{x} \in S$ that is closest to x. Let $\hat{x} = a_1 z_1 + a_2 z_2 + \cdots + a_n z_n$. We can formulate the problem as one of finding the scalars

---

25 *Proof:* Please see Luenberger (1969).

26 The inner product $\sum_{i=1}^{n} <a_i x_i, x_j> = <\bar{0}, x_j>$; that is, $a_j <x_j, x_j> = 0$. Therefore, $a_j = 0, \forall j$. The fact that the vectors are independent was implied earlier.

a_i, $i = 1, 2, 3, ..., n$, that minimize the norm $\| x - a_1 z_1 - a_2 z_2 - a_3 z_3 - \cdots - a_n z_n \|$. By the projection theorem, $\hat{x}$ is the unique minimizing vector, and it is the orthogonal projection of x onto S. Also, $x - \hat{x}$ is orthogonal to each vector z_i, and thus

$$< (x - a_1 z_1 - a_2 z_2 - a_3 z_3 - \cdots - a_n z_n), z_i > = 0, \forall i = 1, 2, 3, \ldots, n$$

or

$$< z_1, z_1 > a_1 + < z_2, z_1 > a_2 + \cdots + < z_n, z_1 > a_n = < x, z_1 >$$
$$< z_1, z_2 > a_1 + < z_2, z_2 > a_2 + \cdots + < z_n, z_2 > a_n = < x, z_2 >$$
$$\vdots$$
$$< z_1, z_n > a_1 + < z_2, z_n > a_2 + \cdots + < z_n, z_n > a_n = < x, z_n >$$

The n equations are called *normal equations*, and the corresponding $n \times n$ matrix corresponding to the vectors z_i is called the *Gram matrix*, which is the transpose of the coefficient matrix of the normal equations and is given by[27]

$$G = G(z_1, z_2, z_3, ..., z_n) \equiv \begin{bmatrix} < z_1, z_1 > & < z_1, z_2 > & \cdots & < z_1, z_n > \\ < z_2, z_1 > & < z_2, z_2 > & \cdots & < z_2, z_n > \\ \vdots & \vdots & \vdots & \vdots \\ < z_n, z_1 > & < z_n, z_2 > & \cdots & < z_n, z_n > \end{bmatrix}$$

The determinant $g = g(z_1, z_2, z_3, ..., z_n)$ is called the *Gram determinant*. The approximation problem posed earlier can be uniquely solved by solving the normal equations as long as the Gram determinant is nonzero.

1.7 Dual Spaces

Given a normed linear space, its corresponding *dual space* refers to all the continuous linear functionals on the first space (referred to as the *primal space*). In a multitude of optimization problems, the dual to a given problem, which may be a minimization problem, is a maximization problem, and vice versa. The two problems are equivalent because the solutions of optimizing their objective functions are equal. Dual spaces are important in the calculus of

---

27 If the space is real, the matrix is symmetric.

variations approach to optimization problems, as well as constrained optimization problems involving Lagrangian equations that append the constraints to the objective functions via a multiplier known as a *Lagrangian multiplier*. We will be studying both in Chapter 2 because they form the basis of most of the key concepts in portfolio selection problems in modern financial economic theory and practice. The fact that a problem in a dual space may be easier to solve than the original problem in the primal space in itself is enough reason to spend some time discussing the concept in detail. The applications of duality and dual spaces in physics and engineering are well known. In the next section of this chapter, we will focus on their applications in finance.[28]

1.7.1 Hahn–Banach Theorem

Let X be a normed linear vector space X^*, the space of all bounded linear functionals on the space is called the *normed dual space* of X, and X^* is a Banach space.[29]

The Projection theorem of the preceding section could be generalized from Hilbert space to normed spaces and to minimum norm problems, which are very important in optimization and estimation problems. The Hahn–Banach theorem is essential for this purpose.

Define g as a continuous *sublinear functional* on X such that for all $x, y \in X$, $a \geq 0$, $g(x + y) \leq g(x) + g(y)$, and $g(ax) = ag(x)$. Let f be a linear functional in a subspace S of a vector space X. A linear functional F is the extension of f if F is defined on a subspace S' that properly contains S and if on S, F is identical with f. In this case, F is an extension of f from S to S'.

Theorem 10 (Hahn–Banach): Let X be a real linear normed space and g a sublinear functional on X. Let f be a linear functional defined on $S \subseteq X$ satisfying

---

28 It may be of interest to some readers that the duality concept could be used in deriving resource-allocation algorithms by constructing a dual algorithm from a primal one. A well-known example is the case of the Arrow–Hurwicz algorithm and its dual the Marglin–Heal algorithm (please see Arrow and Hurwicz 1960, Marglin 1969, and Heal 1973). The first is a planning algorithm that is price directed, whereas the second is quantity directed. The way to construct one from the other is an interesting example of the use of duality and isomorphisms between resource allocation and electrical circuits and networks (Hakanoglu 1982).

29 *Proof:* Note that the dual space is a normed linear space, so the exercise for the reader is to show that it is also complete.

$f(s) \le g(s)$ for all $s \in S$. Then there is an extension F of f from S to X such that $F(x) \le g(x)$ on X.[30]

The Hahn–Banach theorem basically states that a bounded linear functional f defined on a subspace S of a normed space can be extended to a bounded linear functional F defined by the entire space and with norm equal to the norm of f on S; that is, $\| F \| = \| f \|_S = \sup_{s \in S} \dfrac{f(s)}{\| s \|}$.

Theorem 11 (Corollary of Hahn–Banach Theorem): Let f be a bounded linear functional on a subspace S of a real normed vector space X; then there is a bounded linear functional F defined on X that is an extension of f with a norm $\| F \| = \| f \|_S$.[31]

Theorem 12 (Corollary of Hahn–Banach Theorem): Let $x \in X$. Then there is a nonzero bounded linear functional F on X such that $F(x) = \| F \| \| x \|$.[32]

With the Hahn–Banach theorem and its corollaries, we have essentially an existence theorem for a minimization (or maximization) problem.

1.7.2 Inverse Operators and Adjoint Operators

In most optimization problems in discrete and continuous time, we will encounter the objective functions as well as the constraint equations, which could involve difference equations, differential equations, and matrix equations that could be described by the linear operators defined earlier.

A linear operator on a normed space X is continuous in every point in the space if it is continuous at a single point. A linear operator from a normed space to another normed space $A: X \to Y$ is *bounded* if there is a constant k such that $\| Ax \| \le k \| x \|$, $\forall x \in X$. The smallest of constant k that satisfies this condition is called the *norm* of A and denoted as $\| A \|$.

For a linear operator A, let us analyze equation $Ax = y$. For a given $y \in Y$, the equation may have a unique solution, more than one solution, or no solution

30 For rigorous proofs of this important theorem, please see Rudin (1991).
31 *Proof:* Let $g(x) = \| f \|_S \| x \|$ in Theorem 10.
32 *Proof:* For nonzero x, define $f(ax) = a \| x \|$, which implies that f is a bounded linear functional with unit norm by Theorem 11 that can be extended to F, another bounded linear functional on normed vector space X. For $x = 0$, the proof is trivial because any bounded functional is sufficient.

in X. The first case is true if and only if $\forall\, y \in Y \leftrightarrow A{:}\, X \to Y$ is one to one and has a range equal to Y. In this case, the linear operator A has an *inverse* A^{-1} such that $Ax = y \Rightarrow A^{-1}(y) = x$. If A has an inverse, A^{-1} is also linear.

The solutions of the optimization problems we speak about often invoke duality and another type of operator that is known as *adjoint operator* defined in the dual space. Adjoint operators are facilitators in establishing orthogonality and duality relations, which are ubiquitous in optimization theory and its applications in engineering and financial economics.

1.8 Convex Sets and Separating Hyperplanes
1.8.1 Convex Sets

Two of the most used mathematical concepts in economics and finance are convex sets and convexity. A point or a vector set S is defined as a *convex* set if for any scalar $0 \le a \le 1$, $ax + (1 - a)y \in S$ for all $x,\, y \in S$. $\Re^n$, linear subspaces, a line, and a hyperplane are all examples of convex sets. If $x_1, x_2, \ldots, x_n$ are points in a convex set S, and $0 \le a_i \le 1$ and $\sum_{i=1}^{n} a_i = 1$, point $x = \sum_{i=1}^{n} a_i x_i \in S$.

The following properties result:

1. The intersection of convex sets is convex.
2. The union of convex sets is not necessarily convex.
3. $Co(x_1, x_2, \ldots, x_n)$ is the intersection of all convex sets containing $x_1, x_2, \ldots, x_n$. It is the smallest convex set containing $x_1, x_2, \ldots, x_n$, the convex hull of $x_1, x_2, \ldots, x_n$ or the convex closure of $x_1, x_2, \ldots, x_n$.
4. If S' is a set of points which are not necessarily convex but in $\Re^n$, the convex hull or convex closure of S', $Co(S')$ is the smallest convex set containing S', or the convex combination of the points of S'. If S' is a closed convex set, then $Co(S') = S'$.
5. The set of solutions to a system of linear inequalities is convex.
6. The set of nonnegative solutions to a system of linear equations is convex.
7. The product of a scalar and a convex set is convex.
8. Linear mappings of convex sets are convex.

A point $z^* \in S$ is an *extreme point* of S if the following expression is never valid:

$$z^* = ax_i + (1 - a)x_j,\, 0 < a < 1;\, x_i,\, x_j \in S$$

1.8.2 Hyperplanes and Separation Theorem

The applications of the hyperplane separation theorem in asset pricing and capital market theory are fundamental to understanding the mathematical foundations of both. We conclude this chapter with definitions that lead to the theorem.

A linear subspace in a vector space is a *hyperplane*. In a vector space, a hyperplane defines two half-spaces. If we have two convex sets, we can find a *separating hyperplane* such that the first set lies in a half-space that is separated from the second. A *supporting hyperplane* is one where a single convex set is contained in a half-space and at least one point of the set lies in the hyperplane itself.

For a nonzero linear functional f on a linear vector space X, a hyperplane H defined by $H = \{x: f(x) = k\}$, the *half-spaces* determined by H will be the two positive half-spaces and the two negative half-spaces.[33]

Theorem 13 (Minkowski): If S is a closed convex set and y^* is an exterior point to S, there exists a vector v and a point $x^* \in S$ such that $vx \geq vx^* > vy^*$ for all $x \in S$.[34]

Corollaries of Minkowski Theorem[35]

1. If x^* is a boundary point of a closed convex set S, there is a supporting hyperplane through it.
2. A closed convex set is the intersection of its supporting half-spaces.
3. Two closed bounded convex sets with no intersection points have a separating hyperplane.
4. Two closed convex sets that intersect at a single point have a separating hyperplane that is a supporting hyperplane to both.

Theorem 14 (Supporting Hyperplane): Let $S \subseteq \mathfrak{R}^n$ be a nonempty convex set. Let x_0 be either in the boundary of S. Then there exists a closed hyperplane H passing through x_0 and containing S in one of its half-spaces; that is, there exists a nonzero vector $a \in \mathfrak{R}^n$ such that $\sup_{z \in S} a'z \leq d'x_0$.[36]

---

33 $\{x: f(x) \geq k\}$; $\{x: f(x) > k\}$; $\{x: f(x) \leq k\}$; $\{x: f(x) < k\}$. The strict inequalities are open sets, and the inequalities are closed sets.
34 *Proof:* See Boyd and Vandenberghe (2004) and Lancaster (1968).
35 *Proof:* See Lancaster (1968).
36 *Proof:* Please see Boyd and Vandenberghe (2004).

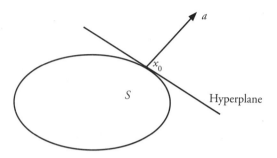

FIGURE 1.3 Supporting hyperplane

Theorem 15 (Separating Hyperplane): If S_1 and S_2 are convex sets in X such that S_1 has an interior point and S_2 has no interior point of S_1, then there exists a closed hyperplane H separating S_1 and S_2. This implies that there is a nonzero vector $a \in \Re^n$ such that $\sup_{x \in S_1} a'x \leq \inf_{z \in S_2} a'z$ and that S_1 and S_2 lie in opposite half-spaces H_1 and H_2 contained by H.[37]

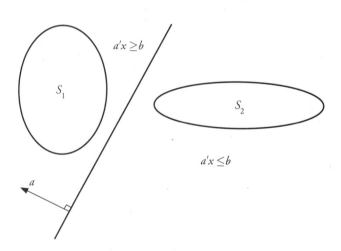

FIGURE 1.4 Separating hyperplane

---

37 *Proof:* Please see preceding footnote.

2
Optimization in Discrete Time

Summary

Asset allocation models range from basic single-period mean-variance analysis to continuous-time models with long horizons employing sophisticated analytical frameworks all dependent on optimization theory. A function $f(x)$ has a maximum at a point x_o if $f(x_o) \geq f(x)$ for all x. The *gradient* of the function is given by

$$\nabla f(x) = \frac{\partial f}{\partial x} = \left(\frac{\partial f}{\partial x_1}, \frac{\partial f}{\partial x_2}, \cdots, \frac{\partial f}{\partial x_n} \right)$$

When f is a function of several variables, at a maximum point each of its partial derivatives, that is, the components of its gradient, vanishes, $\nabla f(x) = 0$. The *Hessian matrix* of the function is given by $Hf = \dfrac{\partial^2 f}{\partial x \partial x'}$

Conditions for optimality: For a function $f(x) = f(x_1, x_2, x_3, \ldots, x_n)$ of several variables, there exist a gradient vector ∇f and a Hessian matrix Hf with respect to x such that

$\nabla f = 0$.

$w'Hfw > 0$ for all nonzero vectors w (unconstrained minimization).

$w'Hfw < 0$ for all nonzero vectors w (unconstrained maximization).

It is seldom that the optimization of a function has any practical use without incorporating constraints pertaining to the specific situation we are dealing with. The constrained maximization problem can be formulated as

$$\max_{x} f(x) \text{ subject to } g_i(x) \leq 0, \, i = 1, 2, \ldots, m$$

By appending the constraint equation with a multiplier λ and formalizing the problem for the maximization of a function subject to constraints, we define the Lagrangian

$$L(x,\lambda) \equiv f(x) - \sum_{i=1}^{m} \lambda_i [g_i(x)], \, i = 1, 2, \ldots, m$$

The *Lagrangian multiplier* λ indicates the marginal increase in the value of what we are trying to maximize achieved by marginally relaxing the constraint.

If we were to include nonbinding as well as binding constraints while requiring $\lambda_i = 0$ if the constraint i is nonbinding, such that $\lambda_i g_i(x) = 0$, $\forall i = 1, 2 \ldots, m$, we could state the *Karush-Kuhn-Tucker conditions for optimality* as

$$-\nabla f(x) = \sum_{i=1}^{m} \lambda_i [- \nabla g_i(x)]$$

$$\lambda_i \geq 0; \, g_i(x) \leq 0; \, \lambda_i g_i(x) = 0, \, i = 1, 2, \ldots, m$$

Asset allocation models frequently use the duality concepts and theorems. At times, the mean-variance portfolio optimization problem can be solved with more computational ease by using the duality properties.

2.1 Unconstrained Optimization

A function $f(x)$ has a maximum at a point x_0 if $f(x_0) \geq f(x)$ for all x. The *gradient* of the function is given by

$$\nabla f(x) = \frac{\partial f}{\partial x} = \left(\frac{\partial f}{\partial x_1}, \frac{\partial f}{\partial x_2}, \ldots, \frac{\partial f}{\partial x_n} \right)$$

When f is a function of n variables, at a maximum or minimum point, each of its partial derivatives, that is, the components of its gradient, is

$$\nabla f(x) = \frac{\partial f}{\partial x} = \left(\frac{\partial f}{\partial x_1}, \frac{\partial f}{\partial x_2}, \ldots, \frac{\partial f}{\partial x_n} \right) = 0$$

That is,

$$\frac{\partial f(x_1, x_2, \ldots, x_n)}{\partial x_1} = 0$$

$$\frac{\partial f(x_1, x_2, \ldots, x_n)}{\partial x_2} = 0$$

$$\vdots$$

$$\frac{\partial f(x_1, x_2, \ldots, x_n)}{\partial x_n} = 0$$

The set of n equations with the same number of unknowns can be solved for x_1, $x_2, \ldots x_n$. The value of the function would be at a maximum or a minimum for those values of x_i where $i = 1, 2, \ldots, n$.

The *Hessian* of the function is given by

$$Hf = \frac{\partial^2 f}{\partial x \partial x'} = \begin{pmatrix} \dfrac{\partial^2 f}{\partial x_1^2} & \dfrac{\partial^2 f}{\partial x_1 \partial x_2} & \cdots & \dfrac{\partial^2 f}{\partial x_1 \partial x_n} \\ \dfrac{\partial^2 f}{\partial x_2 \partial x_1} & \dfrac{\partial^2 f}{\partial x_2^2} & \cdots & \dfrac{\partial^2 f}{\partial x_2 \partial x_n} \\ \vdots & \vdots & & \vdots \\ \dfrac{\partial^2 f}{\partial x_n \partial x_1} & \dfrac{\partial^2 f}{\partial x_n \partial x_2} & \cdots & \dfrac{\partial^2 f}{\partial x_n^2} \end{pmatrix}$$

where x' is the transpose of vector x.

For a function $f(x) = f(x_1, x_2, \ldots, x_n)$ of several variables, there exists a gradient vector ∇f and a Hessian matrix Hf with respect to x such that

$\nabla f = 0$.

$w'Hfw > 0$ for all nonzero vectors w (unconstrained minimization).

$w'Hfw < 0$ for all nonzero vectors w (unconstrained maximization).

Example:

$$f(x) = ax_1^3 + bx_1^2 x_2 + cx_2^4$$

$$\nabla f = \left(\frac{\partial f}{\partial x_1}, \frac{\partial f}{\partial x_2} \right) = \left(3ax_1^2 + 2bx_1 x_2, bx_1^2 + 4cx_2^3 \right)$$

$$Hf = \begin{bmatrix} 6ax_1 + 2bx_2 & 2bx_1 \\ 2bx_1 & 12cx_2^2 \end{bmatrix}$$

2.2 Constrained Optimization

Rarely can the optimization of a function have any practical use without incorporating constraints specific to the situation we are dealing with. Incorporation of such constraints into the formulation of the problem is of paramount importance, and it should be done rigorously and as realistically as possible.

Pension funds maximize their asset values while meeting the constraints imposed by the actuarial and financial liabilities of their contributors. Educational, research, and art institutions maximize their endowment values while meeting their liabilities, fulfilling their future strategic plans, and paying for their present operational costs. Sovereign treasuries manage their asset values as well as their debt and other liabilities. Sovereign wealth funds maximize the value of their financial assets and resource wealth while being constrained by their fiscal budgets as well as their plans relating to the future welfare of their citizens.

If we are trying to maximize the function $f(x)$ of several variables x_i where $i = 1, 2, \ldots, n$ subject to a constraint $g(x_1, x_2, \ldots x_n) = a$, we can formulate the following constrained maximization problem:

$$\max_x f(x)$$

$$\text{subject to } g(x) = a$$

By appending the constraint equation with a multiplier λ to the function, we are trying to maximize the so-called Lagrangian:

$$L = f(x) - \lambda [g(x) - a]$$

Maximizing L is done the same way as maximizing $f(x)$. We take the partial derivatives with respect to x_i and set them to zero. We will end up with n equations and $n + 1$ unknowns, including the multiplier λ. We have an extra equation which is $g(x_1, x_2, \ldots, x_n) = a$, so we end up with the same number of equations and unknowns to solve for.

For cases where we have several constraint equations $g_j(x_1, x_2, ..., x_n) = a_j$ with $j = 1, 2, ..., m$, we can repeat the process by appending each to f after multiplying it with a multiplier λ_j. When the constraints are inequalities in the form $g_j(x_1, x_2, ..., x_n) \leq a_j$, we can still use the Lagrangian multiplier approach. If strict inequality always holds, a multiplier is not needed because the constraint will not be *active*. If the constraint is not always satisfied, then the multiplier is introduced as before. In this case, it is nonnegative.

The Lagrangian multiplier indicates the marginal increase in the value of what we are trying to maximize by marginally relaxing the constraint. For example, if a budget is relaxed by an additional amount of cash inflow from a new source of funds, what would that contribute to the value of the portfolio? As such, the Lagrangian multiplier is really a *shadow price*, or an opportunity cost associated with the constraint in the sense that its relaxation produces additional value.

2.2.1 Lagrangian Method

Let us start with a simple example of constrained optimization:

$$\min_{x_1, x_2}(x_1^2 + x_2^2)$$

$$\text{subject to } x_1 - x_2 = 2$$

The Lagrangian is formed by appending the linear constraint with a multiplier λ:

$$L(x_1, x_2, \lambda) = (x_1^2 + x_2^2) + \lambda(x_1 - x_2 - 2)$$

$$\frac{\partial L}{\partial x_1} = 2x_1 + \lambda = 0$$

$$\frac{\partial L}{\partial x_2} = 2x_2 - \lambda = 0$$

$$\frac{\partial L}{\partial \lambda} = x_1 - x_2 - 2 = 0$$

Solving the three equations with three unknowns, we obtain the minimum to be the points $x_1 = 1$, $x_2 = -1$, and $\lambda = -2$. Thus the objective function has a minimum value of 2 subject to the linear constraint. As can be seen from the geometry of the problem in Figure 2.1, we are trying to minimize the distance (the length of the vector indicated) from the origin imposed by the linear constraint. With no constraint, the objective function would be minimized at the origin.

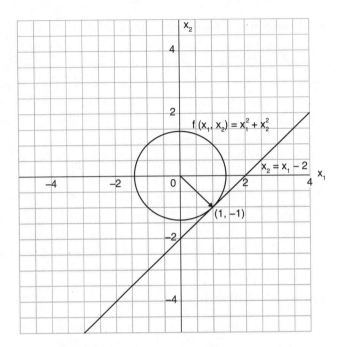

FIGURE 2.1 Optimization with equality constraint

In order to formalize the problem for the maximization of a function subject to equality constraints, we define the Lagrangian:

$$L(x, \lambda) \equiv f(x) - \sum_{i=1}^{m} \lambda_i [g_i(x) - a_i]$$

First-order conditions with respect to x and λ give us

$$\nabla f - \sum_{i=1}^{m} \lambda_i \nabla g_i = 0$$

$$g_i(x) - a_i = 0, \forall i = 1, 2, 3, \dots, m$$

Second-order conditions are given by

$$w' \begin{pmatrix} Hf & \nabla g \\ \nabla g' & 0 \end{pmatrix} w \leq 0 \text{ for all vectors } w$$

Let's generalize the problem by allowing inequality as well as equality constraints for the optimization problem:

$$\min_{x} f(x)$$

subject to $g_i(x) \leq 0$, for $i = 1, 2, \dots, m$

2.2.2 Karush–Kuhn–Tucker Method

Let us start by a simple constrained optimization problem (Lasdon 1970) stated as

$$\min_{x_1, x_2} f(x_1, x_2) = (x_1 - 3)^2 + (x_2 - 1)^2$$
$$\text{subject to} \quad g_1(x_1, x_2) = x_1^2 - x_2 \le 0$$
$$g_2(x_1, x_2) = x_1 + x_2 - 2 \le 0$$

From Figure 2.2 it is clear that the constrained minimum is reached at the point (1, 1), where the second (linear) constraint meets the tangent of the first (parabolic) constraint. This is where the line $x_2 = 2 - x_1$ crosses $x_2 = 2x_1 - 1$. The feasible set is the *cone* generated by those two lines. Let us depict the geometry of the problem by drawing contours of the objective function starting at the origin (3, 1). The gradient vector $-\nabla f$ points at the direction of maximum decrease of the objective function such that any deviation from along any direction making an angle less than 90° with $-\nabla f$ will decrease

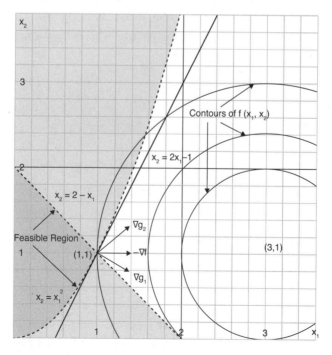

FIGURE 2.2 Geometry of Karush–Kuhn–Tucker conditions

the objective function $f(x_1, x_2)$. At the optimum point, no feasible direction defined by the cone can have an angle less than 90° between itself and $-\nabla f$.

From Figure 2.2 we observe that $-\nabla f$ is necessarily within the cone generated by the gradients of the two constraints ∇g_1 and ∇g_2. Had this not been the case, and, say, ∇g_1 was above $-\nabla f$, the latter would make an angle less than 90° with a feasible direction just above the tangency line $x_2 = 2x_1 - 1$. And, of course, similarly if ∇g_2 were below $-\nabla f$, the latter would form an angle less than 90° with the line depicted by $x_2 = 2 - x_1$.

Using the example, we can state that for the gradient of the objective function ∇f to be inside the cone generated by the negative gradient vectors of the m *binding* constraints g_i, $\forall i = 1,2, \ldots, m$, it must be a nonnegative linear combination of the latter. That is, there must exist numbers λ_i such that

$$\nabla f(x) = \sum_{i=1}^{m} \lambda_i \left[-\nabla g_i(x) \right]$$

where $\lambda_i \geq 0$, $\forall i = 1,2, \ldots, m$.

If we were to include nonbinding as well as binding constraints while requiring $\lambda_i = 0$ if the constraint i is nonbinding, such that $\lambda_i g_i(x) = 0$, $\forall i = 1,2, \ldots, m$, we can state the *Karush–Kuhn–Tucker conditions for minimization* as

$$\nabla f(x) = \sum_{i=1}^{m} \lambda_i \left[-\nabla g_i(x) \right] \qquad (2.1)$$

$$\lambda_i \geq 0$$

$$g_i(x) \leq 0$$

$$\lambda_i g_i(x) = 0, \forall i = 1, 2, \ldots, m$$

For maximization, we only need to reverse the sign of $\nabla f(x)$ in Equation (2.1).

2.2.3 Duality and Its Applications

Given a normed linear space, its corresponding *dual space* refers to all the continuous linear functions on the first space (referred to as the *primal space*). In a multitude of optimization problems, the dual to a given maximization problem may be a minimization problem, and vice versa. For many but not all cases, the two problems are equivalent because the solutions of optimizing their objective functions are equal. That a problem in a dual space may be easier to solve than the original problem in the primal space is important to consider. Asset allocation models frequently use duality concepts and theorems. The mean-variance portfolio optimization problem can be written as a *primal quadratic program*:

$$\min_{x} \frac{1}{2} x^T \Sigma x - b^T x$$

$$\text{subject to } Ax \leq c$$

where x is an n-dimensional vector, b and c are n- and m-dimensional vectors, Σ is an $n \times n$ positive-definite matrix, and A is an $m \times n$ matrix', where m is much smaller than n. We assume that there is an x that satisfies the constraint $Ax \leq c$.

The *primal* problem is equivalent to

$$\max_{\lambda \geq 0} \min_{x} \left\{ \frac{1}{2} x^T \Sigma x - b^T x + \lambda^T (Ax - c) \right\}$$

Here the minimum is achieved by $x = \Sigma^{-1} (b - A^T \lambda)$. Substituting this result into the primal problem, we arrive at the dual problem given by,

$$\max_{\lambda \geq 0} \left\{ -\frac{1}{2} \lambda^T A \Sigma^{-1} A^T \lambda - \lambda^T (c - A\Sigma^{-1}b) - \frac{1}{2} b^T \Sigma^{-1} b \right\} \tag{2.2}$$

which is also a quadratic program. Given that m is much smaller than n, the dual problem is much easier to solve than the primal problem because the constraint set is simpler and of lower dimensionality.

3

Optimization in Continuous Time

Summary

Optimization problems include the allocation of scarce and costly resources, financial and real assets to individuals and entities that are maximizing the utility of their present and future consumption. They also include planning problems in which utility functions of economic agents are optimized over time. Some of these problems are formulated as control theoretic problems where *deterministic* dynamic processes drive and constrain the objective functions that are optimized using costly *controls*. Others are stochastic control problems that formulate the maximization of utility over time with *stochastic* dynamic processes as drivers and when observations of the processes are *noisy* and need to be *approximated* or *estimated*.[1]

Optimal Control Problem (Calculus of Variations Approach): We describe a dynamic system by a differential equation called the *system equation,*

---

1 Of the excellent texts on optimal control and dynamic programming theory and applications, we follow closely Bryson and Ho (1975) as well as Athans and Falb (1966), Bellman (1959), and Luenberger (1979).

$$\frac{dx}{dt} = f[x(t),\, u(t),\, t] \text{ and } x(t_0) \equiv x_0,\, x(T) \equiv x_T, \text{ for } t_0 \le t \le T$$

where $x(t)$ is an n-dimensional vector function described as the *state variable* determined by an m-dimensional vector function described as the *control variable* $u(t) \in U$, a bounded set in $\Re^m$.

The control variable is a decision lever we use to optimize a *performance measure* or *index*:

$$\bar{J} = Q[x(T),T] + \int_{t_0}^{T} L(x, u, t)dt$$

The optimal control problem is the one that searches for functions $u(t)$ that optimize $\bar{J}$. In financial economic problems, the performance index typically takes the form of a *utility function*.

Similar to adjoining a constraint in a Lagrangian formulation, we can adjoin the differential system equation to $\bar{J}$ with Lagrangian multiplier $\lambda(t)$, a vector-valued function also known as the *costate variable*, to obtain

$$J = Q(x_T, T) + \int_{t_0}^{T} \left[L[x(t), u(t), t] + \lambda'(t) \left\{ f[x(t), u(t), t] - \frac{dx(t)}{dt} \right\} \right] dt$$

The *Hamiltonian* is defined as $H \equiv L(x,\, u,\, t) + \lambda'f(x,\, u,\, t)$, and to find a control vector function $u(t)$ that produces a stationary value of the performance index J, we solve the deterministic differential equations known as the *Euler–Lagrange equations of optimality*:

$$\frac{dx}{dt} = f(x(t),\, u(t),\, t)$$

$$\frac{d\lambda}{dt} = -\left(\frac{\partial L}{\partial x}\right)' - \left(\frac{\partial f}{\partial x}\right)'$$

$$\frac{\partial H}{\partial u} = \left(\frac{\partial f}{\partial u}\right)'\lambda + \left(\frac{\partial L}{\partial u}\right)' = 0$$

Optimal Control Problem (Dynamic Programming Approach): Here we look at the optimal control problem from a different point in time. Starting at any arbitrary point (x, t) and proceeding to a terminal hypersurface, there is a unique optimal value of the performance index $J^* \equiv J^*(x, t)$. As in the calculus of variations case, the performance index is

$$\bar{J} = Q[x(T), T] + \int_t^T L(x, u, \tau) d\tau$$

The system equations are $\dfrac{dx}{dt} = f[x(t), u(t), t]$, and the terminal boundary conditions are given by $\Omega[x(T), T] = 0$.

The optimal performance function can be written as

$$J^* = \max_{u(t)} \left\{ Q[x(T), T] + \int_t^T L(x, u, \tau) d\tau \right\}$$

with boundary conditions $J^*(x, T) = Q(x, T)$ on the terminal hypersurface $\Omega[x(T), T] = 0$.

For the Hamiltonian defined similarly as in the calculus of variations case, the solution to the problem yields the partial differential equation: the *Hamilton–Jacobi–Bellman (HJB) equation*:

$$-\frac{\partial J^*}{\partial t} = H^*\left(x, \frac{\partial J^*}{\partial x}, t\right) = \max_u H\left(x, \frac{\partial J^*}{\partial x}, u, t\right)$$

The HJB equation implies that u^* is the value of u that maximizes the Hamiltonian $H\left(x, \dfrac{\partial J^*}{\partial x}, t\right)$ holding $x, \dfrac{\partial J^*}{\partial x}$, and t constant, which gives us a description of the *Pontryagin maximum principle*.

3.1 Introduction to Optimal Control: Calculus of Variations Approach

Let us consider a dynamic system described by a differential equation:

$$\frac{dx}{dt} = f[x(t), u(t), t] \tag{3.1}$$

$$x(t_0) \equiv x_0, x(T) \equiv x_T, \text{ for } t_0 \le t \le T$$

where $x(t)$ is an *n*-dimensional vector function described as the *state variable* determined by an *m*-dimensional vector function described as the *control variable* $u(t) \in U$, a bounded set in $\Re^m$.

We can think of the control variable as a decision lever that we use to optimize a *performance measure* or *index*. Later we will bring in concepts from utility theory to define this measure in the context of financial economics in general and asset allocation in particular.

Consider a scalar performance index given by

$$\bar{J} = Q[x(T), T] + \int_{t_0}^{T} L(x, u, t)dt$$

The optimal control problem is the one that searches for functions $u(t)$ that maximize (or minimize) $\bar{J}$.

Similar to adjoining a constraint in a Lagrangian formulation, we can adjoin the differential system (3.1) to $\bar{J}$ with Lagrangian multiplier $\lambda(t)$, a vector-valued function also known as the *costate variable*, to obtain

$$J = Q(x_T, T) + \int_{t_0}^{T}\left(L[x(t), u(t), t] + \lambda'(t)\left\{ f[x(t), u(t), t] - \frac{dx(t)}{dt}\right\}\right)dt \quad (3.2)$$

We now define the Hamiltonian as

$$H \equiv L(x, u, t) + \lambda'f(x, u, t)$$

Integrating the last term in (3.2) by parts, we obtain

$$J = Q(x_T, T) - \lambda'(T)x_T + \lambda'(t_0)x_0 + \int_{t_0}^{T}[H(x, u, t) + \frac{d\lambda'(t)}{dt}x(t)]\, dt$$

Let us now take the calculus of variations approach to determine the solution by perturbing or varying J by a small amount δ:

$$\delta J = \left[\left(\frac{\partial Q}{\partial x} - \lambda'\right)\delta x\right]_{t=T} + (\lambda'\delta x)_{t=t_0} + \int_{t_0}^{T}\left[\left(\frac{\partial H}{\partial x} + \frac{d\lambda'}{dt}\right)\delta x + \frac{\partial H}{\partial u}\delta u\right]dt \quad (3.3)$$

By choosing the Lagrangian multiplier function such that the coefficients of the perturbation δx on the state variable x vanishes in (3.3), we obtain the *adjoin equation*:

$$\frac{d\lambda'}{dt} = -\frac{\partial H}{\partial x} = -\frac{\partial L}{\partial x} - \lambda'\frac{\partial f}{\partial x} \quad (3.4)$$

With the boundary conditions

$$\lambda'_t = \frac{\partial Q}{\partial x_T} \quad (3.5)$$

We now can write (3.3) as

$$\delta J = \lambda'(t_0)\delta x(t_0) + \int_{t_0}^{T}\frac{\partial H}{\partial u}\delta u\, dt$$

For an extremum $\delta J = 0$ for arbitrary δu, therefore,

$$\frac{\partial H}{\partial u} = 0, \text{ for } t \in [t_0, T] \quad (3.6)$$

Equations (3.4), (3.5) and (3.6) are known as the *Euler–Lagrange equations* in the calculus of variations.

Summarizing, to find a control vector function $u(t)$ that produces a stationary value of the performance index J, we must solve the following deterministic ordinary and partial differential equations:

$$\frac{dx}{dt} = f[x(t), u(t), t] \tag{3.7}$$

$$\frac{d\lambda}{dt} = -\left(\frac{\partial L}{\partial x}\right)' - \left(\frac{\partial f}{\partial x}\right)'\lambda \tag{3.8}$$

where $u(t)$ is determined by

$$\frac{\partial H}{\partial u} = \left(\frac{\partial f}{\partial u}\right)'\lambda + \left(\frac{\partial L}{\partial u}\right)' = 0$$

The boundary conditions for (3.7) and (3.8) are split in time t_0 and T:

$$x(t_0) = x_0$$

$$\lambda(T) = \left(\frac{\partial Q}{\partial x}\right)'\big|_{t=T}$$

This forms a *two-point boundary problem* (i.e., the two boundary conditions are in initial and final time, respectively) to solve.

3.2 Dynamic Programming Approach to Optimal Control

Let's try to approach the optimal control problem but from a different point of view—more precisely, from a different point in time. The initial condition here is an *arbitrary* point (x, t). *Starting* with this point and proceeding to a terminal hypersurface,[2] there is a unique optimal value of the performance index $J^* \equiv J^*(x, t)$.

Similar to the optimal control problem we discussed earlier, the performance index can be written as

---

2 A generalization of an ordinary two-dimensional surface embedded in three-dimensional space to an $(n-1)$-dimensional surface embedded in n-dimensional space. A hypersurface is therefore the set of solutions to a single equation $f(x_1, x_2, ..., x_n) = 0$.

$$\bar{J} = Q[x(T), T] + \int_t^T L(x, u, \tau)d\tau \tag{3.9}$$

The system equations are given by

$$\frac{dx}{dt} = f[x(t), u(t), t] \tag{3.10}$$

And the terminal boundary conditions are

$$\Omega[x(T), T] = 0 \tag{3.11}$$

The optimal performance function can be written as

$$J^* = \max_{u(t)}\left\{Q[x(T), T] + \int_t^T L(x, u, \tau)d\tau\right\} \tag{3.12}$$

with boundary conditions

$$J^*(x, T) = Q(x, T) \text{ on the terminal hypersurface (3.11)} \tag{3.13}$$

We assume that $J^*(x, t)$ exists and is twice differentiable at all points of interest in the (x, t)-space. If our system starts at (x, t) and proceeds for a short time Δt using a nonoptimal control $u(t)$, using the dynamic Equation (3.10), the system will now be at

$$[x + f(x, u, t)\,\Delta t, t + \Delta t] \tag{3.14}$$

If we now use an optimal control function from this point onward, the performance function is given (to first order) by

$$J^*[x + f(x, u, t)\,\Delta t, t + \Delta t] + L(x, u, t)\,\Delta t \equiv J^1(x, t) \tag{3.15}$$

Because nonoptimal control was used in the time interval $t \rightarrow t + \Delta t$, we have

$$J^*(x, t) \geq J^1(x, t) \tag{3.16}$$

The equality will hold only when we choose $u(t)$ in the interval to maximize the right-hand side of (3.16):

$$J^*(x, t) = \max_{u(t)} \{J^*[x + f(x, u, t)\,\Delta t, t + \Delta t] + L(x, u, t)\,\Delta t\} \tag{3.17}$$

Because J^* is continuous and twice differentiable, we can use Taylor series expansion about (x, t) to get[3]

---

3 For Taylor Series Expansion, please see the Appendix.

$$J^*(x,t) = \max_{u(t)} \left(J^* + \frac{\partial J^*}{\partial x} f \Delta t + \frac{\partial J^*}{\partial t} \Delta t + L \Delta t \right) \qquad (3.18)$$

Because J^* and $\dfrac{\partial J^*}{\partial t}$ do not depend explicitly on $u(t)$, we can write (3.18) as

$$-\frac{\partial J^*}{\partial t} = \max_{u(t)} \left(L + \frac{\partial J^*}{\partial x} f \right) \qquad (3.19)$$

As in the calculus of variations derivation, $\lambda(t)$ are Lagrangian multipliers here as well. Small changes in the initial state conditions dx and time conditions dt produce small changes in the performance index according to

$$dJ^* = \lambda'(t)dx - H(t)dt \qquad (3.20)$$

where
$$H(x, \lambda, u, t) = L(x, u, t) + \lambda' f(x, u, t) \qquad (3.21)$$

From (3.20), we obtain

$$\lambda' \equiv \frac{\partial J^*}{\partial x} \text{ on the optimal trajectory} \qquad (3.22)$$

$$H \equiv - \frac{\partial J^*}{\partial t} \qquad (3.23)$$

Using (3.21), we can rewrite (3.19) as

$$-\frac{\partial J^*}{\partial t} = H^* \left(x, \frac{\partial J^*}{\partial x}, t \right) \qquad (3.24)$$

where
$$H^* \left(x, \frac{\partial J^*}{\partial x}, t \right) = \max_u H \left(x, \frac{\partial J}{\partial x}, u, t \right) \qquad (3.25)$$

Equation (3.24) or (3.19) is known as the *Hamilton–Jacobi–Bellman* equation, a partial differential equation to be solved with the boundary condition given by (3.13). Equation (3.25) implies that u^* is the value of u that maximizes the Hamiltonian $H(x, \frac{\partial J^*}{\partial x}, t)$ holding $x, \frac{\partial J^*}{\partial x}, t$ constant, which gives us a description of the *Pontryagin maximum principle*.

If the state variable x and the control variable u are not bounded, it follows our differentiability assumption and (3.25) that there must be a u^* such that

$$\frac{\partial H}{\partial u} \equiv \frac{\partial L}{\partial u} + \frac{\partial J^*}{\partial x} \frac{\partial f}{\partial u} = 0 \qquad (3.26)$$

$$\frac{\partial^2 H}{\partial u^2} \leq 0, \forall t \leq T \qquad (3.27)$$

That is, every component of first partial derivatives of the Hamiltonian with respect to the control variable should vanish, and the second partial derivative should be a nonpositive definite matrix. Equation (3.27) is known as the *Legendre–Clebsch condition* in the calculus of variations.

In order to bridge the two approaches just discussed, we could derive the Euler–Lagrange equation from the HJB equation. Let us consider a particular optimal path associated with the optimal control function. We then have

$$\frac{d\lambda^T}{dt} \equiv \frac{d}{dt}\frac{\partial J^*}{\partial x} = \frac{\partial^2 J^*}{\partial x^2}\frac{dx}{dt} + \frac{\partial^2 J^*}{\partial x \partial t} \tag{3.28}$$

If we differentiate (3.24) with respect to x with $u^* = u^*(x, t)$, we get

$$\frac{\partial^2 J^*}{\partial x \partial t} + \frac{\partial L}{\partial x} + \frac{\partial L}{\partial u}\frac{\partial u^*}{\partial x} + f'\frac{\partial^2 J}{\partial x^2} + \frac{\partial J^*}{\partial x}\left(\frac{\partial f}{\partial x} + \frac{\partial f}{\partial u}\frac{\partial u^*}{\partial x}\right) = 0 \tag{3.29}$$

The coefficient of $\dfrac{\partial u^*}{\partial x}$ in (3.29) vanishes on an optimal path in (3.26).

Using Equation (3.29) in (3.28), we obtain the *adjoint equation*:

$$\frac{d\lambda'}{dt} = -\frac{\partial L}{\partial x} - \lambda'\frac{\partial f}{\partial x}$$

which with (3.26) become the *Euler–Lagrange equations*.

Example (Shortest Path Between Two Points): The shortest path between two points on a plane could be found by formulating the problem as follows: let us find the path $x(t)$ that connects the two points with $x(t_0) \equiv x_0 = 0$ and $x(t_1) = x_1 = 1$ so that we minimize the traveled distance.

$$\frac{dx}{dt} = u$$

with
$$x(0) = 0$$
$$x(1) = 1$$
$$J = \int_0^1 \sqrt{1+u^2}\, dt$$

There are no constraints on the value of $u(t)$. Thus

$$L(x, u, t) = \sqrt{1+u^2}$$

The adjoint equation is given by

$$\frac{d\lambda}{dt} = 0$$

There is no terminal condition on $\lambda(T)$, but it is clear that $\lambda(t) = \lambda$ is constant. The Hamiltonian is given by

$$H = \lambda u - \sqrt{1 + u^2}$$

The optimal $u(t)$ must maximize this at each t. Because all terms in the Hamiltonian other than u do not depend on t, it is clear that $u(t)$ is constant. Thus the slope of $x(t)$ is constant; that is, the minimum-length curve is a straight line.

4

Utility Theory

Summary

The concept of *utility* is used to model worth or value. The term has been adapted by modern economic theory, where a *utility function* represents a consumer's preference ordering over a choice set. A *decision maker* is assumed to be someone who can value various possible alternatives in terms of his or her own subjective *preferences* following a set of axioms, namely the *completeness, reflexivity, transitivity, independence, dominance,* and *continuity axioms.* Consumers are assumed to know the *objective probabilities* associated with the outcomes that their decisions involve. Consumers will be choosing among *lotteries* described by a vector of payoffs $x = (x_1, x_2, ..., x_n)$ and their respective probabilities $p = (p_1, p_2, ..., p_n)$.

Under these axioms, a decision maker selecting between any two or more lotteries will select the one that maximizes the *expectation* of the cardinal utility U function known as the *von Neumann–Morgenstern utility function.* That is, the decision maker maximizes $\sum_{i=1}^{n} p_i U(x_i)$. The utility of wealth $U(W)$ will vary among individuals depending on their attitude toward risk as well as the relationship of expected return to risk.

4.1 Preference Orderings and Ordinal Utility

The consumer is assumed to be a decision maker who can value various possible alternatives in terms of his or her own subjective *preferences*. In finance, possible alternatives often include goods bundled into consumption commodities C_i for all $i = 1, 2, ..., n$, distinguished by time and risk.

4.1.1 Definitions and Notation

Deterministic Case

For every pair of commodities or events C_1, C_2, either $C_1 \sim C_2$ (i.e., the two commodities or events are equivalent) or $C_1 \succ C_2$ (i.e., the first commodity or event is strictly preferred to the second) or $C_1 \succeq C_2$ (i.e., the first commodity or event is weakly preferred to the second) or $C_2 \succ C_1$ (i.e., the second commodity is strictly preferred to the first) or $C_2 \succeq C_1$ (i.e., the second commodity or event is weakly preferred to the first).

The following properties are stated as axioms:

Completeness Axiom: Given two commodities or events C_1, C_2, either $C_1 \sim C_2$, $C_1 \succ C_2$, or $C_2 \succ C_1$.

Reflexivity Axiom: For every commodity or event, $C \sim C$.

Transitivity Axiom: If $C_1 \succeq C_2$ and $C_2 \succeq C_3$, then $C_1 \succeq C_3$.

Stochastic Case

Let us now extend utility theory and preference axioms to the cases that involve uncertainty. The consumers are assumed to know the *objective* probabilities associated with the outcomes that their decisions involve. The consumers will be choosing among lotteries described by a vector of payoffs $x = (x_1, x_2, ..., x_n)$ and their respective probabilities $p = (p_1, p_2, ..., p_n)$.

The axioms of completeness, reflexivity, and transitivity in the deterministic case have their counterparts here just by substituting lotteries L_1, L_2, and L_3 for C_1, C_2, and C_3. These axioms are consistent with an *ordinal* utility function defined over lotteries or an ordinal utility function defined over probability distributions of payoffs. The next three axioms are used to develop a concept of choice through maximization of the expectation of *cardinal* utility functions over payoff complexes.

Independence Axiom: Let $L_1 = [(x_1, x_2, ..., x_h, ..., x_m), p]$ and $L_2 = [(x_1, x_2, ..., H, ..., x_m), p]$. If $x_h \sim H$, then $L_1 \sim L_2$. H is either a payoff complex or another lottery. If H is a lottery $[(x_1^h, x_2^h, ..., x_n^h), p^h]$, then

$$L_1 \sim L_2 \sim [(x_1, ..., x_{h-1}, x_1^h, ..., x_n^h, x_{h+1}, ..., x_m), (p_1, ..., p_{h-1},$$

$$p_h p_1^h, ..., p_h p_n^h, p_{h+1}, ..., p_m)]$$

Elaborating on this axiom, p_i^h is the probability of getting x_i^h conditional on outcome h having been selected by the first lottery L_1. Here $p_h p_i^h$ is the unconditional probability of getting x_i^h. The independence axiom implies that only the utility of the final payoff is relevant and that the exact mechanism for the payoff is irrelevant.

Continuity Axiom: Let x_1, x_2, x_3 be outcomes of lotteries such that

$$x_1 \succeq x_2 \succeq x_3$$

Then there exists a probability p, $0 \leq p \leq 1$, such that the decision maker is indifferent between x_2 and the probability-weighted outcomes of x_1 and x_3, written as

$$x_2 \sim [(x_1, x_3), (p, 1 - p)]$$

The probability p is unique unless $x_1 \sim x_3$.

Dominance Axiom: Let lottery $L_1 = [(x_1, x_2), (p_1, 1 - p_1)]$, and $L_2 = [(x_1, x_2), (p_2, 1 - p_2)]$. If $x_1 \succ x_2$, then $L_1 \succ L_2$ if and only if $p_1 > p_2$.

Theorem (Von Neumann–Morgenstern Utility):[1] Under the axioms introduced earlier, a decision maker selecting between any two or more lotteries will select the one that maximizes the expected utility of the cardinal utility U function known as the von Neumann–Morgenstern utility function. That is, the decision maker maximizes $\sum_{i=1}^{n} p_i U(x_i)$.

4.2 Utility of Wealth and Utility Functions

In order to measure and then maximize the *worth* associated with levels of wealth, we use the basic tenets of utility theory and its representative functions. Because

---

1 *Proof:* Please see von Neumann and Morgenstern (1944).

the maximization of wealth in the future involves unknown events, we can only speak of a combination of probabilistic outcomes and therefore an *expected* utility that appropriately accounts for the probabilistic nature of these outcomes.

The utility of wealth $U(W)$ will vary among individuals depending on their attitude toward risk as well as the relationship of expected return to risk. We may assume that more is preferred to less, and therefore, the first derivative of the utility function with respect to wealth $U'(W) \geq 0$. This derivative, or the slope of the utility function, is the marginal change in utility with changes in wealth.

It may also be assumed that the change in the marginal utility, the second derivative of utility with respect to wealth, is negative, that is, $U''(W) < 0$, because it gets harder to increase utility derived from wealth as it increases.

4.3 Risk Aversion

Absolute risk aversion function is defined as

$$A(W) \equiv - \frac{\dfrac{\partial^2 U(W)}{\partial W^2}}{\dfrac{\partial U(W)}{\partial W}}$$

And *relative risk aversion* is defined as

$$R(W) \equiv - \frac{W\dfrac{\partial^2 U(W)}{\partial W^2}}{\dfrac{\partial U(W)}{\partial W}} = WA(W)$$

4.4 Examples of Typical Utility Functions

Some of the most popular utility functions used in modern finance are as follows:

Linear utility: $U(W) = a + bW$

Quadratic utility[2]: $U(W) = W - \dfrac{1}{2}\lambda W^2, \lambda > 0$

---

2 This happens to be the utility function for the basic mean-variance optimization for asset allocation. In that case, wealth W is defined in terms of the portfolio weights and asset returns.

Exponential utility (CARA): $\qquad U(W) = -e^{-aW}, a > 0$

Constant relative risk aversion (CRRA): $\quad U(W) = \dfrac{W^{(1-\lambda)} - 1}{1 - \lambda}, \lambda > 1$

Logarithmic utility:[3] $\qquad\qquad\qquad U(W) = \log(W)$

Illustrative Example: Let us assume that an investor has an exponential utility function $U(W) = -e^{-aW}$ with an initial level of wealth W_0. The investor can invest an amount x to obtain a random payoff r. We can show that the investor's decision does not depend on his or her initial wealth W_0. The criteria for a rational investor to invest are

$$E[U(W_0 - x + r)] > U(W_0)$$
$$E[-e^{-aW_0} e^{-a(r-x)}] > -e^{-aW_0}$$

Dividing both sides by $-e^{-aW_0}$, investment will be made if $e^{ax}E[e^{-ar}] < 1$, which is independent of initial wealth W_0.

4.5 Certainty Equivalence

Because it is desirable to measure the value assigned to risk aversion, we can ask what amount of *certain* wealth has the same utility as the *expected* utility (the probability-weighted average) of uncertain wealth that depends on the probability of outcomes in the future by solving the equation

$$U(W_{CE}) = E[U(W)]$$

where W_{CE} is called the *certainty equivalent* wealth, the quantity that leaves the decision maker indifferent to uncertainty. Another investor will be considered more or less risk averse if his or her certainty equivalent wealth is smaller or larger than that of the first investor.

For concave utility functions,

$$E[U(W)] < U(E[W])$$

---

3 Logarithmic utility is a special case of the CRRA utility when $\lambda = 1$. Because $W^{(1-\lambda)} = e^{(1-\lambda)\log W}$, applying L'Hôpital's rule and taking derivatives of both the numerator and the denominator, we have

$$\lim_{\lambda \to 1} \frac{e^{(1-\lambda)\log W} - 1}{1 - \lambda} = \lim_{\lambda \to 1} \frac{-\log(W)W^{1-\lambda}}{-1} = \log(W).$$

Therefore, it follows that

$$U(W_{CE}) < U(E[W])$$

and because $U'(W) > 0$,

$$W_{CE} < E[W]$$

which means that the risk-averse investor will prefer the average outcome over an uncertain one.

Example: An investor has a utility function for wealth $U(W) = W^{1/3}$. Her initial wealth is $100 and the investment she is considering has a payoff of $0, $20, $40 or $60 with equal probabilities of 1/4. The certainty equivalent of her investment can be found by calculating the utility of each outcome added to her initial wealth and probability weighting the results first. The utilities of the outcomes are given by

$$U(\$100) = 100^{1/3} = 4.64$$
$$U(\$120) = 120^{1/3} = 4.93$$
$$U(\$140) = 140^{1/3} = 5.19$$
$$U(\$160) = 160^{1/3} = 5.43$$

The expected utility $= \dfrac{1}{4} \times 4.64 + \dfrac{1}{4} \times 4.93 + \dfrac{1}{4} \times 5.19 + \dfrac{1}{4} \times 5.43 = 5.05$.

The certainty equivalent W_{CE} is obtained by solving $W_{CE}^{1/3} = 5.05$, which gives $W_{CE} = \$128.7$. Therefore, the certainty equivalent of her investment is $28.7.

5

Uncertainty: Basics of Probability and Statistics

Summary

A discrete *random variable* X is one that can take on any one of a finite number of specific values, say x_1, x_2, ..., x_n. A probability p_i corresponds to the relative chance of an occurrence of x_i with $\sum_{i=1}^{n} p_i = 1$ and $p_i \geq 0$ for all $i \in [1, ..., n]$. The *expected value* of a discrete random variable X is the average value obtained by reading the probabilities as frequencies of occurrence. The expected value, often called the *mean* or *mean value* of X, is $\mu_X \equiv$

$$E(X) = \sum_{i=1}^{n} p_i x_i.$$

The cumulative distribution function (CDF) of a random variable X represents the probability that it will take on a value less than or equal to x. A continuous random variable is a random variable whose cumulative density function is continuous everywhere. A probability density function (PDF) of a continuous random variable X is an integrable function $f(x)$

whose integral across an interval provides the probability that the value of the random variable lies within that interval.

The expected value or mean of a continuous random variable X is

$$E(X) = \int_{-\infty}^{\infty} x f(x) dx$$

A random variable's deviation from its expected value $(X - \mu_X)$ is a random variable with an expected value of zero. The expectation of the square of that deviation is always nonnegative and is defined as the *variance* of the random variable $\sigma^2 \equiv E[(X - \mu_X)^2] = E(X)^2 - \mu_X^2$. The *standard deviation* σ is the square root of the variance.

For two random variables x, y with expected values μ_X, μ_Y, their covariance is given by

$$\text{Cov}(X, Y) = E[(X - \mu_X)(Y - \mu_Y)] = E(XY) - \mu_{XY} \equiv \sigma_{XY} = \sigma_{YX}$$

If X and Y have a covariance $\sigma_{XY} = 0$, they are said to be *uncorrelated* random variables.

The expected rate of return of an n-asset portfolio, where x_i is the fraction of the portfolio invested in asset i with an expected rate of return μ_i, is $\mu_p \equiv \sum_{i=1}^{n} x_i \mu_i$. Its variance is

$$(\sigma_p)^2 = \sum_{i,j=1}^{n} x_i x_j \sigma_{ij}$$

One of the reasons that the concepts of covariance and correlation are important is their explanatory role in portfolio diversification.

A random variable X has a *normal distribution* with mean μ and variance σ^2 if X has a continuous distribution with a *probability density function*

$$f(x \mid \mu, \sigma^2) = \frac{1}{\sqrt{2\pi}\sigma} \exp\left[-\frac{1}{2}\left(\frac{x - \mu}{\sigma}\right)^2\right], \text{ for } -\infty < x < \infty, \sigma > 0$$

The moment-generating function for the random variable X is given by

$$M(t) = e^{\mu t + (1/2)\sigma^2 t^2}, \text{ for } -\infty < t < \infty$$

The first two derivatives of the moment-generating function evaluated at zero give us the expected value and the variance of the random variable X:

$$E(X) = M'(0) = \mu \text{ and } \text{Var}(X) = M''(0) - [M'(0)]^2 = \sigma^2$$

Central Limit Theorem (CLT): If random variables X_1, X_2, ..., X_n form a random sample of size n from a given distribution with a mean μ and a finite variance σ^2, then for each fixed number x,

$$\lim_{n \to \infty} \Pr\left[\frac{\bar{X}_n - \mu}{\sigma / \sqrt{n}} \leq x\right] = \Phi(x)$$

which is the CDF of the *standard normal distribution*.

The CLT is one of the most basic, well-known, and powerful results in statistics; it pertains to the distribution of any large random sample taken from any distribution with a mean and variance regardless of whether the distribution is discrete or continuous.

If an event B has already occurred and we wish to compute the probability of another event A taking into account that we know that B has occurred, the new probability of A is called the *conditional probability* of the event A given that the event B has occurred and is denoted $P(A|B)$. If $P(B) > 0$, this new conditional probability is

$$P(A|B) = \frac{P(A \cap B)}{P(B)}$$

$P(A|B)$ is the *proportion* of the probability $P(B)$ that is represented by $P(A \cap B)$.

Bayes' theorem is highly important in decision theory and behavioral economics and is really a *rule* for determining the *conditional probability* of an individual event A_i, given another event B, from the *conditional probability* of B given each event A_i and the *unconditional probability* of each A_i.

Bayes' Theorem: Let events A_1, A_2, A_3, ..., A_n form a partition of the sample space S such that the *prior* probabilities $P(A_i) > 0$, $i \in [1, ..., n]$, and let event B have a nonzero probability. Then the *posterior* probabilities are given by the following set of equations for all i:

$$P(A_i | B) = \frac{P(A_i)P(B \mid A_i)}{\sum_{j=1}^{n} P(A_j)P(B \mid A_j)}$$

5.1 Basic Properties of Random Variables

Let us assume that X is a discrete *random variable* that can take on any one of a finite number of specific values, say x_i, x_2, ..., x_n. Also assume that there is a probability p_i that corresponds to the relative chance of an occurrence of x_i. The p_i's satisfy the following equations:

$$\sum_{i=1}^{n} p_i = 1 \text{ and } p_i \geq 0, \text{ for all } i = 1, 2, ..., n$$

because each p_i is the relative frequency with which x_i would occur if an experiment of observing X were repeated infinitely.

The *expected value* of a discrete random variable X is the average value obtained by reading the probabilities as frequencies of occurrence. When the possibilities are finite, the expected value, often called the *mean* or *mean value* of X (also depicted as μ_X) is defined as

$$E(X) = \sum_{i=1}^{n} p_i x_i$$

The CDF of a random variable X represents the probability that it will take on a value less than or equal to x. A continuous random variable is a random variable whose CDF is continuous everywhere.

A PDF of a continuous random variable X is an integrable function $f(x)$ whose integral across an interval provides the probability that the value of the random variable lies within that interval. The expected value or mean of a continuous random variable X is

$$E(X) = \int_{-\infty}^{\infty} x f(x) dx$$

A random variable's deviation from its expected value $X - \mu_X$ is a random variable with an expected value of zero. The expectation of the square of that deviation is always nonnegative and is defined as the *variance* of the random variable. That is,

$$\sigma^2 \equiv \text{Var}(X) = E[(X - \mu_X)^2] = E(X^2) - 2E(X)\mu_X + \mu_X^2 = E(X^2) - \mu_X^2$$

The square root of variance is denoted by σ and is referred to as the *standard deviation* of the random variable X.

When considering two or more random variables, their mutual dependence is defined by their *covariance*. For two random variables X, Y with expected values μ_X, μ_Y, their covariance is

$$\text{Cov}(X, Y) = E[(X - \mu_X)(Y - \mu_Y)] = E(XY) - \mu_{XY} \equiv \sigma_{XY} = \sigma_{YX}$$

If X and Y have a covariance $\sigma_{XY} = 0$, they are said to be *uncorrelated* random variables. This happens when the value of one random variable does not provide any information about the other and the two variables are independent. (Note that independence implies zero correlation, but that the reverse is not true.) The two variables are *positively correlated* when $\sigma_{XY} > 0$ and the information given by one is in the same direction as the other. The opposite is true when two random variables have $\sigma_{XY} < 0$, and they are said to be *negatively correlated*.

The covariance of two random variables satisfies the following inequality:

$$|\sigma_{XY}| \leq \sigma_X \sigma_Y$$

Two random variables are *perfectly correlated* if $\sigma_{XY} = \sigma_X \sigma_Y$, and they are *perfectly negatively correlated* if $\sigma_{XY} = -\sigma_X \sigma_Y$.

The *correlation coefficient* of two random variables is defined as

$$\rho_{XY} \equiv \frac{\sigma_{XY}}{\sigma_X \sigma_Y}, \text{ where } -1 \leq \rho_{XY} \leq 1$$

The variance of a random variable is the covariance of that variable with itself; that is, $\sigma_X^2 = \sigma_{XX}$.

The variance of the sum of two random variables X, Y could be written as

$$\text{Var}(X + Y) = E[(X - \mu_X + Y - \mu_Y)^2] = E[(X - \mu_X)^2] + 2E[(X - \mu_X)(Y - \mu_Y)] + E[(Y - \mu_Y)^2]$$

which leaves us with

$$\text{Var}(X + Y) = \sigma_X^2 + 2\sigma_{XY} + \sigma_Y^2 = \sigma_X^2 + 2\rho_{XY}\sigma_X \sigma_Y + \sigma_Y^2$$

For the case where X and Y are uncorrelated (i.e., $\rho_{XY} = 0$), the expression reduces to

$$\text{Var}(X + Y) = \sigma_X^2 + \sigma_Y^2$$

There is a geometric interpretation of these expressions. If we think of x and y as two vectors, we can interpret the correlation coefficient ρ_{XY} as the angle between the vectors θ. Thus

$$\sigma_X^2 + 2\rho_{XY}\sigma_X\sigma_Y + \sigma_Y^2 = \sigma_X^2 + 2\cos(\theta)\sigma_X\sigma_Y + \sigma_Y^2$$

Here $\theta = 90°$ corresponds to uncorrelated random variables. Acute angles correspond to positive correlation with $\theta = 0°$ indicating perfect positive correlation and obtuse angles to negative correlation with $\theta = 180°$ indicating perfectly negative correlation.

5.2 Expected Value and Variance of an Investment Portfolio

Let us assume that there are n assets with random rates of return r_i with expected values $E(r_i) = \mu_i$, for all $i = 1, 2, \ldots, n$. If we were to invest a fraction x_i for all $i = 1, 2, \ldots, n$, the rate of return on our portfolio would be given by

$$r = x_1 r_1 + x_2 r_2 + \cdots + x_n r_n$$

and the expected rate of its return would be given by

$$\mu_P \equiv E(r) = x_1 E(r_1) + x_2 E(r_2) + \cdots + x_n E(r_n)$$
$$\mu_P = x_1 \mu_1 + x_2 \mu_2 + \cdots + x_n \mu_n$$

which is the weighted sum of the individual asset expected return rates.

The variance of the portfolio return can be written as

$$\sigma_P^2 = E[(r - \mu)^2]$$

$$= E[(\sum_{i=1}^{n} x_i r_i - \sum_{i=1}^{n} x_i \mu_i)^2]$$

$$= E\left\{ [\sum_{i=1}^{n} x_i (r_i - \mu_i)][\sum_{j=1}^{n} x_j (r_j - \mu_j)] \right\}$$

$$= E[\sum_{i,j=1}^{n} x_i x_j (r_i - \mu_i)(r_j - \mu_j)]$$

$$= \sum_{i,j=1}^{n} x_i x_j \sigma_{ij}$$

Hence the variance of a portfolio's return can be determined from the covariances of the asset returns and their weights.

Example: Let us look at a simple portfolio of two assets: a stock market index fund with an expected return of $\mu_S = 7\%$ and a bond market index fund with an expected return $\mu_B = 2\%$. Let us further assume that the standard deviations of the two assets are $\sigma_S = 15\%$ and $\sigma_B = 4\%$. The two assets are assumed to have a correlation coefficient $\rho_{SB} = 0.05$.

If we hold 60% of the first asset and 40% of the second, our expected return would be

$$\mu = 0.6 \times 7\% + 0.4 \times 2\% = 5\%$$

and the portfolio variance would be

$$\sigma^2 = (0.6)^2(0.15)^2 + 2 \times 0.05 \times 0.6 \times 0.4 \times 0.15 \times 0.04 + (0.4)^2(0.04)^2 = 0.0085$$

and the portfolio standard deviation is

$$\sigma = 9.2\%$$

5.3 Diversification and Its Value

One of the reasons that the concepts of covariance and correlation are important is their explanatory role in the concept of diversification. To see the effect of diversification, let us modify the preceding example by setting everything the same as before, but if we assume that the correlation of the two assets is 50% instead of 5%, we would have a standard deviation of 9.9%. The first portfolio would have a standard deviation that is 70 basis points lower because of the diversification associated with the lower correlation between its two components. Had the correlation been −50%, the standard deviation would have been 8.3%, producing a diversification benefit over the original portfolio of 90 basis points.

We can generalize this in two directions: (1) increasing the number of assets in the portfolio but letting all weights and individual standard deviations be equal and the assets not be correlated and (2) doing the same thing but assuming that all pairs of assets in the portfolio are 50% correlated. We will find that in the first case, the portfolio variance shrinks quickly with the number of assets increasing. In the case of the correlated assets, the shrinkage will be limited; no matter how many assets we add to the portfolio, the variance will not be reduced below $0.5 \, \sigma^2$ or $\rho_{ij} \times \sigma^2$ in general.

Uncorrelated Assets with Equal Portfolio Weights, Expected Returns, and Variances

The return of a portfolio of such assets would be

$$\mu = \frac{1}{n}\sum_{i=1}^{n}\mu_i$$

and its variance would be

$$\sigma_p^2 = \frac{1}{n^2}\sum_{i=1}^n \sigma^2 = \frac{\sigma^2}{n}$$

Clearly, the larger the number of assets in the portfolio, the lower is the variance.

Example (Correlated Assets with Equal Portfolio Weights, Expected Returns, and Variances): If we assume that the correlation of each asset is 50% with every other asset in the portfolio (i.e., $\rho_{ij} = 0.5$, for all $i \neq j$), then $\mathrm{cov}(r_i, r_j) = 0.5\,\sigma^2$. We can now write the variance of the portfolio with n equal expected return and variance assets that are equally weighted as

$$\sigma_p^2 = E[\sum_{i=1}^n \frac{1}{n}(r_i - \mu_i)]^2$$

$$= \frac{1}{n^2} E\left([\sum_{i=1}^n (r_i - \mu_i)][\sum_{j=1}^n (r_j - \mu_j)] \right)$$

$$= \frac{1}{n^2} \sum_{i,j=1}^n \sigma_{ij}$$

$$= \frac{1}{n^2}\left(\sum_{i=j}^n \sigma_{ij} + \sum_{i\neq j}^n \sigma_{ij} \right)$$

$$= \frac{1}{n^2}[n\sigma^2 + 0.5\,(n^2 - n)\sigma^2]$$

$$= \frac{\sigma^2}{n} + 0.5\sigma^2\left(1 - \frac{1}{n}\right)$$

$$= \frac{0.5\sigma^2}{n} + 0.5\sigma^2$$

So no matter how large the number of assets, the variance is reduced at the limit to half the individual asset variance.

Example (Diversification Benefits of a Sovereign Wealth Fund): Let us start with a crude oil-producing sovereign that depends on its natural resource wealth for its current and future welfare. As such, the volatility associated with its wealth is mostly driven by the volatility of crude oil $\sigma_o = 26\%$.

Now let us assume that we also have three other single-commodity-producing sovereigns, an aluminum producer facing volatility $\sigma_a = 14.9\%$, a copper producer with a volatility of $\sigma_c = 14.8\%$, and a gold producer with a volatility of $\sigma_g = 7.6\%$. We also know that the four commodities are correlated with each other. The correlation between oil and copper $\rho_{oc} = 0.35$, the correlation between oil and aluminum $\rho_{oa} = 0.3$, the correlation between oil and gold $\rho_{og} = 0.17$, the correlation between aluminum and copper $\rho_{ac} = 0.634$, the correlation between copper and gold $\rho_{cg} = 0.277$, and the correlation between gold and aluminum $\rho_{ga} = 0.214$.

Let us assume that the sovereigns swap their commodity for a portfolio of commodities that have weights $x_i = \dfrac{1}{4}$, where $i = 1$ is oil, 2 is aluminum, 3 is copper, and 4 is gold. The portfolio volatility equation can be written as

$$\sigma = \sqrt{\sum_{i,j=1}^{4} x_i x_j \rho_{ij} \sigma_i \sigma_j} = 11.7\%$$

The simple weighted sum of the volatilities would have been 15.8%, and of course the sovereign with the pure oil exposure would have had a volatility of 26%.

When more realism is built into the problem statement, such as different weights, returns, and variances of individual assets, we may find that diversification may reduce overall expected return without much reduction in the portfolio variance. Therefore, the tradeoff between diversification gains and losses in expected return and variance needs to be better understood. The general mean-variance approach pioneered by Harry Markowitz focuses on the tradeoffs between the expected return and the variance of those returns using basic optimization theory.

5.4 Probability Distribution of Random Variables: The Normal or Gaussian Distribution

Among statistical distributions of random variables, arguably the most important is the normal or Gaussian distribution. Financial economics uses the normal distribution and its properties extensively. We will describe the basics in this section, and they will be referred to extensively in the modeling and applications parts of this book.

A random variable X has a normal distribution with mean μ and variance σ^2 if X has a continuous distribution with a probability density function that is,

$$f(x \mid \mu, \sigma^2) = \frac{1}{\sqrt{2\pi}\sigma} \exp\left[-\frac{1}{2}\left(\frac{x-\mu}{\sigma}\right)^2\right], \text{ for } -\infty < x < \infty, \sigma > 0 \qquad (5.1)$$

Let us show that

$$\int_{-\infty}^{\infty} f(x \mid \mu, \sigma^2) \, dx = 1 \qquad (5.2)$$

$$\int_{-\infty}^{\infty} f(x \mid \mu, \sigma^2) dx = \frac{1}{\sqrt{2\pi}} \int_{-\infty}^{\infty} \exp\left(-\frac{1}{2}y^2\right) dy = \frac{1}{\sqrt{2\pi}} Z$$

where

$$y \equiv \frac{x-\mu}{\sigma}, \ Z \equiv \int_{-\infty}^{\infty} \exp\left(-\frac{1}{2}y^2\right) dy$$

and

$$Z^2 = \int_{-\infty}^{\infty}\int_{-\infty}^{\infty} \exp\left[-\frac{1}{2}(w^2 + y^2)\right] dwdy$$

Let us switch to polar coordinates by defining $y = r\cos\theta$ and $w = r\sin\theta$. Because $w^2 + y^2 = r^2$, $Z^2 = \int_0^{2\pi}\int_0^{\infty} \exp\left(-\frac{1}{2}r^2\right) rdrd\theta = 2\pi$ and $Z = \sqrt{2\pi}$; and therefore,

$$\int_{-\infty}^{\infty} f(x \mid \mu, \sigma^2) dx = 1$$

5.4.1 Moment-Generating Function of the Normal Distribution

For a random variable X with a normal distribution $N(\mu, \sigma^2)$, the *moment-generating function* $M: \Re \rightarrow \Re$ is given by

$$M(t) = E[e^{tX}] = \int_{-\infty}^{\infty} \frac{1}{\sqrt{2\pi}\sigma} \exp\left[tx - \frac{1}{2\sigma^2}(x-\mu)^2\right] dx$$

$$= \int_{-\infty}^{\infty} \frac{1}{\sqrt{2\pi}\sigma} \exp\left(\mu t + \frac{1}{2}\sigma^2 t^2 - \frac{(x-\mu-\sigma^2 t)^2}{2\sigma^2}\right) dx$$

$$= \exp\left(\mu t + \frac{1}{2}\sigma^2 t^2\right) \int_{-\infty}^{\infty} \frac{1}{\sqrt{2\pi}\sigma} \exp\left(-\frac{(x-\mu-\sigma^2 t)^2}{2\sigma^2}\right) dx$$

If we let $\mu' \rightarrow \mu + \sigma^2 t$ and notice that the integral using (5.2) is just 1, we obtain

$$M(t) = e^{\mu t + \frac{1}{2}\sigma^2 t^2}, \text{ for } -\infty < t < \infty$$

The first two derivatives of the moment-generating function evaluated at zero give us the expected value and the variance of the random variable X:

$$E(X) = M'(0) = \mu$$
$$\text{Var}(X) = M''(0) - [M'(0)]^2 = \sigma^2$$

Therefore, we have shown that μ, σ^2 are the mean and variance of the normal distribution given by Equation (5.1).

For a standard normal distribution with zero mean and a variance of one, the PDF is

$$f(x|0,1) = \frac{1}{(2\pi)^{1/2}} \exp\left(-\frac{1}{2}x^2\right), \text{ for } -\infty < x < \infty$$

and the moment-generating function is

$$M(t) = e^{\frac{1}{2}t^2}$$

$$M'(t) = te^{\frac{1}{2}t^2}$$

$$M''(t) = e^{\frac{1}{2}t^2} + t^2 e^{\frac{1}{2}t^2} = (1+t^2)e^{\frac{1}{2}t^2}$$

And, as expected,

$$E(X) = M'(0) = 0$$
$$\text{Var}(X) = M''(0) - [M'(0)]^2 = 1$$

5.4.2 Central Limit Theorem

We now state one of the most basic, well-known, and powerful results in statistics that pertains to the distribution of *any* large random sample taken from *any* distribution with a mean and variance regardless of whether the distribution is discrete or continuous.

Theorem (Central Limit Theorem): If random variables X_1, X_2, ..., X_n form a random sample of size n from a given distribution with a mean μ and a finite variance σ^2, then for each fixed number x,

$$\lim_{n\to\infty} \Pr\left[\frac{\overline{X}_n - \mu}{\sigma/\sqrt{n}} \leq x\right] = \Phi(x)$$

which is the CDF of the standard normal distribution.

In Chapter 6, after discussing the basic elements of stochastic processes, we will present an elegant extension of the central limit theorem known as *Donsker's theorem* or the *functional central limit theorem*.

5.5 Conditional Probability and Bayes' Theorem

5.5.1 Basic Definitions, Axioms, and Theorems

Assuming familiarity with basic set theory, we assign to each event A in a sample space or universal set S a probability $P(A)$ that the event will occur. The sets A, B are disjoint if $A \cap B = \varnothing$. The complement of set A is denoted as A^C and corresponds to the set consisting of all outcomes in S not belonging to A.

The fundamental axioms are stated as follows:

1. For any event A, $P(A) \geq 0$.
2. $P(S) = 1$.
3. For any infinite sequence of disjoint events A_1, A_2, A_3, ...,

$$P\left(\bigcup_{i=1}^{\infty} A_i\right) = \sum_{i=1}^{\infty} P(A_i).$$

We will state some fundamental theorems without proofs next:

4. $P(\varnothing) = 0$.
5. For any finite sequence of disjoint events A_1, A_2, A_3, ..., A_n,

$$P(\bigcup_{i=1}^{n} A_i) = \sum_{i=1}^{n} P(A_i)$$

6. For any event A, $P(A^c) = 1 - P(A)$
7. For any event A, $0 \leq P(A) \leq 1$
8. For any two events A, B, $A \subset B \Rightarrow P(A) < P(B)$
9. For any two events A, B, $P(A \cup B) = P(A) + P(B) - P(A \cap B)$
10. Two events A, B are *independent* if $P(A \cap B) = P(A)P(B)$.

Example: Suppose that two machines are operated independently and that machine A has a probability of failing $P(A) = \dfrac{1}{8}$ and that machine B has a probability of failure $P(B) = \dfrac{1}{6}$ in a given day. What is the probability that at least one machine will be not operational during a typical day?

The probability of both machines failing is $P(A \cap B) = P(A)P(B) = \dfrac{1}{8} \times \dfrac{1}{6} = \dfrac{1}{48}$. The probability that at least one machine is not operational during a typical day will be given by

$$P(A \cup B) = P(A) + P(B) - P(A \cap B) = \frac{1}{8} + \frac{1}{6} - \frac{1}{48} = \frac{13}{48}$$

5.5.2 Conditional Probability

Suppose that we learn that an event B has already occurred and that we wish to compute the probability of another event A taking into account that we know that B has occurred. The new probability of A is called the *conditional probability* of event A given that event B has occurred and is denoted as $P(A|B)$. If $P(B) > 0$, we compute this probability as

$$P(A|B) = \frac{P(A \cap B)}{P(B)}$$

$P(A|B)$ is the proportion of the probability $P(B)$ that is represented by $P(A \cap B)$.

Example: Suppose that two dice are rolled and it is observed that the sum S of the two numbers is even. We shall determine the probability that S was less than 10.

If we let A be the event that $S < 10$ and let B be the event that S is even, then $A \cap B$ is the event that S is 2, 4, 6, or 8. First consider an experiment in which two balanced dice are rolled, and we shall calculate the probability of each of the possible values of the sum of the two numbers that may appear.

Although the experimenter need not be able to distinguish the two dice from one another in order to observe the value of their sum, the specification of a simple sample space in this example will be facilitated if we assume that the two dice are distinguishable. If this assumption is made, each outcome in the sample space S can be represented as a pair of numbers (a, b), where a is the number that appears on the first die and b is the number that appears on the second die. Therefore, S comprises the 36 outcomes $\{(a, b) \mid$ for $a, b \in \{1, 2, 3, 4, 5, 6\}\}$

It is natural to assume that S is a simple sample space and that the probability of each of these outcomes is 1/36.

Let P_i denote the probability that the sum of the two numbers is i for $i = 2$, 3, ..., 12. The only outcome in S for which the sum is 2 is the outcome (1, 1). Therefore, $P_2 = 1/36$. The sum will be 3 for either of the two outcomes (1, 2) or (2, 1). Therefore, $P_3 = 2/36 = 1/18$. By continuing in this manner, we obtain the following probability for each of the possible values of the sum:

$$P_2 = P_{12} = \frac{1}{36}, P_3 = P_{11} = \frac{2}{36}, P_4 = P_{10} = \frac{3}{36}, P_5 = P_9 = \frac{4}{36},$$

$$P_6 = P_8 = \frac{5}{36}, P_7 = \frac{6}{36}$$

From the probabilities for two dice given earlier, we can evaluate $P(A \cap B)$ and $P(B)$ as follows:

$$P(A \cap B) = \frac{1}{36} + \frac{3}{36} + 2 \times \frac{5}{36} = \frac{14}{36} = \frac{7}{18}$$

$$P(B) = \frac{1}{36} + \frac{3}{36} + \frac{5}{36} + \frac{5}{36} + \frac{3}{36} + \frac{1}{36} = \frac{18}{36} = \frac{1}{2}$$

Therefore,

$$P(A \mid B) = \frac{P(A \cap B)}{P(B)} = \frac{7}{9}$$

Let A, B be two events with probabilities of happening given as $P(A)$, $P(B)$; then $P(A \cap B) = P(B)P(A|B) = P(A)P(B|A)$. After a motivating example, we will prove the general case.

Example: Let us assume that we pick two candies one after the other out of a box of candies that contains 20 red candies and 10 green ones. What is the probability of the first one being red (event A) and the second green (event B)? The probability of the first candy being red is $P(A) = \frac{20}{30} = \frac{2}{3}$, and given that the first candy was red, the probability of the second candy being green is $P(B \mid A) = \frac{10}{(30-1)} = \frac{10}{29}$. Therefore, the probability of the first candy being red followed by the second candy being green is given by

$$P(A \cap B) = P(A)P(B|A) = \frac{2}{3} \times \frac{10}{29} = \frac{20}{87}.$$

Theorem (Multiplication Rule for Conditional Probabilities): Let A_1, A_2, A_3, ..., A_n be events such that $P(A_1 \cap A_2 \cap A_3 \cap \cdots \cap A_{n-1}) > 0$. Then

$$P(A_1 \cap A_2 \cap A_3 \cap \cdots \cap A_{n-1} \cap A_n)$$

$$= P(A_1) \, P(A_2|A_1) \, P(A_3|A_1 \cap A_2) \, \dots \, P(A_n|A_1 \cap A_2 \cap A_3 \cap \cdots \cap A_{n-1})$$

Proof: The right-hand side of the equation can be written as follows:

$$P(A_1) \times \frac{P(A_1 \cap A_2)}{P(A_1)} \times \frac{P(A_1 \cap A_2 \cap A_3)}{P(A_1 \cap A_2)} \times \cdots \times \frac{P(A_1 \cap A_2 \cap A_3 \cap \cdots \cap A_n)}{P(A_1 \cap A_2 \cap A_3 \cap \cdots A_{n-1})}$$

Because the denominators are all positive, the equation reduces to the left-hand side of the equation. ∎

5.5.3 Bayes' Theorem

This simple theorem, which is highly important in decision theory and behavioral economics, is really a rule for determining the *conditional probability* of an individual event A_i given another event B from the *conditional probability* of B given each event A_i and the *unconditional probability* of each A_i.

Let the sample space S consist of disjoints events A_i, $i = 1, 2, \ldots, n$, such that their union $\bigcup_{i=1}^{n} A_i = S$ and that each event has a nonzero probability of occurrence. These events form a *partition* of S. If another partition B exists in S for which $P(B) > 0$, the events $A_i \cap B$, $\forall i$, will form a partition of B. Therefore, we can say that $B = (A_1 \cap B) \cup (A_2 \cap B) \cup \cdots \cup (A_n \cap B)$, and because all events on the right-hand side are disjoint,

$$P(B) = \sum_{i=1}^{n} P(A_i \cap B)$$

for $P(A_i) > 0$, $\forall i$, $P(A_i \cap B) = P(A_i)P(B|A_i)$,

$$P(B) = \sum_{i=1}^{n} P(A_i)P(B \mid A_i)$$

We refer to $P(B)$ as the *total probability*.

Theorem (Bayes'): Let events A_1, A_2, A_3, ..., A_n form a partition of the sample space S such that the *prior* probabilities $P(A_i) > 0$, $\forall i = 1, 2, \ldots, n$, and let event B have a nonzero probability. Then the *posterior* probabilities are

$$P(A_i \mid B) = \frac{P(A_i)P(B \mid A_i)}{\sum_{i=1}^{n} P(A_i)P(B \mid A_i)}$$

Proof. By definition,

$$P(A_i \mid B) = \frac{P(A_i \cap B)}{P(B)} = \frac{P(A_i)P(B \mid A_i)}{\sum\limits_{i=1}^{n} P(A_i)P(B \mid A_i)}$$ ∎

Under Bayesian statistics that pivot around this theorem, probability becomes a measure of the strength of one's belief. As such, the proper probabilities correspond to the strength of prior beliefs. As events occur, the observer may *change* the strength of his or her belief on the basis of his or her observations or evidence. *Posterior* probabilities correspond to this *modified* strength of belief. Let us conclude this section with an example that we analyze in some detail.

Example (An Application of Bayes' Theory):[1] A virus has two strains. The first constitutes 80% of the population and is virtually harmless, whereas the second, which constitutes 20% of the population, could cause serious health problems if not treated promptly. The initial symptoms on contracting either strain are exactly the same, so it is not possible to tell which variant the patient is infected with. An oral test is available to detect the strain, and it is 90% effective. What is the probability that a patient who tested positive to the dangerous strain after showing symptoms was indeed affected by the dangerous strain?

Let A represent the case where the strain is dangerous and B represent the case where the test confirms that the strain is dangerous. A^c therefore corresponds to the case where the strain is benign and B^c the case where the test identifies the strain as benign. Thus $P(A) = 0.2$ and $P(A^c) = 0.8$ are the prior probabilities. Let us specify the conditional probabilities first:

The probability of identifying the strain correctly as dangerous given that the strain is dangerous is $P(B|A) = 0.9$.

The probability of identifying the strain correctly as benign given that the strain is benign is $P(B^c|A^c) = 0.9$.

---

1 For excellent discussion and examples of the application of conditional probability and Bayes' Theory, we refer the reader to Kahneman (2011).

The probability of identifying the strain mistakenly as benign given that the strain is dangerous is $P(B^c|A) = 0.1$.

The probability of identifying the strain mistakenly as dangerous given that the strain is benign is $P(B|A^c) = 0.1$.

Now let us calculate the posterior probabilities:

$P(B|A)P(A) = 0.9 \times 0.2 = 0.18$ (True positive)
$P(B|A^c)P(A^c) = 0.1 \times 0.8 = 0.08$ (False positive)
$P(B^c|A)P(A) = 0.1 \times 0.2 = 0.02$ (False negative)
$P(B^c|A^c)P(A^c) = 0.9 \times 0.8 = 0.72$ (True negative)

The probability that the patient has contracting the dangerous strain given that the test shows this strain to be dangerous is given by the ratio of this true positive to the sum of the true and false positives.

The total probability of the strain identified as dangerous $P(B)$ is the sum of true- and false-positive cases earlier; that is $P(B) = P(B|A)P(A) + P(B|A^c)(P(A^c))$. Therefore,

$$P(A \mid B) = \frac{P(A \cap B)}{P(B)} = \frac{P(B \mid A)P(A)}{P(B)} = \frac{P(B \mid A)P(A)}{P(B \mid A)P(A) + P(B \mid A^c)P(A^c)}$$

$$= \frac{0.18}{0.18 + 0.08} \simeq 0.69, \text{ or } 69\%$$

This percentage is significantly less than the percentage effectiveness of the test for determining the strain correctly.

6

Uncertainty: Stochastic Processes and Calculus

Summary[1]

In a random-walk process, the variability around the expectation of distance $X(t)$ traveled in either direction is a linear function of the number of steps taken. If Δx is the size of each step, with n steps taken, and the probabilities of going in either of the two directions are given by $p = q = 0.5$, we have the variance $n(\Delta x)^2$; as such, we can interpret $(\Delta x)^2$ as the variance of $X(t)$ per unit time. As $\Delta x \to 0$, this gives us the instantaneous variance $\sigma(t)^2$ and the instantaneous standard deviation $\sigma(t)$. Similarly, we can obtain the instantaneous mean $\mu(t)$. With p, q, and Δx as the general parameters of the random-walk process, we can derive

$$E[X(t)] = n(p-q)\Delta x = \frac{t}{\Delta t}(p-q)\Delta x \to \mu t$$

$$\text{var}[X(t)] = 4npq(\Delta x)^2 = 4\frac{t}{\Delta t}pq(\Delta x)^2 \to \sigma^2 t$$

---

1 In this chapter, we rely on work on the topic in seminal texts by Karlin and Taylor (1981), Billingsley (1968), and Feller (1957) and the comprehensive applications by Baz and Chacko (2004), Harrison (1985), and Shreve (2004).

The motion of a random walk depicted by the variable X with drift μ and volatility σ and given by $X(t) = \mu t + \sigma B(t)$ with $X(0) = 0$, where $B(t)$ is the *standard Brownian motion*, a special case of the *arithmetic Brownian motion* with instantaneous mean of zero and standard deviation of one. For all t, the increments $X(t + \Delta t) - X(t)$ are independent. $X(t)$ has a mean of μt and a variance of $\sigma^2 t$ and is normally distributed. We can standardize $X(t)$ by defining a normal variable ϕ with zero mean and a variance of one:

$$\phi \equiv \frac{X(t) - \mu t}{\sigma \sqrt{t}}$$

In differential form as a *stochastic differential equation*, the arithmetic Brownian motion equation can be written as $dX(t) = \mu dt + \sigma dB(t)$.

Functional Central Limit Theorem (Donsker's Theorem)—An Extension of the Central Limit Theorem (CLT): If ψ_1, ψ_2, ..., ψ_n are independent and identically distributed random variables with $\mu = 0$ and finite variance σ^2, and if X^n is an appropriately defined random function,[2] then X^n tends toward a Wiener measure or a standard Brownian motion; that is, $\lim_{n \to \infty} X^n \to W$.

A random variable $X(t)$ is said to follow a *geometric Brownian motion* if the stochastic differential equation holds: $dX(t) = \mu X(t)dt + \sigma X(t)dB(t)$. With the initial boundary condition $X(0) \equiv x_0$,

$$X(t) = x_0 e^{[\mu - (\sigma^2/2)]t + \sigma \psi \sqrt{t}}$$

where ψ is a standard normal random variable with a mean of zero and a variance of one.

To understand how the total differential of a function of X and t, $f(X, t)$, behaves, we typically write a *Taylor expansion* of df:

$$df(X,t) = \frac{\partial f}{\partial X} dX + \frac{\partial f}{\partial t} dt + \frac{1}{2}\frac{\partial^2 f}{\partial X^2}(dX)^2 + \frac{\partial^2 f}{\partial X \partial t} dX dt + \frac{1}{2}\frac{\partial^2 f}{\partial t^2}(dt)^2 + \text{higher order terms}$$

When we are dealing with a random variable $X(t)$, the process needs to be modified by taking into consideration the stochasticity of the variable.

---

2 Defined in the main text that follows.

For a random variable $X(t)$ that follows a geometric Brownian motion, the process is $\dfrac{dX}{X} = \mu dt + \sigma dB$, where μ is called the *instantaneous drift* and σ is the *volatility*. dB is a *Wiener process* that has the following properties:

$$dB \equiv \psi \sqrt{dt} \text{ with } \psi \sim N(0, 1)$$

$$\text{Var}(dB) = E(\psi^2 \, dt) - [E(\psi \sqrt{dt}\,)]^2 = E(\psi^2)dt = \{\text{Var}(\psi) + [E(\psi)]^2\} \, dt = dt$$

Furthermore, $(dt)^2 = 0$, $dBdt = dtdB = 0$, and $(dB)^2 = dt$.

We can now write the modified Taylor expansion that is known as *Itô's lemma for geometric Brownian motion*:

$$df = \left(\frac{\partial f}{\partial X}\mu X + \frac{\partial f}{\partial t} + \frac{1}{2}\frac{\partial^2 f}{\partial X^2}\sigma^2 X^2 \right)dt + \frac{\partial f}{\partial X}\sigma X dB$$

We can express Itô's lemma in multidimensions as follows:

$$df(t, X_1, \ldots, X_N) = \left(\sum_{i=1}^{N} \frac{\partial f}{\partial X_i}\mu_i + \frac{\partial f}{\partial t} + \frac{1}{2}\sum_{i=1}^{N}\sum_{j=1}^{N} \frac{\partial^2 f}{\partial X_i \partial X_j}\sigma_i\sigma_j\rho_{ij} \right)dt$$

$$+ \sum_{i=1}^{N} \frac{\partial f}{\partial X_i}\sigma_i dB_i$$

In modeling financial variables as geometric Brownian motion processes, the fact that the variance of returns on financial assets could be unbounded over long time horizons could be problematic. In order to build in the realism we expect from the behavior of financial markets, it is important to model returns in a way that ensures stability. To this effect, stochastic processes with mean-reverting properties become highly desirable in financial modeling.

For a random variable $X(t)$, an *Ornstein–Uhlenbeck process* is $dX(t) = k\,[\theta - X(t)]dt + \sigma dB(t)$, with $X(0) = x_0$ and $k \geq 0$. Here k is the speed that the variable $X(t)$ is pulled toward the long-term mean θ when it deviates from it.

A discrete random process $[M_{n \in N}]$ is a *discrete time martingale* if $E[M_n] < \infty$, $\forall n \in N$, and if $E[M_{n+1} | \, M_0, M_1, M_2, \ldots, M_n] = M_n$; a *submartingale* if $E[M_{n+1} | \, M_0, M_1, M_2, \ldots, M_n] \geq M_n$; and a *supermartingale* if $E[M_{n+1} | \, M_0, M_1, M_2, \ldots, M_n] \leq M_n$.

For continuous random processes, a martingale M can be defined as a process where $E[M_t]$ is finite for all t, and $E_t[M_T] = E[M_T | F_T] = M_t$, with F_t to be interpreted as all the prior information associated with the process accumulated until time t and as such a *filtration*.

If M_n is a martingale and T is the *stopping time* defined as a positive random variable that indicates the end of a procedure, if T is bounded, then, under certain conditions, $E[M_T] = E[M_0]$.[3]

If $Z_{i \in N}$ is a sequence of independent and identically distributed random variables with $E[Z_i] = \mu < \infty$ if stopping time $T < \infty$, and if $E[X_T] < \infty$, with $X_T \equiv \sum_{i=1}^{T} Z_i \Rightarrow E[X_T] = \mu E[T]$.

If M_n is a martingale such that $E[|M_n|] < \infty$, $\forall n$, $\lim_{n \to \infty} M_n$ converges with probability one.

Girsanov's theorem describes how the dynamics of stochastic processes change when the original measure is changed to an equivalent probability measure. The theorem states that for a Brownian motion B_t under a probability measure P and a process v_t, there is a measure Q such that $\overline{B}_t = B_t + \int_0^t v_s ds$ is a Brownian motion under Q.

6.1 Random Walk and Arithmetic Brownian Motion

Let us visualize an inebriated person taking a walk in the woods. Starting in front of a large oak, he takes seemingly random steps on a linear path. Let us assume that every step he takes is of the size Δx with a probability p in the positive direction and with a probability $q = 1 - p$ in the negative direction. If we further assume that each step takes time Δt, we can formulate a random variable $X(t)$ to stand for the distance the person could be at time $t = n\Delta t$.

Assuming that each step taken is exactly of the same length (and only in two directions), say ± 1, and duration, we can formalize the random walk by the following equation:

$$X(t) = \sum_{i=1}^{n} Z_i \tag{6.1}$$

where $Z_i \in \{-1, 1\}$, for all $i = 1, 2, 3, \ldots, n$, are independently and identically distributed. We can write the basic statistical properties of expected value and variance of the random variable $X(t)$ as

$$E[X(t)] = \sum_{i=1}^{n} E[Z_i] = \sum_{i=1}^{n} (p - q)\Delta x = n(p - q)\Delta x \tag{6.2}$$

We expect the person to have traveled a distance in either direction as a function of the number of equal steps. The difference between the probabilities of the

---

3 The general optimal sampling theorem due to Doob can be referred to in Lipster and Shiryaev (1977).

direction of the steps of the linear path determines the distance traveled. If the probabilities are equal, the expected position after n steps is exactly the oak tree at which the inebriated person started. That is,

$$\text{Var}[X(t)] = E[X(t)^2] - E[X(t)]^2 = \sum_{i=1}^{n} E[Z_i^2] - \sum_{i=1}^{n} E[Z_i]^2 = 4npq(\Delta x)^2$$

$$= 4\frac{t}{\Delta t}pq(\Delta x)^2 \tag{6.3}$$

The variability around the expectation of distance traveled in either direction is a linear function of the number of steps taken. If probabilities $p = q = \dfrac{1}{2}$, we have the variance given by $n(\Delta x)^2$; as such, we can interpret $(\Delta x)^2$ as the variance of $X(t)$ per unit time. As $\Delta x \rightarrow 0$, this gives us the *instantaneous variance* $\sigma(t)^2$ and the *instantaneous standard deviation* $\sigma(t)$. Similarly, we can obtain the *instantaneous mean* $\mu(t)$.

More generally, we can calibrate p, q, and Δx, the parameters of the random-walk process, to derive

$$E[X(t)] = n(p-q)\Delta x = \frac{t}{\Delta t}(p-q)\Delta x \rightarrow \mu t \tag{6.4}$$

$$\text{Var}[X(t)] = 4npq(\Delta x)^2 = 4\frac{t}{\Delta t}pq(\Delta x)^2 \rightarrow \sigma^2 t \tag{6.5}$$

$$p = \frac{1}{2} + \frac{\mu\sqrt{\Delta t}}{2\sigma} \tag{6.6}$$

$$q = \frac{1}{2} - \frac{\mu\sqrt{\Delta t}}{2\sigma} \tag{6.7}$$

$$\Delta x = \sigma\sqrt{\Delta t} \tag{6.8}$$

From these last three equations derived from (6.4) and (6.5) by taking continuous-time limits, we can obtain the *arithmetic Brownian motion* for X with drift μ and volatility σ. The following relationships hold:

1. $X(t = 0) = 0$.
2. Increments of $X(t + \Delta t) - X(t)$ are independent.
3. $X(t)$ has a mean of μt and a variance of $\sigma^2 t$ and is normally distributed.[4]

---

4 It can be shown that $X(t)$ is normally distributed using the CLT. For a proof, the reader is referred to Baz and Chacko (1994).

We can standardize $X(t)$ by defining a normal variable ϕ with zero mean and variance of one. Thus

$$\phi = \frac{X(t) - \mu t}{\sigma \sqrt{t}} \tag{6.9}$$

Example (Gambler's Ruin): Let us apply the random walk and conditional probability calculus to a problem where two gamblers G and H play a zero-sum game where G's probability of winning is p and losing is $1 - p$. The gamblers bet 1 dollar each time, and G has g dollars and H has $k - g$ dollars in their pockets. The game ends when one ends up with k dollars and the other with nothing. What is the probability that G will end up with k dollars and her opponent will be "ruined"? Gambler G therefore will win if, throughout the entire game, she never goes to zero and ends up at some point in time with k dollars, knowing that she started off with g dollars.

Let $\pi_k(g)$ be the probability that G will reach k before she reaches zero dollars. If $g = 0$, G is ruined, and if $g = k$, she has won. It is easy to see that $\pi_k(g)$ will satisfy the following recursion:

$$\pi_k(g) = p\pi_k(g+1) + (1-p)\pi_k(g-1) \tag{6.10}$$

This follows from the observation that after the first wager, there is a probability that the gambler wins 1 dollar and then from there onward the probability of winning is the same as that of starting from $g + 1$. Similarly for the second term, if the first wager does not obtain, the new probability of success is the same as that starting from $g - 1$, which proves the preceding equation. This equation can be solved by setting

$$\pi_k(g) = c_1 z_1^g + c_2 z_2^g \tag{6.11}$$

where c_1, c_2, z_1, and z_2 are constants to be determined. Plugging the previous formula into the recursion gives

$$c_1 z_1^g \left(pz_1 + \frac{1-p}{z_1} - 1 \right) + c_2 z_2^g \left(pz_2 + \frac{1-p}{z_2} - 1 \right) = 0$$

Because this last equation must be valid for all g, we need to have

$$\left(pz_1 + \frac{1-p}{z_1} - 1 \right) = \left(pz_2 + \frac{1-p}{z_2} - 1 \right) = 0$$

This implies that $z_1 = 1$, $z_2 = (1 - p)/p$, and thus the solution becomes

$$\pi_k(g) = c_1 + c_2 \left(\frac{1-p}{p} \right)^g$$

Now we know that if gambler G starts off with no money, then she will never win, and if she starts off with k dollars, she has already won. Therefore, we must have

$$\pi_k(0) = 0 = c_1 + c_2$$

$$\pi_k(k) = 1 = c_1 + c_2 \left(\frac{1-p}{p} \right)^k$$

Solving these two equations gives the constants and final expression

$$\pi_k(g) = \frac{p^k}{p^k - (1-p)^k} \left[1 - \left(\frac{1-p}{p} \right)^g \right] \tag{6.12}$$

In the limit of a fair game (i.e. where $p \to 1/2$), we have: $\pi_k(g) = g/k$ (using l'Hôpital's rule to calculate the limit), so the probability of winning and avoiding the gambler's ruin is a function of the initial capital of the players. If the initial wealth for G was 90 dollars and for her opponent H just 10 dollars, the probability of G's ruin would be only 10%.

For a game with unequal probabilities $p \neq 1 - p$, the effect of unequal probabilities in favor of one player could significantly change the wealth effect observed earlier:

$$\pi_g = \frac{1 - ((1-p)/p)^g}{1 - ((1-p)/p)^k}, \text{ for } g = 1, 2, \ldots, k-1 \tag{6.13}$$

Thus $p = 0.4$ would imply

$$\frac{1-p}{p} = \frac{3}{2} \text{ and } \pi_g = \frac{1 - (3/2)^g}{1 - (3/2)^k}$$

If G has an initial wealth of 99 dollars, even though the probability of her winning in any given game is 0.4, her probability of winning a dollar before losing 99 is approximately 0.67. If her initial wealth was 90 dollars, this same probability is only 0.017 and approximately zero if it was 80 dollars!

We conclude this section with an interesting example in which two players play a similar game by flipping a fair coin n times for a dollar each time. If we denote the purse of the first player after n throws as W, what is the probability of W being positive?

Let us define the proportion of the times that W is positive as the random variable A. Common sense would say that for a large enough number of throws, say 1,000, the value of A would be around 50%. It turns out that that is not the case[5]:

$$P(A < a) = \frac{1}{\pi} \int_0^a \frac{1}{\sqrt{x(1-x)}} = \frac{2}{\pi} \arcsin \sqrt{a} \qquad (6.14)$$

We now try different values of probabilities for different a's. First the trivial cases: for $a = 0, 0.5, 1 \Rightarrow P(A < a) = 0\%, 50\%, 100\%$, respectively. But if we deviate toward both tails, we get a very different behavior than expected: significantly denser probability masses:

$a = 0.01 \Rightarrow P(A < a) = 6.38\%$ and $a = 0.1 \Rightarrow P(A < a) = 20.5\%$

$a = 0.8 \Rightarrow P(A < a) = 70.5\%$ and $a = 0.9 \Rightarrow P(A < a) = 79.5\%$

6.2 Formal Definition of Arithmetic Brownian Motion

We now formalize the definition of arithmetic Brownian motion using the statistical properties of the random-walk process $X(t)$. Thus

$$X(t) = \mu t + \sigma B(t), \text{ with } X(0) = 0 \qquad (6.15)$$

$B(t)$ is called the *standard Brownian motion* with the special case of the arithmetic Brownian motion with instantaneous mean of zero and standard deviation of one.

We can write (6.1) in differential form as a *stochastic differential equation:*

$$dX(t) = \mu dt + \sigma dB(t) \qquad (6.16)$$

$$dX(t) \equiv X(t + dt) - X(t) \text{ and } dB(t) \equiv B(t + dt) - B(t) = \psi \sqrt{dt} \qquad (6.17)$$

where ψ is a standard normal random variable with a mean of zero and a variance of one.

---

5 See Feller (1968) and Baz and Chacko (1999)

Because of the fact that

$$\lim_{\Delta t \to 0} \frac{\Delta X(t)}{\Delta t} = \mu + \frac{\sigma \psi}{\sqrt{\Delta t}} \to \pm\infty \tag{6.18}$$

Equation (6.16) is not differentiable with respect to t. It is not surprising, perhaps, that the "randomness" of the walk makes a realization of the variable fundamentally unpredictable over short periods of time and *not differentiable*.

In contrast, because $E_t[B(t + \Delta t)] = B(t)$ at time t and because of Cheybyshev's inequality, which states that for any random variable and any $\delta > 0$, $P([X - E[X] \geq \delta] \leq$ var $[X]/\delta^2$, we obtain

$$\lim_{\Delta t \to 0} P[|\, B(t+\Delta t) - E_t B(t+\Delta t)\,| > \delta] \leq \frac{\mathrm{Var}_t[B(t+\Delta t)]}{\delta^2} = \frac{\Delta t}{\delta^2} \to 0$$

The stochastic process $B(t)$ is therefore *continuous*.

6.3 Distribution of the Maximum and Reflection Principle for Brownian Motion

Let $X(t) = B(t)$ so that we have a *driftless standard Brownian motion* process. Given a point $\rho > 0, T_\rho \equiv \inf_t X(t) = \rho$ as the first time the Brownian motion hits the point. Of course, if no such time exists, $T_\rho = \infty$. Actually, we can show that $T_\rho < \infty$ *almost surely* by observing that if $X(t)$ reaches or hits some level $\gamma \geq \rho$ almost surely, then by continuity and because $X(0) = 0$, it hits ρ almost surely.[6] If ρ is reached or hit at time $T_\rho < t$, then it is equally probable, by symmetry, that $X(t)$ will be either below or above ρ. That is,

$$P[X(t) \geq \rho,\ T_\rho \leq t] = P[X(t) \leq \rho,\ T_\rho \leq t] = 0.5 \tag{6.19}$$

which is known as the *reflection principle*, which we demonstrate below. Recalling the definition of total probability,[7]

$$P[X(t) \geq \rho] = P[X(t) \geq \rho, T_\rho \leq t]P[T_\rho \leq t] + P[X(t) \geq \rho, T_\rho \geq t]P[T_\rho \geq t] \tag{6.20}$$

And because $P[X(t) \geq \rho,\ T_\rho \geq t] = 0$, Equations (6.19) and (6.20) imply that

---

6 An event is said to occur *almost surely* if it happens with probability 1. The set of possible exceptions may be not empty but has a probability of zero. In measure theory, this concept is referred to as *almost everywhere*.

7 $P(B) = P(B|A)P(A) + P(B|A^c)(P(A^c))$, where A^c is the complement of A.

$$P(T_\rho \le t) = 2P[X(t) \ge \rho] \tag{6.21}$$

Given a driftless standard Brownian motion $B(t) = X(t) = X(0) + \sigma\psi\sqrt{t}$, for every $\rho \ge 0$, and the maximum value that the sample path trajectory reaches over the interval $[0, t]$ defined as

$$M(t) \equiv \sup_{0 \le \tau \le t} X(\tau) \tag{6.22}$$

$$P[M(t) \ge \rho] = P(T_\rho \le t) = 2P[X(t) \ge \rho] \tag{6.23}$$

From our definition of driftless Brownian motion, we have

$$X(t) = X(0) + \sigma\psi\sqrt{t} \tag{6.24}$$

$$P[M(t) \ge \rho] = 2P[X(0) + \sigma\psi\sqrt{t} \ge \rho] = 2\Phi\left[\frac{X(0)-\rho}{\sigma\sqrt{t}}\right] \tag{6.25}$$

with the cumulative standard normal distribution function given as

$$\Phi(x) = \frac{1}{\sqrt{2\pi}} \int_{-\infty}^{x} e^{(-1/2)y^2} dy \tag{6.26}$$

Example: If $X(t) = X(0) + \sigma\phi\sqrt{t}$ is the stochastic process describing the slope of the yield curve in the United States depicted by the 6-month T-bill, the 10-year Treasury is 100 basis points, and the volatility is 50 basis points, what are the chances that the slope will reach 150 basis points within 1 year? What if the volatility was given by 100 basis points?

We plug the appropriate values into (6.25) to obtain

$$P[M(1) \ge 150] = P[T_{150} \le 1] = 2\Phi\left[\frac{100-150}{50\sqrt{1}}\right] = 2\Phi[-1] = 31.7\%$$

for the first question and

$$P[M(1) \ge 150] = P[T_{150} \le 1] = 2\Phi\left[\frac{100-150}{100\sqrt{1}}\right] = 2\Phi[-0.5] = 61.7\%$$

for the second question.

For the case of a Brownian motion process with a drift, we get

$$X(t) = X(0) + \mu t + \sigma B(t)$$

We can revise Equation (6.25) for the more general case and obtain

$$P[M(t) \geq \rho] = P(T_\rho \leq t) =$$

$$\Phi\left[\frac{X(0) - \rho + \mu t}{\sigma\sqrt{t}}\right] - e^{2\mu[\rho - X(0)]/\sigma^2}\,\Phi\left[\frac{X(0) - \rho - \mu t}{\sigma\sqrt{t}}\right]$$

6.3.1 Functional Central Limit Theorem

Before we proceed to formally introduce Itô calculus, which is quintessential in the development of asset pricing and portfolio selection theories and models, we take a small detour to fulfill our earlier promise and extend the CLT in a stochastic processes setting.

For a sequence $\psi_1, \psi_2, \ldots, \psi_n$ of independent and identically distributed random variables having a zero mean and a finite variance σ^2, let $S_n = \sum_{i=1}^{n} \psi_i$, $S_0 = 0$. For each integer n and each sample point ρ, construct on the unit interval the polygonal function that is linear on each of the subintervals $[(i-1)/n, i/n]$, $i = 1, 2, \ldots, n$, and the values $S_i(\rho)/\sigma\sqrt{n}$ at the points $\left[\frac{i}{n}\right]$. We can construct the function $X^n(\rho)$ whose value at a point $t \in [(0,1)]$ is given by

$$X_t^n(\rho) = \frac{1}{\sigma\sqrt{n}} S_{i-1}(\rho) + \frac{t - [(i-1)/n]}{1/n}\frac{1}{\sigma\sqrt{n}} \psi_i(\rho), t \in \left[\frac{i-1}{n}, \frac{i}{n}\right] \quad (6.27)$$

For each ρ, $X^n(\rho)$ is an element in a random function in the space of continuous functions C.

We will now state a theorem that concludes that $\lim_{n \to \infty} X^n \Rightarrow W$, where W is a Wiener measure that exists in the space C and that describes the probability distribution of the path followed by a particle in Brownian motion. There also exists a Wiener measure in C that describes the probability distribution of the path traversed by a particle in Brownian motion.

The Wiener measure has the following properties:

1. For each $X_t \sim N(0, \sigma^2 = t)$,

$$W(X_t \leq a) = \frac{1}{\sqrt{2\pi t}} \int_{-\infty}^{a} e^{-u^2/2t}\,du \quad (6.28)$$

with $W[X_0 = 0] = 1$.

2. The stochastic process X_t with $t \in [0,1]$ has independent increments under W. If $0 \leq t_0 \leq t_1 \leq \ldots \leq t_k = 1$, then the random variables $X_{t_1} - X_{t_0}, X_{t_2} - X_{t_1}, \ldots, X_{t_k} - X_{t_{k-1}}$ are independent under W.

With these two properties, if $s \leq t$, X_t is the sum of the independent random variables $X_s \sim N(0, s)$ and $X_t - X_s$, so $X_t - X_s \sim N(0, t - s)$. Therefore, if the ordering for t in property 2 holds,

$$W[X_{t_i} - X_{t_{i-1}} \leq a_i; i = 1,2 \ldots, k] = \prod_{i=1}^{k} \frac{1}{\sqrt{2\pi(t_i - t_{i-1})}} \int_{-\infty}^{a_i} e^{u^2/2(t_i - t_{i-1})} du \quad (6.29)$$

the increments are stationary and independent.

Theorem (Donsker's Theorem or the Functional CLT):[8] If $\psi_1, \psi_2, \ldots, \psi_n$ are independent and identically distributed with zero mean and finite variance σ^2, and if X^n is the random function defined by (6.27), then X^n tends toward a Wiener measure or a standard Brownian motion; that is, $\lim_{n \to \infty} X^n \to W$.

6.4 Itô Calculus

Let's start by defining a few notions that will be useful in the following sections. First let us define the abstract space Ω where $\omega \in \Omega$ are individual points representing possible outcomes for an experiment. Let's define a subset of the abstract space as a set of events to which we can assign a probability of happening. Let F be the set of all these events. The probability numbers $P(\cdot)$ are the relative likelihood of these events.

In a probability context, a *σ-algebra* defines an ordered set of events that can be clearly measured in time. A *filtration F* is an indexed set of objects $\{S_i\}_{i \in I}$, where I is an ordered set with $i \leq j$ in I; then $S_i \subset S_j$. If the index is a time parameter of a stochastic process, then the filtration could be seen as all the historical data available about the stochastic process up to the present. A stochastic process that is adapted to a filtration F does not have a predictive ability with respect to the future. In a mathematical finance context, a filtration F represents information available to and including each time t which becomes increasingly more precise as, say, more price information becomes available.

A stochastic process X adapted to the filtration F has the *Markov property* if for a discrete σ-algebra $\{S_i\}_{i \in I}$,

---

8 Please see Billingsley (1968) and Schondorf (2019) for further details and proof.

$$P(X_n = x_n | X_{n-1} = x_{n-1}, X_{n-2} = x_{n-2}..., X_0 = x_0)$$
$$= P(X_n = x_n | X_{n-1} = x_{n-1})$$

A Brownian motion $B(t)$ satisfies the Markov property if for $t > s$, $B(t)$ depends only on $B(F_s)$. F_s is given by $B(s)$.

The strong Markov property says the same thing with s replaced by a stopping time T. That is, if T is a stopping time and $t > T$, then $B(t)$ depends only on F_T.

Theorem 6.1: Suppose that $B(t)$ is Brownian motion. If $t > T$ and T is a stopping time, then $B(t) - B(T)$ is independent of F_T.

6.4.1 Itô Integral of a Simple Process, Quadratic Variation, and Itô Isometry

Let B be a Brownian motion defined on a probability space (Ω, F, P). A process $\Delta(s, \omega)$, a function $s \geq 0$ with $\omega \in \Omega$, is *adapted* if the dependence of $\Delta(s, \omega)$ on ω is as a function of the initial path fragment $B(\mu, \omega)$, $0 \leq \mu \leq s$. Then $\Delta(s)$ is independent of $B(t) - B(s)$, for $0 \leq s \leq t$.

Let $\tau = \{t_0, t_1, t_2,...,t_n\}$ of the closed set $[0, T]$ with $0 = t_0 \leq t_1 \leq t_2 \leq ... \leq t_n = T$. If we assume that $\Delta(s)$ is constant on each subinterval $[t_j, t_{j+1})$, Δ is called a *simple process*. A trivial example is $\Delta(s) = B(t_j)$ for $t_j \leq s \leq t_{j+1}$.

Let $B(s)$ be the price of a share of a financial asset at time s and let the t_j's be the trading dates in the asset and the $\Delta(t_j)$'s be the number of shares acquitted at each trading date and held until the next trading date. We could write the following equations as the payoffs from trading over time:

$$I(t) = \Delta(t_0)[B(t) - B(t_0)] = \Delta(t_0)B(t), 0 \leq t \leq t_1$$

$$I(t) = \Delta(t_0)[B(t_1) - B(t_0)] + \Delta(t_1)[B(t) - B(t_1)], t_1 \leq t \leq t_2$$

$$I(t) = \Delta(t_0)[B(t_1) - B(t_0)] + \Delta(t_1)[B(t_2) - B(t_1)] + \Delta(t_2)[B(t) - B(t_2)], t_2 \leq t \leq t_3$$

$$...$$

The process I is the *Itô integral* of the simple process Δ:

$$I(t) = \int_0^t \Delta(s)dB(s), 0 \leq t \leq T$$

Theorem 6.2: The Itô integral of a simple process has an expectation of zero.

Proof: By definition $I(T) = \sum_{i=0}^{n-1}\Delta(t_i)[B(t_{i+1}) - B(t_i)]$, and $\Delta(t_j)$ is independent of $B(t_{i+1}) - B(t_i)$. Thus

$$E\{\Delta(t_i)[B(t_{i+1}) - B(t_i)]\} = E\Delta(t_i)E[B(t_{i+1}) - B(t_i)] = E\Delta(t_i) \times 0 = 0$$

Theorem 6.3 (Quadratic Variation): The simple Itô integral $I(t) = \int_0^t \Delta(s)dB(s)$ has a *quadratic variation* $[I, I](T) = \int_0^T \Delta^2(s)ds$, which is random.

Proof: Letting $s \in [t_i, t_{i+1}]$, we have $\Delta(s) = \Delta(t_i)$:

$$I(s) = I(t_i) + \Delta(t_i)[B(s) - B(t_i)] = [I(t_i) - \Delta(t_i)B(t_i)] + \Delta(t_i)B(s)$$

$$[I, I](t_{i+1}) - [I, I](t_i) = \Delta^2(t_i)([B, B](t_{i+1}) - [B, B](t_i)) = \Delta^2(t_i)(t_{i+1} - t_i)$$
$$= \int_{t_i}^{t_{i+1}} \Delta^2(s)ds$$

Summing over all the intervals, we get

$$[I, I](T) = \sum_{i=0}^{n-1}([I, I](t_{i+1}) - [I, I](t_i)) = \int_0^T \Delta^2(s)ds \quad \blacksquare$$

Theorem 6.4 (Itô's Isometry): The simple Itô integral $I(t) = \int_0^t \Delta(s)dB(s)$ has a variance given by

$$E[I^2(T)] = E\int_0^T \Delta^2(s)ds$$

that is *not* random. This variance is called *Itô's isometry.*

Proof:

$$I(T) = \sum_{i=0}^{n-1}\Delta(t_i)[B(t_{i+1}) - B(t_i)]$$

Squaring and taking the expected values of both sides,

$$E[I^2(T)] = \sum_{i=0}^{n-1}E\{\Delta^2(t_i)[B(t_{i+1}) - B(t_i)]^2\}$$

$$+ 2\sum_{i<j}E\{\Delta(t_i)\Delta(t_j)[B(t_{i+1}) - B(t_i)][B(t_{j+1}) - B(t_j)]\}$$

Because $\Delta(s)$ is independent of $B(t) - B(s)$, for $0 \le s \le t$,

$$E\{\Delta^2(t_i)[B(t_{i+1}) - B(t_i)]^2\} = E[\Delta^2(t_i)]E\{[B(t_{i+1}) - B(t_i)]^2\}$$
$$= E[\Delta^2(t_i)](t_{i+1} - t_i) = \int_{t_i}^{t_{i+1}} E[\Delta^2(s)]ds$$

We now show that the cross-terms have an expectation of zero. For $i < j$, we know that $B(t_{j+1}) - B(t_j)$ is independent of $\Delta(t_i)\,\Delta(t_j)\,[B(t_{i+1}) - B(t_i)]$. Therefore,

$$E\{\Delta(t_i)\,\Delta\,(t_j)[B(t_{j+1}) - B(t_j)][B(t_{i+1}) - B\,(t_i)]\}$$
$$= E\{\Delta(t_i)\,\Delta\,(t_j)[B(t_{i+1}) - B(t_i)]E[B(t_{j+1}) - B\,(t_j)]\}$$
$$= E\{\Delta(t_i)\,\Delta\,(t_j)[B(t_{i+1}) - B(t_i)]\} \times 0 = 0 \quad \blacksquare$$

6.4.2 Geometric Brownian Motion

A random variable $X(t)$ is said to follow a geometric Brownian motion if the stochastic differential equation holds. That is,

$$dX(t) = \mu X(t)dt + \sigma X(t)dB(t) \qquad (6.30)$$

with the initial condition $X(0) \equiv x_0$. Integrating (6.30) we have

$$X(t) = x_0 e^{[\mu - (\sigma^2/2)]t + \sigma\psi\sqrt{t}} \qquad (6.31)$$

where ϕ is a standard normal variable with zero mean and a variance of one. With these two equations, it is clear that $\log X(t)$ is normally distributed conditional on the initial condition above. That is,

$$\log[X(t)] = \log x_0 + \left(\mu - \frac{\sigma^2}{2}\right)t + \sigma\psi\sqrt{t}$$

with the mean and variance at $t = 0$ given by

$$E_{t=0}[\log X(t)] = \log x_0 + \left(\mu - \frac{\sigma^2}{2}\right)t$$

$$\mathrm{Var}_{t=0}[\log X(t)] = \sigma^2 t$$

The log-normal cumulative distribution function is

$$P[X(t) \le x] = \int_{-\infty}^{x} \frac{1}{\sigma X\sqrt{2\pi t}} e^{-\frac{[\log X - \log x_0 + (\mu - \sigma^2/2)t]^2}{2\sigma^2 t}} dX$$

The change of variables $u = \dfrac{[\log X - \log x_0 + (\mu - \sigma^2/2)t]}{\sigma\sqrt{t}}$ implies that

$$P[X(t) \le x] = \frac{1}{\sqrt{2\pi}} \int_{-\infty}^{} \frac{[\log x - \log x_0 + (\mu - \sigma^2/2)t]^2}{\sigma^2 t} e^{-u^2/2} du$$

$$= \Phi \left\{ \frac{\log x - \log x_0 + (\mu - \sigma^2/2)t}{\sigma \sqrt{t}} \right\}$$

We can express (6.31) as

$$\frac{dX(t)}{X(t)} = d \log X(t) = \mu dt + \sigma dB(t)$$

which makes it easier to see the fractional change of the random variable in time.

6.4.3 Itô's Lemma

Let the random variable $X(t)$ follows the process

$$\frac{dX}{X} = \mu dt + \sigma dB$$

where μ is called the *instantaneous drift*, t is time, σ is the volatility, and dB a Wiener process. Here dB is defined as

$$dB \equiv \psi \sqrt{dt}$$

with $\psi \sim N(0,1)$.[9] It is easy to see that

$$\text{Var}(dB) = E(\psi^2 dt) - [E(\psi \sqrt{dt})]^2 = E \ (\psi^2) dt = (\text{Var}(\psi) + [E(\psi)]^2) dt = dt$$

We go on to fill the following multiplication table:

x	dt	dB
dt	?	?
dB	?	?

---

9 Normally distributed with mean zero and variance one.

Bearing in mind that $(dt)^n$, for $n > 1$, is a negligible quantity $o(dt)$, the following three rules hold:

Rule 1: $(dt)^2 = 0$ because $(dt)^2 = o(dt)$ given that $\lim\limits_{\Delta t \to 0} \dfrac{(\Delta t)^2}{\Delta t} = 0$.

Rule 2: $dBdt = dtdB = 0$ because $dBdt$ is a random variable with

$$E[dBdt] = dtE[dB] = 0$$

$$\text{Var}[dBdt] = (dt)^2\text{Var}(dB) = (dt)^2\text{Var}[\psi\sqrt{dt}] = (dt)^3 = o(dt)$$

Rule 3: $(dB)^2 = dt$

$$E[(dB^2)] = E[(\psi\sqrt{dt})^2] = dt$$

$$\text{Var}((dB)^2) = \text{Var}(\psi^2)(dt)^2 = \{E(\psi^4) - [E(\psi^2)]^2\}(dt)^2 = (3-1)(dt)^2 = 2(dt)^2 = o(dt)$$

where $E(\psi^4) = 3$ is the kurtosis of a standard normal distribution.

Because $\text{Var}((dB)^2)$ is negligible, $(dB)^2$ is equal to expectation dt. Therefore, we can write the following as a multiplication table for stochastic calculus.

x	dt	dB
dt	0	0
dB	0	dt

6.4.4 Itô's Lemma for Geometric Brownian Motion

We want to understand how the total differential of a function of S and t, $f(S, t)$, behaves. Write a Taylor expansion of df up to the first two terms:

$$df(X,t) = \frac{\partial f}{\partial X}dX + \frac{\partial f}{\partial t}dt + \frac{1}{2}\frac{\partial^2 f}{\partial X^2}(dX)^2 + \frac{\partial^2 f}{\partial X\partial t}dXdt + \frac{1}{2}\frac{\partial^2 f}{\partial t^2}(dt)^2$$
$$+ \text{ higher order term}$$

It is easy to see, in reference to the multiplication table, that higher-order terms of the Taylor expansion are negligible.

Since

$$(dX)^2 = (\mu X dt + \sigma X dB)^2 = \sigma^2 X^2 (dB)^2 = \sigma^2 X^2 dt$$

it follows that

$$df = \left(\frac{\partial f}{\partial X} \mu X + \frac{\partial f}{\partial t} + \frac{1}{2} \frac{\partial^2 f}{\partial X^2} \sigma^2 X^2 \right) dt + \frac{\partial f}{\partial X} \sigma X dB$$

This is the simple expression of Itô's lemma when the underlying asset price X follows a geometric Brownian motion.

Example: What is $d(\ln X)$?
If $f(X, t) = \ln X$

then $\dfrac{\partial f}{\partial X} = \dfrac{1}{X}, \dfrac{\partial^2 f}{\partial X^2} = -\dfrac{1}{X^2}, \dfrac{\partial f}{\partial t} = 0$

From Itô's lemma,

$$d(\ln X) = \left(\mu - \frac{\sigma^2}{2} \right) dt + \sigma dB$$

Integrating both sides between zero and T, we get

$$\ln X_T = \ln X_0 + \left(\mu - \frac{\sigma^2}{2} \right) T + \sigma (B_T - B_0)$$

Take exponential on both sides to obtain the expression of X_T as a function of X_0:

$$X_T = X_0 e^{[\mu - (\sigma^2/2)]T + \sigma B_T} = X_0 e^{[\mu - (\sigma^2/2)]T + \sigma \psi \sqrt{T}}$$

6.4.5 Multidimensional Itô's Lemma

In the general case where many underlying variables $X_1, X_2, ..., X_N$ follow the random process

$$dX_i = \mu_i(t, X_1, ..., X_N) dt + \sum_{j=1}^{N} \sigma_{ij} dB_j, i = 1, ..., N$$

with $dB_i dB_j = \rho_{ij} dt$, where ρ_{ij} is in $[-1, 1]$, with $\rho_{ij} = 1$ when $i = j$, then Itô's lemma becomes

$$df(t,X_1,...,X_N) = \left(\sum_{i=1}^{N} \frac{\partial f}{\partial X_i} \mu_i + \frac{\partial f}{\partial t} + \frac{1}{2} \sum_{i=1}^{N} \sum_{j=1}^{N} \frac{\partial^2 f}{\partial X_i \partial X_j} \sigma_i \sigma_j \rho_{ij} \right) dt + \sum_{i=1}^{N} \frac{\partial f}{\partial X_i} \sigma_i dB_i$$

Example: If $\dfrac{dX_1}{X_1} = \mu_1 dt + \sigma_1 dB_1$ and $\dfrac{dX_2}{X_2} = \mu_2 dt + \sigma_2 dB_2$ with $dB_1 \, dB_2 = \rho dt$,

then what is the process followed by $f(X_1, X_2) = \dfrac{X_1}{X_2}$?

We note the following

$$\frac{\partial f}{\partial X_1} = \frac{1}{X_2}, \frac{\partial f}{\partial X_2} = -\frac{X_1}{X_2^2}, \frac{\partial f}{\partial t} = 0, \frac{\partial^2 f}{\partial X_1^2} = 0, \frac{\partial^2 f}{\partial X_2^2} = \frac{2X_1}{X_2^3}, \frac{\partial^2 f}{\partial X_1 \partial X_2} = -\frac{1}{X_2^2}$$

Then

$$\frac{df}{f} = (\mu_1 - \mu_2 - \rho\sigma_1\sigma_2 + \sigma_2^2) dt + \sigma_1 dB_1 - \sigma_2 dB_2$$

We can re-express this by defining

$$dB_f \equiv \frac{\sigma_1 dB_2 - \sigma_2 dB_2}{\sigma_f} \text{ with } \sigma_f \equiv \sqrt{\sigma_1^2 + \sigma_2^2 - 2\rho\sigma_1\sigma_2}$$

Then

$$\frac{df}{f} = \mu_f dt + \sigma_f dB_f \text{ with } \mu_f \equiv \mu_1 - \mu_2 - \rho\sigma_1\sigma_2 + \sigma_2^2$$

6.5 Mean-Reverting Processes

We can see from the preceding discussion that a potential problem in using geo-metric Brownian motion is the fact that the variance of returns on financial assets could be unbounded over long time horizons. In order to build in the realism we expect from the behavior of financial markets, it is important to model returns in a way that ensures stability. To this effect, a stochastic process with mean-reverting properties becomes a highly desirable tool in modeling. The Ornstein–Uhlenbeck process is arguably the best known of such processes. We will briefly discuss its properties.

6.5.1 The Ornstein–Uhlenbeck Process

For the random variable $X(t)$, the general Ornstein–Uhlenbeck process is written as

$$dX(t) = k[\theta - X(t)]dt + \sigma dB(t) \tag{6.32}$$

with $X(0) = x_0$ and $k \geq 0$. k is the speed that the variable $X(t)$ is pulled toward the long-term mean θ when it deviates from it. To obtain the integral version of the process equation, we use Itô's lemma to get

$$d(Xe^{kt}) = e^{kt}(k\theta dt + \sigma dB) \tag{6.33}$$

and integrating (6.33), we get

$$\int_0^t d(Xe^{kt}) = \int_0^t e^{ks}[k\theta ds + \sigma dB(s)] \tag{6.34}$$

$$X(t) = \theta + (x_0 - \theta)e^{-kt} + \sigma \int_0^t e^{-k(t-s)}dB(s) \tag{6.35}$$

which implies that $X(t)$ is normally distributed because the integral is at the limit the sum of normal variables, which is normal.

Because the expectation at $t = 0$ of the second integral is zero, we can write

$$E[X(t)] = \theta + (x_0 - \theta)e^{-kt} \tag{6.36}$$

and the variance at $t = 0$ is given by

$$\text{Var}[X(t)] = E[X(t) - E(X(t))]^2 = \sigma^2 \int_0^t E[e^{-k(t-s)}dB(s)]^2 = \sigma^2 \int_0^t e^{-2k(t-s)}ds$$

$$= \frac{\sigma^2(1-e^{-2kt})}{2k} \tag{6.37}$$

The distribution of $X(t)$ now can be written as

$$P[X(t) \leq x] = \int_{-\infty}^x \frac{1}{\sqrt{2\pi \text{Var}[X(t)]}} e^{-\{X(t)-E[X(t)]\}/\{2\text{Var}[X(t)]\}} dX(t) \tag{6.38}$$

6.6 Poisson Processes

Some stochastic processes involve events that are expected to occur individually and with an expected frequency or average rate per time λ. The number of occurrences of $q(t)$ at a time t and the frequency of occurrences, as well as the fact that the increments of the process are independent, help define the process usually known as *Poisson*. The process starts at $q(0) = 0$, and jumps are expected at a rate or probability $\lambda \Delta t$ in a short interval $(t, t + \Delta t)$. The process is defined by the initial condition $q(0) = 0$ and the probabilities

$$P[q(t + \Delta t) - q(t) = 0] = 1 - \lambda \Delta t + o(\Delta t) \qquad (6.39)$$

$$P[q(t + \Delta t) - q(t) = 1] = \lambda \Delta t + o(\Delta t) \qquad (6.40)$$

$$P[q(t + \Delta t) - q(t) > 1] = o(\Delta t) \qquad (6.41)$$

We define $P_n(t) \equiv P[q(t) = n]$ as the probability distribution of occurrences $q(t)$. Using the Equations (6.39)–(6.41) and the independence of the increments, we obtain

$$P_n(t + \Delta t) = P_n(t)[1 - \lambda \Delta t + o(t)] + P_{n-1}(t)\lambda \Delta t + P_{n-2}(t)o(\Delta t) \qquad (6.42)$$

which implies that

$$\lim_{\Delta t \to 0} \frac{P_n(t + \Delta t) - P_n(t)}{\Delta t} = \frac{P_{n-1}(t)\lambda \Delta t - P_n(t)\lambda \Delta t}{\Delta t} \qquad (6.43)$$

which can be written as

$$\frac{dP_n(t)}{dt} = -\lambda P_n(t) + \lambda P_{n-1}(t) \qquad (6.44)$$

When $n = 0$ and $P_{-1} = 0$, we have

$$\frac{dP_0(t)}{dt} = -\lambda P_0(t) \text{ and } P_0(0) = 1 \qquad (6.45)$$

The solution to (6.45) is then given by $P_0(t) = e^{-\lambda t}$.

To show the case for $n > 0$ we proceed as follows.

From (6.44), we can write

$$e^{\lambda t}\left[\frac{dP_n(t)}{dt} + \lambda P_n(t)\right] = \lambda e^{\lambda t} P_{n-1}(t) = \frac{d[e^{\lambda t} P_n(t)]}{dt} \qquad (6.46)$$

and $P_{n-1}(t)$ can be assumed to be $\dfrac{e^{-\lambda t}(\lambda t)^{n-1}}{(n-1)!}$. Thus

$$\frac{d[e^{\lambda t}P_n(t)]}{dt} = \frac{\lambda^n t^{n-1}}{(n-1)!} \tag{6.47}$$

Integrating both sides, we obtain

$$P_n(t) = \frac{e^{-\lambda t}(\lambda t)^n}{n!} + C \text{ and } P_n(0) = 0 \Rightarrow C = 0$$

Therefore, by induction, we have obtained the desired probability distribution of the random occurrence $q(t)$ as

$$P_n(t) = \frac{e^{-\lambda t}(\lambda t)^n}{n!} \tag{6.48}$$

6.7 Martingales

A discrete random process $[M_{n \in N}]$ is a *martingale* if $E[M_n] < \infty$, $\forall n \in N$, and if

$$E[M_{n+1}|M_0, M_1, M_2,..., M_n] = M_n$$

a *submartingale* if

$$E[M_{n+1}|M_0, M_1, M_2,..., M_n] \geq M_n$$

and a *supermartingale* if

$$E[M_{n+1}|M_0, M_1, M_2,..., M_n] \leq M_n$$

For continuous random processes, a martingale M can be defined a process where $E[M_t]$ is finite $\forall t$,

$$E_t[M_T] = E[M_T | F_t] = M_t$$

with F_t to be interpreted as all the prior information associated with the process accumulated until time t and as such a filtration.[10]

Example: Let the price of financial asset S follow a geometric Brownian motion:

$$\frac{dS}{S} = \mu dt + \sigma dB$$

---

10 This section will simplify the treatment that involves measure theoretical concepts as well as the concepts of Markov chains and processes. We refer the interested reader to Harrison (1985), Hoel, Port, and Stone (1972), Billingsley (1968), and Shreve (2004).

We know that $E(S_T) = S_t e^{\mu(T-t)}$, and therefore we conclude that $S_T e^{-\mu(T-t)}$ follows a martingale because

$$E_t[S_T e^{-\mu(T-t)}] = S_t$$

Because the increments are driven by a Brownian motion that is a martingale, this should not be surprising.[11]

6.7.1 Properties of Martingales

The following three theorems are stated without proofs.[12]

Theorem 6.5 (Optimal Sampling): M_n is a martingale, and T is the *stopping time*, defined as a positive random variable that indicates the end of a procedure. If T is bounded, then under certain conditions,

$$E[M_T] = E[M_0]$$

Theorem 6.6 (Wald): If $Z_{i\in N}$ is a sequence of independent and identically distributed random variables with $E[Z_i] = \mu < \infty$, if stopping time $T < \infty$, and if

$$E[X_T] < \infty \text{ with } X_T \equiv \sum_{i=1}^{T} Z_i \Rightarrow E[X_T] = \mu E[T]$$

Theorem 6.7 (Martingale Convergence): If M_n is a martingale such that $E[|M_n|] < \infty$, $\forall n$, then $\lim_{n\to\infty} M_n$ converges with probability one.

Example (Gambler's Ruin Revisited): Our gambler now has k dollars in her pocket, and she would like to play until she reaches K dollars or loses all she has. Her probability of winning is (where p is not $\frac{1}{2}$) and her probability of losing is $q = 1 - p$. Let us also define her probability of getting to her goal p_K before bankrupting herself. What is her expected stopping time $E[T]$?

$$E[X_T] = (K - k)p_K - k(1 - p_K) = Kp_K - k$$

From Theorem 6.6,

$$E[X_T] = (p - q)E[T]$$

$$E[T] = \frac{p_K K - k}{p - q}$$

---

11 The results hold trivially if the Brownian motion is driftless.
12 See Lipster and Shiryayev (1977), Harrison (1985), and Karlin and Taylor (1981).

and we know form Equation (6.13) that

$$p_K = \frac{1-(q/p)^k}{1-(q/p)^K}$$

6.8 Girsanov's Theorem

Girsanov's theorem describes how the dynamics of stochastic processes change when the original measure is changed to an equivalent probability measure. The theorem states that for a Brownian motion B_t under a probability measure P and a process v_t, there is a measure Q such that[13]

$$\bar{B}_t = B_t + \int_0^t v_s ds$$

is a Brownian motion under Q.

A technical condition for this to happen is

$$E^P(e^{\frac{1}{2}\int_0^t v_s^2 ds}) < \infty$$

The probability measures are rotated by the so-called *Radon–Nikodym* derivative:

$$\frac{dQ}{dP} = e^{-\int_0^t v_s dB_s - \frac{1}{2}\int_0^t v_s^2 ds}$$

We now show why $\bar{B}_t$ is a Brownian motion under Q when v is a scalar:

$$E^Q\left(e^{\theta \bar{B}_t}\right) = E^P\left(\frac{dQ}{dP}e^{\theta \bar{B}_t}\right) = E^P(e^{-vB_t-(v^2t/2)+\theta B_t + v\theta t})$$

Note that $E^P\left(e^{(\theta-v)B_t}\right) = e^{(\theta-v)^2(t/2)}$ because this is a standard moment-generating function of a normal variable. It follows that

$$E^Q(e^{\theta \bar{B}_t}) = e^{\theta^2 t/2}e^{-v\theta t}e^{v\theta t} = e^{\theta^2 t/2}$$

which is the moment-generating function of a normal variable $\bar{B}_t \sim N(0, t)$.

Example: In order to understand the context that Girsanov's theorem could be seen applicable in finance, especially in the pricing of financial derivatives, let us simply state that it helps us transform all stochastic processes in an economy

---

13 Girsanov (1960). Also, please see Billingsley (1968) for a good introduction to measure theory.

into a risk-neutral economy by transforming them using the theorem. The transformation of the Brownian motion B_t into $\bar{B}_t$ lets us do that. Let us assume that the price of a risky financial instrument follows the stochastic process. That is,

$$\frac{dS}{S} = \mu dt + \sigma dB_t$$

Then, for $v = (\mu - r)/\sigma$,

$$d\bar{B}_t = dB_t + \frac{\mu - r}{\sigma} dt \text{ and } \frac{dS}{S} = \mu dt + \sigma\left(d\bar{B}_t - \frac{\mu - r}{\sigma}\right) = rdt + \sigma d\bar{B}t$$

Thus, under Q-measure $\bar{B}_t$, S earns a risk-free rate r:

$$E^Q(S_t) = S_0 e^{rt} \text{ and } E^Q\left(e^{-rt} S_t\right) = S_0$$

meaning that the risky asset discounted at the riskless rate is a martingale under the Q probability measure.

PART II

Portfolio Models

7

Single-Period and Continuous-Time Portfolio Choice

Summary

Single-period portfolio choice

A risky asset and a risk-free asset: The risky asset has expected return μ with variance of returns σ^2, and the risk-free asset earns the risk-free rate r with variance zero. The efficient frontier boils down to a straight line:

$$\mu_p = \frac{\mu - r}{\sigma}\sigma_p + r$$

Two risky assets: We are given risky asset 1 with expected return μ_1 and variance of returns σ_1^2 and asset 2 with expected return μ_2 and variance of returns σ_2^2. Asset returns have correlation ρ. Expressing the standard deviation of the portfolio as a function of μ_p, we get

$$\sigma_p = \sqrt{A_1\mu_p^2 + A_2\mu_p + A_3}$$

which is a hyperbola and

where

$$A_1 = \frac{\sigma_1^2 + \sigma_2^2 - 2\rho\sigma_1\sigma_2}{(\mu_1 - \mu_2)^2}$$

$$A_2 = \frac{-2\mu_2\sigma_1^2 - 2\mu_1\sigma_2^2 + 2\rho\sigma_1\sigma_2(\mu_1 + \mu_2)}{(\mu_2 - \mu_1)^2}$$

$$A_3 = \frac{\mu_2^2\sigma_1^2 + \mu_1^2\sigma_2^2 - 2\rho\sigma_1\sigma_2\mu_1\mu_2}{(\mu_1 - \mu_2)^2}$$

N risky assets: We want to minimize the variance of the portfolio return subject to two constraints: (1) the portfolio weight must add up to one, and (2) the portfolio return is equal to a given target. Therefore, we want to solve

$$\min_x \frac{1}{2} x^T \Sigma x$$

$$\text{subject to } x^T \mu = \mu_p$$

$$\text{and } x^T \mathbf{1} = 1$$

where $x_{(N \times 1)}$ is the column vector of portfolio weights, $\Sigma_{(N \times N)}$ is the covariance matrix of asset returns, $\mathbf{1}_{(N \times 1)}$ is a column vector of ones, $\mu_{(N \times 1)}$ is the column vector of expected asset returns, and μ_p is the portfolio return target, a scalar. Defining

$$A \equiv \mu^T \Sigma^{-1} \mathbf{1}$$

$$B \equiv \mu^T \Sigma^{-1} \mu$$

$$C \equiv \mathbf{1}^T \Sigma^{-1} \mathbf{1}$$

$$D \equiv BC - A^2$$

$$E \equiv \frac{C\Sigma^{-1}\mu - A\Sigma^{-1}\mathbf{1}}{D}$$

$$F \equiv \frac{B\Sigma^{-1}\mathbf{1} - A\Sigma^{-1}\mu}{D}$$

The optimal weight is

$$x = E\mu_p + F$$

In mean-volatility space, the equation of the efficient frontier will be

$$\sigma_p = \sqrt{\frac{C\mu_p^2 - 2A\mu_p + B}{D}}$$

These results follow:

The optimal portfolio weights are a linear function of expected portfolio returns.

The efficient frontier in mean-variance space is a parabola.

The efficient frontier in mean-volatility space is a hyperbola.

N risky assets with a risk-free asset: We now need to solve

$$\min_{x} \frac{1}{2} x^T \Sigma x$$

$$\text{subject to } x^T \mu + (1 - x^T \mathbf{1}) \, r = \mu_p$$

where, as before, $x_{(N \times 1)}$ is the column vector of risky asset weights. The mean-volatility boils down to two half-lines:

$$\mu_p = r \pm \sigma_p \sqrt{B - 2rA + r^2 C}$$

The minimum variance problem could be written in vector form as

$$\min_{x} \sigma_P^2(x) = x^T \Sigma x$$

$$\text{subject to } x^T \mathbf{1} = 1$$

where $x = (x_1, x_2, ..., x_n)$, $\mathbf{1}$ is a vector of n ones, Σ is the $n \times n$ covariance matrix with elements σ_{ij}, with $i, j = 1, 2, 3, ..., n$, and σ_P^2 is the portfolio variance. We can write the optimal weights of a global minimum variance portfolio as

$$x = \frac{\Sigma^{-1}}{\mathbf{1}^T \Sigma^{-1} \mathbf{1}} \mathbf{1}$$

The expected return and variance of the global minimum variance portfolio thus are given by

$$\mu_P = x^T \mu = \frac{\mathbf{1}^T \Sigma^{-1} \mu}{\mathbf{1}^T \Sigma^{-1} \mathbf{1}}$$

$$\sigma_P^2 = x^T \Sigma x = (\mathbf{1}^T \Sigma^{-1} \mathbf{1})^{-1}$$

Because the return of a portfolio W_0 continuously compounded at a rate r yields $W_T = W_0 e^{rT}$ after T periods, it follows that a compounded return or portfolio growth r is

$$r = \frac{\ln \dfrac{W_T}{W_0}}{T}$$

In an uncertain world, because W_0 and T are known quantities at time zero, maximizing the expected growth is equivalent to maximizing $E(\ln W_T)$. This is the so-called Kelly rule.

Continuous-time portfolio choice. Under constant relative risk aversion (CRRA) utility, optimal mean-variance allocation to the risky asset is

$$x^* = \frac{\mu - r}{\gamma \sigma^2}$$

The optimal growth portfolio is

$$x^* = \frac{\mu - r}{\sigma^2}$$

The difference between the mean log (or geometric) return and the mean arithmetic return is not far from half the variance of the arithmetic return. This relationship holds exactly in continuous time when the asset price follows a geometric Brownian motion.

Volatility pumping is more potent with higher volatilities and lower correlations. For single-period portfolio optimizations, mean-variance analysis is consistent with the theoretically popular expected utility maximization framework if the investor's utility is quadratic or if returns are normally distributed.

When $\gamma = 1$, $x_{MV} = x_{OG}$; that is, the mean-variance optimal portfolio is also the optimal growth portfolio. We illustrate this point with two examples where stochastic control and martingales methods lead to the same solution.

7.1 Single-Period Portfolio Choice

7.1.1 Mean-Variance

A Risky Asset and a Risk-Free Asset

The risky asset has expected return μ with variance of returns σ^2, and the risk-free asset earns the risk-free rate r with variance zero. Then the portfolio will have expected return and variance

$$\mu_p = x\mu + (1-x)r \tag{7.1}$$

$$\sigma_p^2 = x^2 \sigma^2 \tag{7.2}$$

From (7.1),

$$x = \frac{\mu_p - r}{\mu - r}$$

(7.3)

Inserting (7.3) into (7.2) gives

$$\sigma_p^2 = \left(\frac{\mu_p - r}{\mu - r}\right)^2 \sigma^2$$

We define the efficient frontier as the set of portfolios with the highest expected return at given risk level. Then, the efficient frontier boils down to a straight line as shown in Figure 7.1:

$$\mu_p = \frac{\mu - r}{\sigma} \sigma_p + r$$

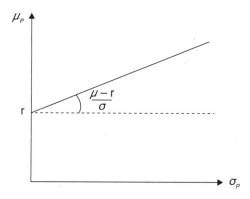

FIGURE 7.1   A risky asset and a risk-free asset

Example: If

$$\mu = 4\%$$
$$r = 1\%$$
$$\sigma = 15\%$$

Then the efficient frontier equation is

$$\mu_p = 0.2\,\sigma_p + 0.01$$

Two Risky Assets

We are given risky asset 1 with expected return μ_1 and variance of returns σ_1^2 and asset 2 with expected return μ_2 and variance of returns σ_2^2. Asset returns have correlation ρ. Thus a portfolio that allocates a proportion $(1 - x)$ to asset 1 and x to asset 2 will have an expected return and covariance of

$$\mu_p = (1 - x)\mu_1 + x\mu_2 \tag{7.4}$$

$$\sigma_p^2 = (1 - x)^2 \sigma_1^2 + x^2 \sigma_2^2 + 2\rho\sigma_1\sigma_2 x(1 - x) \tag{7.5}$$

From (7.4),

$$x = \frac{\mu_p - \mu_1}{\mu_2 - \mu_1} \tag{7.6}$$

Inserting (7.6) into (7.5), we get the equation expressing σ_p^2 as a function of μ_p. A bit of algebra shows that

$$\sigma_p^2 = A_1\mu_p^2 + A_2\mu_p + A_3 \tag{7.7}$$

where

$$A_1 = \frac{\sigma_1^2 + \sigma_2^2 - 2\rho\sigma_1\sigma_2}{(\mu_1 - \mu_2)^2}$$

$$A_2 = \frac{-2\mu_2\sigma_1^2 - 2\mu_1\sigma_2^2 + 2\rho\sigma_1\sigma_2(\mu_1 + \mu_2)}{(\mu_2 - \mu_1)^2}$$

$$A_3 = \frac{\mu_2^2\sigma_1^2 + \mu_1^2\sigma_2^2 - 2\rho\sigma_1\sigma_2\mu_1\mu_2}{(\mu_1 - \mu_2)^2}$$

Equation (7.7) is a parabola.

Expressing the volatility of the portfolio as a function of μ_p, we get

$$\sigma_p = \sqrt{A_1\mu_p^2 + A_2\mu_p + A_3} \tag{7.8}$$

Equation (7.8) is a hyperbola.

Example: If

$$\sigma_1 = 20\%$$

$$\sigma_2 = 30\%$$

$$\rho = 50\%$$

$$\mu_1 = 10\%$$
$$\mu_2 = 20\%,$$

then

$$A_1 = 7$$
$$A_2 = -1.6$$
$$A_3 = 0.13$$

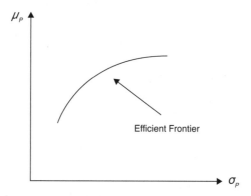

FIGURE 7.2 Two risky assets

The efficient frontier equation (as shown in Figure 7.2) is

$$\sigma_p = \sqrt{7\mu_p^2 - 1.6\mu_p + 0.13}$$

From (7.5), note that if $\rho = 1$, then $\sigma_p = |(1 - x)\,\sigma_1 + x\sigma_2|$, and

$$x = \frac{\pm\sigma_p - \sigma_1}{\sigma_2 - \sigma_1} \tag{7.9}$$

Combining (7.6) and (7.9) gives

$$\mu_p = \pm\frac{\mu_2 - \mu_1}{\sigma_2 - \sigma_1}\sigma_p + \frac{\mu_1\sigma_2 - \mu_2\sigma_1}{\sigma_2 - \sigma_1} \tag{7.10}$$

In the perfect correlation case, the efficient frontier becomes a straight line. When $\rho = -1$, we have $\sigma_p = |(1 - x)\,\sigma_1 - x\sigma_2|$. Then

$$x = \frac{\sigma_1 \pm \sigma_p}{\sigma_1 + \sigma_2}$$

and

$$\mu_p = \pm \frac{\mu_1 - \mu_2}{\sigma_1 + \sigma_2} \sigma_p + \frac{\mu_1 \sigma_2 + \mu_2 \sigma_1}{\sigma_2 + \sigma_1} \tag{7.11}$$

Lastly, note that to determine the minimum variance portfolio, we differentiate σ_p^2 with respect to x using (7.5). Thus

$$\frac{\partial \sigma_p^2}{\partial x} = -2(1-x)\sigma_1^2 + 2x\sigma_2^2 - 2(2x-1)\rho\sigma_1\sigma_2 = 0$$

$$\rightarrow x_{\text{min variance}} = \frac{\sigma_1^2 - \rho\sigma_1\sigma_2}{\sigma_1^2 - 2\rho\sigma_1\sigma_2 + \sigma_2^2}$$

Equations (7.10) and (7.11) describe the efficient frontier when $\rho = 1$ and $\rho = -1$ (see Figure 7.3).

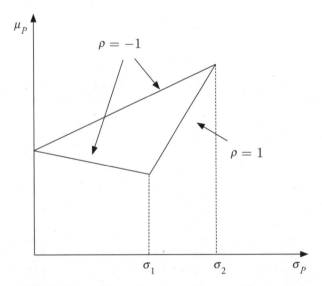

FIGURE 7.3 Efficient frontiers with two risky assets

N Risky Assets

We want to minimize the variance of the portfolio return subject to two constraints: (1) the portfolio weight must add up to one, and (2) the portfolio return is equal to a given target. Therefore, we want to solve

$$\min_{x} \frac{1}{2} x^T \Sigma x$$

$$\text{subject to } x^T \mu = \mu_p$$

$$\text{and } x^T \mathbf{1} = 1$$

where $x_{(N \times 1)}$ is the column vector of portfolio weights, $\Sigma_{(N \times N)}$ is the covariance matrix of asset returns, $\mathbf{1}_{(N \times 1)}$ is a column vector of ones, $\mu_{(N \times 1)}$ is the column vector of expected asset returns, and μ_p is the portfolio return target, a scalar. The Lagrangian is

$$L(x, \lambda_1, \lambda_2) = \frac{1}{2} x^T \Sigma x + \lambda_1 (\mu_p - x^T \mu) + \lambda_2 (1 - x^T \mathbf{1})$$

To solve the problem, we first differentiate the L function with respect to the vector x and the scalars λ_1 and λ_2 and set the derivatives equal to zero.

The first order conditions are

$$\frac{\partial L}{\partial x} = \Sigma x - \lambda_1 \mu - \lambda_2 \mathbf{1} = 0 \tag{7.12}$$

$$\frac{\partial L}{\partial \lambda_1} = \mu_p - x^T \mu = 0 \tag{7.13}$$

$$\frac{\partial L}{\partial \lambda_2} = 1 - x^T \mathbf{1} = 0 \tag{7.14}$$

From $\partial L / \partial x = 0$, we get

$$x = \lambda_1 \Sigma^{-1} \mu + \lambda_2 \Sigma^{-1} \mathbf{1} \tag{7.15}$$

Replacing x by its expression in (7.13) and (7.14) gives

$$\lambda_1 \mu^T \Sigma^{-1} \mu + \lambda_2 \mu^T \Sigma^{-1} \mathbf{1} = \mu_p$$

$$\lambda_1 \mu^T \Sigma^{-1} \mathbf{1} + \lambda_2 \mathbf{1}^T \Sigma^{-1} \mathbf{1} = 1$$

These expressions follow from $x^T = \lambda_1 \mu^T \Sigma^{-1} + \lambda_2 \mathbf{1}^T \Sigma^{-1}$ (recall that because Σ is symmetric, Σ^{-1} is symmetric and $(\Sigma^{-1})^T = \Sigma^{-1}$) and from $\mathbf{1}^T \Sigma^{-1} \mu = \mu^T \Sigma^{-1} \mathbf{1}$ (because the transpose of a scalar is this scalar). These expressions represent two equations with two unknowns, λ_1 and λ_2. Defining

$$A \equiv \mu^T \Sigma^{-1} \mathbf{1}$$

$$B \equiv \mu^T \Sigma^{-1} \mu$$

$$C \equiv \mathbf{1}^T \Sigma^{-1} \mathbf{1}$$

$$D \equiv BC - A^2$$

the results follow:

$$\lambda_1 = \frac{C\mu_p - A}{D} \tag{7.16}$$

$$\lambda_2 = \frac{B - A\mu_p}{D} \tag{7.17}$$

We now define E and F as

$$E \equiv \frac{C\Sigma^{-1}\mu - A\Sigma^{-1}1}{D}$$

$$F \equiv \frac{B\Sigma^{-1}1 - A\Sigma^{-1}\mu}{D}$$

We immediately obtain the expression for optimal weight from (7.15)–(7.17):

$$x = E\mu_p + F \tag{7.18}$$

The expression of the efficient frontier in mean-variance space also follows from (7.13)–(7.17):

$$\begin{aligned}
\sigma_p^2 &= x^T \Sigma x \\
&= x^T \Sigma (\lambda_1 \Sigma^{-1}\mu + \lambda_2 \Sigma^{-1}1) \\
&= \lambda_1 \mu_p + \lambda_2 \\
&= \frac{C\mu_p^2 - 2A\mu_p + B}{D}
\end{aligned} \tag{7.19}$$

In mean-volatility space, the equation of the efficient frontier thus will be

$$\sigma_p = \sqrt{\frac{C\mu_p^2 - 2A\mu_p + B}{D}} \tag{7.20}$$

These results follow:

1. From (7.18), we can see that the optimal portfolio weights are a linear function of expected portfolio returns.
2. From (7.19), it appears that the efficient frontier in mean-variance space is a parabola.
3. From (7.20), it can be inferred that the efficient frontier in mean volatility space is a hyperbola.

N Risky Assets with a Risk-Free Asset

We now need to solve the following problem:

$$\min_{x} \frac{1}{2} x^T \Sigma x$$

$$\text{subject to } x^T \mu + (1 - x^T \mathbf{1}) \, r = \mu_p$$

where, as before, $x_{(N \times 1)}$ is the column vector of risky asset weights. Note that $x^T \mathbf{1} = 1$ is no longer a constraint because we can buy and sell a risk-free asset that earns risk-free rate r. The Lagrangian is

$$L(x, \lambda) = \frac{1}{2} x^T \Sigma x + \lambda[\mu_p - x^T \mu - (1 - x^T \mathbf{1})r]$$

The first-order conditions are

$$\frac{\partial L}{\partial x} = \Sigma x - \lambda \mu + \lambda r \mathbf{1} = 0 \tag{7.21}$$

$$\frac{\partial L}{\partial \lambda} = \mu_p - x^T \mu - (1 - x^T \mathbf{1}) \, r = 0 \tag{7.22}$$

From (7.21), we get

$$x = \lambda \Sigma^{-1}(\mu - r\mathbf{1})$$

Premultiply by $(\mu - r\mathbf{1})^T$, and use (7.22) to find λ:

$$\lambda = \frac{\mu_p - r}{(\mu - r\mathbf{1})^T \Sigma^{-1}(\mu - r\mathbf{1})}$$

Note that

$$(\mu - r\mathbf{1})^T \Sigma^{-1}(\mu - r\mathbf{1}) = B - 2rA + r^2 C$$

Hence the mean-variance equation becomes

$$\sigma_p^2 = x^T \Sigma x$$

$$= x^T \Sigma \lambda \Sigma^{-1}(\mu - r\mathbf{1})$$

$$= \lambda(x^T \mu - r x^T \mathbf{1})$$

$$= \lambda(\mu_p - r)$$

$$= \frac{(\mu_p - r)^2}{B - 2rA + r^2 C}$$

And the mean-volatility boils down to two half-lines:

$$\mu_p = r \pm \sigma_p \sqrt{B - 2rA + r^2 C}$$

A Geometric Interpretation

Let us assume that we have a market with n risky assets and one risk-free asset. Let us further depict their return-risk characteristics in a mean-standard deviation diagram as shown in Figure 7.4. If we were to construct any portfolio from all the possible weighted combinations of the *risky assets* such that $\Sigma_{i=1}^{n} x_i = 1$, the set of points corresponding to all these portfolios will be known as the *feasible set* or *region*.

The left boundary of this feasible set is the *minimum variance set* because for any expected return, the feasible point with the smallest standard deviation will be the left boundary point. The left-most point of this boundary will be the *minimum variance point*. The upper part of the minimum variance set (to the right of the minimum variance point) is known as the *efficient frontier*. It contains all portfolios with the best possible mean-variance combinations.[1]

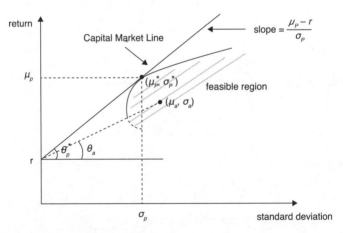

FIGURE 7.4   Geometric interpretation of mean-variance optimization

From Figure 7.4, if we draw a line between the risk-free rate of return r and any point in the feasible region and denote the angle between the line and the horizontal axis by θ, for any *feasible* risky asset portfolio we obtain

---

1 We can think of this efficiency as being Pareto optimal in the sense that deviating from a point on it in order to achieve a better risk and return is not possible.

$$\tan \theta = \frac{\mu - r}{\sigma} \equiv \text{Sharpe ratio}$$

The tangent portfolio P is the feasible point on the efficient frontier that maximizes the angle θ. Any portfolio with an expected return of μ_a and a standard deviation of σ_a in the feasible region including its boundary forms an angle $\theta_a \leq \theta_P$ with the horizontal axis, and its tangent (or its Sharpe ratio) is smaller in magnitude than or equal to the optimal portfolio's. The Sharpe ratio, a common measure of risk-reward tradeoff, is defined as the excess return of a portfolio over the risk-free asset to the portfolio's standard deviation.

Let us assume that we have n risky assets with weights x_i that sum up to one in the tangent portfolio (there is no risk-free asset in the portfolio, and short selling is allowed). Thus

$$\mu_P = \Sigma_{i=1}^n x_i \mu_i \text{ and } r = \Sigma_{i=1}^n x_i r$$

We can write the following:

$$\tan \theta = \frac{\mu_P - r}{\sigma_P} = \frac{\Sigma_{i=1}^n x_i (\mu_i - r)}{(\Sigma_{i,j=1}^n \sigma_{ij} x_i x_j)^{1/2}} = \frac{x^T (\mu - r)}{(x^T \Sigma x)^{1/2}}$$

To get the maximum value of the tangent, we differentiate the preceding expression with respect to each asset weight x_k and set it equal to zero. Thus

$$\frac{\partial \tan \theta}{\partial x_k} = 0 = \frac{(\mu_k - r)(\Sigma_{i,j=1}^n \sigma_{ij} x_i x_j)^{1/2} - (\Sigma_{i=1}^n x_i \mu_i - r)\frac{\partial}{\partial x_k}(\Sigma_{i,j=1}^n \sigma_{ij} x_i x_j)^{1/2}}{\Sigma_{i,j=1}^n \sigma_{ij} x_i x_j}$$

or in vector form

$$\frac{\partial \tan \theta}{\partial x} = 0 = \frac{(\mu - r)(x^T \Sigma x)^{1/2} - (\mu_P - r)\frac{\partial}{\partial x}(x^T \Sigma x)^{1/2}}{x^T \Sigma x}$$

Note that

$$\frac{\partial}{\partial x_k}\left(\sum_{i,j=1}^n \sigma_{ij} x_i x_j\right)^{1/2} = \left(\sum_{i,j=1}^n \sigma_{ij} x_i x_j\right)^{-1/2} \sum_{j=1}^n \sigma_{kj} x_j$$

or in vector form

$$\frac{\partial}{\partial x}(x^T \Sigma x)^{1/2} = (x^T \Sigma x)^{-1/2} \Sigma x$$

Therefore, we have

$$\mu_k - r = \frac{\sum_{i=1}^n x_i(\mu_i - r)}{\sum_{i,j=1}^n \sigma_{ij} x_i x_j} \sum_{i=1}^n \sigma_{ki} x_i, \text{ for all } k = 1, 2, \ldots, n$$

or in vector form

$$\mu - r = \frac{x^T \mu - r}{x^T \Sigma x} \Sigma x$$

Define

$$\lambda \equiv \frac{\sum_{i=1}^n x_i(\mu_i - r)}{\sum_{i,j=1}^n \sigma_{ij} x_i x_j} = \frac{x^T(\mu - r)}{x^T \Sigma x}$$

which is the ratio of the expected excess return of the portfolio over the risk-free rate to the portfolio variance.

We can also interpret the coefficient as the ratio of the Sharpe ratio to the portfolio standard deviation. Rewriting the first-order conditions using the definition of λ, we get

$$\sum_{i=1}^n \sigma_{ki} \lambda x_i = \mu_k - r, \text{ for } k = 1, 2, .., n \qquad (7.23)$$

And the optimal weights are given by solving the n equations and normalizing, we get

$$x_i = \frac{\lambda x_i}{\sum_{k=1}^n \lambda x_k} \qquad (7.24)$$

Illustrative Example: Suppose that we have three uncorrelated assets x_1, x_2, and x_3 with expected returns $\mu_1 = 1\%$, $\mu_2 = 2\%$, and $\mu_3 = 3\%$. The variances are all equal to 1%. Let's assume that the risk-free rate is $r = 0.5\%$. We can write (7.23) as

$$z_1 \equiv \lambda x_1 = (1\% - 0.5\%)/1\% = 0.5$$
$$z_2 \equiv \lambda x_2 = (2\% - 0.5\%)/1\% = 1.5$$
$$z_3 \equiv \lambda x_3 = (3\% - 0.5\%)/1\% = 2.5$$

Now using (7.24), where

$$\sum_{i=1}^3 z_i \equiv \sum_{i=1}^3 \lambda x_i = 0.5 + 1.5 + 2.5 = 4.5$$

we obtain the optimal allocations:

$$x_1 = \frac{0.5}{4.5} = \frac{1}{9}$$

$$x_2 = \frac{1.5}{4.5} = \frac{1}{3}$$

$$x_3 = \frac{2.5}{4.5} = \frac{5}{9}$$

Global Minimum Variance Portfolio

Let us start with a special case of mean-variance optimization problems in which the portfolio contains only risky assets. We are not constrained to the choice of asset weights, except that they add up to one even after short selling is allowed.

This global mean-variance problem could be written in vector form as

$$\min_{x} \frac{1}{2}\sigma_P^2(x) = \frac{1}{2}x^T \Sigma x$$
$$\text{subject to} \quad x^T \mathbf{1} = 1$$

where $x = (x_1, x_2, ..., x_n)$ and $\mathbf{1}$ is a vector of n ones. Here Σ is the $n \times n$ covariance matrix with elements σ_{ij}, with $i,j = 1, 2, 3, ..., n$, and σ_P^2 is the portfolio variance.

We attempt to solve the problem using the Lagrange multiplier method. The Lagrangian for this problem could be written as

$$L(x) = \frac{1}{2}x^T \Sigma x + \lambda(1 - x^T \mathbf{1})$$

By setting the derivative of the Lagrangian with respect to x equal to zero, we obtain

$$\frac{\partial L(x)}{\partial x} = \Sigma x - \lambda \mathbf{1} = 0$$

Therefore, the *optimal* portfolio weights are given by

$$x = \lambda \, \Sigma^{-1} \mathbf{1}$$

and the Lagrange multiplier is

$$\lambda = (\mathbf{1}^T \Sigma^{-1} \mathbf{1})^{-1}$$

We can write the optimal weights of a global minimum variance portfolio as

$$x = \frac{\Sigma^{-1}\mathbf{1}}{\mathbf{1}^T \Sigma^{-1}\mathbf{1}}$$

The expected return and variance of the global minimum variance portfolio are thus given by

$$\mu_p = x^T\mu = \frac{\mathbf{1}^T \Sigma^{-1}\mu}{\mathbf{1}^T \Sigma^{-1}\mathbf{1}}$$

$$\sigma_p^2 = x^T\Sigma x = (\mathbf{1}^T\Sigma^{-1}\mathbf{1})^{-1}$$

The volatility of the global minimum variance portfolio is given by

$$\sigma_p = (\mathbf{1}^T \Sigma^{-1}\mathbf{1})^{-1/2}$$

7.1.2 Optimal Growth

Compounded Returns

Because the return of a portfolio W_0 continuously compounded at a rate r yields $W_T = W_0 e^{rT}$ after T periods, it follows that a compounded return or portfolio growth r is

$$r = \frac{\ln \dfrac{W_T}{W_0}}{T}$$

In an uncertain world, because W_0 and T are known quantities at time zero, maximizing expected growth is equivalent to maximizing $E(\ln W_T)$. This is the so-called Kelly rule. A nice property of the Kelly strategy is that the probability that it will outperform an alternative fixed-mix strategy over time is always higher than 50% and converges to 100% as the investment horizon goes to infinity (see Appendix for the derivation for a simple example with one risky asset).

Optimal Growth Portfolio with a Risky Asset and a Risk-Free Asset in Discrete Time

We want to allocate a portfolio between a risky asset and a risk-free asset to maximize the expected growth of the portfolio. Denote by x the portfolio allocation to the risky asset and by $(1 - x)$ the allocation to the risk-free asset. Assume that the risky asset doubles in value with probability p and is worth zero with probability $(1 - p)$, then

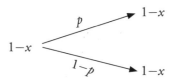

the risk-free asset earns zero interest. Therefore,

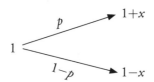

And the portfolio will evolve as follows:

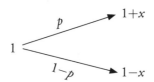

Hence

$$E(\ln W) = p \ln (1 + x) + (1 - p) \ln(1 - x)$$

To maximize the expected portfolio growth, choose x such that

$$\frac{\partial E(\ln W)}{\partial x} = \frac{p}{1+x} - \frac{1-p}{1-x} = 0$$

$$\rightarrow x^* = 2p - 1$$

and the optimal growth will be

$$p \ln(2p) + (1 - p) \ln(2 - 2p)$$

Table 7.1 shows optimal expected growth as a function of p after one game.

$p(\%)$	Optimal growth(%)
50	0
52	0.08
54	0.33
60	2.01
70	8.23
80	19.27
90	36.81

Similarly, if the risky asset value is multiplied by $m \geq 1$ with probability p or divided by m with probability $(1 - p)$, then

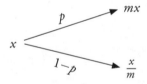

As before, the risk-free asset earns no interest. Then

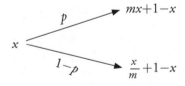

and

$$E(\ln W) = p\ln[(m-1)x+1]+(1-p)\ln\left(\frac{x}{m}+1-x\right)$$

The first-order condition stemming from $\partial E(\ln W)/\partial x = 0$ is

$$\frac{p(m-1)}{x^*(m-1)+1} = \frac{(1-p)\left(1-\dfrac{1}{m}\right)}{1+x^*\left(\dfrac{1}{m}-1\right)}$$

The optimal asset allocation to risky asset is therefore

$$x^* = \frac{p(m+1)-1}{m-1} \tag{7.25}$$

Example: An asset value that is multiplied by 3 with probability 1/2 and by 1/3 with probability 1/2. There is also a risk-free asset that yields zero interest. The expected growth on the risky asset is

$$\frac{1}{2}\ln 3 + \frac{1}{2}\ln\frac{1}{3} = 0$$

Both assets have an expected growth rate of zero. What happens when we combine the assets in a portfolio?

Say that we invest a quarter of our initial wealth in the risky asset and three quarters in the risk-free assets: the payoff t will be

In the upstate:

$$\left(\frac{1}{4}\times 3\right)+\left(\frac{3}{4}\times 1\right)=\frac{3}{2}$$

In the downstate:

$$\left(\frac{1}{4}\times\frac{1}{3}\right)+\left(\frac{3}{4}\times 1\right)=\frac{5}{6}$$

And the expected growth rate will be

$$\frac{1}{2}\ln\frac{3}{2}+\frac{1}{2}\ln\frac{5}{6}=11.57\%$$

By combining two zero-expected-growth assets, the portfolio has an expected growth of 11.57%! It appears that diversification increases the expected portfolio growth. This is the so-called volatility pumping (we will discuss this more later).

The next question in this example is: Can we reach an expected growth even higher than 11.57%? We can use Equation (7.25) to find the risky allocation x that maximizes expected growth.

The answer is

$$\frac{\frac{1}{2}(3+1)-1}{3-1}=\frac{1}{2}$$

meaning that we allocate half the initial wealth to each of the risky and risk-free assets. The payoff is now

In the upstate:

$$\left(\frac{1}{2}\times3\right)+\left(\frac{1}{2}\times1\right)=2$$

In the downstate:

$$\left(\frac{1}{2}\times\frac{1}{3}\right)+\left(\frac{1}{2}\times1\right)=\frac{2}{3}$$

The optimal growth is then

$$\frac{1}{2}\ln2+\frac{1}{2}\ln\frac{2}{3}=14.38\%$$

7.2 Continuous-Time Portfolio Choice

7.2.1 Mean-Variance in Continuous Time

We posit a constant relative risk aversion (CRRA) utility function

$$U(W)=\frac{W^{1-\gamma}}{1-\gamma}$$

where W is wealth and γ is the risk aversion coefficient. We choose the allocations to a risky and a risk-free asset so as to maximize $E[U(W)]$. Note that maximizing $E[W^{1-\gamma}/(1-\gamma)]$ is equivalent to maximizing $E(W^{1-\gamma})$. Define $U\equiv W^{1-\gamma}$, Then, by Itô's lemma,

$$dU=(1-\gamma)W^{-\gamma}dW-\frac{\gamma(1-\gamma)}{2}W^{-\gamma-1}(dW)^2$$

and

$$\frac{dU}{U} = (1-\gamma)\frac{dW}{W} - \frac{\gamma(1-\gamma)}{2}\left(\frac{dW}{W}\right)^2 \qquad (7.26)$$

The risky asset price S follows:

$$\frac{dS}{S} = \mu dt + \sigma dB$$

The risk-free asset earns rdt. And the portfolio allocates x to the risky asset and $(1-x)$ to the risk-free asset and therefore obeys the following process:

$$\frac{dW}{W} = [r + x(\mu - r)]dt + x\sigma dB \qquad (7.27)$$

From (7.26) and (7.27), we obtain the process followed by dU/U:

$$\frac{dU}{U} = (1-\gamma)\left\{[r + x(\mu - r)] - \frac{\gamma}{2}x^2\sigma^2\right\}dt + (1-\gamma)x\sigma dB$$

The expression for $E(U_T)$ follows:

$$E(U_T) = U_0 e^{(1-\gamma)[r + x(\mu-r) - (\gamma/2)x^2\sigma^2]T}$$

and $\underset{x}{max}\, E(U_T)$ is equivalent to

$$\frac{\partial[r + x(\mu - r) - (\gamma/2)x^2\sigma^2]}{\partial x} = 0$$

which yields the allocation to the risky asset:

$$x^* = \frac{\mu - r}{\gamma\sigma^2} \qquad (7.28)$$

Vital statistics of the mean-variance portfolios are found by plugging (7.28) into (7.27). Thus

$$\frac{dW}{W} = \left[r + \frac{1}{\gamma}\left(\frac{\mu-r}{\sigma}\right)^2\right]dt + \frac{1}{\gamma}\frac{\mu-r}{\sigma}dB$$

The expected excess return of the portfolio is $1/\gamma[(\mu - r)/\sigma]^2$, that is, the square of the Sharpe ratio of the risky asset divided by the risk aversion coefficient. The volatility of the portfolio returns is $(\mu - r)/(\gamma\sigma)$, that is, the Sharpe ratio of the risky asset divided by the risk aversion coefficient. And the Sharpe ratio of the mean-variance portfolio is

$$\frac{\frac{1}{\gamma}[(\mu-r)/\sigma]^2}{\frac{\mu-r}{\gamma\sigma}} = \frac{\mu-r}{\sigma}$$

which is the Sharpe ratio of the risky asset.

Example: If the risky asset is the Standard & Poor's 500 Index (S&P 500) and the risk-free asset is T-bills and these assets earn an expected return of μ and r and $\mu - r = 3\%$, $\sigma = 20\%$, and $\gamma = 3$, then this portfolio allocation to the S&P 500 is $(\mu - r)/(\gamma\sigma^2) = 3\%/(3 \times 4\%) = 25\%$. The volatility of the portfolio is $3\%/(3 \times 20\%) = 5\%$, and the Sharpe ratio of the portfolio is 15%. The expected excess return of the portfolio is $(15\%)^2/3 = 0.75\%$.

7.2.2 Optimal Growth in Continuous Time

We want to allocate a portfolio between a risky and a risk-free asset to maximize the geometric growth rate of the portfolio. The risky asset price follows a geometric Brownian motion. Thus

$$\frac{dS}{S} = \mu dt + \sigma dB$$

whereas the risk-free asset yields rdt. If x is the weight of the risky asset in the portfolio, then

$$\frac{dW}{W} = x(\mu dt + \sigma dB) + (1-x)rdt = [r + x(\mu - r)]dt + x\sigma dB \qquad (7.29)$$

To maximize portfolio growth, first note that, by Itô's lemma,

$$d\ln W = \left[r + x(\mu - r) - \frac{x^2\sigma^2}{2}\right]dt + x\sigma dB$$

or

$$\ln W_T = \ln W_0 + \left[r + x(\mu - r) - \frac{x^2\sigma^2}{2}\right]T + x\sigma B_T$$

and

$$E(\ln W_T) = \ln W_0 + \left[r + x(\mu - r) - \frac{x^2\sigma^2}{2}\right]T$$

We pick x such that

$$\frac{\partial E(\ln W_T)}{\partial x} = [(\mu - r) - x\sigma^2]T = 0$$

Hence

$$x = \frac{\mu - r}{\sigma^2} \tag{7.30}$$

Replace x by its value in (7.30) into (7.29) to get

$$\frac{dW}{W} = \left[r + \left(\frac{\mu - r}{\sigma}\right)^2\right]dt + \frac{\mu - r}{\sigma}dB$$

Hence the excess return of an optimal growth portfolio over the risk-free rate is $[(\mu - r)/\sigma]^2$, that is, the square of the Sharpe ratio of the risky asset. The volatility of the portfolio is $(\mu - r)/\sigma$, that is, the Sharpe ratio of the risky asset. The Sharpe ratio of the optimal portfolio is

$$\frac{\left(\frac{\mu - r}{\sigma}\right)^2}{\frac{\mu - r}{\sigma}} = \frac{\mu - r}{\sigma}$$

also the Sharpe ratio of the risky asset.

Example: Consider an optimal portfolio comprised of the S&P 500 and T-bills earning expected returns of μ and r, respectively. If $\mu - r = 3\%$ and $\sigma = 20\%$, then the portfolio allocation to the S&P 500 should be $(\mu - r)/\sigma^2 = 3\%/4\% = 75\%$. The volatility of the portfolio is $3\%/20\% = 15\%$, and the Sharpe ratio of the portfolio would also be equal to 15%. The expected excess return of the portfolio is $(15\%)^2 = 2.25\%$.

7.2.3 Geometric and Arithmetic Growth Rates

If r is an arithmetic rate of returns, then a second-order Taylor expansion of $\ln(1 + r)$ around $E(r)$ gives

$$\ln(1+r) \approx \ln[1 + E(r)] + \frac{r - E(r)}{1 + E(r)} - \frac{[r - E(r)]^2}{2[1 + E(r)]^2}$$

Taking expectations on both sides, we have

$$E[\ln(1+r)] \approx \ln[1+E(r)] - \frac{\text{var}(r)}{2[1+E(r)]^2}$$

When $E(r)$ is small, then $\ln[1+E(r)] \approx E(r)$ and $[1+E(r)]^2 \approx 1+2E(r)$. Hence

$$E[\ln(1+r)] - E(r) \approx \frac{1}{2}\frac{\text{var}(r)}{1+2E(r)}$$

This relationship says that the difference between the mean log (or geometric) return and the mean arithmetic return is not far from half the variance of the arithmetic return. This relationship holds exactly in continuous time when the asset price follows a geometric Brownian motion:

$$\frac{dP}{P} = \mu dt + \sigma dB$$

By Itô's lemma,

$$d\ln P = \left(\mu - \frac{\sigma^2}{2}\right)dt + \sigma dB$$

Then the mean arithmetic return is

$$E\left(\frac{dP/P}{dt}\right) = \mu$$

and the mean geometric return is

$$E\left(\frac{d\ln P}{dt}\right) = \mu - \frac{\sigma^2}{2}$$

The difference between the mean returns is exactly half the variance.

7.2.4 Volatility Pumping

A related difference between the mean arithmetic return and a mean geometric return is additivity. Posit a portfolio of two assets 1 and 2 priced at P_1 and P_2. Hence

$$\frac{dP_1}{P_1} = \mu_1 dt + \sigma_1 dB_1$$

$$\frac{dP_2}{P_2} = \mu_2 dt + \sigma_2 dB_2$$

with $dB_1 dB_2 = \rho dt$. The portfolio allocates a weight x to asset 1 and $(1 - x)$ to asset 2. Then the value of the portfolio has motion:

$$\frac{dW}{W} = x\frac{dP_1}{P_1} + (1-x)\frac{dP_2}{P_2} = [x\mu_1 + (1-x)\mu_2]dt + x\sigma_1 dB_1 + (1-x)\sigma_2 dB_2$$

and

$$E\left(\frac{dW / W}{dt}\right) = x\mu_1 + (1-x)\mu_2 = xE\left(\frac{dP_1 / P_1}{dt}\right) + (1-x)E\left(\frac{dP_2 / P_2}{dt}\right)$$

The mean arithmetic return of the portfolio is hence the weighted average of the mean arithmetic returns of its constituent assets. Let us now turn to the mean geometric return. By Itô's lemma,

$$d\ln W = \left\{x_1\mu_1 + (1-x)\mu_2 - \frac{1}{2}[x_1^2\sigma_1^2 + (1-x)^2\sigma_2^2 + 2\rho x(1-x)\sigma_1\sigma_2]\right\}dt$$
$$+ x\sigma_1 dB_1 + (1-x)\sigma_2 dB_2$$

One can then see that the additivity property does not hold for the mean geometric return because

$$E\left(\frac{d\ln W}{dt}\right) = x\mu_1 + (1-x)\mu_2 - \frac{1}{2}[x^2\sigma_1^2 + (1-x)^2\sigma_2^2 + 2\rho x(1-x)\sigma_1\sigma_2] \quad (7.31)$$

whereas

$$xE\left(\frac{d\ln P_1}{dt}\right) + (1-x)E\left(\frac{d\ln P_2}{dt}\right) = x\mu_1 + (1-x)\mu_2 - \frac{1}{2}x\sigma_1^2 - \frac{1}{2}(1-x)\sigma_2^2$$

The difference between the mean geometric return on the portfolio and the weighted geometric return of its components with an extra growth turn from volatility pumping is

$$E\left(\frac{d\ln W}{dt}\right) - \left[xE\left(\frac{d\ln P_1}{dt}\right) + (1-x)E\left(\frac{d\ln P_2}{dt}\right)\right] = \frac{1}{2}x(1-x)(\sigma_1^2 + \sigma_2^2 - 2\rho\sigma_1\sigma_2)$$

Volatility pumping is more potent with higher volatilities and lower correlations.

Example: Assume that asset 1 has drift $\mu_1 = 8\%$ and volatility 40%. Asset 2 is a risk-free bond earning zero interest. Then asset 1 has a mean geometric return of $8\% - (40\%)^2/2 = 0$. The mean geometric return of asset 2 is $0 - (0/2) = 0$. Recalling that $\rho = 0$, then the mean geometric return on expected growth of a portfolio allocating x to asset 1 and $(1 - x)$ to asset 2 is

$$E\left(\frac{d \ln W}{dt}\right) = \frac{1}{2}x(1-x)\sigma_1^2$$

and

$$\max_x E\left(\frac{d \ln W}{dt}\right) = 2\%, \text{ with } x = \frac{1}{2}$$

Example: From (7.31), we can calculate x to maximize the expected growth of a portfolio with two risky assets:

$$\frac{\partial E\left(\dfrac{d \ln W}{dt}\right)}{\partial x} = 0$$

$$\rightarrow x = \frac{\mu_1 - \mu_2 + \sigma_2^2 - \rho\sigma_1\sigma_2}{\sigma_1^2 + \sigma_2^2 - 2\rho\sigma_1\sigma_2} \tag{7.32}$$

Consider asset 1 with parameters $\mu_1 = 22\%$ and $\sigma_1 = 60\%$ and asset 2 with parameters $\mu_2 = 12\%$ and $\sigma_2 = 40\%$. The correlation ρ is –0.1. First note that the expected growth on both assets is the same: $\mu_1 - \sigma_1^2/2 = \mu_2 - \sigma_2^2/2 = 4\%$. From Equation (7.32), we get the optimal growth allocations: $x = 50\%$ and $(1 - x) = 50\%$. Plugging the parameter values in Equation (7.31), we find the optimal growth $E(d \ln W/dt) = 11.1\%$.

If each of two investors owns either asset 1 or asset 2, the expected growth rate on each portfolio would be 4%. If they pool their assets in a growth-optimal portfolio comprising assets 1 and 2, the expected growth on their portfolio increases to 11.1%. The difference can be attributed to volatility pumping. Put differently, diversification reduces portfolio volatility. This, in turn, increases geometric growth.

7.3 Analogies

7.3.1 Utility Functions and Mean-Variance

A mean-variance utility function is defined as: $E(r_p) - \frac{1}{2}\lambda V(r_p)$, where λ is a measure of risk aversion. Consider the case of a risky asset and a risk-free asset:

$$E(r_p) = (1-x)r + x\mu = r + x(\mu - r)$$

$$V(r_p) = x^2\sigma^2$$

The mean-variance portfolio is then

$$\max_x r + x(\mu - r) - \frac{1}{2}\lambda x^2\sigma^2$$

The first-order condition is

$$\mu - r - \lambda\sigma^2 x = 0$$

and

$$x^* = \frac{\mu - r}{\lambda\sigma^2}$$

Similarly, in the CRRA utility case with continuous rebalancing[2] and log-normal prices, we had seen that

$$x^* = \frac{\mu - r}{\gamma\sigma^2}$$

The risk aversion parameter λ in the mean-variance problem therefore coincides with the risk aversion parameter γ of the CRRA utility function.

For single-period portfolio optimizations, mean-variance analysis is consistent with the theoretically popular expected utility maximization framework if the investor's utility is quadratic or if returns are normally distributed. Even if the utility function is not quadratic, Levy and Markowitz (1979) showed that mean-variance optimization is equivalent to maximizing the expectation of the

---

2 Continuous rebalancing is the limiting case of small rebalancing intervals. It makes it easy or possible to derive analytical solutions that provide economic insights that are difficult to obtain from numerical solutions and allows us to distinguish general properties of the solutions from those relying on specific parameter values. Continuous rebalancing can be a good approximation for frequently rebalanced portfolios, especially when the investment horizon is long.

second-order Taylor approximations of standard utility functions, such as power utility and exponential utility. Thus the consistency of the mean-variance analysis with expected utility maximization for single-period optimization problems depends on the degree of nonnormality of returns, the investment horizon, and the specific functional form of the investor's utility.

7.3.2 Mean-Variance and Optimal-Growth Portfolios

Recall that with a risky and a risk-free asset, the optimal mean-variance allocation to the risky asset consistent with CRRA utility maximization under continuous rebalancing and lognormal prices was found to be

$$x_{MV} = \frac{\mu - r}{\gamma \sigma^2}$$

and the optimal growth allocation to the risky asset was

$$x_{OG} = \frac{\mu - r}{\sigma^2}$$

It is straightforward to see that the optimal-growth portfolio is a mean-variance portfolio with $\gamma = 1$.

Indeed, recall that the CRRA utility function is

$$U(W) = \frac{W^{1-\gamma}}{1-\gamma} \tag{7.33}$$

The mean-variance solution was shown to to maximize the expectation of (7.33), whereas an optimal-growth investor maximizes

$$U(W) = \ln W$$

As discussed in Chapter 4, the log utility is a special case of a CRRA utility with $\gamma = 1$.

We give the same analogy with N risky assets and a risk-free asset. The optimal-growth rule maximizes

$$E(\ln W_T) = r + x^T (\mu - r) - \frac{1}{2} x^T \Sigma x$$

$$\rightarrow x_{OG} = \Sigma^{-1} (\mu - r)$$

with x, μ, and r being $N \times 1$ column vectors and Σ an $N \times N$ matrix. The mean-variance rule maximizes

$$r + x^T (\mu - r) - \frac{1}{2} \gamma x^T \Sigma x$$

$$\to x_{MV} = \Sigma^{-1} \frac{\mu - r}{\gamma}$$

Again, for $\gamma = 1$, $x_{MV} = x_{OG}$.

7.3.3 Stochastic Control and Martingales

Two-Period Portfolio Selection

We now solve a simple two-period portfolio selection problem using, first, stochastic control and, then, martingale.

Posit a risky asset price that follows the following process:

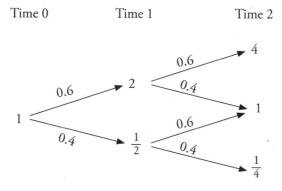

whereas a dollar invested in the risk-free asset earns zero interest. We want to determine the optimal portfolio allocation α^* to the risky asset. Call the nodes on the tree

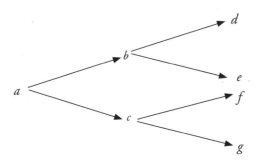

We need to make decisions at nodes *a*, *b*, and *c*. We will assume logarithmic utility.

Stochastic Control Method

The basic principle of dynamic control is to solve the problem recursively by optimizing subsequences. At every node, with an initial wealth of $1, the wealth tree is as follows:

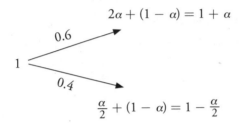

$$2\alpha + (1 - \alpha) = 1 + \alpha$$

$$\frac{\alpha}{2} + (1 - \alpha) = 1 - \frac{\alpha}{2}$$

Stand at node *b*. You want to maximize

$$0.6 \ln(2\alpha_b + 1 - \alpha_b) + 0.4 \ln\left(\frac{\alpha_b}{2} + 1 - \alpha_b\right)$$

which is the mathematical expectation (at node *b*) of the utility at nodes *d* and *e*. The first-order condition is

$$\frac{0.6}{1+\alpha_b^*} = \frac{0.2}{1 - \frac{\alpha_b^*}{2}}$$

$$\rightarrow \alpha_b^* = 0.8$$

Thus it is easily checked that α_c^* and α_a^* are also equal to 0.8.

Martingale Method

We proceed to solve the same discrete-time asset allocation using the martingale method. The approach is to produce the highest expected utility under cost constraint. An asset-allocation strategy can be viewed as a contingent claim. We can price it or cost it using elementary derivative pricing.

In the case at hand, if we call the attainable wealth at time 2 w_d, w_e, w_f, and w_g, then we know that the probability of reaching these wealth levels will be 0.36, 0.24, 0.24, and 0.16:

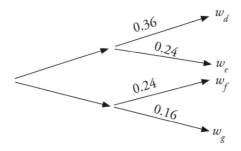

So we seek to

$$\max 0.36 \ln w_d + 0.24 \ln w_e + 0.24 \ln w_f + 0.16 \ln w_g$$

under cost constraint. The cost of the asset allocation is

$$C = E^Q(W) = q^2 w_d + q(1-q)w_e + q(1-q)w_f + (1-q)^2 w_g$$

with[3]

$$q \equiv \frac{1+r-d}{u-d} = \frac{1+0-\dfrac{1}{2}}{2-\dfrac{1}{2}} = \frac{1}{3}$$

So the cost constraint is

$$C = \frac{1}{9}w_d + \frac{2}{9}w_e + \frac{2}{9}w_f + \frac{4}{9}w_g$$

Form a Lagrangian:

$$L = 0.36 \ln w_d + 0.24 \ln w_e + 0.24 \ln w_f + 0.16 \ln w_g +$$

$$\lambda\left(C - \frac{1}{9}w_d - \frac{2}{9}w_e - \frac{2}{9}w_f - \frac{4}{9}w_g\right)$$

---

3 See Appendix for the derivation of q.

$$\frac{\partial L}{\partial w} = 0$$

$$\frac{0.36}{w_d} = \frac{1}{9}\lambda$$

$$\frac{0.24}{w_e} = \frac{2}{9}\lambda$$

$$\frac{0.24}{w_f} = \frac{2}{9}\lambda$$

$$\frac{0.16}{w_g} = \frac{4}{9}\lambda$$

We can solve for the maximum attainable wealth levels. We get $\lambda = 1/C$ and

$$w_d^* = 3.24C$$
$$w_e^* = 1.08C$$
$$w_f^* = 1.08C$$
$$w_g^* = 0.36C$$

Finally, we compute the optimal allocations α_a^*, α_b^*, and α_c^* that will generate w_d^*, w_e^*, w_f^*, and w_g^*:

$$(1+\alpha_a^*)(1+\alpha_b^*)C = 3.24C$$

$$(1+\alpha_a^*)\left(1-\frac{\alpha_b^*}{2}\right)C = 1.08C$$

$$\left(1-\frac{\alpha_a^*}{2}\right)(1+\alpha_c^*)C = 1.08C$$

$$\left(1-\frac{\alpha_a^*}{2}\right)\left(1-\frac{\alpha_c^*}{2}\right)C = 0.36C$$

As in the stochastic control example, we find

$$\alpha_a^* = \alpha_b^* = \alpha_c^* = 0.8$$

Continuous-Time Portfolio Selection

Consider the problem

$$J(x,0) = \max_u E_0\left\{\int_0^T f(x,t,u)dt + \phi[x(T),T]\right\}$$

subject to the constraint

$$dx = \mu(x,t,u)dt + \sigma(x,t,u)dB$$

Stochastic Control Method

Bellman's principle of optimality states that at any point t,

$$J(x,t) = \max_u E_t \int_t^{t+\Delta t} f(x,s,u)ds + J(x+\Delta x, t+\Delta t)$$

By the mean-value theorem,

$$\int_t^{t+\Delta t} f(x,s,u)ds \approx f(x,t,u)\Delta t$$

A Taylor expansion on the J term shows that

$$J(x+\Delta x, t+\Delta t) = J(x,t) + J_x \Delta x + J_t \Delta t + \frac{1}{2} J_{xx}(\Delta x)^2 + o(\Delta t)$$

where $o(\Delta t)$ denotes the higher-order terms in the Taylor expansion.

From the constraint, and recalling that $(\Delta x)^2 = \sigma^2 \Delta t$, we get

$$0 = \max_u \left(f\Delta t + J_x \mu \Delta t + J_t \Delta t + \frac{1}{2} J_{xx} \sigma^2 \Delta t \right)$$

Dividing through by Δt, we end up with the Bellman equation:

$$-J_t = \max_u f + J_x \mu + \frac{1}{2} J_{xx} \sigma^2$$

This is a partial differential equation with boundary condition

$$J[x(T),T] = \phi[x(T),T]$$

Consider now the infinite-horizon problem

$$J(x,t) = \max_u E_t \left[\int_t^\infty e^{-\beta s} f(x,u)ds \right]$$

subject to the constraints

$$dx = \mu(x,u)dt + \sigma(x,u)dB$$
$$x(0) = x_0$$

Then

$$J(x,t) = e^{-\beta t} V(x)$$

with $V(x)$ defined as

$$V(x) \equiv \max_{u} E_t\left[\int_t^\infty e^{-\beta(s-t)} f(x,u)ds\right]$$

Then

$$J_t = -\beta e^{-\beta t} V(x)$$
$$J_x = e^{-\beta t} V_x$$
$$J_{xx} = e^{-\beta t} V_{xx}$$

Replacing in the finite-horizon Bellman equation, we get

$$\beta V = \max_{u} f + V_x \mu + \frac{1}{2} V_{xx} \sigma^2$$

The infinite-horizon problem boils down to an ordinary differential equation. Noting that f can be interpreted as a dividend and by Itô's lemma,

$$E(dV) = V_x \mu + \frac{1}{2} V_{xx} \sigma^2$$

which is a capital gain. Then the ordinary differential equation (also the infinite-horizon Bellman equation) can be interpreted as follows: βV, the interest on the value function V, is equal, at equilibrium, to the maximum attainable dividend and capital gain from the value function.

Example: The consumption problem

$$\max E \int_0^\infty e^{-\beta t} \left(\frac{C^{1-\gamma}}{1-\gamma}\right) dt$$

subject to $dW = \{[r + \alpha(\mu - r)]W - C\}dt + \alpha W \sigma dB$

where C is consumption, γ is the risk aversion parameter, W is the total wealth, r is the risk-free rate, μ is the instantaneous expected return on the risky asset, and σ is the instantaneous volatility of the risky asset return.

Replacing the f, μ, and σ^2 functions in the Bellman equation for an infinite horizon by these values, we have

$$\beta V = \max_{a,C} \left\{\frac{C^{1-\gamma}}{1-\gamma} + V_W([r + \alpha(\mu - r)]W - C)\right\} + \frac{V_{WW}}{2}\alpha^2 W^2 \sigma^2 \quad (7.34)$$

The first-order conditions are

$$C = (V_W)^{-1/\gamma}$$

$$\alpha = -\frac{V_W}{WV_{WW}} \frac{\mu - r}{\sigma^2}$$

Guessing a solution of form $V = KW^{1-\gamma}$ and replacing values of V, C, and α in Equation (7.34), a little algebra yields the optimal asset allocation and consumption:

$$\alpha^* = \frac{\mu - r}{\gamma\sigma^2}$$

and

$$C^* = \frac{1-\gamma}{\gamma}\left[\frac{\beta}{1-\gamma} - r - \frac{1}{2\gamma}\left(\frac{\mu - r}{\sigma}\right)^2\right]W$$

Let us use some plausible values of the parameters to size an optimal consumption and asset allocation with $\mu = $ 4%, $r = $ 1%, $\beta = $ 2%, $\gamma = $ 3, and $\sigma = $ 15%. Thus $\alpha^* = $ 44% and $C^* = 0.018W$, meaning that an optimization allocates 44% of the wealth to the risky asset and consumes 1.8% of the wealth per year.

Lastly, note that for $\gamma = 1$, the utility function is logarithmic, and the asset-allocation ratio becomes

$$\alpha^* = \frac{\mu - r}{\sigma^2}$$

We will prove this result using martingale methods in the next section.

Martingale Method

As in the discrete-time case, we maximize the utility of terminal wealth subject to the cost of the asset allocation. The asset allocation is a contingent claim that can be priced under the martingale measure Q. That is,

$$\max E[U(C)]$$
$$\text{subject to } E^Q(e^{-rt}C) = W_0 \qquad (7.35)$$

Then the Lagrangian is

$$L = E[U(C)] + \lambda[W_0 - E^Q(e^{-rt}C)]$$

Transform this E^Q term into an expectation under the physical probability measure by plugging in the Radon–Nikodym derivative:

$$L = E[U(C)] + \lambda W_0 - \lambda e^{-rt} E\left(\frac{dQ}{dP}C\right)$$

with

$$\frac{dQ}{dP} = e^{-\frac{(\mu-r)^2}{2\sigma^2}t - \frac{\mu-r}{\sigma}B_t}$$

Hence

$$L = E\left[U(C) - \lambda e^{-rt}\frac{dQ}{dP}C\right] + \lambda W_0$$

We use $dL/dC = 0$ to get

$$U'(C) = \lambda e^{-rt}\frac{dQ}{dP} \qquad (7.36)$$

As an example, solve for a logarithmic utility function

$$U(C) = \ln C \rightarrow U'(C) = \frac{1}{C}$$

Thus, from (7.36),

$$C = \frac{1}{\lambda e^{-rt}\dfrac{dQ}{dP}} \qquad (7.37)$$

And combining (7.35) and (7.37), we get

$$E^Q(e^{-rt}C) = E\left(e^{-rt}\frac{dQ}{dP}C\right) = W_0 = \frac{1}{\lambda} \qquad (7.38)$$

Hence the expression for C from (7.37) and (7.39) is

$$C = \frac{W_0 e^{rt}}{dQ/dP} = W_0 e^{rt} e^{\frac{1}{2}(\frac{\mu-r}{\sigma})^2 t + \frac{\mu-r}{\sigma}B_t} \qquad (7.39)$$

But recall that a portfolio valued at W that allocates α to stocks and $(1 - \alpha)$ to bonds has the dynamics

$$\frac{dW}{W} = [r + \alpha(\mu - r)]dt + \alpha\sigma dB_t$$

or, equivalently,

$$W_t = W_0 e^{\left[r+\alpha(\mu-r)-\frac{\alpha^2\sigma^2}{2}\right]t+\alpha\sigma B_t} \tag{7.40}$$

Comparing (7.39) and (7.40) and identifying terms, it appears that

$$\alpha^* = \frac{\mu - r}{\sigma^2}$$

This is the same result obtained using stochastic optimal control techniques.

8

An Example of Asset Allocation for a Sovereign

Summary

For sovereigns endowed with natural resources who accumulate wealth in specially managed funds from the proceeds of selling commodities in domestic and international markets, optimal portfolio allocation is of fundamental importance. Such a sovereign would try to maximize the expected present value of its utility of consumption by choosing the weights x_i of financial assets in its portfolio subject to a budget constraint. If there are n assets to chose from with expected returns μ_i and volatilities σ_i, $i \in [1, n]$, with the nth asset being the risk-free security with a return r and a volatility $\sigma_n = 0$, the problem could be formulated as a stochastic control problem:

$$J(W, t) = \max_{C, x_i} E_t \left\{ \int_t^\infty U[C(\tau)] e^{-\eta(\tau - t)} d\tau \right\}$$

$$dW = \sum_{i=1}^n x_i (\mu_i - r) W dt + (rW - C) dt + \sum_{i=1}^n x_i W \sigma_i dB_i$$

where $W = \sum_{i=1}^{n} P_i N_i$ is the portfolio value, P_i is the price of the ith asset, and N_i is the number of shares held. The *control* variable $x_i = \dfrac{P_i N_i}{W}$ such that $W = \sum_{i=1}^{n} x_i W$.

Each asset follows a Brownian motion process

$$dP_i = \mu_i P_i\, dt + \sigma_i P_i\, dB_i,\ i \in [1, n-1]$$

where dB_i is a *Wiener* process with $dB_i\, dB_j = \rho_{ij}\, dt$ and $\rho_{ii} = 1$ for all i. The covariance matrix is Σ with elements $\sigma_{ij} = \rho_{ij}\sigma_i\sigma_j$.

Assuming a constant relative risk-aversion (CRRA) utility function for the sovereign and solving the Hamilton–Jacobi–Bellman (HBJ) equation, we obtain the optimal portfolio size as well as the allocation to risky assets as $x_i = \omega_i x$, where

$$\omega_i \equiv \frac{1}{y}\sum_{j=1}^{n-1} y_{ij}(\mu_i - r)$$

and y_{ij} is the ij-th entry of the inverse of the covariance matrix Σ^{-1}.

The share of the sum of risky assets in the portfolio is given by

$$x = \frac{y}{\lambda},\ \text{where}\ y \equiv \sum_{i=1}^{n-1}\sum_{j=1}^{n-1} y_{ij}(\mu_i - r)$$

λ is the risk aversion coefficient and the share of the riskless asset in the portfolio is given by $1 - x$.

The correlation between the risky assets themselves impacts the risk-adjusted return. The higher the positive correlation, the larger is the portfolio variance and the lower is the risk-adjusted return, implying a smaller component of risky assets in the portfolio.

The proportion of *individual* risky assets in the portfolio is independent of the coefficient of risk aversion; only the total amount of risky assets is.

When the dependence of the sovereign on a natural resource is *explicit* and the production quantity Q is constant over time, if we assume that the price of the commodity is P_Q and that there exists an asset in the market that is perfectly correlated with P_Q so that all hedging can be done with this single asset, the portfolio allocation optimization problem could be written in terms of the HJB formulation:

$$J(W, P_Q, t) = \max_{C, x_i} E_t\left\{\left[\int_t^\infty U[C(\tau)]e^{-\eta(\tau-t)}d\tau\right]\right\}$$

with the budget constraint

$$dW = \sum_{i=1}^{n-1} x_i(\mu_i - r)W dt + (rW + P_Q Q - C) dt + \sum_{i=1}^{n-1} x_i W \sigma_i dB_i$$

where the commodity price follows a Brownian motion given by

$$P_Q = \mu_Q P_Q dt + \sigma_Q P_Q dB_Q$$

Let us assume the existence of the asset $k \in [1, n-1]$ that is perfectly correlated with the returns of the commodity follows the Brownian motion process $dB_K = dB_Q$. With asset k and the risk-free asset n, we can replicate the commodity revenue of the sovereign.

The value of this combination is the *capitalized value* of the commodity revenue

$$V(P_Q, t) \equiv P_Q(t)Q[1 - e^{-\alpha_k(T-t)}] \frac{1}{\alpha_k}$$

where

$$\alpha_k \equiv r - \mu_Q + \beta_k(\mu_k - r)$$

and

$$\beta_k \equiv \frac{\sigma_Q}{\sigma_k}$$

The total wealth that is the combination of financial and underground assets $\overline{W} \equiv W + V$ has a dynamic equation given by

$$d\overline{W} = \sum_{i=1}^{n-1} \overline{x}_i(\mu_i - r)\overline{W} dt + (r\overline{W} - C) dt + \sum_{i=1}^{n-1} \overline{x}_i \overline{W} \sigma_i dB_i$$

where $\overline{x}_i \equiv \dfrac{x_i W}{W + V}$, for $i \neq k$ and $\overline{x}_k \equiv \dfrac{x_k W + \beta_k V}{W + V}$.

The *difference* of a sovereign *taking account* of its natural resource wealth in making decisions on the optimal asset allocation versus one that does not *is the additional demand* for a *hedge asset* that is perfectly correlated with the commodity and given by $-\dfrac{V}{W}\beta_k$ on top of additional leveraged demand for each risky asset $\dfrac{V}{W}\overline{x}_i$, for $i \neq k$, $i \in [1, n-1]$.

8.1 Asset Allocation Without Explicit Dependence on Natural Resources

A wealth fund of a sovereign with a major natural resource endowment is trying to maximize the expected present value of its utility of consumption by choosing the weights (the control variable) of financial assets in its portfolio subject to a budget constraint. There are $i = 1, 2, ..., n$ assets to chose from with expected returns μ_i and volatilities σ_i, with the nth asset being the risk-free security with a return r and a volatility $\sigma_n = 0$. Thus

$$J(W, t) = \max_{C, x_i} E_t \left\{ \int_t^\infty U[C(\tau)] e^{-\eta(\tau - t)} d\tau \right\}$$

$$dW = \sum_{i=1}^n x_i (\mu_i - r) W dt + (rW - C) dt + \sum_{i=1}^n x_i W \sigma_i dB_i$$

Let us assume that the portfolio's value is given by

$$W = \sum_{i=1}^n P_i N_i$$

where P_i is the price of the ith asset, and N_i is the number shares held. If we define our control variable x_i as $\dfrac{P_i N_i}{W}$ so that $W = \sum_{i=1}^n x_i W$ and assume that each asset follows a Brownian motion given by

$$dP_i = \mu_i P_i dt + \sigma_i P_i dB_i \text{ for all } i = 1, ..., n - 1$$

where dB_i is a Wiener process with $E[dB_i dB_j] = \rho_{ij} dt$ and $\rho_{ii} = 1$, $\mu_n \equiv r$, the risk-free rate, and $\sigma_n = 0$, the covariance matrix is Σ with elements $\sigma_{ij} = \rho_{ij} \sigma_i \sigma_j$.

$x_n = 1 - \sum_{i=1}^{n-1} x_i$ is positive if all of the asset positions are long and could be negative if borrowing at the riskless asset rate to invest in risky assets is allowed.

Let us choose the familiar CRRA type of utility function for the sovereign. We can now solve the HJB equation and obtain the optimal portfolio size as well as the allocation to risky assets:

$$x_i = \omega_i x$$

$$\omega_i \equiv \frac{1}{y} \sum_{j=1}^{n-1} y_{ij} (\mu_i - r) \tag{8.1}$$

where y_{ij} is the ijth entry of the inverse of the covariance matrix Σ^{-1}. The share of the sum of risky assets in the portfolio will be given by

$$x = \frac{y}{\lambda}, \text{ where } y \equiv \sum_{i=1}^{n-1}\sum_{j=1}^{n-1} y_{ij}(\mu_i - r) \qquad (8.2)$$

The share of the riskless asset in the portfolio is given by $x_n = 1 - x$. Here y can be seen as the risk-adjusted expected return over the riskless rate. The magnitude of the risky asset portfolio is given by Equation (8.2) and is proportional to the risk-adjusted return of the portfolio and inversely proportional to the coefficient of risk aversion λ.

We can make the observation that when we limit the number of risky assets to one, the optimal amount of that risky asset in the portfolio is given by the familiar equation already seen in the context of the Markowitz formulation:

$$x = \frac{(\mu - r)}{\lambda \sigma^2}$$

The correlation between the risky assets themselves impacts the risk-adjusted return. The higher the positive correlation, the larger is the portfolio variance and lower is the risk-adjusted return, implying a smaller component of risky assets in the portfolio.

We also observe that the proportion of *individual* risky assets in the portfolio is independent of the coefficient of risk aversion. Only the total amount of risky assets is. The lower correlation that a particular asset has to other assets will increase its representation in the portfolio of risky assets because of diversification benefits.

8.2 Asset Allocation with Explicit Dependence on Natural Resources

Let us now include the dependence on natural resources in the analysis we presented earlier. After obtaining the optimal portfolio characteristics, we will compare and contrast the portfolio with the results of Section 8.1.[1]

We assume that the natural resource production quantity Q is constant over time. Let us also assume that the price of the commodity is P_Q. Let us further

---

1 For a detailed specific example, please see Baz et al. (2020a).

assume that there exists an asset in the market that is perfectly correlated with P_Q so that all hedging can be done with this single asset.

The optimization problem could be written in terms of the Bellman formulation:[2]

$$J(W, P_Q, t) = \max_{C, x_i} E_t \left\{ \int_t^\infty U[C(\tau)] e^{-\eta(\tau-t)} d\tau \right\}$$

subject to the budget constraint

$$dW = \sum_{i=1}^{n-1} x_i (\mu_i - r) W dt + (rW + P_Q Q - C) dt + \sum_{i=1}^{n-1} x_i W \sigma_i dB_i$$

and that the price of the commodity follows the Brownian process given by

$$P_Q = \mu_Q P_Q dt + \sigma_Q P_Q dB_Q$$

Let us also assume the asset $k \in [1, 2, ..., n-1]$ that is perfectly correlated with the returns of the commodity follows the Brownian process $dB_K = dB_Q$ (please note that it is not necessary that the volatilities σ_Q, σ_k are equal to each other). With asset k and the risk-free asset n, we can replicate the commodity revenue of the sovereign. The value of this combination is the *capitalized value* of the commodity revenue:

$$V(P_Q, t) \equiv P_Q(t) Q (1 - e^{-\alpha_k(T-t)}) \frac{1}{\alpha_k}$$

$$\alpha_k \equiv r - \mu_Q + \beta_k(\mu_k - r) \tag{8.3}$$

$$\beta_k \equiv \frac{\sigma_Q}{\sigma_k}$$

The total wealth $\overline{W} \equiv W + V$ (financial plus underground assets) has a dynamic equation given by

$$d\overline{W} = \sum_{i=1}^{n-1} \overline{x}_i (\mu_i - r) \overline{W} dt + (r\overline{W} - C) dt + \sum_{i=1}^{n-1} \overline{x}_i \overline{W} \sigma_i dB_i$$

where

$$\overline{x}_i \equiv \frac{x_i W}{W + V}, \text{ for } i \neq k, \quad \text{and} \quad \overline{x}_k \equiv \frac{x_k W + \beta_k V}{W + V}$$

---

2 See van den Bremer et al. (2016) which we follow closely.

The number of shares in asset k is chosen such that the replicating portfolio has the same variance as the commodity. The number of risk-free assets is chosen so that the replicating portfolio has the same expected return (drift) of the commodity price. As such, the commodity wealth and the replicating portfolio behave identically, and the markets are complete. The price of the replicating portfolio is the value of the commodity wealth. Commodity wealth is the present value of the commodity revenues discounted at the rate given by Equation (8.3).

This formulation assumes that the exposure the sovereign has to commodity price risk dB_Q is replicated by combining the revenue from the commodity with an amount of the replicating bundle. By choosing the weights in each risky asset $\overline{x}_i$ in *total wealth* $\overline{W}$, we can simplify the problem to the one in Section 8.1.

If there exists a financial asset $k \in [1, 2, ..., n-1]$ whose revenue is perfectly correlated with the commodity return of the sovereign, the weight of each risky asset will be constant and will be given by

$$\overline{x}_i = \omega_i x$$

$$\overline{x} \equiv \sum_{i=1}^{n-1} \overline{x}_i = x$$

where x and ω_i are defined in Equations (8.1) and (8.2). The weights of each risky asset in the sovereign wealth fund will be

$$x_i = \overline{x}_i \frac{W+V}{W}, i \neq k, i = 1, 2, ..., n-1$$

$$x_k = \overline{x}_k \frac{W+V}{W} - \beta_k \frac{V}{W} = \overline{x}_k + \overline{x}_k \frac{V}{W} - \beta_k \frac{V}{W} \qquad (8.4)$$

The difference of a sovereign taking account of its natural resource wealth in making decisions on the optimal asset allocation (versus one that does not in Section 8.1) is the additional demand (actually a negative quantity) for a *hedge asset* that is perfectly correlated with the commodity and given by $-\frac{V}{W}\beta_k$ on top of additional/leveraged demand for each risky asset $\frac{V}{W}\overline{x}_i$, $i \neq k, i = 1, 2, ..., n-1$.

Both additional demands are proportional to the ratio of commodity wealth V to financial wealth W. The weight of every asset in the fund is leveraged by the ratio of total wealth to financial wealth, allowing for the additional commodity wealth outside the financial fund.

The demand for hedging is proportional to the beta relevant to the commodity, the replication asset $\beta_k = \dfrac{\sigma_Q}{\sigma_k} > 0$ and the leverage factor $\dfrac{V}{W}$. The assumption that asset k perfectly replicates the commodity implies that the hedging demand is negative and that the commodity risk can be perfectly offset by shorting this asset.

The dynamics of the allocation over time should take into consideration the fact that the natural endowment in the commodity is one that depletes over time. Initially, the endowment is rich in the commodity, and the sovereign is highly exposed to commodity price volatility. The weight of the riskless asset in the portfolio given by

$$x_n = 1 - \bar{x} + (\beta_k - \bar{x})\frac{V}{W}$$

therefore will be relatively higher if the negative demand for the hedge asset is larger than the total demand for risky assets in the absence of the commodity, that is, $\beta_k > \bar{x}$. As the commodity depletes and $V \to 0$, the leverage factor declines, and the leveraged demand for each risky asset converges back $x_i \to \bar{x}_i$, for $i \neq k$, and $x_k \to \bar{x}_k$, and the negative hedging demand for asset k approaches zero. By continuously adjusting asset weights, in particular as the commodity is extracted to the limit, the assets should be reallocated from risky to riskless assets.

Illustrative Example: What does this optimization problem look like in practice? We consider a numerical example to illustrate the key insights derived from the joint optimization framework. The parameters used to evaluate this example are given below. The hypothetical situation is that of a country that has proven reserves with an initial stock equal to 200 and the present value of this stock is equal to $V = 500$. We assume an exogenous extraction rate to do away with the problem of the feedback loop, when the portfolio allocations influence commodity extraction decisions. Let us further assume that the value of the sovereign financial portfolio is $W = 1,000$.

Parameter Descriptions and Values

$r \equiv$ risk-free rate $= 3\%$
$\mu_Q \equiv$ drift commodity return process $= 2\%$
$\mu_s \equiv$ expected return on risky asset $= 10\%$
$\mu_k \equiv$ expected return on hedging asset $= 3\%$

$\sigma_Q \equiv$ volatility of commodity return process $= 40\%$

$\sigma_s \equiv$ volatility of risky asset $= 20\%$

$\sigma_k \equiv$ volatility of hedging asset $= 36\%$

$\lambda \equiv$ risk aversion parameter CRRA $= 3$

$$\beta_k \equiv \frac{\sigma_Q}{\sigma_k} = 1.1$$

The optimal amount of risky asset without considering the wealth in natural resource endowment is simply given as

$$\frac{(\mu_s - r)}{\lambda \sigma_s^2} = \frac{(0.10 - 0.03)}{3 \times 0.2^2} = 0.58$$

If we include the natural resource wealth that has a present value of $V = 765$, we can now write Equation (8.4) as

$$x_s = \bar{x}_s + \bar{x}_s \frac{V}{W} - \beta_k \frac{V}{W}$$

$$= 0.58 + 0.58 \frac{765}{1,000} - \frac{0.4}{0.36} \frac{765}{1,000} = 0.58 + 0.765 \times 0.58 - 0.765 \times 1.1 = 0.182$$

The second term is additional investment in the risky asset because of the leverage, and the last term is the decrease because of the hedging asset.

As cited earlier, the *additional* demands are proportional to the ratio of commodity wealth V to financial (fund) wealth W. The weight of every asset in the fund is leveraged by the ratio of total wealth to financial wealth, 0.765, allowing for the additional commodity wealth outside the financial fund. Obviously, as the extraction of natural resource progresses in time, the ratio will eventually go to zero, and the investment in the risky asset will converge back to its original value, *ceteris paribus*.[3]

---

3 See van der Bremer et al. (2016) and Baz et al. (2020a) provide an example of a metal extracting sovereign where the values of investments in the risky, riskless, and hedging assets over time are tracked until the resource is exhausted.

9

Liability-Driven Asset Allocation

Summary

The asset-allocation process is often practiced in tandem with a liability management process. Typically, the latter acts like a binding constraint on the former and can be thought as a portfolio *floor* that has to be maintained throughout. We can simply think of the floor as the present value of the liabilities of a pension fund or a sovereign wealth fund, for example.

The idea of *buying insurance* on a portfolio is a way to define the problem. This insurance could be purchased directly in the markets in the form of an appropriately structured put on the portfolio value with the strike price set at the value of the floor. It also could be created synthetically by a dynamic trading strategy to replicate the option.

Constant-Proportion Portfolio Insurance (CPPI): The idea behind CPPI involves managing a portfolio dynamically so that its terminal value W_T at the end of the investment horizon at time T does not fall below the floor F_T, which is given as a percentage of the initial portfolio value $\gamma_t W_0$. The difference between the portfolio value and the floor at any time is called the *cushion* C_t. We invest the portfolio in a risky *active asset* in an amount that is a positive multiple *m* of the cushion and a *reserve asset* with similar characteristic dynamics of the liabilities.

The market exposure is represented by E_t and is a function of the price of the underlying active asset S_t, which follows a geometric Brownian motion process $\frac{dS}{S} = \mu dt + \sigma dz$.

The sum of the exposure E_t to the active asset and the amount invested in the reserve asset B_t, is the value of the portfolio W_t. The rebalancing trade is triggered when the market moves by an amount about equal to or greater than what we call the *tolerance* τ. We buy the active asset when the market is up and sell it when the market is down. We do exactly the reverse with the reserve asset, always maintaining the multiple constant, hence the name CPPI.

The value of the cushion is

$$C_t = C_0 \left(\frac{S_t}{S_0} \right)^m e^{(1-m)(r+\frac{1}{2}m\sigma^2)t}$$

The mean and variance of the value to the end of the investment horizon of the portfolio W_T are

$$\mu(W_T) \equiv E[W_T] = \gamma_T W_0 + C_0 e^{[r+m(\mu-r)]T}$$

$$\sigma^2(W_T) \equiv C_0^2 e^{2[r+m(\mu-r)]T} (e^{m^2\sigma^2 T} - 1)$$

where $C_0 = W_0(1 - \gamma_T e^{-rT})$.

For a *constant relative risk-aversion utility* (CRRA) function,

$$U(C_t) = \frac{C_t^{1-\lambda}}{1-\lambda}, \text{ for } C_t \geq k$$

The maximization of the discounted expected value over time abiding to a minimum consumption constraint, that is,

$$\max_{C_t} E\left[\int_0^\infty e^{-\rho t} U(C_t) dt \right]$$

$$\text{subject to } C_T \geq C_{\min}$$

implies that CPPI is the optimal investment strategy.

The expected return of CPPI could be compared with that of an appropriately structured option. The expected return of the cushion in the CPPI strategy is $E_T[C_{\text{CPPI}}] = e^{[r + m(\mu - r)]T}$, whereas the expected value of a call option V with a strike price that is obtained using the Black–Scholes formula is $E_T[\text{option}] = e^{\mu T} \dfrac{V(S_0, F, \mu, \sigma, t)}{V(S_0, F, r, \sigma, t)}$.

A useful variation of CPPI is its application to *fixed-income markets* where the active and reserve assets are both fixed-income assets with different durations.

9.1 Dynamic Rebalancing of Asset Portfolios with Floors

The asset allocation process is often practiced in tandem with a liability management process. Typically, the latter acts like a binding constraint on the former and can be thought as a portfolio floor that has to be maintained throughout. We can simply think of the floor as the present value of the liabilities. Let us take a pension fund as an example; the process involved is highly similar to the ones taken by endowments or sovereign wealth funds.

In the case of a corporate pension fund, the floor of the asset portfolio needs to be maintained at a level very close to the present value of its liabilities. Because of regulatory and accounting constraints, failure to do so will affect the earnings negatively and erode shareholder value.[1]

The idea of *buying insurance* on a portfolio is a way to define the problem. This insurance could be purchased directly in the markets in the form of a put option on the portfolio value with the strike price set at the value of the floor. It also could be created synthetically by a dynamic trading strategy to replicate the option. We will start by describing a simple strategy called CPPI and then compare it to a strategy involving the purchase of an option on the portfolio with the appropriate strike price reflecting the liability-driven constraints.

---

1 The components of the floor are the accumulated benefit obligations (ABOs)—the present value of earned benefits based on past and current compensation levels—and the projected benefit obligations (PBOs)—the present value of earned benefits based on expected compensation benefits. The discounting is done on market-specific interest rates. The calculations take into consideration turnover and mortality estimates.

In the most basic version of CPPI, we need to know the current value of the portfolio of assets and the floor to implement the strategy.[2] The floor could be made variable by slightly modifying the basic formulation. The difference between the portfolio value and the floor at any time is called the *cushion* or the surplus.

The idea behind the strategy can be illustrated by assuming a two-asset world: a risky asset we will call the *active asset*, such as an index fund, and a *reserve asset*, such as Treasury securities of an appropriate duration matching the liabilities and that have an acceptable return.[3] As the cushion decreases as a result of market moves, we trade out of the active asset and into the reserve asset, and as the cushion increases, we do the reverse. For a pension fund, a good choice of a reserve asset would be one that has a similar sensitivity to interest rates as drivers of the floor (e.g., accumulated benefit obligations). A Treasury security of appropriate duration would be a good choice.

At time t, E_t represents the exposure we have to the market and is a function of the price of the underlying active asset S_t. This exposure is a function of the cushion C_t as well as our measure of risk aversion. Let us call the latter the *multiple m*, giving us a simple formula $E_t = mC_t$ for the exposure. The rebalancing or dynamic strategy we follow is to manage the exposure to the active asset by trading into and out of it (and out of and into the reserve asset) such that the constant proportion m is maintained—hence the name CPPI. The sum of the exposure E_t to the active asset and the amount invested in the reserve asset B_t is the value of the portfolio W_t. The rebalancing trade is triggered when the market moves by an amount about equal to or greater than what we call the *tolerance τ*.

The higher the multiple, the more participation there is in the active asset as it rallies, and the reverse, when it declines. As the cushion declines and approaches zero, the allocation to the reserve asset approaches 100%. When the exposure

---

2 The formulation of the CPPI problem we discuss will be following the models developed by Fischer Black and his team at Goldman Sachs & Co. in the late eighties. Please see Black and Jones (1987, 1988), Black and Hakanoglu (1988), and Black and Rouhani (1988a, 1988b). A more elaborate theoretical version of those models was developed by Black and Perold (1992) linking CPPI with Merton models on university endowment management (please see Merton, 1990). The models were extended to fixed-income markets by Hakanoglu, Kopprasch, and Roman (1989a, 1989b).

3 Duration is the sensitivity of bond prices to the change in interest rates. *Macaulay duration D* is given by the equation $\frac{dP}{P} = -\frac{D}{1+r}dr$, where P is the price of the bond, and r is the interest rate to maturity, the zero-coupon rate, or the forward rate. *Modified duration* $D_{mod} \equiv \frac{D}{1+r}$. See Chapter 13.

reaches 100% of the portfolio value, we stop trading until the cushion declines enough for the exposure to be less than 100% again. The cushion stays nonnegative unless the markets move sharply such that the value of the assets decline sharply against the liabilities (or floor) before you can rebalance[4] or when the value of the reserve assets falls below the floor (in the case of the pension fund, the accumulated benefit obligation).[5]

The lower the tolerance, the more rebalancing transactions are necessary to ensure accuracy and the higher are transaction costs. In nontrending and volatile markets, the rebalancing will erode value, which can be defined as the *cost of volatility*.

Example (Mechanics of the CPPI Strategy): For the E_t, C_t, F_t, B_t, W_t and m values given below at the outset, let the tolerance τ be 2% and transaction costs κ be 0.5% of the total traded amounts in each rebalancing. Let us also assume that the floor does not move during the period examined. Let us analyze a portfolio during a period of time when the market moved twice at or above the set tolerance level with the following values at the outset: $t = 0$, $m = 5$, $W_0 = 100$, $F_0 = 90$, $C_0 = 10$, $E_0 = 50$, and $B_0 = 50$. After a market move, the exposure is denoted by E_{t-} and after a rebalancing as E_{t+}.

TABLE 9.1

t	S_t	W_t	F_t	C_t	E_{t-}	E_{t+}	B_t
0	4,000	100	90	10	50	50	50
1	4,100	101.25	90	11.25	51.25	56.25	44.97
2	3,900	98.47	90	8.5	53.51	42.53	55.89

In this example, the volatility in the market and the tolerance determine the frequency of trades. There is obviously a tradeoff between trading frequently and keeping the "constancy" of the strategy and the cost of doing so. For a given period, say a year, if volatility is high, the value of the portfolio will erode toward the floor, even if the market has not really changed from the beginning of the analysis period. The size of the multiple clearly determines your participation in the market appreciation; it also determines the speed of moving into the riskless or reserve asset when the market drops. The higher the multiple, the more you

---

4 What happened on October 19, 1987, is an excellent example.
5 The correlation between the liabilities and the reserve asset breaks down.

will lose in markets that go up and then down and down and then up, even without any clear drift.

The basic CPPI strategy is simple and easy to implement without requiring any sophisticated algorithms or computer programs. One can even change the parameters of the strategy to accommodate new information. The multiple, the floor, and the tolerance are the investor's controls.

We could use the strategy for an investor who does not have a floor and could *sell* portfolio insurance by taking the other side of the trades.[6]

9.2 Theoretical Exposition

The differential equation for the risky asset S_t that is governed by a geometric Brownian motion is[7]

$$\frac{dS_t}{S_t} = \mu dt + \sigma dz$$

where μ is the instantaneous mean and $\sigma_S \equiv \sigma$ the standard deviation; dz is a Wiener process with $E[dz] = 0$ and $dz^2 = dt$. The differential equation for the reserve asset is given by

$$\frac{dB_t}{B_t} = rdt$$

where r is the risk-free rate of return with volatility equal to zero.

The idea behind CPPI involves managing a dynamic portfolio so that its terminal value W_T at the end of the investment horizon never falls below the floor F_T with γ_T a nonnegative fraction relating the floor to the initial portfolio value W_0:

$$F_T = \gamma_T W_0$$

Given that we can only claim a return that is guaranteed by investing in a risk-free security, $\gamma_T \leq e^{rT}$. The present value of the guaranteed floor F_t, for $t \in [0, T]$, is therefore

$$F_t = \gamma_t W_0$$

---

6 Please see Black and Hakanoglu (1988).

7 For more detail about the theoretical construction of the CPPI strategy and its comparison with other synthetic and bought-option strategies, please see Brennan and Solanki (1981), Leland and Rubinstein (1988), Perold (1986), Black and Perold (1992), Grossman and Vila (1992), Black and Rouhani (1989), Zagst and Kraus (2011), and Maalej and Prigent (2016).

where

$$\gamma_t = \gamma_T e^{-r(T-t)} \text{ and } d\gamma_t = \gamma_T r e^{-r(T-t)} dt$$

For $0 \le t \le T$, from the definitions of the floor, cushion, exposure, and investment in the reserve asset, we get

$$C_t = \max[W_t - F_t, 0]$$

In order to ensure that $W_T \ge F_T$, as we have stated before, the method involves investing a constant proportion m of the cushion. We assume that $m \ge 1$; therefore, the payoff function of the strategy is convex. The amount invested in the active asset is given by

$$E_t = mC_t = m \max[W_t - F_t, 0]$$

whereas the reserve asset investment is the rest of the portfolio. That is,

$$B_t = W_t - E_t$$
$$W_t = F_t + C_t = \gamma_t W_0 + C_t$$

Proposition 1: The value of the cushion C_t is given by

$$C_t = C_0 \left(\frac{S_t}{S_0}\right)^m e^{(1-m)(r+\frac{1}{2}m\sigma^2)t}$$

Proof: Because $W_t = F_t + C_t$, $E_t = mC_t$, $F_t = \gamma_t W_0$ and $d\gamma_t = \gamma_t r dt$; $\forall t \in [0, 1]$,

$$dW_t = (W_t - mC_t)\frac{dB_t}{B_t} + mC_t\frac{dS_t}{S_t} = [W_t(1-m) + m\gamma_t W_0]r dt + mC_t\frac{dS_t}{S_t}$$

which implies that

$$dC_t = d(W_t - \gamma_t W_0) = dW_t - W_0 d\gamma_t = [W_t(1-m) + m\gamma_t W_0]r dt$$

$$+ mC_t\frac{dS_t}{S_t} - W_0\gamma_t r dt$$

$$= [(W_t - W_0\gamma_t)(1-m)]r dt + mC_t\frac{dS_t}{S_t} = C_t(1-m)r dt + mC_t\frac{dS_t}{S_t}$$

Let us use the definition of the risky asset dynamics in this equation to get

$$\frac{dC_t}{C_t} = [m\mu + r(1-m)]dt + m\sigma\,dz_t$$

Using Itô's lemma, the cushion follows from the following[8]

$$\ln C_t - \ln C_0 = m(\ln S_t - \ln S_0) + (1-m)\left[r + \frac{1}{2}m\sigma^2\right]t$$

$$C_t = C_0\left(\frac{S_t}{S_0}\right)^m e^{(1-m)\left(r + \frac{1}{2}m\sigma^2\right)t} \quad \blacksquare$$

Proposition 2: The mean and variance of the portfolio value at the end of the investment horizon are given by

$$\mu(W_T) = E[W_T] = \gamma_T W_0 + C_0 e^{[r + m(\mu - r)]T}$$

$$\sigma^2(W_T) = C_0^2 e^{2[r + m(\mu - r)]T}\left(e^{m^2\sigma^2 T} - 1\right)$$

where $C_0 = W_0(1 - \gamma_T e^{-rT})$.

Proof: Because $\ln S_t \sim N\left[\ln S_0 + (\mu - \frac{\sigma^2}{2})t, \sigma^2 t\right]$, the cushion C_t is log-normally distributed as

$$\ln C_t \sim N\left\{\ln C_0 + [r + m(\mu - r) - \frac{1}{2}m^2\sigma^2]t, m^2\sigma^2 t\right\}$$

From the properties of the log-normal distribution,

$$\mu(X) = E[X] = e^{(\mu + \frac{1}{2}\sigma^2)}$$

$$\sigma^2(X) = \mathrm{var}[X] = e^{2\mu + \sigma^2}\left(e^{\sigma^2} - 1\right)$$

---

8 See Brennan and Solanki (1981), Perold (1986), Black and Perold (1992), Grossman and Vila (1992), and Zagst and Kraus (2011).

We know from the two equations just above Proposition 1 that

$$W_T = \gamma_T W_0 + C_T$$

$$\mu(W_T) = E[W_T] = \gamma_T W_0 + E[C_T] = \gamma_T W_0 + e^{\left\{\ln C_0 + \left[r + m(\mu-r) - \frac{1}{2}m^2\sigma^2\right]T\right\} + \frac{m^2\sigma^2 T}{2}}$$

$$= \gamma_T W_0 + C_0 e^{[r+m(\mu-r)]T}$$

And the variance is

$$\sigma^2(W_T) = \text{Var}[\gamma_t W_0 + C_T] = \text{Var}[C_T]$$

$$= e^{2\left\{\ln C_0 + \left[r + m(\mu-r) - \frac{1}{2}m^2\sigma^2\right]T\right\} + m^2\sigma^2 T} (e^{m^2\sigma^2 T} - 1)$$

$$= C_0^2 e^{2[r+m(\mu-r)]T} (e^{m^2\sigma^2 T} - 1) \quad \blacksquare$$

Finally, we also want to point out the link between the CPPI and the extensive literature deriving from Merton's optimal consumption models in continuous time, which the interested reader can find in the references.[9] For a CRRA utility function discussed earlier and given by

$$U(C_t) = \frac{C_t^{1-\lambda}}{1-\lambda}, \text{ for } C_t \geq k$$

the maximization of the discounted expected value over time subject to a minimum consumption constraint[10]

$$\max_{C_t} E\left[\int_0^\infty e^{-\rho t} U(C_t) dt\right]$$

subject to $C_T \geq C_{\min}$

implies that the optimal investment strategy is CPPI.[11]

9 See Merton (1971), Perold (1986), and Black and Perold (1992).
10 $\rho > 0$ is the discounting factor for time preference of consumption, $\lambda > 0$ is the risk-aversion coefficient, and $k > 0$ is a constant related to the minimum consumption level and the given parameters of the CPPI strategy. We assume that the utility function is concave and differentiable at k.
11 See Perold (1986) and Black and Perold (1992).

9.3 Traded Options Versus CPPI

Let us formulate a traded options-based strategy and compare it with CPPI. Given the initial value of the floor or the present value of the liabilities as before, we would like the portfolio value not to fall below the floor at exercise time or expiration T. If we invest the initial cushion in S and the floor in B, we purchase n call options on S with a strike price of K. Given the standard Black–Scholes formula to price call options, that is,

$$V(S, K, r, t, \sigma) = SN(d) - Ke^{-rt}N\left(d - \frac{1}{2}\sigma^2\right)$$

we can write the following as the value of the initial cushion:

$$C_0 = W_0 - F_0 = nV[S, K, r, T, \sigma]$$

and because the total exercise price is equal to the value of the floor at exercise time T,

$$nK = F_T = F_0 e^{rT}$$

At any time t between the initiation of the strategy and the termination, the value of the portfolio is

$$W_t = F_t + nV(S, K, r, \sigma, t, T) = F_T e^{-(T-t)} + nV(S, K, t, \sigma, t, T)$$

The stylized payoff diagram of a call option in Figure 9.1 and the payoff diagram of a CPPI strategy have obvious similarities for good reason. It may be interesting to give a simple numerical example of a CPPI strategy with given parameters and determine the equivalent purchased-option strategy.

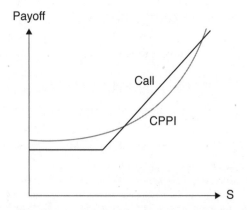

FIGURE 9.1 Payoff of CPPI versus traded options

We start by observing that the expected return of the cushion in the CPPI strategy is described by

$$E_T[C_{CPPI}] = e^{[r + m(\mu - r)]T}$$ (9.1)

whereas the expected value of a call option V with a strike price that is obtained using the Black–Scholes formula is given by[12]

$$E_T[call] = e^{\mu T} \frac{V(S_0, F, \mu, \sigma, t)}{V(S_0, F, r, \sigma, t)}$$ (9.2)

Can we now find a multiple m that will make the two strategies equivalent in terms of expected returns? That is, setting the two equations above equal to each other and solving for the multiple.

Adding some parameters to the introductory example, we let $S_0 = 100$, $F_0 = 90$, $\mu = 6\%$, $r = 1\%$, $\sigma = 15\%$, and $T = 1$. Inserting these into the Black–Scholes formula, we obtain the expected value of the option strategy to be 34.8%. We now use the expected return formula from equation (9.1) and after taking logarithms of both sides:

$$\ln(1.348) = [r + m(\mu - r)]t$$
$$\ln(1.348) = 0.01 + 0.05m$$

Solving for a CPPI multiple that makes the two expectations equal, we obtain $m = 5.77$.

9.4 An Extension of CPPI to Fixed Income

In many ways the definitions and methods of CPPI apply to investors trying to use it solely in the fixed-income markets. We choose both the active and passive assets among the instruments with different maturities in the credit spectrum. The concept uses *duration* as the basic driver for the strategy. Besides its temporal reference, duration is a measure of the price sensitivity of the portfolio to changes in interest rates. As such, it could be used as a measure of volatility. Yield movements of similar duration are highly correlated, which gives us the ability to substitute different securities for the active asset as long as the overall dollar duration is preserved.

---

12 Rubinstein, M. "A simple formula for the expected rate of return of an option over a finite holding period," *Journal of Finance*, December 1984.

As in the case of equity CPPI, we need to monitor the value of the reserve as well as the active asset. The overall portfolio, not just the active component, has a target volatility level measured by the portfolio duration. Because there is a significant correlation between the variations in the active and reserve assets, we are not concerned as much with the source of volatility as with its overall level.

In equity-based CPPI, the exposure is expressed in terms of the value of investment in the active asset. The reserve asset is typically invested in Treasury securities with durations approximating the durations of the liabilities. In fixed-income CPPI, the active and reserve assets could be combined into a single duration measure. We can then manage the exposure by adjusting the overall portfolio duration and therefore the volatility.

Let us illustrate how CPPI would work with duration being the variable we control. The investment is in the active asset $E = mC$, with m and C defined as before. The total portfolio value is $P = E + R$. The duration of the total portfolio d_p is a linear combination of the durations of the two underlying assets, d_E and d_R:

$$d_p = \alpha d_E + (1 - \alpha)d_R$$

where $\alpha = \dfrac{E}{P} = \dfrac{mC}{P}$ and $(1 - \alpha) = \dfrac{R}{P}$ are the respective fractions of the active and reserve assets in the portfolio. Thus

$$d_p = d_E m \frac{C}{P} + d_R\left(1 - m\frac{C}{P}\right)$$

We call he *excess* duration over the reserve-asset duration e_d, the *duration exposure*:

$$e_d \equiv d_p - d_R = (d_E - d_R)m\frac{C}{P}$$

Let us define $m_d \equiv (d_E - d_R)m$ as the *duration-adjusted multiple*. This coefficient is the excess duration of the active asset over the reserve asset that tracks the floor or liabilities. Finally, we define $c \equiv \dfrac{C}{P}$ as the proportional cushion value to the total portfolio value. We now get

$$e_d = m_d c.$$

The larger difference between the durations of the active and reserve assets amplifies the adjusted multiple and increases the size of the trade (in either direction) for adjusting the duration given a market move equal or larger than the tolerance level. In turn, the duration exposure e_d becomes more sensitive to market moves.

In traditional CPPI, we trade when the market moves sufficiently. *Sufficiency* is defined by the preset tolerance level, which is the amount by which our actual exposure can deviate from the target exposure defined as the constant multiple m times the *absolute* dollar value of the cushion. In the duration-adjusted CPPI case, we target the portfolio duration. We therefore must define the tolerance as the maximum acceptable percentage change in the duration exposure $e_d = d_P - d_R$. A tolerance of 5% means that the product of the proportional cushion and the excess duration of assets over liabilities $d_E - d_R$ multiplied by constant multiple m must change by 5% before a rebalancing trade is triggered.

As the value of the active asset rises relative to that of the reserve asset, the proportional cushion expands, causing the duration of the portfolio d_p to increase toward the duration of the active asset d_E. At the limit, $d_p = d_E$, and the portfolio value just depends on the active asset and its duration. In contrast, if the reverse happens, the cushion shrinks, causing d_p to decrease toward the duration of the reserve asset. At the limit, $d_p = d_R$, and the CPPI strategy emulates traditional immunization. The duration-adjusted CPPI strategy protects the value of the asset from falling below the floor or the present value of the liabilities, assuming that no downward *jumps* occur along the way.

PART III

Asset Pricing

10
Equilibrium Asset Pricing

Summary

Asset pricing looks for the right discount rate. Asset pricing models relate the discount rate to how asset payoffs covary with states of the world.

The price of an Arrow–Debreu security $A(\omega)$ that pays \$1 in state of the world ω is

$$A(\omega) = P(\omega)M_{t+1}(\omega)$$

with

$$M_{t+1}(\omega) \equiv \delta\frac{U'[C_{t+1}(\omega)]}{U'(C_t)}$$

Here $P(\omega)$ is the probability of state of the world ω occurring, δ is the subjective discount factor, and $U'[C_{t+1}(\omega)]/[U'(C_t)]$ is the ratio of marginal utilities of future and present consumptions.

$M_{t+1}(\omega)$ is called the *stochastic discount factor*. It turns out that the gross risk-free rate is the inverse of the expected stochastic discount factor under the probability measure P:

$$1+r = \frac{1}{E_t^P[M_{t+1}(\omega)]}$$

The price of an arbitrary security is given by

$$\pi = E_t^Q\left[\frac{\pi_{t+1}(\omega)}{1+r}\right]$$

with Q defined by the Radon–Nikodym derivative $\frac{dQ(\omega)}{dP(\omega)} \equiv$ $\delta\frac{U'[c_{t+1}(\omega)]}{U'(C_t)}(1+r)$.

With the constant relative risk-aversion (CRRA) utility and log-normal consumption, the expected return on a risky asset is the risk-free rate plus the product of the risk-aversion coefficient and the covariance between the risky return and consumption growth:

$$E(R_i) = R_f + \gamma\mathrm{cov}\left[\ln\frac{C_{t+1}}{C_t}, R_i\right]$$

The capital asset pricing model (CAPM) is an equilibrium pricing model that states the following:

$$\mu_i - r = \frac{\sigma_{iM}}{\sigma_M^2}(\mu_M - r)$$

with

$$\beta_i \equiv \frac{\sigma_{iM}}{\sigma_M^2}$$

where μ_i is the expected return on asset i, r is the risk-free rate, and μ_M is the expected market return. The difference between the expected market return and the risk-free rate is called the *market risk premium*. The asset beta is defined as the covariance of the asset return with the market return divided by the variance of the market return.

The intertemporal CAPM (ICAPM) extends the static, single-period CAPM and states the following:

$$\mu_i - r = \beta_{iM}(\mu_M - r) + \sum_{j=1}^m \beta_{iH_j}\left(\mu_{H_j} - r\right)$$

where μ_{H_j} is the expected return of the hedging portfolio with the maximum (absolute) correlation with the jth state variable determining the investment opportunities. When there is only one state variable,

$$\mu_i - r = \frac{\sigma_H^2 \sigma_{iM} - \sigma_{MH}\sigma_{iH}}{\sigma_M^2 \sigma_H^2 - \sigma_{MH}^2}(\mu_M - r) - \frac{\sigma_{MH}\sigma_{iM} - \sigma_M^2 \sigma_{iH}}{\sigma_M^2 \sigma_H^2 - \sigma_{MH}^2}(\mu_H - r)$$

$$\equiv \beta_{iM}(\mu_M - r) + \beta_{iH}(\mu_H - r)$$

We can think of β_{iM} and β_{iH} as the coefficients of the multivariate regression of asset i's excess returns on the excess returns of the market and hedging portfolios.

10.1 Arrow–Debreu Securities and State Price Densities

Posit an economy at time t that can move into n possible states of the world at time $t + 1$. The probability of each state is $P(\omega)$, for $\omega = 1, 2, \ldots, n$. Evidently, $P(1) + \ldots + P(n) = 1$. An Arrow–Debreu security, priced at time t at $A(\omega)$, is defined by a payoff of \$1 in a state of the world ω and a payoff of zero otherwise, meaning in all other states of the world.

10.1.1 Optimal Consumption Problem

Start with $n = 2$ (only two states of the world). An investor seeks to maximize utility by consuming at time t and $t + 1$ and by investing wealth appropriately in the collection of Arrow–Debreu securities. The optimization problem is

$$\max_{C_t, C_{t+1}, N(1), N(2)} U(C_t) + E_t\{\delta U[C_{t+1}(\omega)]\}$$

subject to the following budget constraint:

$$W_t - C_t = A(1)N(1) + A(2)N(2)$$

where C_t is consumption at time t, $C_{t+1}(\omega)$ is consumption at time $t + 1$ and is state dependent, δ is the subjective discount factor (the more impatient the investor, the lower is δ), W_t is initial wealth, and $N(\omega)$ is the number of Arrow–Debreu securities paying \$1 in state ω.

First note that what is left for consumption at $t + 1$, meaning $C_{t+1}(\omega)$, is equal to $N(1)$ if $\omega = 1$ or $N(2)$ if $\omega = 2$. We use this expression for future consumption and the expression for the budget constraint to rewrite the optimization problem as

$$\max_{N(1),N(2)} U[W_t - A(1)N(1) - A(2)N(2)] + P(1)\delta U[N(1)] + P(2)\delta U[N(2)]$$

10.1.2 Arrow–Debreu Security Prices

From first-order conditions, we obtain

$$A(1) = P(1)\delta \frac{U'[C_{t+1}(1)]}{U'(C_t)}$$

and

$$A(2) = P(2)\delta \frac{U'[C_{t+1}(2)]}{U'(C_t)}$$

More generally,

$$A(\omega) = P(\omega)M_{t+1}(\omega)$$

with

$$M_{t+1}(\omega) \equiv \delta \frac{U'[C_{t+1}(\omega)]}{U'(C_t)}$$

Here $M_{t+1}(\omega)$ is called the *stochastic discount factor* (SDF) or *state-price density*. It is stochastic because it depends on $C_{t+1}(\omega)$, which is, in turn, state dependent.

Note that $P(\omega)$ is the expected value of an Arrow–Debreu security that pays off $\$1$ if state ω prevails. $M_{t+1}(\omega)$ determines whether the market is willing to pay more (if the SDF is more than one) or less (if the SDF is less than one) than the expected value of the security (more on this when we discuss consumption-based pricing).

Example: In a world with two states, the probability of state 1 is 60% and that of state 2 is 40%. If the SDF is valued at 0.97 in state 1 and 0.95 in state 2, what are the values of the Arrow–Debreu securities for states 1 and 2?

The value of the Arrow–Debreu security for state 1 is

$$A(1) = P(1)\delta \frac{U'[C_{t+1}(1)]}{U'(C_t)} = 0.6 \times 0.97 = 0.582$$

Similarly,

$$A(2) = P(2)\delta \frac{U'[C_{t+1}(2)]}{U'(C_t)} = 0.4 \times 0.95 = 0.38$$

10.1.3 The Risk-Free Rate

A zero-coupon bond paying \$1 at $t + 1$ will replicate the payoff of all n Arrow–Debreu securities—because each security pays \$1 in each of the n states of the world. By arbitrage, the zero-coupon price at time t, $B(t, t + 1)$, will therefore be equal to the sum of the prices of the Arrow–Debreu securities. When $n = 2$, we have

$$B(t, t+1) = A(1) + A(2) = P(1)\delta \frac{U'[C_{t+1}(1)]}{U'(C_t)} + P(2)\delta \frac{U'[C_{t+1}(2)]}{U'(C_t)}$$

In general, the zero-coupon bond price is

$$B(t, t+1) = \sum_{\omega=1}^{n} P(\omega)\delta \frac{U'[C_{t+1}(\omega)]}{U'(C_t)}$$

This happens to be the mathematical expectation of the stochastic discount factor under the probability measure P. Thus

$$B(t, t+1) = E_t^P[M_{t+1}(\omega)]$$

Define r as the risk-free rate. Then we have

$$B(t, t+1) = \frac{1}{1+r}$$

and

$$r = \frac{1}{E_t^P[M_{t+1}(\omega)]} - 1$$

Example: From the preceding example, what is the value of the zero-coupon bond? What is the interest rate?

The value of the zero-coupon bond is $B(t, t+1) = A(1) + A(2) = 0.582 + 0.38 = 0.962$. The interest rate is $1/B(t, t+1) - 1 \approx 3.95\%$.

10.1.4 Pricing Assets with Arbitrary Payoffs

Suppose that a security has payoff $\pi_{t+1}(\omega)$, for $\omega = 1, 2, \ldots, n$. How do we price this security? Consider a portfolio consisting of $\pi_{t+1}(\omega)$ Arrow–Debreu securities for $\omega = 1, 2, \ldots, n$. Then this portfolio replicates the security exactly. The price of the portfolio and therefore of the security is

$$\pi_t = \sum_{\omega=1}^{n} P(\omega)\delta \frac{U'[C_{t+1}(\omega)]}{U'(c_t)} \pi_{t+1}(\omega) \tag{10.1}$$

That is,

$$\pi_t = E_t^P[M_{t+1}(\omega)\pi_{t+1}(\omega)]$$

For notational simplicity, call the stochastic discount factor M and the gross return on the security $R \equiv \pi_{t+1}/\pi_t$. Then we obtain a standard equation of asset pricing:

$$E_t^P(MR) = 1$$

10.1.5 Change-of-Probability Measure and Radon–Nikodym Derivative

Define a probability measure $Q(\omega)$ as

$$Q(\omega) \equiv \frac{P(\omega)\delta \dfrac{U'[C_{t+1}(\omega)]}{U'(C_t)}}{\sum_{\omega=1}^{n} P(\omega)\delta \dfrac{U'[C_{t+1}(\omega)]}{U'(C_t)}}$$

We use the risk-free rate expression to re-formulate this equation as

$$Q(\omega) = P(\omega)\delta \frac{U'[C_{t+1}(\omega)]}{U'(C_t)}(1+r)$$

The coefficient relating $Q(\omega)$ to $P(\omega)$, that is, $\dfrac{dQ(\omega)}{dP(\omega)} \equiv \delta \dfrac{U'[C_{t+1}(\omega)]}{U'(C_t)}(1+r),$ is called the *Radon–Nikodym derivative*. Using this probability change, Equation (10.1) can be rewritten as

$$\pi_t = \sum_{\omega=1}^{n} P(\omega)\delta \frac{U'[C_{t+1}(\omega)]}{U'(C_t)} \pi_{t+1}(\omega) = \sum_{\omega=1}^{n} P(\omega)\frac{dQ(\omega)}{dP(\omega)}\frac{\pi_{t+1}(\omega)}{1+r}$$

This yields

$$\pi_t = \sum_{\omega=1}^{n} Q(\omega)\frac{\pi_{t+1}(\omega)}{1+r}$$

or

$$\pi_t = E_t^{Q}\left[\frac{\pi_{t+1}(\omega)}{1+r}\right]$$

The sleight of hand just described allows us to price an asset by discounting its payoffs at the risk-free rate. The only complication involved is to change the real-life probabilities P of the states of the world into so-called risk-neutral probabilities Q. When we price derivative assets or contingent claims, we will see that this method is more convenient because it is way handier to change a probability measure than to find the right discount rate. The following example will show how to price a stock and a call option through a change in probabilities.

Example: Going back to the preceding example, calculate the risk-neutral probabilities $Q(1)$ and $Q(2)$. Then compute the value of a stock that pays 10 in state 1 and 3 in state 2. Lastly, price a call struck at 2 on this stock. A call payoff is $\max[S_T(\omega) - K, 0]$, where $S_T(\omega)$ is the stock price at expiration at state ω (10 or 3), and K is the strike price, 2 in this case.

The risk-neutral probabilities are

$$Q(1) = 0.6 \times 0.97 \times 1.0395 = 0.605$$
$$Q(2) = 0.4 \times 0.95 \times 1.0395 = 0.395$$

The stock price is valued at

$$S = \frac{(0.605 \times 10) + (0.395 \times 3)}{1.0395} = 6.96$$

And the call option price is

$$\sum_{\omega=1}^{n} Q(\omega) \frac{\max[S_{t+1}(\omega) - K, 0]}{1+r} = \frac{(0.605 \times 8) + (0.395 \times 1)}{1.0395} = 5.04$$

10.2 Consumption-Based Asset Pricing

10.2.1 Stochastic Discount Factor

We now solve the same problem without assuming the existence of Arrow–Debreu securities and will reach similar results.

Start with a representative agent who maximizes the discounted utility of a consumption stream over periods t and $t + 1$. The agent has endowment e_t at time t and e_{t+1} during the next period. She buys N units of an asset at time t at price p_t and consumes at $t + 1$ the payoff x_{t+1} from these N units of assets (sales proceeds and dividends) in addition to e_{t+1}. This can be written as

$$\max_N U(C_t) + E_t[\delta U(C_{t+1})]$$

subject to the following constraints:

$$C_t = e_t - Np_t \text{ and } C_{t+1} = e_{t+1} + Nx_{t+1}$$

Differentiating the expression

$$U(e_t - Np_t) + E_t[\delta U(e_{t+1} + Nx_{t+1})]$$

with respect to N, we get the first-order condition

$$1 = E_t\left[\delta \frac{U'(C_{t+1})}{U'(C_t)} \frac{x_{t+1}}{p_t}\right]$$

As before, define the stochastic discount factor as

$$M_{t+1} \equiv \delta \frac{U'(C_{t+1})}{U'(C_t)}$$

and the gross asset return as

$$R_{t+1} \equiv \frac{x_{t+1}}{p_t}$$

As in the Arrow–Debreu model, we have

$$E_t(M_{t+1}R_{t+1}) = 1$$

This equation holds for all assets including the risk-free asset. Because the gross risk-free rate R_f is known, it does not have to live within the expectation operator. We obtain an expression of the expected stochastic discount factor as the inverse of the gross risk-free rate

$$E_t(M_{t+1}) = \frac{1}{R_f}$$

As an example, if the risk-free rate is 2%, then $R_f = 1.02$, and the stochastic discount factor will average about 0.98.

10.2.2 Consumption Capital Asset Pricing Model (CCAPM)

Using shorthand notation and recalling that

$$E(MR) = 1 = E(M)E(R) + \text{cov}(M, R)$$

we can now replace $E(M)$ by $1/R_f$ to calculate the difference between the expected return on an asset i and the risk-free return. Thus

$$E(R_i) - R_f = R_f \text{cov}(-M, R_i) \tag{10.2}$$

From the definition of M and $E(M) = 1/R_f$, we know that

$$R_f = \frac{U'(C_t)}{\delta E[U'(C_{t+1})]} \tag{10.3}$$

Equations (10.2) and (10.3) boil down to the expression for the CCAPM:

$$E(R_i) - R_f = \frac{\text{cov}[-U'(C_{t+1}), R_i]}{E[U'(C_{t+1})]} \tag{10.4}$$

Note that $U'(C_{t+1})$ decreases with future consumption C_{t+1} because of satiation, meaning that $U''(C_{t+1}) < 0$. Thus $-U'(C_{t+1})$ increases with future consumption, and the covariance term is positive when asset returns are positively correlated with consumption. In this case, the asset is procyclical. A procyclical asset will not protect you against the business cycle. Instead, it will reinforce it. It acts like anti-insurance, and you will pay a low price for it. Low price means high expected return. This is exactly what the CCAPM Equation (10.4) is saying. When an asset return covaries positively with consumption, its price is low, and its expected return is in excess of the risk-free rate. Conversely, an insurance asset will deliver higher returns when consumption is low. As such, it is a desirable asset. Its price is high and its expected return is lower than the risk-free rate.

Also, note that Equation (10.4) can be rewritten as

$$
E(R_i) = R_f - \frac{\mathrm{cov}\left[\dfrac{U'(C_{t+1})}{U'(C_t)}, R_i\right]}{E\left[\dfrac{U'(C_{t+1})}{U'(C_t)}\right]} = R_f - \frac{\sigma_{\frac{U'(C_{t+1})}{U'(C_t)}}\sigma_{R_i}\,\mathrm{corr}\left[\dfrac{U'(C_{t+1})}{U'(C_t)}, R_i\right]}{E\left[\dfrac{U'(C_{t+1})}{U'(C_t)}\right]}
$$

This equation will help us parametrize expected returns for specific utility functions.

10.2.3 CCAPM with CRRA Utility and Log-Normal Consumption

Useful Properties of a Log-Normal Distribution

Recall that the moment-generating function of a normal random variable Y with mean m and variance v^2 is

$$
E(e^{\lambda Y}) = e^{\lambda m + \frac{\lambda^2 v^2}{2}}
$$

This expression allows us to calculate all the moments of a log-normal distribution. For example, a log-normal variable X is defined as $X \equiv e^{Y}$. Then, with $\lambda = 1$, the mean of a log-normal distribution is

$$
E(X) = e^{m + \frac{v^2}{2}}
$$

And with $\lambda = 2$,

$$
E(X^2) = e^{2m + 2v^2}
$$

Also, from the moment-generating expression of a normal variable, simple algebra shows that

$$
\mathrm{var}(e^{\lambda Y}) = \left(e^{\lambda m + \frac{\lambda^2 v^2}{2}}\right)^2 (e^{\lambda^2 v^2} - 1)
$$

These properties will allow us to derive expected returns with CRRA utilities.

The Risk-Free Rate

We now put more structure on the model by assuming a CRRA utility function and a log-normal random walk for consumption. The CRRA utility function is

$$U(C) = \frac{C^{1-\gamma} - 1}{1 - \gamma}$$

The ratio of marginal utilities is then

$$\frac{U'(C_{t+1})}{U'(C_t)} = \left(\frac{C_{t+1}}{C_t} \right)^{-\gamma}$$

And the expectation of the ratio can be expressed as

$$E\left[\frac{U'(C_{t+1})}{U'(C_t)} \right] = E\left[e^{-\gamma \ln\left(\frac{C_{t+1}}{C_t} \right)} \right]$$

If consumption growth follows a log-normal distribution, that is, if

$$\ln\left(\frac{C_{t+1}}{C_t} \right) \sim N(g, \sigma^2)$$

then from the moment-generating function of a normal distribution discussed earlier, we obtain

$$E\left[\frac{U'(C_{t+1})}{U'(C_t)} \right] = e^{-\gamma g + \frac{\gamma^2 \sigma^2}{2}}$$

Define the rate of time preference as $\theta = -\ln \delta$, then

$$E(M_{t+1}) = E\left[\delta \frac{U'(C_{t+1})}{U'(C_t)} \right] = e^{-\theta - \gamma g + \frac{\gamma^2 \sigma^2}{2}}$$

And the continuously compounded risk-free rate defined as $r \equiv \ln R_f$ is equal to

$$r = -\ln[E(M_{t+1})] = \theta + \gamma g - \frac{\gamma^2 \sigma^2}{2}$$

Note that with a logarithmic utility function, $\gamma = 1$, and the risk-free rate becomes

$$r = \theta + g - \frac{\sigma^2}{2}$$

Risky Assets

We now derive expected returns on risky assets with CRRA utility and log-normal consumption. From the properties of a log-normal distribution, as discussed earlier, note that

$$\frac{\sigma_{\frac{U'(C_{t+1})}{U'(C_t)}}}{E\left[\dfrac{U'(C_{t+1})}{U'(C_t)}\right]} = \sqrt{e^{\gamma^2\sigma^2}-1} \approx \gamma\sigma$$

where the approximation follows from $e^x - 1 \approx x$ for small x. Similarly,

$$\frac{U'(C_{t+1})}{U'(C_t)} = \left(\frac{C_{t+1}}{C_t}\right)^{-\gamma} = e^{-\gamma\ln\frac{C_{t+1}}{C_t}} \approx 1 - \gamma\ln\frac{C_{t+1}}{C_t}$$

Then it follows that

$$\operatorname{corr}\left[\frac{U'(C_{t+1})}{U'(C_t)}, R_i\right] \approx \operatorname{corr}\left[-\gamma\ln\frac{C_{t+1}}{C_t}, R_i\right] = \frac{-\gamma\operatorname{cov}\left(\ln\frac{C_{t+1}}{C_t}, R_i\right)}{\gamma\sigma_{\ln\frac{C_{t+1}}{C_t}}\sigma_{R_i}} = -\operatorname{corr}\left[\ln\frac{C_{t+1}}{C_t}, R_i\right]$$

Using these approximations, the generic CCAPM expression becomes

$$E(R_i) = R_f - \frac{\sigma_{\frac{U'(C_{t+1})}{U'(C_t)}}\sigma_{R_i}\operatorname{corr}\left[\dfrac{U'(C_{t+1})}{U'(C_t)}, R_i\right]}{E\left[\dfrac{U'(C_{t+1})}{U'(C_t)}\right]} = R_f + \gamma\sigma\sigma_{R_i}\operatorname{corr}\left[\ln\frac{C_{t+1}}{C_t}, R_i\right]$$

Hence the expression for the expected return of a risky asset

$$E(R_i) = R_f + \gamma\operatorname{cov}\left[\ln\frac{C_{t+1}}{C_t}, R_i\right]$$

The expected return on a risky asset is the risk-free rate plus the product of the risk-aversion coefficient and the covariance between the risky return and consumption growth.

We shall revisit this expression when we discuss the equity risk premium.

10.2.4 Hansen–Jagannathan Bounds

Writing symbols in shorthand, we know that

$$E(MR_i) = E(MR_f) = 1$$

We also know that

$$\text{cov}(M, R_i) = E(MR_i) - E(M)E(R_i)$$

This equation therefore can be rewritten as

$$\sigma_M \sigma_{R_i} \text{corr}_{M, R_i} = R_f E(M) - E(M)E(R_i)$$

Because $-1 \le \text{corr}_{M, R_i}$, we have

$$\frac{E(R_i) - R_f}{\sigma_{R_i}} \le \frac{\sigma_M}{E(M)}$$

This inequality says that the Sharpe ratio (the excess return over the risk-free rate divided by its standard deviation) for any asset i must be smaller than the ratio of the standard deviation to the expectation of the stochastic discount factor. Because this inequality holds for any asset i, it can be formulated as

$$\max_i \left[\frac{E(R_i) - R_f}{\sigma_{R_i}} \right] \le \frac{\sigma_M}{E(M)}$$

By definition of the stochastic discount factor and using an approximation from the preceding section, we obtain

$$\frac{\sigma_M}{E(M)} = \frac{\sigma_{\frac{U'(C_{t+1})}{U'(C_t)}}}{E\left[\frac{U'(C_{t+1})}{U'(C_t)}\right]} = \sqrt{e^{\gamma^2 \sigma^2} - 1} \approx \gamma \sigma$$

Hence the simplified expression of the Hansen–Jagannathan bound:

$$\max \text{ (Sharpe ratio across assets)} \le \gamma \sigma$$

Market practitioners are well aware that the best expected Sharpe ratio opportunities can reach 0.5, if not more. It would not be unreasonable to estimate σ, the yearly standard deviation of log consumption, at about 1%. What this means is that the risk-aversion coefficient γ that will satisfy this inequality should be at least 50, a number that beggars belief. "CRRA experts" believe γ to be between 2 and 5.

10.2.5 Miscellaneous

Marginal Utility of Consumption with Quadratic Utility

Under specific assumptions, it can be shown that the marginal utility of consumption is linear in market returns. For example, in a bare-bone one-period model, if the representative agent has no labor income, does not consume at time t, and consumes only accumulated wealth at time $t + 1$, then

$$C_{t+1} = W_{t+1}$$
$$W_{t+1} = R_M W_t$$

If the utility function is quadratic,

$$U(C_{t+1}) = -AC_{t+1}^2 + BC_{t+1}$$

then

$$U'(C_{t+1}) = -2AC_{t+1} + B$$

and

$$U'(C_{t+1}) = -aR_M + b$$

with $a \equiv 2AW_t$ and $b \equiv B$. While trivial, this result will be used in a derivation of the CAPM.

Price of the Consumption Claims with Log Utility

As established, the value of any payoff (future consumption in this case) is given by

$$V = E_t \left[\delta \frac{U'(C_{t+1})}{U'(C_t)} C_{t+1} \right]$$

When $U(C_t) = \ln(C_t)$, $U'(C_{t+1})/U'(C_t) = C_t/C_{t+1}$ and $V = \delta C_t$. The value of future consumption is independent of future consumption. This is because under logarithmic utility, the income effect (say higher future consumption) and the substitution effect (lower marginal utility of a higher future consumption) cancel each other. Good news (higher future consumption expenditure) does not impact the market because the discount rate increases to offset the good news.

10.3 Capital Asset Pricing

We proceed to discuss the CAPM, which is an equilibrium pricing model that states the following:

$$\mu_i - r = \frac{\sigma_{iM}}{\sigma_M^2}(\mu_M - r)$$

with

$$\beta_i \equiv \frac{\sigma_{iM}}{\sigma_M^2}$$

where μ_i is the expected return on asset i, r is the risk-free rate, and μ_M is the expected market return. The difference between the expected market return and the risk-free rate is called the *market risk premium*. The asset beta is defined as the covariance of the asset return with the market return divided by the variance of market return. The CAPM equation describes a line called the *security market line* (SML) that plots the expected return of an asset against its beta, with the slope being the market risk premium.

Example: $\mu_M = 0.05$ and $r = 0.01$. What is the expected return on asset A with beta of 1.25 and asset B with beta of –0.35?

$$\mu_A = r + \beta_A(\mu_M - r) = 0.01 + 1.25 \times (0.05 - 0.01) = 0.06$$

$$\mu_B = r + \beta_B(\mu_M - r) = 0.01 - 0.35 \times (0.05 - 0.01) = -0.004$$

Literally, the CAPM says that the expected return on an asset is the risk-free rate plus the product of the asset beta and the market risk premium. It also says that the expected return of an asset does not depend on the volatility of this asset but rather on its covariance with the market return. This may fly against intuition.

Example: $\mu_M = 0.05$ and $r = 0$. What is the expected return of a bet that pays 1 million if it rains and zero otherwise, assuming that the market return and the weather are independent?

The answer is zero. This is clearly a volatile bet, but its covariance with the market return is zero. It therefore should earn the risk-free rate, zero in this case. In a risk-neutral world, the price of this bet is 1 million times the probability of rain.

We now present three proofs of the CAPM.

10.3.1 Proof 1: CAPM as a Corollary of Tangency Portfolios

Reminiscence from the Preceding Section

Recall that the capital market line, defined as the tangent of the efficient frontier with N risky assets, is the locus of all efficient portfolios in the presence of a risk-free asset. Depending on the investor's risk appetite, one can be to the left or to the right of the tangency point. Investors with low risk aversion will borrow to leverage up their risky portfolios and will be to the right of the tangency point. Risk-averse investors will be to the left of the tangency point, will lend money, and will own less than their entire wealth in risky assets.

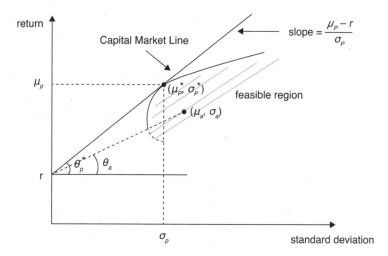

FIGURE 10.1 CAPM and the tangency portfolio

As stated in Chapter 7, the equation of the capital market line is

$$\mu_P = r + \frac{\mu_M - r}{\sigma_M} \sigma_P$$

where μ_P and σ_P are, respectively, the expected return and the volatility of the return of any efficient portfolio.

Of note is the market equilibrium point: when supply and demand are equated, the market owns, well, the market. Tautologically, M is the market equilibrium point where supply and demand are aggregated.

Proof: Now form a portfolio with portion α in a risky asset with mean return μ_i and return volatility σ_i and $1 - \alpha$ in the market portfolio. The expected return on the portfolio is

$$\mu_\alpha = \alpha\mu_i + (1-\alpha)\mu_M$$

and the return volatility is

$$\sigma_\alpha = \sqrt{\alpha^2\sigma_i^2 + 2\alpha(1-\alpha)\sigma_{iM} + (1-\alpha)^2\sigma_M^2}$$

Then

$$\frac{d\mu_\alpha}{d\alpha} = \mu_i - \mu_M$$

and

$$\frac{d\sigma_\alpha}{d\alpha} = \frac{\alpha\sigma_i^2 + (1-2\alpha)\sigma_{im} + (\alpha-1)\sigma_M^2}{\sigma_\alpha}$$

Note that

$$\frac{d\mu_\alpha}{d\sigma_\alpha} = \frac{\dfrac{d\mu_\alpha}{d\alpha}}{\dfrac{d\sigma_\alpha}{d\alpha}} = \frac{\sigma_\alpha(\mu_i - \mu_M)}{\alpha\sigma_i^2 + (1-2\alpha)\sigma_{iM} + (\alpha-1)\sigma_M^2}$$

Evidently, at equilibrium, it makes no sense to add any portion of asset i, meaning that $\alpha = 0$. Evaluating $d\mu_\alpha / d\sigma_\alpha$ at $\alpha = 0$ and equating this derivative to the slope of the capital market line, we obtain

$$\frac{\sigma_M(\mu_i - \mu_M)}{\sigma_{iM} - \sigma_M^2} = \frac{\mu_M - r}{\sigma_M}$$

Solving for μ_i, we get the expression for the CAPM:

$$\mu_i - r = \frac{\sigma_{iM}}{\sigma_M^2}(\mu_M - r)$$

10.3.2 Proof 2: CAPM with a Mean-Variance Utility Function

Posit a representative investor with a mean-variance utility function

$$U(r_P) = \mu_P - \frac{1}{2}\lambda\sigma_P^2$$

where λ measures risk aversion, and r_p, μ_p, and σ_p^2 are the return, expected return, and return variance of the investor's portfolio, respectively.

The investor's portfolio consists of portion α in risky assets and $1 - \alpha$ in the risk-free asset with return r. The portfolio of risky assets comprises N assets with weights $x_1, \ldots, x_N$ ($\sum_{i=1}^{N} x_i = 1$), expected returns $\mu_1, \ldots, \mu_N$, and return variances $\sigma_1^2, \ldots, \sigma_N^2$. The optimal solution satisfies

$$\frac{\partial U}{\partial x_i} = 0$$

Therefore,

$$\frac{\partial \mu_\alpha}{\partial x_i} = \frac{1}{2}\lambda\frac{\partial \sigma_\alpha^2}{\partial x_i}$$

With the expected return on the portfolio

$$\mu_\alpha = r + \alpha\sum_{i=1}^{N} x_i(\mu_i - r)$$

and the variance of returns

$$\sigma_\alpha^2 = \alpha^2\left(\sum_{i=j} x_i^2\sigma_i^2 + \sum_{i\neq j}\rho_{ij}x_i x_j\sigma_i\sigma_j\right)$$

At equilibrium, $\alpha = 1$ and $x = [x_1\ x_1\ \cdots\ x_N]' = x_M$.

It is easy to show that evaluated at $\alpha = 1$,

$$\frac{\partial \mu_\alpha}{\partial x_i} = \mu_i - r$$

and

$$\frac{\partial \sigma_\alpha^2}{\partial x_i} = 2\sum_{j=1}^{N}\text{cov}(x_j r_j, r_i) = 2\sigma_{iM}$$

And hence

$$\mu_i - r = \lambda\sigma_{iM}$$

Multiplying both sides by x_i and summing over i, we have

$$\sum_{i=1}^{N} x_i (\mu_i - r) = \mu_M - r = \lambda \sum_{i=1}^{N} x_i \sigma_{iM} = \lambda \sigma_M^2$$

The CAPM follows from the last two equations:

$$\mu_i - r = \frac{\sigma_{iM}}{\sigma_M^2}(\mu_M - r)$$

10.3.3 Proof 3: CAPM from CCAPM with Quadratic Utility

We now derive the CAPM from the CCAPM equation. Suppose, as shown in the simple quadratic utility example earlier, that the marginal utility of future consumption is perfectly negatively correlated with the market gross return. That is,

$$U'(C_{t+1}) = -aR_M + b$$

Then the CCAPM equation applied to some asset i will give

$$E(R_i) - R_f = \frac{\text{cov}[-U'(C_{t+1}), R_i]}{E[U'(C_{t+1})]} = \frac{a\,\text{cov}(R_i, R_M)}{E[U'(C_{t+1})]}$$

The same equation applied to the market portfolio will yield

$$E(R_M) - R_f = \frac{\text{cov}[-U'(C_{t+1}), R_M]}{E[U'(C_{t+1})]} = \frac{a\,\text{var}(R_M)}{E[U'(C_{t+1})]}$$

Dividing through, the denominators drop, and we obtain

$$\frac{E(R_i) - R_f}{E(R_M) - R_f} = \frac{\text{cov}(R_i, R_M)}{\text{var}(R_M)}$$

The CAPM follows:

$$\mu_i - r = \frac{\sigma_{iM}}{\sigma_M^2}(\mu_M - r)$$

Viewed from this angle, the CAPM is a special case of the CCAPM.

10.3.4 Systematic and Idiosyncratic Risk

The CAPM states that the market will pay investors for the covariance of the asset with the market but not for the total variance of the asset return. To make the distinction between systematic and idiosyncratic risk, we show first the "testable" expression of the CAPM in regression format:

$$r_i = r + \beta_i(r_M - r) + \varepsilon_i$$

where r_i and r_M are, respectively, the observed asset return and market return, and ε_i is the error term with mean zero. Note that

$$\text{cov}(r_M, \varepsilon_i) = \text{cov}[r_M, r_i - r - \beta_i(r_M - r)] = \sigma_{iM} - \beta_i \sigma_M^2 = 0$$

and it follows that

$$\text{var}(r_i) = \beta_i^2 \sigma_M^2 + \text{var}(\varepsilon_i)$$

Thus the total risk is equal to the sum of the systematic risk (asset beta squared times the variance of the market return) and the variance of the error term.

Example: If the market has a volatility of 20% and the asset has a volatility of 30% with a beta of 1.1, then what is the systematic variance? How about the idiosyncratic risk?

The total variance is $0.3^2 = 0.09$. The systematic variance is $\beta_i^2 \sigma_M^2$; that is, $1.1^2 \times 0.2^2 = 0.0484$. The idiosyncratic variance $\text{var}(\varepsilon_i)$ is the difference between the total variance and the systematic variance; that is, $0.09 - 0.0484 = 0.0416$. The R^2 of the regression is 0.0484/0.09, about 54%.

10.3.5 Capital Market Line and Security Market Line

The capital market line (CML) and the security market line (SML) are both statements about expected returns. The CML expresses the expected return of an efficient portfolio as a function of the volatility of that portfolio. In contrast, the SML states that *any* asset or portfolio expected return is a function of the beta or covariance of that asset or portfolio with the market portfolio.

Because any portfolio will be on the SML in a CAPM world, we can express the expected portfolio return as

$$\mu_P = r + \frac{\sigma_{PM}}{\sigma_M^2}(\mu_M - r) = r + \frac{\rho_{PM}\sigma_P}{\sigma_M}(\mu_M - r)$$

whereas the CML has equation

$$\mu_P = r + \frac{\mu_M - r}{\sigma_M}\sigma_P$$

This means that a portfolio lies on both the CML and the SML (that is, the CML and the SML equations are the same) when $\rho_{PM} = 1$. If $\rho_{PM} < 1$, then the portfolio will lie on the SML but not the CML (of course, all portfolios on the CML, being combinations of the risk-free asset and the market, are perfectly correlated with the market).

10.3.6 CAPM: A Couple of Observations

The CAPM has been widely viewed as convenient to use: its inputs, covariance between market returns and individual asset returns and market risk premium, are easy to understand. Proxies for these inputs are observable at high frequency.

Convenience generally comes at a cost. To state the obvious, models are as good as their assumptions: investor rationality, the ability to lend and borrow at no transaction costs, and perhaps more importantly, the assumptions of a risk-free asset and an observable market portfolio are all reasons for skepticism or further inquiry.

While the assumption of a risk-free asset has been tackled by Fischer Black (1972) in a CAPM version called *zero-beta CAPM*, the inability to observe a market portfolio (think about illiquid assets and, worse, about human capital) appears to be a rather serious issue. Famously, Roll (1977) showed that any valid test of the CAPM presupposed knowledge of a market portfolio.

Also, as will be discussed later, it is likely that assets can be remunerated for their exposure to systematic factors beyond the market factor.

10.4 Intertemporal Capital Asset Pricing

The classic CAPM is a static, single-period model. In reality, investors live for more than just one period and make investment and consumption decisions over time. The *intertemporal capital asset pricing model* (ICAPM) is a dynamic model that relaxes this unrealistic assumption of the static CAPM. Here we present a simplified version of the continuous-time model in Merton (1973b).

Suppose that there are n risky assets, one "instantaneously risk-free" asset, and a state variable S that determines the investment opportunities. The asset returns and the state variable follow:

$$\frac{dP_i}{P_i} = \mu_i(S)dt + \sigma_i(S)dz_i, \text{ for } i = 1, \dots, n$$

$$\frac{dP_{n+1}}{P_{n+1}} = r(S)dt$$

$$dS = \mu_S(S)dt + \sigma_S(S)dz_S$$

where the dz_i's are standard Wiener processes with $E[dz_i dz_j] = \rho_{ij}dt$ and $\rho_{ii} = 1$. The covariance matrix is Σ with elements $\sigma_{ij} = \rho_{ij}\sigma_i\sigma_j$.

Consider a consumer-investor who chooses the amount of consumption and the investment portfolio continuously to maximize lifetime expected utility:

$$J(W,S,0) = \max_{\{c,w\}} E_0\left\{\int_0^T U[c(t),t]dt + B[W(T),T]\right\}$$

$$\text{subject to}\ \ dW = \sum_{i=1}^{n+1} w_i W \frac{dP_i}{P_i} - cdt$$

where $W(t)$ is his wealth at time t and w_i is the fraction of his wealth invested in asset i. Plugging in the expressions for dP_i/P_i, we can rewrite the budget constraint as

$$dW = \left[\sum_{i=1}^{n} w_i(\mu_i - r)W + (rW - c)\right]dt + \sum_{i=1}^{n} w_i W \sigma_i dz_i$$

The optimality conditions are

$$\max_{\{c,w\}} U[c(t),t] + J_W\left[\sum_{i=1}^{n} w_i(\mu_i - r)W + (rW - c)\right] + J_S\mu_S + J_t + \frac{1}{2}J_{WW}W^2\sum_{i=1}^{n}\sum_{j=1}^{n}w_i w_j \sigma_{ij}$$

$$+ \frac{1}{2}J_{SS}\sigma_S^2 + J_{WS}W\sum_{i=1}^{n}w_i\sigma_{iS} = 0$$

$$\text{subject to}\ J(W, S, T) = B(W, T)$$

where subscripts for the value function J denote partial derivatives.

The first-order condition with respect to consumption c is

$$U_c = J_W$$

This is the usual intertemporal envelope condition, which equates the marginal utility of current consumption with the marginal utility of wealth, that is, future consumption.

The first-order condition with respect to portfolio weights w is (in matrix form)

$$0 = WJ_W(\mu - r) + J_{WW}W^2\Sigma w + J_{WS}W\sigma_S$$

where

$$\sigma_S = \begin{bmatrix} \sigma_{1S} \\ \vdots \\ \sigma_{nS} \end{bmatrix}$$

Therefore, the optimal allocation

$$w^* = -\frac{J_W}{WJ_{WW}}\Sigma^{-1}(\mu - r) - \frac{J_{WS}}{WJ_{WW}}\Sigma^{-1}\sigma_S$$

or, equivalently,

$$w^*W = -\frac{J_W}{J_{WW}}\Sigma^{-1}(\mu - r) - \frac{J_{WS}}{J_{WW}}\Sigma^{-1}\sigma_S = A\Sigma^{-1}(\mu - r) + H\Sigma^{-1}\sigma_S$$

where $A \equiv -\dfrac{J_W}{J_{WW}}$ and $H \equiv -\dfrac{J_{WS}}{J_{WW}}$.

Note that the first term on the right-hand side resembles the usual demand function for risky assets in a static, single-period mean variance optimization problem, where $A = -J_W/J_{WW} = -U_c/(U_{cc}c_W) > 0$ is proportional to the reciprocal of the investor's relative risk-aversion coefficient. It is sometimes referred to as the *myopic demand* as opposed to the *hedging demand*, which is the second term, as explained below.

The second term reflects the investor's demand for risky assets to hedge against future "undesirable" shifts in the investment opportunity set, defined as changes in S that would lead to lower consumption at a given level of wealth. For example, if $c_S \equiv \partial c/\partial S < 0$, then $\Delta S > 0$ would be undesirable.

Assume for simplicity that Σ is diagonal. Then the second term for asset i becomes $H\sigma_{ii}^{-1}\sigma_{iS}$. Because $H = -J_{WS}/J_{WW} = -c_S/c_W > 0$ if $c_S < 0$, this means that the investor will invest more in asset i than she would in the single-period optimization problem if the return of this asset is positively correlated with the state variable S.

If $\sigma_S = 0$, we have

$$w^* = -\frac{J_W}{WJ_{WW}}\Sigma^{-1}(\mu - r)$$

This is the traditional CAPM formula. In this case, investors cannot hedge future undesirable changes in investment opportunities with assets, so there is no hedging demand for assets.

Next, we derive the equilibrium expected asset returns. We first rewrite the asset demand function for investor k by rearranging terms and adding a superscript to variables that are investor specific:

$$\Sigma W^k w^k = A^k (\mu - r) + H^k \sigma_S$$

Summing over k and dividing both sides by $\sum_k A^k$, we have

$$\mu - r = \frac{\sum_k W^k}{\sum_k A^k} \Sigma \frac{\sum_k W^k w^k}{\sum_k W^k} - \frac{\sum_k H^k}{\sum_k A^k} \sigma_S$$

To simplify notation, define $\lambda \equiv \dfrac{\sum_k W^k}{\sum_k A^k}$ and $h \equiv \dfrac{\sum_k H^k}{\sum_k A^k}$. In equilibrium, $\dfrac{\sum_k W^k w^k}{\sum_k W^k}$ has to be the market portfolio w_M. Therefore,

$$\mu - r = \lambda \Sigma w_M - h \sigma_S$$

Premultiplying both sides by $w_M{'}$, we get

$$w'_M (\mu - r) = \mu_M - r = \lambda w'_M \Sigma w_M - h w'_M \sigma_S = \lambda \sigma_M^2 - h \sigma_{MS}$$

Construct another portfolio w_H that maximizes the squared (or absolute) correlation between the portfolio and the state variable S for best hedging:

$$w_H = \frac{\Sigma^{-1} \sigma_S}{1' \Sigma^{-1} \sigma_S}$$

Premultiplying both sides by w'_H, we get

$$w'_H (\mu - r) = \mu_H - r = \lambda w'_H \Sigma w_M - h w'_H \sigma_S = \lambda \sigma_{MH} - h \sigma_{HS}$$

Therefore, we can express λ and h as functions of the risk premia of the market portfolio and the hedging portfolio:

$$\lambda = \frac{\sigma_{HS} (\mu_M - r) - \sigma_{MS} (\mu_H - r)}{\sigma_M^2 \sigma_{HS} - \sigma_{MH} \sigma_{MS}}$$

$$h = \frac{\sigma_H^2 (\mu_M - r) - \sigma_M^2 (\mu_H - r)}{\sigma_M^2 \sigma_{HS} - \sigma_{MH} \sigma_{MS}}$$

Therefore,

$$\mu - r = \lambda \Sigma w_M - h\sigma_S = \frac{\sigma_{HS}\,\sigma_M - \sigma_{MH}\,\sigma_S}{\sigma_M^2 \sigma_{HS} - \sigma_{MH}\,\sigma_{MS}}(\mu_M - r) - \frac{\sigma_{MS}\,\sigma_M - \sigma_M^2 \sigma_S}{\sigma_M^2 \sigma_{HS} - \sigma_{MH}\,\sigma_{MS}}(\mu_H - r)$$

where

$$\sigma_M = \begin{bmatrix} \sigma_{1M} \\ \vdots \\ \sigma_{nM} \end{bmatrix}$$

or, for asset i,

$$\mu_i - r = \frac{\sigma_{HS}\,\sigma_{iM} - \sigma_{MH}\,\sigma_{iS}}{\sigma_M^2 \sigma_{HS} - \sigma_{MH}\,\sigma_{MS}}(\mu_M - r) - \frac{\sigma_{MS}\,\sigma_{iM} - \sigma_M^2 \sigma_{iS}}{\sigma_M^2 \sigma_{HS} - \sigma_{MH}\,\sigma_{MS}}(\mu_H - r)$$

To see how this equation relates to the multivariate regression of the asset's excess return on the excess returns of the market and the hedging portfolios, recall that

$$w_H = \frac{\Sigma^{-1}\sigma_S}{1'\Sigma^{-1}\sigma_S}$$

Therefore,

$$\sigma_H \equiv \begin{bmatrix} \sigma_{1H} \\ \vdots \\ \sigma_{nH} \end{bmatrix} = \Sigma w_H = \frac{1}{1'\Sigma^{-1}\sigma_S}\sigma_S \equiv \frac{1}{c}\sigma_S$$

Then

$$\mu_i - r = \frac{c\sigma_H^2 \sigma_{iM} - \sigma_{MH}\,c\sigma_{iH}}{\sigma_M^2 c\sigma_H^2 - \sigma_{MH}\,c\sigma_{MH}}(\mu_M - r) - \frac{c\sigma_{MH}\,\sigma_{iM} - \sigma_M^2 c\sigma_{iH}}{\sigma_M^2 c\sigma_H^2 - \sigma_{MH}\,c\sigma_{MH}}(\mu_H - r)$$

$$= \frac{\sigma_H^2 \sigma_{iM} - \sigma_{MH}\,\sigma_{iH}}{\sigma_M^2 \sigma_H^2 - \sigma_{MH}^2}(\mu_M - r) - \frac{\sigma_{MH}\,\sigma_{iM} - \sigma_M^2 \sigma_{iH}}{\sigma_M^2 \sigma_H^2 - \sigma_{MH}^2}(\mu_H - r)$$

$$\equiv \beta_{iM}(\mu_M - r) + \beta_{iH}(\mu_H - r)$$

We can think of β_{iM} and β_{iH} as the coefficients for the multivariate regression of asset i's excess returns on the excess returns of the market and hedging portfolios.

If the state variable S is uncorrelated with the market portfolio, that is, $\sigma_{MH} = 0$, the relationship can be further simplified to

$$\mu_i - r = \frac{\sigma_{iM}}{\sigma_M^2}(\mu_M - r) + \frac{\sigma_{iH}}{\sigma_H^2}(\mu_H - r)$$

This is similar to the case of orthogonal predictors in a multivariate regression where the multivariate coefficients are equal to the univariate ones. Compared with the traditional CAPM, which is a single-factor model, we now have two factors to explain the excess return of each asset in equilibrium. If there is more than one state variable, we generally will have one additional factor for each additional state variable:

$$\mu_i - r = \beta_{iM}(\mu_M - r) + \sum_{j=1}^{m}\beta_{iH_j}\left(\mu_{H_j} - r\right)$$

11
Factor Models

Summary

The *arbitrage pricing theory* (APT) is a general theory of asset pricing developed by Ross (1976) as an alternative to the capital asset pricing model (CAPM).

Suppose that the random returns for n assets follow a linear k-factor model

$$r_i = \mu_i + \sum_{j=1}^{k} \beta_{ij} f_j + \varepsilon_i$$

or, in matrix form,

$$r = \mu + \beta f + \varepsilon$$

where μ is an $n \times 1$ vector of asset-specific constants, ε is an $n \times 1$ vector of idiosyncratic risks, f is a $k \times 1$ vector of systematic or common factor returns, and β is an $n \times k$ matrix (β_{ij} is asset i's beta or factor loading on factor j).

The APT states that under some additional assumptions, the absence of arbitrage for a linear factor structure such as that above implies that the expected asset returns have the following approximate representation:

$$E[r_i] - r_f = \sum_{j=1}^{k} \beta_{ij} \lambda_j$$

where r_f is the risk-free rate, and λ_j is the risk premium for factor j, that is, the excess return for any asset or portfolio with unit beta to factor j and zero betas to all other factors.

Many researchers have attempted to identify additional such factors over the past few decades (see Harvey, Liu, and Zhu [2016] and Harvey and Liu [2021] for comprehensive reviews and critique). The factors studied generally fall into two categories: macro and style factors. *Macro* factors are the fundamental drivers for absolute returns across multiple asset classes in the economy, such as growth, inflation, and real interest rate. These factors usually have directional impact on asset returns and are typically implemented with long-only portfolios. In contrast, *style* factors explain relative returns within asset classes, such as small cap versus large cap within equities and high-quality versus low-quality bonds within fixed income. Except for time-series momentum, these factors are often implemented with long-short strategies within each asset class that are beta neutral.

Carry, momentum, and value are three popular style factors studied by a large and still growing body of research. They are also some of the most robust style factors identified in the literature across asset classes and markets.

The Fama–French three-factor model (Fama and French [1993]) has been one of the most empirically successful and prominent factor models for stock returns since the intertemporal CAPM and APT were developed. It introduced two new factors to the single-factor CAPM, size and value.

11.1 Arbitrage Pricing Theory

The *arbitrage pricing theory* (APT) is a general theory of asset pricing developed by Ross (1976) as an alternative to the CAPM. It starts from a statistical characterization of realized asset returns and ends with certain implications for expected asset returns or asset pricing. Compared with the CAPM, which states that expected returns depend only on a single nondiversifiable risk (the market risk), the APT allows a variety of risk sources and is therefore more realistic and intuitive. The linear risk factor structure of the APT is the theoretical foundation of the risk-management systems for many large asset managers today.

11.1.1 The Heuristic Argument

There are three basic assumptions underlying the APT:

- Asset returns can be characterized by a linear factor model.
- Idiosyncratic risk can be sufficiently diversified away.
- There are no arbitrage opportunities.

Suppose that the random returns for n assets follow a linear k-factor model

$$r_i = \mu_i + \sum_{j=1}^{k} \beta_{ij} f_j + \varepsilon_i$$

or, in matrix form,

$$r = \mu + \beta f + \varepsilon$$

where μ is an $n \times 1$ vector of asset-specific constants, ε is an $n \times 1$ vector of idiosyncratic risks, f is a $k \times 1$ vector of systematic or common factor returns, and β is an $n \times k$ matrix (β_{ij} is asset i's beta or factor loading on factor j).

We follow the simplification convention to normalize the expected returns for the systematic factors and the idiosyncratic terms to be zero; that is, $E[f] = 0$ and $E[\varepsilon] = 0$. This implies that $E[r] = \mu$. For simplicity, we also assume that $E[\varepsilon|f] = 0$ and that $\Omega \equiv E[\varepsilon\varepsilon']$ is a diagonal matrix, although these assumptions can be relaxed for some versions of the APT.

The APT states that under some additional assumptions,[1] the absence of arbitrage for a linear factor structure such as that above implies that the expected asset returns have the following approximate representation:

$$E[r_i] - r_f = \sum_{j=1}^{k} \beta_{ij} \lambda_j$$

---

1 Formal proof of the APT usually requires some assumptions on β and Ω that are not overly restrictive. See, for example, Ross (1976), Huberman (1982), and Ingersoll (1984). Huberman and Wang (2008) provide a comprehensive overview of the original theory and subsequent developments.

where r_f is the risk-free rate, and λ_j is the risk premium for factor j, that is, the excess return for any asset or portfolio with unit beta to factor j and zero betas to all other factors.

To see why this is the case, we can construct a zero-cost arbitrage portfolio w; that is, $w'\mathbf{1} = 0$. We also require w to be well diversified with each weight w_i of order $1/n$ in (absolute) magnitude. By the law of large numbers, for large enough n, the influence of the idiosyncratic random noises on the arbitrage portfolio will become negligible. Thus

$$w'r = w'\mu + w'\beta f + w'\varepsilon \approx w'\mu + w'\beta f$$

Assuming further that the arbitrage portfolio has zero net systematic factor loadings, that is, $w'\beta = 0$, we have

$$w'r \approx w'\mu$$

The zero-cost and (approximately) zero-risk portfolio should earn zero return because there would be arbitrage opportunities otherwise. We have

$$w'\mu \approx 0$$

Because this holds for any w satisfying $w'\mathbf{1} = 0$ and $w'\beta = 0$, μ must be spanned by $\mathbf{1}$ and β; that is,

$$\mu = c\mathbf{1} + \beta\lambda$$

where c is a constant, and λ is a $k \times 1$ vector.

For each asset i,

$$\mu_i = c + \sum_{j=1}^{k} \beta_{ij}\lambda_j$$

If there exists a risk-free asset, c should be the risk-free rate of return, and λ_j is the risk premium for factor j ($j = 1, \ldots, k$).

The intuition behind the APT is similar to that behind the Arrow–Debreu security pricing model discussed in Chapter 10. Because the idiosyncratic risks become negligible under the law of large numbers, there are k fundamental securities (or factors) spanning all possible systematic risks that drive returns. If the systematic risks in each asset's return can be represented by a linear combination of the k fundamental securities, then no arbitrage implies that the asset's expected return should be the same linear combination of the k fundamental securities' expected returns.

11.1.2 APT Versus CAPM and ICAPM

The CAPM is a single-factor model that states that an asset expected return is linearly related to its covariance with the market portfolio (or its beta) based on the assumption that the market portfolio is mean variance optimal. Developed as a substitute for the CAPM, the APT starts from a statistical characterization of asset returns and allows potentially more than one factor for asset pricing. Its simplicity and flexibility have contributed to the practical popularity of the theory. However, unlike the CAPM, the APT is silent about the identities of the factors.

The ICAPM extends the static, single-period CAPM and allows for multiple factors for asset pricing as well, so the model looks similar to the APT at first glance. However, the derivations for the APT and ICAPM are different. This mostly leads to different inspirations for factors in empirical work.[2] The derivation for the ICAPM suggests that one should look for state variables that can potentially predict the distributions of future asset returns or future marginal utility from consumptions. Macroeconomic variables naturally fall into this category, as well as shocks to noninvestment income such as labor income. In contrast, derivation of the APT suggests that one can start by analyzing the historical covariance matrix for returns to find the common drivers of asset returns.

11.1.3 Factor Identification

The linear factor model, which was the basic assumption for the APT, resembles a linear regression model:

$$r_i = \mu_i + \sum_{j=1}^{k} \beta_{ij} f_j + \varepsilon_i$$

where $E[\varepsilon_i] = E[\varepsilon_i \mid f] = 0$. If the factors are known, we can run empirical models to estimate the factor structure. However, in most cases, we don't know the factors in advance and must identify them first. There are several approaches one can consider.

2 The difference between the APT and the ICAPM in empirical work is not as clear-cut as the difference between their derivations. Cochrane (2005) provides two examples of well-known papers that can potentially be categorized under either the APT or the ICAPM.

The first approach is based on statistical techniques such as factor analysis and principal component analysis. For example, one can estimate the covariance matrix of asset returns and its eigenvalue decomposition and set the smallest eigenvalues to zero to estimate a factor structure.

The second approach is almost the opposite of the first one in the sense that researchers start from economic theories and intuitions to find possible factors, estimate the factor loadings, and evaluate how the factor structure explains the cross-sectional returns.

The third approach combines statistical analysis with economic reasoning to identify factors, so it is neither purely statistical nor purely judgmental. Compared with the preceding two extreme approaches, it is more popular among economists. One of the most famous examples is the Fama–French factor model to explain stock returns, which is discussed in Section 11.3.

Since the early tests of the CAPM found that the market beta explained a significant fraction of the cross section of asset returns, many researchers have attempted to identify additional such factors over the past few decades.[3] The factors studied in the empirical literature generally fall into two categories: macro and style factors. Macro factors are the fundamental drivers for absolute returns across multiple asset classes in the economy, such as growth, inflation, nominal and real interest rates, and the exchange rate. They usually have directional impact on asset returns and are typically implemented with long-only portfolios. In contrast, style factors explain mostly relative returns within asset classes, such as small cap versus large cap within equities and high-quality versus low-quality bonds within fixed income. Except for time-series momentum, these factors are often implemented with long-short strategies within each asset class that are beta neutral.

11.2 Carry, Momentum, and Value

Carry, momentum, and value[4] are three popular style factors studied by a large and growing body of research. They are also some of the most robust style factors identified in the literature across asset classes and markets. We discuss below the taxonomy and some economic rationales for these factors or the corresponding strategies.

---

3 Harvey et al. (2016) provide a comprehensive review of 316 factors selected from the literature and argue that most claimed factors found in financial economics are likely false.
4 This section follows closely Baz et al. (2015).

11.2.1 Carry

Carry can be defined as the difference between the spot price and the forward/futures price of an asset if price does not change. A simple example of carry for a currency pair is the interest-rate differential between the foreign and base currencies. The carry trade is one of the most popular trading strategies in the foreign exchange market. A simple currency carry trade can be long high-yielding currencies and short low-yielding currencies.

A carry trade bets on the difference between the forward price and expected future spot price of the asset. If the two were equal, there would be no long-term risk premium for the carry factor. We show below mathematically why they should not be equal in general. Take currency forward as an example. Suppose that the forward price of currency F in terms of currency B is the unbiased estimator for future spot exchange rate:

$$F_{t,T} = E_t[S_T]$$

where $F_{t,T}$ is the forward price between time t and expiry T, and S_T is the spot price at time T. This is a case where uncovered interest parity holds or the forward bias is zero. However, if this is a general principle, it also should hold for the price of currency B expressed as units of currency F:

$$\frac{1}{F_{t,T}} = E_t\left[\frac{1}{S_T}\right]$$

which means that

$$E_t\left[\frac{1}{S_T}\right] = \frac{1}{E_t[S_T]}$$

This cannot hold because of Jensen's inequality. Therefore, forward prices cannot be unbiased estimators for future spot prices in general. This is called *Siegel's paradox*, which we will revisit in Chapter 14 to show that as long as there is randomness, risk premia are prevalent in all asset classes.

Example (Forward Bias for Equity): To quantify the forward bias, consider a dividend-paying asset as an example. The forward price and the spot price have the following relation:

$$F_{t,T} = S_t e^{(r-d)(T-t)}$$

where r and d are the continuously compounded risk-free rate and dividend yield, respectively. The sign of carry for this asset depends on the difference between r and d. If the interest rate is higher than the dividend yield, carry will be positive, and vice versa.

Let's assume that the CAPM holds; then the expected spot price of the asset is

$$E_t[S_T] = S_t e^{(r+\beta\pi-d)(T-t)}$$

where β is the asset's equity market beta, and π is the equity risk premium. If $\beta\pi > 0$, which is the case most of the time, we have

$$E_t[S_T] > F_{t,T}$$

Based on the simple CAPM, we have shown a systematic forward bias for this generic dividend-paying asset, and the sign of the bias depends on the asset's equity market beta but not on carry. We can use richer asset pricing models to link forward bias to carry (see Baz et al. [2015] for more examples).

11.2.2 Momentum

A *momentum* strategy is defined as selling losers and buying winners. It is based on the belief that asset returns are persistent; that is, recent outperformance predicts future outperformance and recent underperformance predicts future underperformance.

Based on this simple principle, there are various ways to implement a momentum trade. It could be cross sectional or time series. The look-back window also could vary, although the most common trade, especially in the academic literature, uses 12 months past performance as the signal.

The choice of look-back window sometimes can materially impact the backtest results. This is not surprising because asset returns tend to exhibit different patterns in terms of momentum versus mean reversion in different horizons. For example, mean aversion (or negative autocorrelation) for some assets is more prominent for very short windows (days or weeks) or very long windows (years), and momentum (positive autocorrelation) is common for moderate horizons such as 6–12 months. This is also the typical look-back window most momentum trades would focus on.

Researchers have explored the reasons for the persistent and positive performance of momentum strategies from a theoretical perspective. The first group of hypotheses searches for the type of aggregate, nondiversifiable risk embedded in momentum strategies. For example, Liu and Zhang (2008) found that recent winners tend to be more exposed to the growth rate of industrial production, which is a priced risk factor in standard asset-pricing tests. They claimed that this macroeconomic risk factor explains more than half of momentum profits. In this case, risk seems to play an important role in driving the positive performance of momentum strategies.

Chapter 14 shows an example of momentum trading strategy where we argue that negative skewness may help explain its positive performance. The momentum strategy is effectively long long-dated variance and short short-dated variance. It indicates that a momentum buyer is exposed to crash risk to the extent that a crash is generally associated with a spike in short-dated variance. Therefore, the momentum risk premium is sometimes interpreted as compensation for crash risk.

Investors' behavioral bias and sentiment also may help explain the origin of momentum profits. For example, Barberis, Shleifer, and Vishny (1998) argued that investors tend to underreact to news because of conservatism bias and slow updates of their beliefs. The disposition effect among investors also can help to explain momentum profits. Investors tend to sell their winning stocks too early while holding onto their losers, causing positive autocorrelation in asset returns that do not fully reflect the asset's fundamental value.

11.2.3 Value

Value refers to the difference between an asset's market price and its fair or fundamental price. A value strategy involves buying cheap and selling expensive assets. The fair or fundamental price for an asset is usually not observed but modeled and estimated. To evaluate the impact of a value signal on an asset's expected return, we also need to estimate how fast the asset's price is expected to revert to its fair or fundamental price.

Example (Equity Valuation): Based on the Gordon growth model, a stock's price should be the present value of its future dividends, with the initial dividend D growing at a real rate g and discounted at a real equity yield r. Thus

$$P = \frac{D}{r - g}$$

Hence

$$r = \frac{D}{P} + g$$

The equity risk premium (ERP) is

$$ERP = r - R = \frac{D}{P} + g - R$$

where R is the real bond yield. Let i be the real internal rate of return and b the earnings retention rate, that is

$$b \equiv \frac{E_R}{E}$$

where E_R is the retained earnings, and E is earnings. Then g can be written as

$$g = bi$$

This is true because dividend growth is equal to earnings growth (i.e., $g = dE/E$), and earnings grow at the real internal rate of return achieved on retained earnings, so $i = dE/E_R$. In equilibrium, we have $i = r$ because firms will keep investing until the two are equalized. We then have

$$P = \frac{D}{r - br} = \frac{D}{r(1-b)} = \frac{E}{r}$$

Therefore,

$$\frac{E}{P} = r$$

To the extent that real dividend growth, the real bond yield, and real gross domestic product (GDP) growth are equal, the equity risk premium can be approximated by the dividend yield as well. Thus

$$ERP = \frac{D}{P}$$

Dividend yields then can be used as a measure of value for broad equity markets. Another measure of value for equities is the price-to-book ratio, which is similar to Tobin's Q, another statistic used by investors to gauge value in stocks.

11.3 Fama–French Factor Models

The ICAPM and APT frameworks developed by Robert Merton and Stephen Ross, respectively, in the 1970s laid the theoretical groundwork for potential factors beyond the market portfolio return. Since then, many researchers have tried to construct better factor models with higher explanatory power for asset returns. Among them, the Fama–French three-factor model (Fama and French 1993) has been one of the most empirically successful and prominent models for stock returns.

Motivated by two empirical observations (also called *puzzles* or *anomalies* at the time because they could not be explained by the CAPM) that stocks for smaller companies and stocks with higher book-to-market ratios tend to perform better than what's implied by their exposures to the market portfolio return, Fama and French (1993) introduced two new factors beyond the market return in CAPM to explain common return variations in 25 US equity portfolios.

The regression model is

$$R_t - R_{f,t} = a + \beta_M(R_{M,t} - R_{f,t}) + \beta_S SMB_t + \beta_H HML_t + \varepsilon_t$$

The dependent variables, $R_t - R_{f,t}$, are the excess returns on the equity portfolios formed based on size and book-to-market quintiles. $R_{M,t} - R_{f,t}$ is the excess return on the broad market portfolio. SMB_t and HML_t are the returns of two new factor-mimicking portfolios described below. β_M, β_S, and β_H are the stock portfolio's sensitivities or loadings to the three factors, which can be estimated using the time-series regression.

SMB stands for "small (market capitalization) minus big" and is often called the *size factor*. It is the difference between the return for a portfolio of small stocks and the return for a portfolio of large stocks, such as the return differential between the bottom 50% and the top 50% of stocks in terms of market capitalization.

HML stands for "high (book-to-market) minus low" and is often called the *value factor*. It is the difference between the return of a portfolio of high book-to-market stocks and the return of a portfolio of low book-to-market stocks such as the excess return of value stocks over growth stocks.

Fama and French (1996) summarized the three-factor model and discussed the competing stories for its successes. They also showed empirical evidence that the model helped explain most of the CAPM average-return anomalies beyond just the size and value effects that motivated it, such as earnings/price, cash flow/price, and sales growth, because many of them are related.

Before introducing the two new factors, the CAPM explained around 60%–80% of the return variations for the 25 stock portfolios. By introducing only two factors, the Fama–French three-factor model was able to explain over 90%

of the return variations for many of these diversified equity portfolios. This was a significant improvement in the model's explanatory powers. With R^2 so high, we can think of the Fama–French three-factor model as an APT model. However, this doesn't mean that the model cannot be interpreted as an ICAPM model.

What aggregate, undiversifiable risk can be proxied by the size and value factors? In other words, what are the state variables in the aggregate economy that can create hedging demand from consumer-investors to justify the positive premiums found for the factors? Fama and French (1996) provided one possible explanation for the value factor. They interpreted the average *HML* return as a premium for relative distress by noting that many value firms had persistently low earnings and were in financial distress and more sensitive to market downturns.

The Fama–French three-factor model not only works for the US stock market, on which the original study focused, but Griffin (2002) also found that the country-specific (or domestic) version of the three-factor model worked well at explaining time-series variation in portfolio and individual stock returns for Canada, the United Kingdom, and Japan, with an average R^2 of 90%.

Fama and French (2015) proposed a five-factor model by introducing two additional factors:

$$R_t - R_{f,t} = a + \beta_M(R_{M,t} - R_{f,t}) + \beta_S SMB_t + \beta_H HML_t + \beta_R RMW_t$$
$$+ \beta_C CMA_t + \varepsilon_t$$

RMW stands for "robust (operating profitability) minus weak" and is often called the *profitability factor*. It is the difference between the return of stocks with high operating profitability minus the return of stocks with low operating profitability.

CMA stands for "conservative (investment) minus aggressive" and is called the *investment factor*. It is the difference between the return of the stocks of companies that invest conservatively because they require little ongoing capital investment to maintain and grow their businesses minus the return of the stocks of companies that invest aggressively to catch up.

The value factor of the three-factor model, *HML*, became redundant for describing average returns in the sample in Fama and French (2015) with the addition of profitability and investment factors.

12
Derivatives Pricing

Summary

If a risky asset price evolves in discrete time according to the following tree:

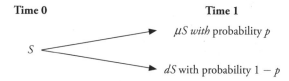

then a derivative of this asset that has payoff C^u in the upstate and C^d in the downstate is valued at

$$C = \frac{qC^u + (1-q)C^d}{1+r}$$

with q defined as

$$q \equiv \frac{1+r-d}{u-d}$$

with r the risk-free rate.

The option value does not depend on the probability p but on q, which can be interpreted as a pseudo probability or a martingale probability measure.

To price a derivative in continuous time, we must solve the Black–Scholes–Merton (BSM) partial differential equation

$$\frac{\partial C}{\partial S}rS + \frac{\partial C}{\partial t} + \frac{1}{2}\frac{\partial^2 C}{\partial S^2}\sigma^2 S^2 = rC$$

subject to relevant boundary conditions. C is the derivative price, S is the price of the underlying asset, σ is the volatility of the underlying asset returns, and t is time.

A derivative value can be computed from a basic arbitrage argument, from convergence between discrete and continuous time, from the CAPM, from Kelly portfolios, from martingale methods, or from a naive risk-neutral argument.

Corporate liabilities can be reinterpreted as derivatives of company assets.

Preliminaries

We show alternative methods to price derivative securities (in this book, we call them *contingent claims* interchangeably). We aim at an intuitive presentation, not overburdened by complex mathematics. To this end, we start with a simple binomial model and then discuss pricing in continuous time and alternative proofs of the celebrated BSM formula. We also show applications of derivative pricing to the capital structure of a firm and to exotic options.

Before we embark on these topics, we provide a quick description of standard derivative securities. A forward contract is an obligation to buy (or sell if you are short the contract) an underlying asset at a future date and at a prespecified price. A European call option is the right (but not the obligation) to buy an underlying asset at a future date and at a prespecified price. A European put option is the right (but not the obligation) to sell an underlying asset at a future date and at a prespecified price.

Example: Suppose that an asset can take five values in one year: 80, 90, 100, 110, and 120. Describe the payoffs of a one-year forward, a one-year European call option, and a one-year European put option. The prespecified price is 100 for all three instruments.

Clearly, a rational investor would only exercise her call, meaning her option to buy, at 100 if the asset price were above 100. That same investor would only exercise her put, meaning her option to sell, at 100 if the asset price were below 100. There is no choice for an investor who enters a forward because she will have to buy at 100 regardless of the asset value. The payoff (profit and loss) of the call, put, and forward is shown in the following table:

Final Asset Price	Call Payoff	Put Payoff	Forward Payoff
80	0	20	−20
90	0	10	−10
100	0	0	0
110	10	0	10
120	20	0	20

Our reader will readily see that the final payoff of a call is $C_T = \max(0, S_T - K)$, that of a put is $P_T = \max(0, K - S_T)$, and that of a forward is $f_T = S_T - K$, where S_T is the asset price at expiration of the contract, and K is the prespecified price (called a *strike price* for options and *delivery price* for forwards).

Call, put, and forward values are linked. For example, the put-call parity at time t says that

$$C + Ke^{-r(T-t)} = P + S$$

where C, P, and S are, respectively, the European call, European put, and underlying (non-dividend-paying) asset prices at time t, and T is the time to expiration of the call and put. The put-call parity says that buying a call and lending the present value of the strike price are equivalent to buying a put and the underlying asset. It is easy to see why this holds:

Instrument	Value at T (when $S_T \leq K$)	Value at T (when $S_T \geq K$)
C	0	$S_T - K$
Lend $Ke^{-r(T-t)}$	K	K
Total	K	S_T
P	$K - S_T$	0
S	S_T	S_T
Total	K	S_T

For a given strike and asset price, once you know one of the call (or put) value, you can infer the put (or call) value from the put-call parity.

You can also find the value of a forward contract by identifying payoffs as in the preceding table. The value of a forward contract at time t is

$$f = S - Ke^{-r(T-t)}$$

as can be easily checked from the following table:

Instrument	Value at T
S	S_T
Borrow $Ke^{-r(T-t)}$	$-K$
Total	$S_T - K$
F	$S_T - K$

By combining put-call parity and forward valuation, one can infer that

$$f = C - P$$

One can also infer that $f = 0$ and $C = P$ when $K = Se^{r(T-t)}$, meaning that call and put values are equal when the strike price is the underlying asset compounded at the risk-free rate. This strike at which the value of the forward contract is zero is called the *forward price*. By borrowing the money to buy a risky asset, you replicate a forward contract on that asset. The maturity of the loan matches that of the forward contract.

12.1 The Binomial Model

12.1.1 Binomial Option Formula from a Replicating Portfolio

Consider an asset priced at S that can take value uS or value dS (where $u > d$) in one period with probabilities p and $1 - p$, respectively. There exists a risk-free asset earning a rate r. Graphically, the risky asset price evolves as in the following tree:

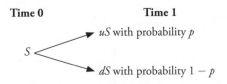

Note that $u > 1 + r > d$. This must hold in the absence of arbitrage. Say that $1 + r > u > d$; then the risk-free asset would dominate the risky asset in both states of the world. The price of the risk-free asset would rise, and the risk-free rate would fall relative to the risky asset until inequality $u > 1 + r > d$ is reestablished. If $u > d > 1 + r$, then the risk-free asset is always dominated. Again, its price would fall, and its yield would rise versus the risky asset until $u > 1 + r > d$.

Now consider a claim contingent on the risky asset. The contingent claim can also be called a *derivative*. The derivative has a payoff that depends formulaically on the risky asset payoff at time 1. Call this payoff C^u in the upstate and C^d in the downstate. Derivative assets or contingent claims will be defined by their terminal payoffs. For example, a European call option is the right, but not the obligation, to purchase the underlying asset at time 1 at a preset price K, also called a *strike price*. At time 1, its payoffs in the upstate and the downstate are, respectively,

$$C^u = \max(uS - K, 0)$$
$$C^d = \max(dS - K, 0)$$

As another example, a forward contract is the obligation to buy the underlying asset at a specified price, called the *delivery price*, on a future date. In this case,

$$C^u = uS - K$$
$$C^d = dS - K$$

In the general case, the derivative price will evolve as in the following tree:

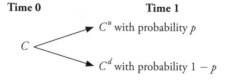

C^u and C^d are known because they are predetermined functions of uS and dS that are themselves known. The only unknown in this exercise is the derivative price C—*the aim of derivative pricing is to determine the price C of the contingent claim at time zero.*

One could conjecture that

$$C = \frac{pC^u + (1-p)C^d}{1+r}$$

because an asset price is a discounted expected payoff. But it would be wrong because uncertain cash flows cannot be discounted at the risk-free rate in general. To pick the proper discount rate, one needs an appropriate asset-pricing theory. We will discuss later how to apply the CAPM to derivative pricing.

It turns out that the task at hand is much simpler. By forming an appropriate portfolio of risky and risk-free assets, one can replicate the derivative payoffs and find C. A portfolio consisting at time zero of Δ units of the risky asset and an amount of dollars B of the risk-free asset will have the following dynamics:

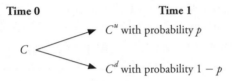

Time 0 **Time 1**

C^u with probability p

C

C^d with probability $1 - p$

To find the derivative price C, set Δ and B *such that the portfolio replicates exactly the payoff of the claim.* This is the central intuition of derivative pricing. It boils down to two equations with two unknowns:

$$uS\,\Delta^* + B^*(1 + r) = C^u$$
$$dS\,\Delta^* + B^*(1 + r) = C^d$$

Solving, we get

$$\Delta^* = \frac{C^u - C^d}{(u - d)S}$$

and

$$B^* = \left[C^u - \frac{u(C^u - C^d)}{u - d}\right]\frac{1}{1 + r}$$

The value of the derivative is hence

$$C = S\Delta^* + B^* = \frac{C^u - C^d}{u - d} + \left[C^u - \frac{u(C^u - C^d)}{u - d}\right]\frac{1}{1 + r}$$

Simplifying, we get

$$C = \frac{qC^u + (1 - q)C^d}{1 + r}$$

with q defined as

$$q \equiv \frac{1+r-d}{u-d}$$

Note that because $u > 1 + r > d$ as stated above, q is between zero and one. Like p, it walks and talks like a probability. Unlike p, however, it is not the true probability of the upstate. q is called a *pseudo probability*.

It is also called a *risk-neutral probability measure*. Why? Note that $C = \dfrac{qC^u + (1-q)C^d}{1+r}$ is close to our initial (wrong) conjecture $C = \dfrac{pC^u + (1-p)C^d}{1+r}$.

By replacing p by q, it is suddenly appropriate to discount the "expected" payoff at the risk-free rate: payoffs are thus treated as risk free. And derivatives are priced *as if* economic agents were risk neutral.

To confirm this intuition, apply our formula to the risky asset price S. After all, a risky asset is tautologically a derivative of that same asset. Calculate the expression

$$\frac{quS + (1-q)dS}{1+r}$$

with $q = \dfrac{1+r-d}{u-d}$, and we find indeed that

$$\frac{quS + (1-q)dS}{1+r} = S$$

So the risky asset value is the expected value of its payoffs under the risk-neutral probability measure q.

Example: As stated earlier, a European call option on an asset pays the difference, if positive, between the asset price at expiration and the strike price. The asset price is 10 and will be 15 in the upstate with probability $p = 0.6$ and 7 in the downstate with probability $1 - p = 0.4$. The strike price is 8, and the risk-free rate is 10%.

To value the European call option, note that $C^u = \max(0, 15 - 8) = 7$ and $C^d = \max(0, 7 - 8) = 0$. With $u = 1.5$ and $d = 0.7$, we can calculate the risk-neutral probability

$$q = \frac{1.1 - 0.7}{1.5 - 0.7} = 0.5$$

and

$$C = \frac{(0.5 \times 7) + (0.5 \times 0)}{1.1} \approx 3.18$$

To calculate the option value, notice that we did not use the real-world probabilities p and $1 - p$. We only used the risk-neutral probability $q = 0.5$.

We will show further down the line in this chapter how to use real-world probabilities to price options by deriving the binomial model from the CAPM. Of course, the binomial formula applies to all types of contingent claims. We now give an example of put pricing.

Example: A European put option is the right, but not the obligation, to sell at expiration an underlying asset at a strike price K. Its terminal payoff is therefore $(0, K - S_T)$, where S_T is the price of the underlying asset at option expiration T. We use the same data as in the preceding example. The asset price is 10 and will be 15 in the upstate with probability $p = 0.6$ and 7 in the downstate with probability $1 - p = 0.4$. The strike price is 8, and the risk-free rate is 10%. To value the European put option, note that $P^u = \max(0, 8 - 15) = 0$ and $P^d = \max(0, 8 - 7) = 1$.

With $u = 1.5$ and $d = 0.7$, the risk-neutral probability is, as before,

$$q = \frac{1.1 - 0.7}{1.5 - 0.7} = 0.5$$

And the put option value is

$$P = \frac{(0.5 \times 0) + (0.5 \times 1)}{1.1} \approx 0.45$$

In the next example, we use the binomial formula to price a forward contract.

Example: As stated earlier, the payoffs of a forward contract are $C^u = uS - K$ and $C^d = dS - K$. Replacing these values of C^u and C^d in the binomial formula gives

$$C = \frac{q(uS - K) + (1 - q)(dS - K)}{1 + r}$$

And a bit of algebra shows that

$$C = S - \frac{K}{1 + r}$$

The value of a forward contract is the asset price minus the present value of the delivery price.

12.1.2 Martingale Pricing

Define X as the price of a risk-free claim paying $(1 + r)$ at time 1. Then $X(0) = 1$ and $X(1) = 1 + r$. Further defining $M \equiv \dfrac{S}{X}$, then it can be seen that

$$M(0) = S$$
$$E_0^q[M(1)] = \frac{quS + (1-q)dS}{1+r}$$

and by replacing q with its value $\dfrac{1+r-d}{u-d}$, it follows that

$$M(0) = E_0^q[M(1)]$$

This defines a martingale. The value of M today is today's expectation of its value in one period.

Similarly, defining $M' \equiv \dfrac{C}{X}$, then it follows that

$$M'(0) = C$$
$$E_0^q[M'(1)] = \frac{qC^u + (1-q)C^d}{1+r}$$

Again, replacing q by its value $\dfrac{1+r-d}{u-d}$, it follows that

$$M'(0) = E_0^q[M'(1)]$$

The price of any contingent asset (including the underlying asset itself) discounted at the risk-free rate is a martingale under the q probability measure. This is why q is also called the *martingale probability measure*. Reexpressing $M'(0)$ as C, the equation says something we already know—that an asset price is the expected payoff of that asset under the q measure, discounted at the risk-free rate:

$$C = \frac{E_0^q[C(1)]}{1+r}$$

Yet another way to say this is that the expected return of contingent claims is the risk-free rate:

$$E_0^q\left(\frac{\Delta C}{C}\right) = r$$

12.2 The Black–Scholes–Merton (BSM) Equation

We switch to a continuous-time framework to prove the celebrated BSM equation and related formulas. The BSM partial differential equation is the master equation used to solve for the value of contingent claims. The precise nature of the claim is expressed by boundary conditions, which, together with the partial differential equation (PDE), yield the solution. The BSM equation for a non-dividend-paying asset is

$$\frac{\partial C}{\partial S} rS + \frac{\partial C}{\partial t} + \frac{1}{2}\frac{\partial^2 C}{\partial S^2}\sigma^2 S^2 = rC$$

where C is the price of the contingent claim, S the price of the underlying asset, t is time, r is the risk-free rate, and σ is the standard deviation (or volatility) of the underlying asset return.

We now try our hand at several versions of the proof of the BSM equation.

12.2.1 Proof 1: Merton No-Arbitrage Portfolio

Posit a risky-asset price that follows the standard geometric Brownian motion dynamics

$$\frac{dS}{S} = \mu dt + \sigma dB$$

The risk-free asset price P obeys $dP/P = rdt$, with r being the risk-free rate.

By Itô's lemma, the option price C satisfies the equation

$$dC(S,t) = \frac{\partial C}{\partial S} dS + \frac{\partial C}{\partial t} dt + \frac{1}{2}\frac{\partial^2 C}{\partial S^2}(dS)^2$$

which boils down to

$$dC(S,t) = \left(\frac{\partial C}{\partial S}\mu S + \frac{\partial C}{\partial t} + \frac{1}{2}\frac{\partial^2 C}{\partial S^2}\sigma^2 S^2\right)dt + \frac{\partial C}{\partial S}\sigma SdB$$

The instantaneous expected return of the option μ_C is hence

$$\mu_C = E\left(\frac{\frac{dC}{C}}{dt}\right) = \frac{\frac{\partial C}{\partial S}\mu S + \frac{\partial C}{\partial t} + \frac{1}{2}\frac{\partial^2 C}{\partial S^2}\sigma^2 S^2}{C}$$

While the volatility of the option return σ_C is

$$\sigma_C = \frac{\frac{\partial C}{\partial S}\sigma S}{C}$$

We form a zero-investment portfolio made of N_1 dollars invested in the risky asset, N_2 dollars invested in the derivative security, and N_3 dollars in the risk-free asset. That is,

$$N_1 + N_2 + N_3 = 0$$

The instantaneous dollar return of this portfolio π is

$$d\pi = N_1\frac{dS}{S} + N_2\frac{dC}{C} + N_3\frac{dP}{P}$$

Remembering that $N_3 = -N_1 - N_2$, this, in turn, is equal to

$$d\pi = [N_1(\mu - r) + N_2(\mu_C - r)]dt + (N_1\sigma + N_2\sigma_C)dB$$

Setting $N_1 = -N_2\,\sigma_C/\sigma$, the dB term drops out, and the portfolio, because it is a hedged zero-investment portfolio, has zero return. In other words, $d\pi = 0$. Under these conditions, we get the following relationship:

$$\frac{\mu - r}{\sigma} = \frac{\mu_C - r}{\sigma_C}$$

The Sharpe ratio of the contingent claim is equal to the Sharpe ratio of the underlying asset. Replacing μ_C and σ_C by their expressions in this equation, we obtain the BSM partial differential equation

$$\frac{\partial C}{\partial S}rS + \frac{\partial C}{\partial t} + \frac{1}{2}\frac{\partial^2 C}{\partial S^2}\sigma^2 S^2 = rC$$

12.2.2 Proof 2: Binomial Model Convergence

This proof describes the convergence of the binomial model toward its continuous-time equivalent, namely the BSM pricing equation. The spirit of the proof is to shrink the time interval to an infinitesimal period dt and map the binomial model parameters into continuous-time parameters. We use, in turn, Taylor expansions to order dt to approximate the continuous-time parameters.

Consider the following mappings:

$$u = e^{\sigma\sqrt{dt}} \approx 1 + \sigma\sqrt{dt} + \frac{\sigma^2 dt}{2}$$

$$d = e^{-\sigma\sqrt{dt}} \approx 1 - \sigma\sqrt{dt} + \frac{\sigma^2 dt}{2}$$

whereas the gross risk-free rate is now $e^{rdt} \approx 1 + rdt$.

Under these conditions, the binomial formula becomes

$$C(1 + rdt) = qC^u + (1 - q)C^d$$

with the risk-neutral measure approximated by

$$q = \frac{e^{rdt} - d}{u - d} \approx \frac{1}{2} + \left(\frac{r}{2\sigma} - \frac{\sigma}{4}\right)\sqrt{dt}$$

A Taylor expansion of C^u and C^d yields

$$C^u \approx C + \frac{\partial C}{\partial S}(uS - S) + \frac{\partial C}{\partial t}dt + \frac{1}{2}\frac{\partial^2 C}{\partial S^2}(u - 1)^2 S^2$$

$$\approx C + \frac{\partial C}{\partial S}\left(\sigma\sqrt{dt} + \frac{\sigma^2 dt}{2}\right)S + \frac{\partial C}{\partial t}dt + \frac{1}{2}\frac{\partial^2 C}{\partial S^2}\sigma^2 S^2 dt$$

$$C^d \approx C + \frac{\partial C}{\partial S}(dS - S) + \frac{\partial C}{\partial t}dt + \frac{1}{2}\frac{\partial^2 C}{\partial S^2}(d - 1)^2 S^2$$

$$\approx C + \frac{\partial C}{\partial S}\left(-\sigma\sqrt{dt} + \frac{\sigma^2 dt}{2}\right)S + \frac{\partial C}{\partial t}dt + \frac{1}{2}\frac{\partial^2 C}{\partial S^2}\sigma^2 S^2 dt$$

The last step is to replace q, C^u, and C^d by their values in the binomial formula. Eliminating all $(dt)^n$ terms with $n > 1$, a bit of algebra leaves us with the BSM equation:

$$\frac{\partial C}{\partial S} rS + \frac{\partial C}{\partial t} + \frac{1}{2}\frac{\partial^2 C}{\partial S^2}\sigma^2 S^2 = rC$$

12.2.3 Proof 3: Derivatives Pricing with the CAPM

A Digression on the CAPM

As discussed earlier, the CAPM states that the expectation of an asset return is

$$E(R_S) = r + \beta_S[E(R_M) - r]$$

with $\beta_S \equiv \dfrac{\text{cov}(R_S, R_M)}{\text{var}(R_M)}$.

Similarly, the expectation of the contingent claim return is

$$E(R_C) = r + \beta_C[E(R_M) - r]$$

with $\beta_C \equiv \dfrac{\text{cov}(R_C, R_M)}{\text{var}(R_M)}$.

We can then express $E(R_C)$ as a function of $E(R_S)$ by combining these two equations:

$$\frac{E(R_C) - r}{E(R_S) - r} = \frac{\text{cov}(R_C, R_M)}{\text{cov}(R_S, R_M)}$$

Multiplying the numerator and denominator by R_S/R_M yields

$$\frac{E(R_C) - r}{E(R_S) - r} = \frac{\text{cov}(R_C, R_S)}{\text{var}(R_S)}$$

Hence the CAPM version of option pricing relative to the underlying asset is

$$E(R_C) = r + \beta_{CS}[E(R_S) - r]$$

with $\beta_{CS} \equiv \dfrac{\text{cov}(R_C, R_S)}{\text{var}(R_S)} = \dfrac{\beta_C}{\beta_S}$.

The Beta of an Option

Let us now calculate the beta of an option β_{CS} under standard BSM assumptions. By definition of a covariance and a variance (and simplifying all the dt terms),

$$\beta_{CS} \equiv \frac{\mathrm{cov}(R_C, R_S)}{\mathrm{var}(R_S)} == \frac{E\left[\left(\frac{dC}{C}\right)\left(\frac{dS}{S}\right)\right] - E\left(\frac{dC}{C}\right)E\left(\frac{dS}{S}\right)}{E\left[\left(\frac{dS}{S}\right)^2\right] - \left[E\left(\frac{dS}{S}\right)\right]^2}$$

Remembering that

$$\frac{dC}{C} = \frac{\left(\frac{\partial C}{\partial S}\mu S + \frac{\partial C}{\partial t} + \frac{1}{2}\frac{\partial^2 C}{\partial S^2}\sigma^2 S^2\right)dt + \frac{\partial C}{\partial S}\sigma S dB}{C}$$

and

$$\frac{dS}{S} = \mu dt + \sigma dB$$

It follows, by the simple rules of Itô multiplication, that the beta of an option relative to the underlying asset is

$$\beta_{CS} = \frac{\dfrac{\dfrac{\partial C}{\partial S}\sigma^2 S}{C}dt}{\sigma^2 dt} = \frac{\partial C}{\partial S}\frac{S}{C}$$

and

$$\beta_C = \frac{\partial C}{\partial S}\frac{S}{C}\beta_S$$

Here β_{CS} is called the *elasticity* (or the *omega*) of the option. It represents the relative change in the option value divided by the relative change in the underlying asset value. We will have more to say about this elasticity when we discuss the expected return of options in Chapter 14.

Derivation

We are now ready to derive the BSM equation from the CAPM. Recall that

$$E\left(\frac{\frac{dC}{C}}{dt}\right) = r + \beta_{CS}\left[E\left(\frac{\frac{dS}{S}}{dt}\right) - r\right]$$

Replacing the beta and the expectation terms by their values, we obtain

$$\frac{\frac{\partial C}{\partial S}\mu S + \frac{\partial C}{\partial t} + \frac{1}{2}\frac{\partial^2 C}{\partial S^2}\sigma^2 S^2}{C} = r + \frac{\partial C}{\partial S}\frac{S}{C}(\mu - r)$$

which simplifies to the standard BSM pricing equation

$$\frac{\partial C}{\partial S}rS + \frac{\partial C}{\partial t} + \frac{1}{2}\frac{\partial^2 C}{\partial S^2}\sigma^2 S^2 = rC$$

For the reader's reference, Black and Scholes derived their option pricing formula from the CAPM. Merton was responsible for the no-arbitrage proof discussed earlier. The CAPM implies no arbitrage (otherwise, we would not be in equilibrium). But no arbitrage does not imply the CAPM. The Merton proof is more powerful and its scope broader because its assumptions are weaker.

12.2.4 Proof 4: BSM with Risk Neutrality

This proof favors brevity over rigor but retains the spirit of the risk-neutral argument. We know that

$$E\left(\frac{\frac{dC}{C}}{dt}\right) = \frac{\frac{\partial C}{\partial S}\mu S + \frac{\partial C}{\partial t} + \frac{1}{2}\frac{\partial^2 C}{\partial S^2}\sigma^2 S^2}{C} \text{ and } E\left(\frac{\frac{dS}{S}}{dt}\right) = \mu$$

Recall from the binomial model that for option pricing purposes, investors live in a world that walks and talks as if it were a risk-neutral world.

In such a world (the * sign refers to the risk-neutral world)

$$E^*\left(\frac{\frac{dC}{C}}{dt}\right) = E^*\left(\frac{\frac{dS}{S}}{dt}\right) = r$$

which means that we should replace μ by r to get

$$\frac{\frac{\partial C}{\partial S}rS + \frac{\partial C}{\partial t} + \frac{1}{2}\frac{\partial^2 C}{\partial S^2}\sigma^2 S^2}{C} = r$$

Hence the BSM equation

$$\frac{\partial C}{\partial S} rS + \frac{\partial C}{\partial t} + \frac{1}{2}\frac{\partial^2 C}{\partial S^2}\sigma^2 S^2 = rC$$

12.2.5 Proof 5: BSM with Kelly Portfolios

A Property of Kelly Portfolios

Recall that a portfolio with a proportion α invested in a risky asset (with motion $dS/S = \mu dt + \sigma dB$) and $(1 - \alpha)$ invested in a risk-free asset earning rdt will obey the following equation:

$$\frac{d\pi}{\pi} = [r + \alpha(\mu - r)]dt + \alpha\sigma dB$$

How to find an allocation that maximizes the expected growth rate of the portfolio? This, as the reader may recall, defines a Kelly portfolio. By Itô's lemma, $\ln \pi = \left[r + \alpha(\mu - r) - \frac{\alpha^2\sigma^2}{2}\right]dt + \alpha\sigma dB$. We want to find an α that maximizes the geometric growth rate of the portfolio. This means maximizing $\left[r + \alpha(\mu - r) - \frac{\alpha^2\sigma^2}{2}\right]$, which gives $\alpha^* = \frac{\mu - r}{\sigma^2}$. Plugging α^* back in the initial differential equation driving the portfolio, we obtain

$$\frac{d\pi}{\pi} = \left[r + \left(\frac{\mu - r}{\sigma}\right)^2\right]dt + \left(\frac{\mu - r}{\sigma}\right)dB$$

Now calculate the covariance of $\frac{d\pi}{\pi}$ and $\frac{dS}{S}$:

$$\mathrm{cov}\left(\frac{d\pi}{\pi}, \frac{dS}{S}\right) = E\left(\frac{d\pi}{\pi}\frac{dS}{S}\right) - E\left(\frac{d\pi}{\pi}\right)E\left(\frac{dS}{S}\right) = E\left(\frac{d\pi}{\pi}\frac{dS}{S}\right)$$

$$= \left(\frac{\mu - r}{\sigma}\right)dB \times \sigma dB$$

and hence

$$(\mu - r)dt = \mathrm{cov}\left(\frac{d\pi}{\pi}, \frac{dS}{S}\right)$$

The excess expected return of the risky asset is equal to the covariance of the instantaneous Kelly portfolio return and the risky-asset instantaneous return. Thus, to calculate the expected excess return on an asset, all one needs is its covariance with the Kelly portfolio including this asset.

In the case of a Kelly portfolio with n risky assets, it is easily checked that

$$(\mu_i - r)dt = \text{cov}\left(\frac{d\pi}{\pi}, \frac{dS_i}{S_i}\right), \forall i = 1, \ldots, n$$

Deriving the BSM from the Kelly Property

We now use the preceding property to derive the BSM equation. Take the risky asset to be the derivative asset itself (no harm in that a derivative is a redundant asset and can be replicated by a combination of its underlying asset and cash). Then

$$(\mu_C - r)dt = \text{cov}\left(\frac{d\pi}{\pi}, \frac{dC}{C}\right)$$

Recall that

$$\frac{dC}{C} = \frac{\left(\frac{\partial C}{\partial S}\mu S + \frac{\partial C}{\partial t} + \frac{1}{2}\frac{\partial^2 C}{\partial S^2}\sigma^2 S^2\right)dt + \frac{\partial C}{\partial S}\sigma S dB}{C}$$

Therefore,

$$\mu_C = \frac{\frac{\partial C}{\partial S}\mu S + \frac{\partial C}{\partial t} + \frac{1}{2}\frac{\partial^2 C}{\partial S^2}\sigma^2 S^2}{C}$$

and

$$\text{cov}\left(\frac{d\pi}{\pi}, \frac{dC}{C}\right) = E\left(\frac{d\pi}{\pi}\frac{dC}{C}\right) = \left[\left(\frac{\mu-r}{\sigma}\right)dB\right]\left[\left(\frac{\partial C}{\partial S}\right)\left(\frac{\sigma S}{C}\right)dB\right] = \frac{\partial C}{\partial S}\frac{S}{C}(\mu-r)dt$$

Equating $(\mu_C - r)dt$ with $\text{cov}[(d\pi/\pi), (dC/C)]$, we obtain

$$\frac{\frac{\partial C}{\partial S}\mu S+\frac{\partial C}{\partial t}+\frac{1}{2}\frac{\partial^2 C}{\partial S^2}\sigma^2 S^2}{C}-r=\frac{\partial C}{\partial S}\frac{S}{C}(\mu-r)$$

The BSM pricing equation follows:

$$\frac{\partial C}{\partial S}rS+\frac{\partial C}{\partial t}+\frac{1}{2}\frac{\partial^2 C}{\partial S^2}\sigma^2 S^2=rC$$

12.2.6 Proof 6: BSM with Martingales

From the Merton proof earlier, the self-financed portfolio led to the following arbitrage condition:

$$\frac{\mu-r}{\sigma}=\frac{\mu_C-r}{\sigma_C}=v$$

where v is the Sharpe ratio of both the underlying asset and the derivative. It is also called the *market price of risk*. As seen with the Girsanov theorem, we define a new Wiener process $\tilde{B}_t$ such that $d\tilde{B}_t=dB_t+vdt$.

It follows that the instantaneous expected return of the call is now the risk-free rate under the probability measure Q (as defined by the Girsanov theorem for a choice of a market price of risk v):

$$\frac{dC}{C}=\mu_C dt+\sigma_C dB=(r+\sigma_C v)dt+\sigma_C(d\tilde{B}_t-vdt)=rdt+\sigma_C d\tilde{B}_t$$

(Also note that $dS/S=\mu dt+\sigma dB=(r+\sigma v)dt+\sigma(d\tilde{B}_t-vdt)=rdt+\sigma d\tilde{B}_t$.)

Define $b_t\equiv e^{rt}$ as a money-market instrument earning the risk-free rate r. Define further $C^*\equiv C/b$. Then, by Itô's lemma,

$$\frac{dC^*}{C^*}=\sigma_C d\tilde{B}_t$$

which implies that C^* is a martingale under Q. Thus

$$C_t^*=E_t^Q(C_T^*)$$

By the definition of C^*, we have

$$\frac{C_t}{e^{rt}} = E_t^Q \left(\frac{C_T}{e^{rT}} \right)$$

Hence the fundamental derivative-pricing equation is

$$C_t = e^{-r(T-t)} E_t^Q (C_T)$$

This equation states that the value of a derivative is the expected value of its discounted payoff under the Q probability measure, with the discount rate being the risk-free rate. It is the continuous-time equivalent of the binomial pricing equation $= E_0^q [C(1)] / (1+r)$.

12.3 Derivatives Prices

12.3.1 Partial Differential Equations and Martingale Pricing

As discussed earlier, we can price a derivative by solving a partial differential equation (PDE)

$$\frac{\partial C}{\partial S} rS + \frac{\partial C}{\partial t} + \frac{1}{2} \frac{\partial^2 C}{\partial S^2} \sigma^2 S^2 = rC$$

subject to the relevant boundary conditions.

Or we can price a derivative by calculating a discounted expectation of its payoffs under a martingale probability measure:

$$C_t = e^{-r(T-t)} E_t^Q (C_T)$$

This is the so-called probabilistic approach. The two methods are equivalent. *But it turns out that the probabilistic approach is computationally more convenient.*

12.3.2 The Underlying Asset and the Forward Contract as Derivatives

Recalling that the risky asset is a derivative of itself and that a forward contract on a risky asset is obviously a derivative of this asset, we can use these two examples as sanity checks to convince ourselves that both the PDE approach and the probabilistic approach to pricing appear to work.

Start with the PDE. We first check whether the risky asset itself satisfies the PDE. In this case,

$$C = S, \frac{\partial C}{\partial S} = 1, \frac{\partial C}{\partial t} = 0, \text{ and } \frac{\partial^2 C}{\partial S^2} = 0$$

so we get indeed $rC = rC$.

We now check whether the value of the forward contract verifies the PDE. As established at the beginning of this chapter,

$$f = S - Ke^{-r(T-t)}$$

When $C = f$, then

$$\frac{\partial C}{\partial S} = 1, \frac{\partial C}{\partial t} = -rKe^{-r(T-t)}, \text{ and } \frac{\partial^2 C}{\partial S^2} = 0$$

Replacing these values in the PDE, we obtain

$$rS - rKe^{-r(T-t)} = r[S - Ke^{-r(T-t)}]$$

The forward value satisfies the PDE as hoped.

How about the probabilistic approach? Now we solve for the values of the derivatives (instead of just verifying that they satisfy the pricing equation).

First note that under the Q probability measure, the risky-asset price follows the following stochastic differential equation:

$$\frac{dS}{S} = rdt + \sigma d\tilde{B}$$

Therefore,

$$E_t^Q(S_T) = Se^{r(T-t)}$$

When the derivative is the risky asset itself, we find that

$$C = S = e^{-r(T-t)}E_t^Q(S_T) = e^{-r(T-t)}Se^{r(T-t)} = S$$

To our relief, the stock, viewed as a derivative, is indeed equal to itself. When the derivative is the forward contact, then $C_T = S - K$, and

$$C = e^{-r(T-t)}E_t^Q(S_T - K) = e^{-r(T-t)}(Se^{r(T-t)} - K) = S - Ke^{-r(T-t)}$$

as expected. Away from trivial examples, we now address the pièce de résistance: European call and put options.

12.3.3 Pricing European Calls and Puts: The BSM Formula

We value a European call option on a risky asset priced at S with strike price K and expiration T using the probabilistic method. As established earlier, a call, like any derivative, is the discounted payoff under the martingale probability measure

$$C = e^{-r(T-t)} E_t^Q (S_T - K)^+$$

The terminal payoff is $(S_T - K)^+$, which is shorthand for $\max(S_T - K, 0)$.

The expression can be split into the sum of two discounted expectations:

$$C = e^{-r(T-t)} E_t^Q (S_T 1_{S_T > K}) - e^{-r(T-t)} E_t^Q (K 1_{S_T > K})$$

where $1_{S_T > K}$ is an indicator function that takes the value 1 if $S_T > K$ and 0 otherwise. This equation is saying that

- The call buyer is entitled to receive the underlying asset if $S_T > K$ (if the call option is in the money). The call buyer is long (owns) this option, also called an *asset-or-nothing option* worth $S_T 1_{S_T > K}$ at expiration.
- In this same event where $S_T > K$, the call buyer pays K. The call buyer is short (owes) a digital option worth $K 1_{S_T > K}$ at expiration: A digital option pays a fixed amount K if the terminal value of the underlying asset is greater than K.

Let us first price the digital option:

$$e^{-r(T-t)} E_t^Q (K 1_{S_T > K}) = K e^{-r(T-t)} E_t^Q (1_{S_T > K}) = K e^{-r(T-t)} Q(S_T > K)$$

where the second equality is saying that the expectation of the indicator function under Q is simply the risk-neutral probability Q that the underlying terminal value is higher than K. The price of the underlying asset obeys the following dynamics under Q:

$$\frac{dS}{S} = r\,dt + \sigma\,d\tilde{B}$$

Recall from Chapter 6 that this stochastic differential equation can be integrated to get

$$S_T = Se^{\left(r - \frac{\sigma^2}{2}\right)(T-t) + \sigma \varepsilon \sqrt{T-t}}$$

where ε is a standard normal variable. We can now calculate the Q-probability of $S_T > K$:

$$Q(S_T > K) = \Pr\left[Se^{\left(r-\frac{\sigma^2}{2}\right)(T-t)+\sigma\varepsilon\sqrt{T-t}} > K \right]$$

$$= \Pr\left[\ln S + \left(r-\frac{\sigma^2}{2}\right)(T-t) + \sigma\varepsilon\sqrt{T-t} > \ln K \right]$$

From the symmetry of the normal distribution, it follows that

$$Q(S_T > K) = \Phi\left[\frac{\ln\left(\dfrac{S}{K}\right)+\left(r-\dfrac{\sigma^2}{2}\right)(T-t)}{\sigma\sqrt{T-t}} \right]$$

with Φ being the cumulative normal probability operator.
  Define

$$d \equiv \frac{\ln\left(\dfrac{S}{K}\right)+\left(r-\dfrac{\sigma^2}{2}\right)(T-t)}{\sigma\sqrt{T-t}}$$

Then the value of the digital option is

$$Ke^{-r(T-t)}Q(S_T > K) = Ke^{-r(T-t)}\Phi(d)$$

The digital option value is therefore the present value of the payoff $Ke^{-r(T-t)}$ times the risk-neutral probability of option exercise (meaning of $S_T > K$) $\Phi(d)$.
  To price the all-or-nothing option, note that

$$e^{-r(T-t)}E^Q_t(S_T 1_{S_T>K}) = e^{-r(T-t)}\int_{S_T>K} Se^{\left(r-\frac{\sigma^2}{2}\right)(T-t)+\sigma\varepsilon\sqrt{T-t}}\frac{e^{-\varepsilon^2/2}}{\sqrt{2\pi}}\,d\varepsilon$$

Referring to the digital option case, it is easy to check that the domain of the integral $(S_T > K)$ under Q is $(-d, \infty)$. We can simplify the integral to get

$$e^{-r(T-t)}E^Q_t(S_T 1_{S_T>K}) = \frac{S}{\sqrt{2\pi}}\int_{-d}^{\infty} e^{-\frac{\varepsilon^2}{2}+\sigma\varepsilon\sqrt{T-t}-\frac{\sigma^2}{2}(T-t)}\,d\varepsilon$$

With a change of variable $u \equiv \varepsilon - \sigma\sqrt{T-t}$, we get the value of the all-or-nothing option:

$$e^{-r(T-t)}E^Q_t(S_T 1_{S_T>K}) = \frac{S}{\sqrt{2\pi}}\int_{-(d+\sigma\sqrt{T-t})}^{\infty} e^{-\frac{u^2}{2}}\,du = S\Phi(d+\sigma\sqrt{T-t})$$

Because the European call is the asset-or-nothing option minus the digital option, we can infer its value directly. The European call value is given by

$$C = S\Phi(d + \sigma\sqrt{T-t}) - Ke^{-r(T-t)}\Phi(d)$$

with

$$d \equiv \frac{\ln\left(\dfrac{S}{K}\right) + \left(r - \dfrac{\sigma^2}{2}\right)(T-t)}{\sigma\sqrt{T-t}}.$$

This is the celebrated BSM option formula.

To obtain the value of a European put option, recall that from put-call parity,

$$P = C + Ke^{-r(T-t)} - S$$

Hence the BSM formula for a European put:

$$P = Ke^{-r(T-t)}\Phi(-d) - S\Phi(-d - \sigma\sqrt{T-t})$$

For both the call and the put, five inputs are needed: the underlying current price S, the strike price K, the risk-free rate r, the time to expiration $(T-t)$, and the volatility of the underlying asset returns σ.

12.3.4 Option Sensitivity to Inputs

A bit of algebra gives the sensitivity of Europeans puts and calls to various inputs. These sensitivities are described in the following table:

Call and Put Sensitivity to Inputs

Sensitivity	Call	Put
Delta (sensitivity to asset price)	$\dfrac{\partial C}{\partial S} = \Phi(d + \sigma\sqrt{T-t}) > 0$	$\dfrac{\partial P}{\partial S} = -\Phi(-d - \sigma\sqrt{T-t}) < 0$
Sensitivity to strike price	$\dfrac{\partial C}{\partial K} = -e^{-r(T-t)}\Phi(d) < 0$	$\dfrac{\partial P}{\partial K} = e^{-r(T-t)}\Phi(-d) > 0$
Rho (sensitivity to the risk-free rate)	$\dfrac{\partial C}{\partial r} = (T-t)Ke^{-r(T-t)}\Phi(d) > 0$	$\dfrac{\partial P}{\partial r} = -(T-t)Ke^{-r(T-t)}\Phi(-d) < 0$

Sensitivity	Call	Put
Theta (sensitivity to time to expiration)	$$\frac{\partial C}{\partial (T-t)}$$ $$=\frac{\sigma S}{2\sqrt{T-t}}\Phi'(d+\sigma\sqrt{T-t})$$ $$-rKe^{-r(T-t)}\Phi(d)>0$$	$$\frac{\partial P}{\partial (T-t)}$$ $$=\frac{-\sigma S}{2\sqrt{T-t}}\Phi'(d+\sigma\sqrt{T-t})$$ $$+rKe^{-r(T-t)}\Phi(-d)$$ (sign is ambiguous)
Vega (sensitivity to volatility)	$\dfrac{\partial C}{\partial \sigma}=S\sqrt{T-t}\Phi'(d+\sigma\sqrt{T-t})>0$	$\dfrac{\partial P}{\partial \sigma}=S\sqrt{T-t}\Phi'(d+\sigma\sqrt{(T-t)})>0$

Note that $\Phi'(x)$ is the standard normal density function at x. That is,

$$\Phi'(x)=\frac{e^{\frac{-x^2}{2}}}{\sqrt{2\pi}}.$$

12.3.5 Numerical Approximations

At-the-Money-Forward (ATMF) European Options

A particularly useful rule of thumb for ATMF options is due to Brenner and Subrahmanyam (1994). An ATMF option is defined by a strike price equal to the forward price, that is, $K = Se^{r(T-t)}$. Also remember that an ATMF call is equal to an ATMF put by put-call parity.

Replacing the strike by the forward in the BSM formula, we get

$$d \equiv \frac{\ln\left(\frac{S}{K}\right)+\left(r-\frac{\sigma^2}{2}\right)(T-t)}{\sigma\sqrt{T-t}}=\frac{-\sigma\sqrt{T-t}}{2}$$

Under these conditions, the Black–Scholes call price becomes

$$C=S\Phi(d+\sigma\sqrt{T-t})-Ke^{-r(T-t)}\Phi(d)=S\left[\Phi\left(\frac{\sigma\sqrt{T-t}}{2}\right)-\Phi\left(\frac{-\sigma\sqrt{T-t}}{2}\right)\right]$$

And the ratio of an ATMF option value to its underlying asset value is

$$\frac{C}{S}=\frac{P}{S}=\int_{\frac{-\sigma\sqrt{T-t}}{2}}^{\frac{\sigma\sqrt{T-t}}{2}}\frac{e^{\left(\frac{-\mu^2}{2}\right)}}{\sqrt{2\pi}}\,d\mu$$

A Taylor expansion of $e^{-\mu^2/2}$ shows that

$$e^{\frac{-\mu^2}{2}} = 1 - \frac{\mu^2}{2} + \frac{\mu^4}{4} + \cdots$$

Limiting ourselves to the first term of the expansion, we obtain

$$\frac{C}{S} = \frac{P}{S} \approx \int_{\frac{-\sigma\sqrt{T-t}}{2}}^{\frac{\sigma\sqrt{T-t}}{2}} \frac{d\mu}{\sqrt{2\pi}} = \frac{\sigma\sqrt{T-t}}{\sqrt{2\pi}} \approx 0.4\sigma\sqrt{T-t}$$

Example: We want to price a one-year call option on a non-dividend-paying stock. The price of the stock is 100. The strike of the call is 100. The risk-free rate is zero. The volatility is 40%.

We first use the BSM formula. As discussed earlier, $S = 100$, $K = 100$, $r = 0$, $T - t = 1$, and $\sigma = 0.4$. With these inputs, $C = 15.85$. Note that the strike is equal to the forward. We can therefore use the approximation $C = S \times 0.4$ $\sigma\sqrt{T-t} = 16$. The approximation error is about 1%. Note that long times to expiration do not agree as well with the approximation. For example, with all other inputs still the same, a time to expiration of 10 years gives a BSM call value of 47.29, whereas the approximation gives a call value of 50.6. This is a 7% approximation error.

Constant-Elasticity Derivatives
Recall from the BSM proof by the CAPM that the beta of a derivative is

$$\beta_C = \frac{\partial C}{\partial S}\frac{S}{C}\beta_S$$

The ratio of the beta of a derivative to that of the underlying is the so-called omega, or elasticity of the derivative to the underlying asset $\frac{\partial C}{\partial S}\frac{S}{C}$.

Consider a set of constant-elasticity securities that can, in combination, replicate any derivative instrument. Kreuser and Seigel (1995) call them *atomic securities* because they constitute an atomic structure of derivative securities. The constant-elasticity condition can be stated as

$$\frac{\partial C_n}{\partial S}\frac{S}{C_n} = n$$

where n is an arbitrary constant. These atomic securities are derivatives that depend on the underlying value S and time. The solution to the equation is

$$C_n(S, t) = k(t)S^n$$

where $k(t)$ is a function of time only.

Plugging this equation into the BSM PDE $\dfrac{\partial C}{\partial S} rS + \dfrac{\partial C}{\partial t} + \dfrac{1}{2}\dfrac{\sigma^2 C}{\partial S^2}\sigma^2 S^2 = rC$

and solving for $k(t)$, we get an ordinary differential equation:

$$k'(t) + \left[n(n-1)\frac{\sigma^2}{2} + (n-1)r \right]k(t) = 0$$

The solution is

$$k(t) = k(0)e^{-\left[n(n-1)\frac{\sigma^2}{2} + (n-1)r \right]t}$$

Setting $k(0) = 1$, we get the value of the atomic securities:

$$C_n(S,t) = e^{-\left[n(n-1)\frac{\sigma^2}{2} + (n-1)r \right]t} S^n$$

For integer values of n, we get

$$C_0(S,t) = e^{rt}$$
$$C_1(S,t) = S$$
$$C_2(S,t) = e^{-(\sigma^2 + r)t} S^2$$
$$C_3(S,t) = e^{-(3\sigma^2 + 2r)t} S^3$$
$$C_4(S,t) = e^{-(6\sigma^2 + 3r)t} S^4$$

and so on. The central question is then, can we find constant coefficients a_n so that

$$\sum_{n=0}^{m} a_n e^{-\left[n(n-1)\frac{\sigma^2}{2} + (n-1)r \right]t} S^n$$

can replicate arbitrary derivative securities? It turns out that the answer is yes and is confirmed by the Weierstrass approximation theorem that states that for any continuous function on the interval $[c, d]$, for all positive ε's, there exists a polynomial $P_m(x)$ (of sufficiently high degree m) such that for all x in $[c, d]$, $|f(x) - P_m(x)| < \varepsilon$.

To give examples of this approach, if you wanted to replicate a forward contract valued at

$$f = S - Ke^{-r(T-t)}$$

then the contract value at expiration is

$$S - K = a_0 e^{rT} + a_1 S + a_2 e^{-(\sigma^2 + r)T} S^2 + \cdots$$

For this equation to hold, the coefficients will satisfy

$$a_0 = -Ke^{-rT}$$
$$a_1 = 1$$

And with these values of a_0 and a_1 and all other a_n's equal to zero, $a_0 e^{rt} + a_1 S = S - Ke^{-r(T-t)}$.

Similarly, if a security has a terminal payoff $(S - K)^2$, then we can identify coefficients by setting

$$S^2 - 2KS + K^2 = a_0 e^{rT} + a_1 S + a_2 e^{-(\sigma^2 + r)T} S^2 + \cdots$$

Then we get

$$a_0 = K^2 e^{-rT}$$
$$a_1 = -2K$$
$$a_2 = e^{(\sigma^2 + r)T}$$

And the value of this derivative is then

$$K^2 e^{-r(T-t)} - 2KS + e^{(\sigma^2 + r)(T-t)} S^2$$

12.4 Exotic Derivatives
12.4.1 Simple Exotics

Exotic derivatives come in different flavors. Some are straightforward and are not fundamentally more difficult to price than plain-vanilla derivatives. As an example of a simple exotic derivative, consider a European digital power put that pays an amount A if $(S_T)^n < K$, meaning that if the nth power of an underlying asset price is higher than some value K at expiration, we know, by Itô's lemma, that

$$\frac{d(S^n)}{S^n} = \left[n\mu + \frac{n(n-1)}{2}\sigma^2 \right] dt + n\sigma dB$$

Then we use the familiar change of measure to show that the value of the digital power put is

$$P = Ae^{-r(T-t)}Q[(S_T)^n < K] = Ae^{-r(T-t)}\Phi\left[-\frac{\ln\left(\dfrac{S^n}{K}\right) + n\left(r - \dfrac{\sigma^2}{2}\right)(T-t)}{n\sigma\sqrt{T-t}}\right]$$

As another example of a simple exotic option, we use martingale pricing to value an exotic forward contract with terminal payoff $(S - K)^2$, exactly the same as the one we priced in the preceding section.

The value of this forward is given by the expectation of its payoff under the martingale probability measure Q:

$$f = e^{-r(T-t)}E_t^Q[(S_T - K)^2] = e^{-r(T-t)}E_t^Q(S_T^2 - 2KS_T + K^2)$$

From Itô's lemma, when $dS/S = \mu dt + \sigma dB$, then

$$\frac{d(S^2)}{S^2} = (2\mu + \sigma^2)dt + 2\sigma dB$$

and

$$E_t^Q(S_T^2) = S^2 e^{(2r+\sigma^2)(T-t)}$$

With $E_t^Q(S_T) = Se^{r(T-t)}$, it follows that

$$f = e^{-r(T-t)}E_t^Q[(S_T - K)^2] = e^{-r(T-t)}E_t^Q(S_T^2 - 2KS_T - K^2) = S^2 e^{(r+\sigma^2)(T-t)} - 2KS + e^{-r(T-t)}K^2$$

as found previously.

There are, of course, exotic flavors that are more complicated to analyze. One such flavor is the barrier option. Barrier option pricing sometimes requires prior knowledge of first-passage time calculus, something we develop next.

12.4.2 First-Passage Time for an Arithmetic Brownian Motion

We now show some results on first-passage time for a Brownian motion with drift. Consider a variable X that follows an arithmetic Brownian motion under a probability P:

$$dX = \mu dt + \sigma dB$$

where B is a standard Brownian motion under P.

Call $M(t)$ the maximum point reached by X between 0 and t. We want to understand the probability distribution of $M(t)$.

Let us first calculate the joint probability that $X(t)$ is below b when $M(t)$ is above a (of course, $a > b$):

$$\Pr[X(t) \leq b, M(t) \geq a] = E_0^P(1_{[X(t)\leq b, M(t)\geq a]})$$

Define $d\tilde{B}(t) \equiv dB(t) - \gamma dt$, where $\gamma \equiv -\mu/\sigma$. Then, by the Girsanov theorem,

$$dX = \sigma d\tilde{B}(t)$$

under the new probability measure $\tilde{P}$. Note that the probabilities are related to each other by

$$\frac{d\tilde{P}}{dP} = e^{\gamma B(t) - \frac{\gamma^2}{2}t}$$

The probability now is

$$E_0^P(1_{[X(t)\leq b, M(t)\geq a]}) = E_0^{\tilde{P}}\left[\frac{1}{\frac{d\tilde{P}}{dP}}1_{[X(t)\leq b, M(t)\geq a]}\right]$$

$$= E_0^{\tilde{P}}\left[e^{-\gamma B(t) + \frac{\gamma^2}{2}t}1_{[X(t)\leq b, M(t)\geq a]}\right]$$

$$= E_0^{\tilde{P}}\left[e^{-\gamma\{\tilde{B}(t) - \gamma t\} - \frac{\gamma^2}{2}t}1_{[X(t)\leq b, M(t)\geq a]}\right]$$

$$= E_0^{\tilde{P}}\left[e^{-\gamma\tilde{B}(t) - \frac{\gamma^2}{2}t}1_{[X(t)\leq b, M(t)\geq a]}\right]$$

We now use the reflection principle to get

$$E_0^P[1_{[X(t)\leq b, M(t)\geq a]}] = E_0^{\tilde{P}}\left[e^{-\gamma\{\frac{2a}{\sigma} - \tilde{B}(t)\} - \frac{\gamma^2}{2}t}1_{[X(t)\geq 2a-b]}\right]$$

$$= e^{-\frac{2\gamma a}{\sigma}}E_0^{\tilde{P}}\left[e^{\gamma\tilde{B}(t) - \frac{\gamma^2}{2}t}1_{[X(t)\geq 2a-b]}\right]$$

We need to eliminate the $e^{\gamma \tilde{B}(t)-(\gamma^2/2)t}$ term in the expectations operator. To this end, we reuse the Girsanov theorem. Define a new probability $\hat{P}$ by setting

$$\frac{d\hat{P}}{d\widetilde{P}} = e^{\gamma \tilde{B}(t)-\frac{\gamma^2}{2}t}$$

Then $d\hat{B}(t) \equiv d\tilde{B}(t) - \gamma dt$ is a standard Brownian motion, and $dX = \sigma d\tilde{B} = \gamma \sigma dt + \sigma d\hat{B}$. Under the new probability $\hat{P}$, we have

$$E_0^P\left[1_{[X(t)\leq b, M(t)\geq a]}\right] = e^{-\frac{2\gamma a}{\sigma}} E_0^{\hat{P}}\left[\frac{e^{\gamma \tilde{B}(t)-\frac{\gamma^2}{2}t}}{d\hat{P}/d\widetilde{P}} 1_{[X(t)\geq 2a-b]}\right]$$

$$= e^{-\frac{2\gamma a}{\sigma}} E_0^{\hat{P}}\left[1_{[X(t)\geq 2a-b]}\right]$$

With $\gamma \equiv -\mu/\sigma$, we get

$$E_0^P[1_{[X(t)\leq b, M(t)\geq a]}] = e^{\frac{2\mu a}{\sigma^2}} \Phi\left(\frac{b-2a-\mu t}{\sigma\sqrt{t}}\right)$$

We are only a step away from determining the probability of a maximum of a Brownian motion. The reader can easily see that

$$\Pr[M(t) \geq b] = \Pr[X(t) \leq b, M(t) \geq b] + \Pr[X(t) \geq b]$$

But $\Pr[X(t) \geq b] = \Phi\left(\dfrac{\mu t - b}{\sigma\sqrt{t}}\right)$. Hence

$$\Pr[M(t) \geq b] = e^{\frac{2\mu b}{\sigma^2}} \Phi\left(\frac{-b-\mu t}{\sigma\sqrt{t}}\right) + \Phi\left(\frac{\mu t - b}{\sigma\sqrt{t}}\right)$$

12.4.3 First-Passage Time for a Geometric Brownian Motion

How do we adapt the preceding result to a geometric Brownian motion with drift? Suppose that we want to calculate the probability that an asset value S is higher than or equal to K any time between t and T (i.e., $S(t) < K$ and $t < T$). Then we can define $X \equiv \ln S$, and with $dS/S = \alpha dt + \sigma dB$, we have

$$dX = \left(\alpha - \frac{\sigma^2}{2}\right)dt + \sigma dB$$

If we call $M(X, T, t)$ the maximum level that X reaches between t and T, then

$$\Pr[M(S, T, t) \geq K] = \Pr[M(X, T, t) \geq \ln K]$$

And the result in the arithmetic Brownian case can be adapted to this problem by setting

$$\mu = \alpha - \frac{\sigma^2}{2}$$

$$b = \ln\left(\frac{K}{S}\right)$$

and replacing t by $T - t$ to get

$$\Pr[M(S,T,t) \geq K] = \Phi(d_1) + \left(\frac{S}{K}\right)^{1-\frac{2\alpha}{\sigma^2}} \Phi(d_2)$$

with

$$d_1 \equiv \frac{\ln\left(\frac{S}{K}\right) + \left(\alpha - \frac{\sigma^2}{2}\right)(T - t)}{\sigma\sqrt{T - t}}$$

and

$$d_2 \equiv \frac{\ln\left(\frac{S}{K}\right) - \left(\alpha - \frac{\sigma^2}{2}\right)(T - t)}{\sigma\sqrt{T - t}}$$

12.4.4 Digital Barrier Options

Let us price, based on the preceding result, a digital option that pays $1 at expiration if the underlying asset value hits a strike price K before the time to expiration T of the option, in which case the price of the option is the net present value of the Q-probability of the asset value hitting the strike price:

$$C = e^{-r(T-t)} E_t^Q (1_{M(S,t,T) \geq K})$$

Because we go from physical probabilities in the previous paragraph to martingale pricing, we have under the martingale probability measure Q

$$dX = \left(r - \frac{\sigma^2}{2}\right) dt + \sigma \, dB^Q$$

and the option price follows:

$$C = e^{-r(T-t)}\left[\Phi(h_1) + \left(\frac{S}{K}\right)^{1-\frac{2r}{\sigma^2}}\Phi(h_2)\right]$$

with

$$h_1 \equiv \frac{\ln\left(\dfrac{S}{K}\right) + \left(r - \dfrac{\sigma^2}{2}\right)(T-t)}{\sigma\sqrt{T-t}}$$

and

$$h_2 \equiv \frac{\ln\left(\dfrac{S}{K}\right) - \left(r - \dfrac{\sigma^2}{2}\right)(T-t)}{\sigma\sqrt{T-t}}$$

12.5 Corporate Liabilities

One of the most fertile applications of the BSM model is the valuation of corporate liabilities in an option-pricing framework. Both equity and risky bonds are interpreted as derivatives or claims contingent on corporate asset value. To see why, consider the following corporate balance sheet at time t:

Assets		Liabilities	
	Market Value		Market Value
Assets	A	Equity	E
		Zero-coupon bond	b

The corporation has a limited liability, meaning that the owners are not personally liable for the zero-coupon debt owed by the company to its bondholders. It does not pay dividends. The bond has a face value of F and matures at T. The risk-free rate is r for all maturities. The value of the assets (also called the *firm value*) follows a geometric Brownian motion:

$$\frac{dA}{A} = \mu dt + \sigma dB$$

At maturity T of the debt, one of two things may happen: If $A \geq F$, shareholders receive $A - F$ and bondholders are paid their due, F. If $A < F$, shareholders receive nothing and bondholders take over the company and get paid whatever assets are left.

This means the following:

$$E_T = \max(A_T - F, 0)$$

Equity is a European call option on the value of the firm with a strike price equal to the nominal value of the debt. We also have

$$b_T = \min(A_T, F)$$
$$= -\max(-A_T, -F)$$
$$= F - \max(F - A_T, 0)$$

The debt, in this case a zero-coupon bond, is a risk-free bond paying F minus a European put on the assets of the firm with a strike equal to the notional value of the debt. The reader should be able to see how this relates directly to the BSM framework. The equity value at time t is

$$C = A\Phi(d + \sigma\sqrt{T-t}) - Fe^{-r(T-t)}\Phi(d)$$

with

$$d \equiv \frac{\ln\left(\dfrac{A}{F}\right) + \left(r - \dfrac{\sigma^2}{2}\right)(T-t)}{\sigma\sqrt{T-t}}$$

The zero-coupon debt is valued at

$$b = A - E = Fe^{-r(T-t)}\Phi(d) + A\Phi(-d - \sigma\sqrt{T-t})$$

Also, note that

$$b = Fe^{-R(T-t)}$$

where R is the risky corporate yield. Then

$$R = -\frac{\ln\left(\dfrac{b}{F}\right)}{T-t}$$

And the reader can check that the difference $R - r$ between the risky rate and the risk-free rate, also called a *credit spread*, is

$$-\frac{1}{T-t}\ln\left\{\Phi\left[\frac{-\frac{\sigma^2(T-t)}{2}-\ln\frac{Fe^{-r(T-t)}}{A}}{\sigma\sqrt{T-t}}\right]+\frac{A}{Fe^{-r(T-t)}}\Phi\left[\frac{-\frac{\sigma^2(T-t)}{2}+\ln\frac{Fe^{-r(T-t)}}{A}}{\sigma\sqrt{T-t}}\right]\right\}$$

The credit spread $R - r$ increases with the ratio of face present value to assets $Fe^{-r(T-t)}/A$, also called *quasi-leverage*.

This is the bare-bones Merton model of corporate liabilities.[1] Although a higher firm value is in the interest of both shareholders and bondholders, a higher nominal for the zero-coupon bond reduces shareholder value while increasing debt value. Similarly, because shareholders are *long* optionality and bondholders are *short* optionality, higher volatility will help shareholder value and hurt bondholder value. Bondholders often negotiate tougher covenants (by, e.g., limiting the riskiness of corporate investment) so as to limit the volatility of corporate assets.

The Merton model can be extended to value various levels of subordination on the capital structure. The model also can be extended to warrants, rights, convertible debt, and callable debt.

12.6 State Contingent Claims

The reader may recall the pricing of discrete-time state contingent claims, also called *Arrow–Debreu securities*, in Chapter 10. We discuss below the Breeden–Litzenberger model.[2] This model can price state contingent claims in a continuous-time framework; it can also extract the implied risk-neutral density of the underlying asset from existing option prices.

Consider a portfolio with the following terminal payoff:

$$P(K,T,\Delta K) = \frac{1}{\Delta K}[C(K-\Delta K,T)-2C(K,T)+C(K+\Delta K,T)]$$

where $C(K, T)$ is the value of a European call with a strike of K and expiring at T. This portfolio, with payoff $P(K, T, \Delta K)$, is long $\frac{1}{\Delta K}$ units of two calls struck

---

1 See Merton (1973b).
2 See Breeden and Litzenberger (1978).

at $K - \Delta K$ and $K + \Delta K$ and short $\dfrac{1}{\Delta K}$ units of two calls struck at K. This is called a *butterfly spread*.

The underlying asset price S can only move by increments of ΔK. It can take positive values of form $K \pm n\Delta K$, with n a positive integer. That is, the asset price at expiration S_T can take values

$$0, \ldots, K - 2\Delta K, K - \Delta K, K, K - \Delta K, K - 2\Delta K, \ldots$$

The following table shows the payoff of the butterfly spread:

	$S_T \leq K - \Delta K$	$S_T = K$	$S_T \geq K + \Delta K$
$\dfrac{1}{\Delta K} C(K - \Delta K, T)$	0	1	$\dfrac{1}{\Delta K}[S_T - (K - \Delta K)]$
$-\dfrac{1}{\Delta K} 2C(K, T)$	0	0	$-\dfrac{1}{\Delta K} 2(S_T - K)$
$\dfrac{1}{\Delta K} C(K + \Delta K, T)$	0	0	$\dfrac{1}{\Delta K}[S_T - (K + \Delta K)]$
$P(K, T, \Delta K)$	0	1	0

As shown by this table, the butterfly spread payoff is 1 when $S_T = K$ and 0 otherwise. This describes an Arrow–Debreu security that pays 1 at maturity in the state of the world where $S_T = K$.

Note that if the value of the portfolio is divided by the step size, then

$$\frac{P(K,T,\Delta K)}{\Delta K} = \frac{[C(K - \Delta K, T) - 2C(K, T) + C(K + \Delta K, T)]}{(\Delta K)^2}$$

and

$$\lim_{\Delta K \to 0} \frac{P(K,T,\Delta K)}{\Delta K} = \frac{\partial^2 C(K, T)}{\partial K^2}$$

The pricing function $P(K, T)$ is intuitively close to a risk-neutral density function because the price of an Arrow–Debreu security is the discounted risk-neutral probability of a state occurring times the payoff (a payoff of 1 in this case).

To show the result, consider a European call option value

$$C = e^{-r(T-t)} E_t^Q [(S_T - K)^+] e^{-r(T-t)} \int_K^\infty (S_T - K) q(S_T) dS_T$$

where $q(S_T)$ is the risk-neutral probability density function of the terminal underlying asset price S_T. Differentiating with respect to the strike K, we obtain, by Leibniz's rule:[3]

$$\frac{\partial C}{\partial K} = -e^{-r(T-t)} \int_K^\infty q(S_T)dS_T$$

But $\int_K^\infty q(S_T)d S_T = 1 - \int_0^K q(S_T)dS_T$. It follows that

$$\frac{\partial C}{\partial K} = e^{-r(T-t)}\left[\int_0^K q(S_T)dS_T - 1\right]$$

and

$$\frac{\partial^2 C}{\partial K^2}\bigg|_{K=S_T} = e^{-r(T-t)}\frac{\partial}{\partial K}\left[\int_0^K q(S_T)dS_T - 1\right] = e^{-r(T-t)}q(S_T)$$

The risk-neutral density thus can be recovered from the second derivative of the call with respect to the strike:

$$q(S_T) = e^{r(T-t)}\frac{\partial^2 C}{\partial^2 K}\bigg|_{K=S_T}$$

And any derivative can be priced using this density function:

$$C = e^{-r(T-t)} \int_0^\infty f(S_T)q(S_T)dS_T$$

$$= \int_0^\infty f(S_T)\frac{\partial^2 C}{\partial^2 K}\bigg|_{K=S_T} dS_T$$

In a standard Black–Scholes model, differentiating the European call price twice with respect to K gets us

$$\frac{\partial^2 C}{\partial K^2} = \frac{\Phi'(d)e^{r(T-t)}}{K\sigma\sqrt{T-t}}$$

---

3 Leibniz rule:

$$\frac{d}{dx}\left[\int_{a(x)}^{b(x)} f(x,t)\,dt\right] = f[x,b(x)]\frac{db(x)}{dx} - f[x,a(x)]\frac{da(x)}{dx} + \int_{a(x)}^{b(x)} \frac{\partial}{\partial x} f(x,t)\,dt$$

with

$$d \equiv \frac{\ln\left(\dfrac{S}{K}\right) + \left(r - \dfrac{\sigma^2}{2}\right)(T - t)}{\sigma\sqrt{T - t}} \quad \text{and} \quad \Phi'(d) = \frac{e^{\frac{-d^2}{2}}}{\sqrt{2\pi}}$$

Therefore,

$$q(S_T) = \frac{\Phi'(d)}{K\sigma\sqrt{T - t}}$$

Evidently, the probability of a price being equal to a given number is zero in continuous time. But the density function is not zero.

13
Interest Rate Models

Summary

Fixed income derivatives are more complicated than equity derivatives because fixed income is simpler than equity: fixed income has a maturity and pulls to par. Because bond prices are predictable, standard valuation models for equity derivatives such as the Black–Scholes framework do not necessarily work.

Toy interest rate models show that the interest rate tends to increase with the time-preference discount rate and the growth of capital, of consumption, and of population. It tends to decrease with growth uncertainty.

In a one-factor equilibrium model, an interest-rate-sensitive asset price P is obtained by solving the following partial differential equation:

$$\frac{\partial P}{\partial r}[\mu(r,t) - \lambda(r,t)\sigma(r,t)] + \frac{\partial P}{\partial t} + \frac{1}{2}\frac{\partial^2 P}{\partial r^2}\sigma^2(r,t) = rP$$

subject to appropriate boundary conditions. Here r is the instantaneous risk-free rate with drift $\mu(r, t)$ and standard deviation $\sigma(r, t)$, t is time, and $\lambda(r, t)$ is the market price of risk.

Equivalently, the price of a zero-coupon bond paying off \$1 at maturity T is given by

$$P(t,T) = E_t^Q \left\{ \exp\left[-\int_t^T r(s)ds\right] \right\}$$

with E_t^Q defined as the expectation operator at time t under the martingale probability measure Q.

Term-structure-consistent models help value fixed income derivatives accurately. In the Heath–Jarrow–Morton model, it can be showed that to preclude arbitrage, we must have

$$df(t,T) = \left[\sigma(t,T)\int_t^T \sigma(t,s)ds\right]dt + \sigma(t,T)dB(t)$$

The instantaneous short forward $f(t, T)$ is the forward rate at time t that applies to a loan starting at T and maturing at $T + dt$. $\sigma(t, T)$ is the corresponding volatility, and $B(t)$ is a Wiener process.

Preliminaries

We start with a few basic definitions:

■ A yield r of a zero-coupon bond, called a *zero-coupon yield*, solves the following equation:

$$P(t,T) = e^{-r(T-t)} \text{ or } r = \frac{-\ln P}{T-t}$$

where $P(t, T)$ is the price at time t of a zero-coupon bond paying \$1 at maturity T.

■ A duration is (minus) the relative change of a bond price induced by a change in interest rates. For a zero-coupon bond,

$$D = -\frac{\dfrac{dP(t,T)}{P(t,T)}}{dr} = -\frac{\dfrac{dP(t,T)}{dr}}{P(t,T)} = -\frac{-(T-t)P(t,T)}{P(t,T)} = (T-t)$$

So the duration of a zero-coupon bond is the remaining time to maturity.

■ A yield-to-maturity y of a coupon bond solves the equation

$$P(t,T) = \sum_{i=1}^{n} C_i e^{-y(t_i - t)}$$

where C_i is the ith future cash flow paid by the bond at time t_i, and $P(t, T)$ is the price at time t of the coupon bond maturing at time T (defined as t_n).

It is said that fixed income derivatives are more complicated than equity derivatives because fixed income is simpler than equity. There is a lot of truth to this, as the reader will perhaps appreciate. Fixed income has a maturity and pulls to par—a government bond price promising 100 will, absent default, converge to 100 at maturity. Because bond prices are predictable, standard valuation models for equity derivatives such as the Black–Scholes framework do not necessarily work.

Example: You want to calculate the value of a European call on a 1-year T-bill. You use Black–Scholes–Merton (BSM) for this purpose. The parameters are as follows:

$$S = 98.02;\ K = 100;\ r = 0.02;\ \tau = 1;\ \sigma = 1\%$$

You plug these values in the BSM formula:

$$C = S\Phi\left[\frac{\ln\left(\frac{S}{K}\right)+\left(r+\frac{\sigma^2}{2}\right)\tau}{\sigma\sqrt{T-t}}\right] - Ke^{-r(T-t)}\Phi\left[\frac{\ln\left(\frac{S}{K}\right)+\left(r-\frac{\sigma^2}{2}\right)\tau}{\sigma\sqrt{T-t}}\right]$$

to find $C = 0.39$.

But we ask the reader to reconsider: a 1-year T-bill will surely be worth 100 in 1 year, which is the time to expiration of the call. So the European call is worth zero, not 0.39, as claimed by the BSM formula.

The reason for this discrepancy is that BSM assumes that the underlying asset price follows a geometric Brownian motion. One ensuing property is that the asset's return volatility increases with the square root of time. This is clearly not the case for a T-bill, which sees its volatility dampen to zero as it gets close to maturity. We need to modify the random process to take into account the pull to par of the Treasury security.

Because of the certainty about terminal cash flows, the definition of the stochastic process becomes more intricate. For the same reason, there are restrictions on how the yield curve may move. To take an example, a parallel shift of a flat yield curve is not permissible because it allows arbitrage.

Example: Consider three zero-coupon bonds 1, 2, and 3 maturing in that order at $t - \Delta t$, t, and $t + \Delta t$ and paying \$1 at maturity. Also assume a flat yield curve with interest rates equal to r. Then form a zero-cash, zero-duration portfolio that is long the barbell (bonds 1 and 3) and short the bullet (bond 2).

The value- and duration-matching conditions can be expressed, respectively, as

$$N_1 e^{-r(t-\Delta t)} + N_3 e^{-r(t+\Delta t)} = N_2 e^{-rt}$$

$$N_1 (t - \Delta t) e^{-r(t-\Delta t)} + N_3 (t + \Delta t) e^{-r(t+\Delta t)} = N_2 t e^{-rt}$$

where N_1, N_2, and N_3 are the numbers of bonds 1, 2, and 3. Without loss of generality, set $N_2 = 1$. Then we obtain

$$N_1 = \frac{e^{-r\Delta t}}{2}$$

and

$$N_3 = \frac{e^{+r\Delta t}}{2}$$

The portfolio has value $\pi = N_1 e^{-r(t-\Delta t)} + N_3 e^{-r(t+\Delta t)} - e^{-rt} = 0$ by construction. What happens to this portfolio value for a small change dr in the level of interest rates (meaning a parallel shift of the flat yield curve)? Then

$$\pi' = N_1 e^{-(r+dr)(t-\Delta t)} + N_3 e^{-(r+dr)(t+\Delta t)} - e^{-(r+dr)t}$$

Replacing N_1 and N_3 by their value, we get

$$\pi' = \frac{e^{-r\Delta t}}{2} e^{-(r+dr)(t-\Delta t)} + \frac{e^{+r\Delta t}}{2} e^{-(r+dr)(t+\Delta t)} - e^{-t(r+dr)}$$

$$= e^{-t(r+dr)} \left[\frac{e^{(r+dr)\Delta t} e^{-r\Delta t} + e^{-(r+dr)\Delta t} e^{+r\Delta t}}{2} - 1 \right]$$

$$= e^{-t(r+dr)} [\cosh(dr\Delta t) - 1] \geq 0$$

where the inequality holds because $\cosh(x) \geq 1$, $\forall x$. The portfolio generates a net profit regardless of the sign of dr. Therefore, the parallel shift of the flat yield curve is not permissible because it allows arbitrage.

13.1 Toy Models of Interest Rate

We show two naive models of interest rate determination. The Solow–Swan model derives an expression for the return on capital with a deterministic production function; the second model, which is consumption based, involves a simple optimization by a representative agent. As the reader will see, these models are far too parsimonious to be realistic but describe qualitatively the impact of production and consumption parameters on the level of interest rates.

13.1.1 Interest Rates and the Production Function: The Solow–Swan Model

Start with a profit-maximizing firm with a standard production function

$$Y = F(K,L) = K^{\alpha}(AL)^{1-\alpha}$$

where $Y = F(K, L)$ is production or output, and K and L are, respectively, units of capital and labor, A is labor-augmenting technology, and α is the output elasticity of capital. In equilibrium, the return on capital equals the marginal productivity of capital, which is given by

$$R = \frac{\partial F}{\partial K} = \alpha K^{\alpha-1}(AL)^{1-\alpha} = \alpha \frac{Y}{K}$$

If the capital stock K depreciates at a constant rate δ and the households save a fixed fraction s of the total output, then the dynamic of capital stock follows: $\dot{K} = sY - \delta K$.

Also suppose that labor L, or the number of workers, and technology grow at rates n and g—that is, $A_t = A_0 e^{gt}$ and $L_t = L_0 e^{nt}$. Define $k = K/AL$ and $y = Y/AL$ as capital and output per effective worker. Then k will grow at

$$\dot{k} = \frac{\dot{K}}{AL} - k(n+g)$$

Plug in $\dot{K} = sY - \delta K$, and we obtain $\dot{k} = sy - (\delta + n + g)k$. At the steady state, capital per unit of effective labor does not change—that is, $sy = (\delta + n + g)k$. Therefore, at the steady state,

$$\frac{K}{Y} = \frac{k}{y} = \frac{s}{\delta + n + g}$$

and the marginal productivity of capital, or return on capital, is

$$R = \alpha \frac{\delta + n + g}{s}$$

The return on capital is increasing in the output elasticity of capital, technology growth, capital depreciation, and labor growth. It declines with the savings rate. This is because (1) the marginal productivity of capital obviously increases with the output elasticity of capital, and (2) the output-capital ratio increases at a steady state with the growth of other inputs (technology and labor) and decreases with the savings rate.

13.1.2 Interest Rates in a Basic Consumption Model

The expression for the interest rate with log-normal consumption and constant relative risk-aversion (CRRA) utility functions was derived in Chapter 10. We derive it again here from first principles.

An agent maximizes lifetime consumption:

$$\max_{C_t, C_{t+1}} U(C_t) + e^{-\rho} E_t[U(C_{t+1})]$$

$$\text{subject to } C_t + e^{-r}C_{t+1} = W$$

Standard Lagrangian optimization yields the following result:

$$e^r = \frac{1}{E_t\left[e^{-\rho}\dfrac{U'(C_{t+1})}{U'(C_t)}\right]}$$

And hence

$$r = -\ln E_t(M_{t+1})$$

with $M_{t+1} \equiv e^{-\rho}\dfrac{U'(C_{t+1})}{U'(C_t)}$

Assume a CRRA utility of consumption

$$U(C_t) = \frac{C_t^{1-\theta} - 1}{1 - \theta}$$

Therefore,

$$E_t\left[e^{-\rho}\frac{U'(C_{t+1})}{U'(C_t)}\right]=e^{-\rho}E_t[\left(\frac{C_{t+1}}{C_t}\right)^{-\theta}]$$

Now assume that consumption follows a log-normal random walk:

$$C_{t+1}=C_t e^{g-\frac{\sigma^2}{2}+\sigma\varepsilon}$$

Recalling that

$$E_t\left(e^{-\theta\sigma\varepsilon}\right)=e^{\frac{\theta^2\sigma^2}{2}}$$

it follows immediately that

$$r=\rho+\theta g-\frac{\theta(\theta+1)\sigma^2}{2}$$

If ρ, the time preference coefficient, is high, the economic agent would rather consume today than tomorrow and will want to save or lend less, therefore raising interest rates. Similarly, if consumption growth is expected to be high, people will tend to save less today and smooth their consumption. Conversely, with an increased variance of consumption growth, the agent will consume less today for precautionary reasons. This means an incentive to lend and a lower interest rate.

13.2 Models of the Term Structure: Generic Solutions

We show generic solutions for the term structure of interest rates. In line with BSM pricing, we find that interest-rate-sensitive securities can be valued either by solving a partial differential equation or by representing a bond price as an expectation of future cash flows under a risk-neutral or martingale probability measure. We focus on the so-called one-factor models, where the term structure is generated by a single factor, the instantaneous short rate r.

13.2.1 Proof 1: Arbitrage Portfolio

Our first proof develops a partial differential equation to price the term structure. We get this equation by assuming a one-factor model, forming a self-financed portfolio, and invoking absence of arbitrage. The one-factor model assumes that the interest rate derivative's price P is a function of the short rate r and time:

$$P = P(r, t)$$

The short rate follows a general Itô process:

$$dr = \mu(r, t)dt + \sigma(r, t)dB$$

By Itô's lemma,

$$\frac{dP}{P} = a(r, t)dt + b(r, t)dB$$

where $a(r, t)$ and $b(r, t)$ are

$$a(r, t) \equiv \frac{\dfrac{\partial P}{\partial r}\mu(r, t) + \dfrac{\partial P}{\partial t} + \dfrac{1}{2}\dfrac{\partial^2 P}{\partial r^2}\sigma^2(r, t)}{P}$$

and

$$b(r, t) \equiv \frac{\dfrac{\partial P}{\partial r}\sigma(r, t)}{P}$$

Consider now two bonds priced at P_1 and P_2 and maturing at T_1 and T_2. Bond 1 return has drift a_1 and volatility b_1. Bond 2 return has drift a_2 and volatility b_2. If one forms a self-financed portfolio consisting of a position worth V_1 of bond 1, a position worth V_2 of bond 2 while borrowing an amount $V_1 + V_2$ at the instantaneous risk-free rate r, then the instantaneous change $d\pi$ of the value of the portfolio will obey the following equation:

$$d\pi = [V_1(a_1 - r) + V_2(a_2 - r)]dt + (V_1 b_1 + V_2 b_2)dB$$

Now V_1 and V_2 can be chosen to cancel the noise, meaning the dB term, in this equation. Hence

$$V_1 = \frac{-V_2 b_2}{b_1}$$

When the dB term disappears, this means that the self-financed portfolio can only yield zero in the absence of arbitrage. Then

$$d\pi = [V_1(a_1 - r) + V_2(a_2 - r)]dt = 0$$

and it follows that

$$\frac{a_1 - r}{b_1} = \frac{a_2 - r}{b_2}$$

The risk-adjusted excess returns (also called the *Sharpe ratio*) of all interest-rate-sensitive assets will be equal by arbitrage in this one-factor framework. We will call this Sharpe ratio the *market price* of risk $\lambda(r, t)$. In other words,

$$\frac{a_1 - r}{b_1} = \frac{a_2 - r}{b_2} = \lambda(r,t)$$

Because $(a - r)/b = \lambda(r, t)$ for all interest rate derivatives, then replacing the values of a and b in this equation, we obtain the partial differential equation that prices interest-rate-sensitive assets:

$$\frac{\partial P}{\partial r}[\mu(r,t) - \lambda(r,t)\sigma(r,t)] + \frac{\partial P}{\partial t} + \frac{1}{2}\frac{\partial^2 P}{\partial r^2}\sigma^2(r,t) = rP$$

This partial differential equation solves for general interest rate securities. We need to append to this equation boundary conditions defining the nature of the security to be priced. For example, the boundary condition for a zero-coupon bond paying \$1 at maturity T will be written

$$P(r, T, T) = 1$$

meaning that the price at time T of the security maturing at T is \$1.

13.2.2 Proof 2: Risk Neutrality

As we did in the case of the BSM equation in Chapter 10, we show in proofs 2 and 3 the heuristics of risk-neutral valuation of interest-rate-sensitive securities. We conjecture that, in a risk-neutral world,

$$dr = [\mu(r,t) - \lambda(r,t)\sigma(r,t)]dt + \sigma(r,t)dB$$

In such a world,

$$E^*\left(\frac{dP}{P}\right) = rdt$$

By Itô's lemma,

$$dP(r,t) = \left\{ \frac{\partial P}{\partial r}[\mu(r,t) - \lambda(r,t)\sigma(r,t)] + \frac{\partial P}{\partial t} + \frac{1}{2}\frac{\partial^2 P}{\partial r^2}\sigma^2(r,t) \right\} dt + \frac{\partial P}{\partial t}\sigma(r,t)dB$$

and

$$E^*\left(\frac{dP}{P} \right) = \frac{\left\{ \frac{\partial P}{\partial r}[\mu(r,t) - \lambda(r,t)\sigma(r,t)] + \frac{\partial P}{\partial t} + \frac{1}{2}\frac{\partial^2 P}{\partial r^2}\sigma^2(r,t) \right\} dt}{P} = rdt$$

It follows that

$$\frac{\partial P}{\partial r}[\mu(r,t) - \lambda(r,t)\sigma(r,t)] + \frac{\partial P}{\partial t} + \frac{1}{2}\frac{\partial^2 P}{\partial r^2}\sigma^2(r,t) = rP$$

which is exactly the same partial differential equation as in the arbitrage proof. In other words, to price an interest-rate-sensitive security, one can do so in a make-believe world where everyone is risk neutral and the drift of the short rate has been adjusted by $-\lambda(r, t)\,\sigma(r, t)$.

13.2.3 Proof 3: Risk Neutrality Redux

We will now give another angle to the same result by proving that the partial differential equation

$$\frac{\partial P}{\partial r}[\mu(r,t) - \lambda(r,t)\sigma(r,t)] + \frac{\partial P}{\partial t} + \frac{1}{2}\frac{\partial^2 P}{\partial r^2}\sigma^2(r,t) = rP$$

with boundary condition $P(T, T) = 1$ has solution

$$P(t,T) = E_t\left\{ \exp\left[-\int_t^T r(s)ds - \frac{1}{2}\int_t^T \lambda^2(r,s)ds - \int_t^T \lambda(r,s)dB(s) \right] \right\}$$

Define $X[u, B(u)]$ as

$$X[u,B(u)] = \exp\left[-\int_t^u r(s)ds - \frac{1}{2}\int_t^u \lambda^2(r,s)ds - \int_t^u \lambda(r,s)dB(s) \right]$$

Use Itô's lemma to obtain

$$dX[u,B(u)] = \left(\frac{\partial X}{\partial u} + \frac{1}{2}\frac{\partial^2 X}{\partial B^2} \right)du + \frac{\partial X}{\partial B}dB$$

By the Leibniz rule,[1]

$$\frac{\partial X}{\partial u} = -r(u)X[u, B(u)] - \frac{1}{2}\lambda^2(r, u)X[u, B(u)]$$

$$\frac{\partial X}{\partial B} = -\lambda(r, u)X[u, B(u)]$$

and

$$\frac{\partial^2 X}{\partial B^2} = \lambda^2(r, u)X[u, B(u)]$$

Hence

$$dX[u, B(u)] = -r(u)X[u, B(u)]du - \lambda(r, u)X[u, B(u)]dB$$

Also, as established earlier,

$$dP(r, u) = \left\{\frac{\partial P}{\partial r}[\mu(r, u) - \lambda(r, u)\sigma(r, u)] + \frac{\partial P}{\partial u} + \frac{1}{2}\frac{\partial^2 P}{\partial r^2}\sigma^2(r, u)\right\}du + \frac{\partial P}{\partial r}\sigma(r, u)dB$$

We now use bivariate Itô's lemma to calculate $d(PX)$ using short form:

$$d(PX) = XdP + PdX + dPdX$$

$$= \left[\frac{\partial P}{\partial r}(\mu - \lambda\sigma) + \frac{\partial P}{\partial u} + \frac{1}{2}\frac{\partial^2 P}{\partial r^2}\sigma^2 - rP\right]Xdu + \left(X\frac{\partial P}{\partial r}\sigma - \lambda XP\right)dB$$

From the pricing PDE, we know that the term in du is equal to zero.
Integrating from t to T and taking expectations, we get

$$E_t\int_t^T d[P(r, u, T)X(u)] = E_t[P(r, T, T)X(T) - P(r, t, T)X(t)] = 0$$

With $P(r, T, T) = 1$ and $X(t) = 1$, we get

$$P(r, t, T) = E_t[X(T)] = E_t\left\{\exp\left[-\int_t^T r(s)ds - \frac{1}{2}\int_t^T \lambda^2(s)ds - \int_t^T \lambda(s)dB(s)\right]\right\}$$

---

1 The Leibniz integral rule is given by

$$\frac{d}{dz}\int_{a(z)}^{b(z)} f(x, z)dx = \int_{a(z)}^{b(z)}\frac{\partial f}{\partial z}dx + f[b(z), z]\frac{db}{dz} - f[a(z), z]\frac{da}{dz}$$

which is the required result. The last step is to note that in a risk-neutral world, returns on bonds of all maturities are equal to r, and the market price of risk λ is equal to zero. This simplifies the preceding equation to

$$P(r,t,T) = \tilde{E}_t \left\{ \exp\left[-\int_t^T r(s)ds \right] \right\}$$

where $\tilde{E}_t$ is the time t expectation operator in a risk-neutral world. We will establish this result more formally in Proof 4.

13.2.4 Proof 4: Martingale Approach

Dynamics of the Stochastic Discount Factor
In continuous time, the price of an asset, in this case a zero-coupon bond, can be expressed as

$$P(t,T) = E_t \left[\frac{M(T)P(T,T)}{M(t)} \right]$$

meaning that $P(t, T)M(t)$ is a martingale and therefore has zero drift. It follows that

$$E_t \{d[P(t,T)M(t)]\} = 0$$

With P and M following a geometric Brownian motion (for simplicity, we drop the time dependence where not necessary),

$$\frac{dP}{P} = adt + bdB$$

and

$$\frac{dM}{M} = cdt + edB$$

and then, by Itô's lemma,

$$d(PM) = PdM + MdP + dPdM$$

and

$$E_t(dPdM) = (cMP + aMP + beMP)dt = 0$$

The sum of the drifts thus should be equal to minus the product of the volatilities:

$$a + c = -be$$

This relationship should apply to any interest-rate-sensitive security, including to a money-market account with drift $a = r$ and zero volatility ($b = 0$). It follows that the drift of the stochastic discount factor is minus the instantaneous short rate:

$$c = -r$$

We can also infer the value of the volatility e of the stochastic discount factor:

$$e = -\frac{a+c}{b} = -\frac{a-r}{b} = -\lambda$$

where the second equality stems from the definition of the market price of risk λ.

The stochastic discount factor hence follows the process:

$$\frac{dM}{M} = -r(t)dt - \lambda(t)dB$$

The integral form of this stochastic differential equation is straightforward:

$$M(T) = M(t)\exp\left[-\int_t^T r(s)ds - \frac{1}{2}\int_t^T \lambda^2(s)ds - \int_t^T \lambda(s)dB(s) \right]$$

Hence the price of a zero-coupon bond paying \$1 at maturity is

$$P(t,T) = E_t\left[\frac{M(T)}{M(t)} \right] = E_t\left\{ \exp\left[-\int_t^T r(s)ds - \frac{1}{2}\int_t^T \lambda^2(s)ds - \int_t^T \lambda(s)dB(s) \right] \right\}$$

Change of Measure

We can apply Girsanov's theorem to change the probability measure. A process

$$dW^Q = dW + \lambda dt$$

is a Wiener process under probability measure Q, with the Radon–Nikodym derivative defined by

$$\frac{dQ}{dP} = \exp\left[-\frac{1}{2}\int_t^T \lambda^2(s)ds - \int_t^T \lambda(s)dB(s) \right]$$

Recalling that

$$P(t,T) = E_t \left\{ \frac{dQ}{dP} \exp\left[-\int_t^T r(s)ds \right] \right\}$$

the result follows:

$$P(t,T) = E_t^Q \left\{ \exp\left[-\int_t^T r(s)ds \right] \right\}$$

13.3 Single-Factor Models: Examples

We discuss solutions of three specific single-factor models: Merton, Vasicek, and Cox–Ingersoll–Ross. Models are solved by resorting to the partial differential pricing equation or the martingale approach. We have assumed that rates were following a general Itô process:

$$dr = \mu(r,t)dt + \sigma(r,t)dB$$

Merton, Vasicek, and Cox–Ingersoll–Ross are special cases of this stochastic differential equation. The following table describes the process assumed by these models:

TABLE 13.1

	$\mu(r, t)$	$\sigma(r, t)$
Merton	μ	σ
Vasicek	$k(\theta - r)$	σ
Cox-Ingersoll-Ross	$k(\theta - r)$	$\sigma\sqrt{r}$

Here k is the speed of reversion of the short rate to its unconditional mean θ.

13.3.1 The Merton Model

We derive the term structure of the Merton model by first solving the pricing partial differential equation for interest-rate-sensitive securities and then by calculating the expectation under the martingale probability measure.

Solution of the Merton Model: The Pricing Partial Differential Equation

As indicated in the table above, the short rate in the Merton model obeys a simple arithmetic Brownian motion:

$$dr = \mu dt + \sigma dB$$

The market price of risk λ is assumed to be constant. This results into the following partial differential equation:

$$\frac{\partial P}{dr}(\mu - \lambda\sigma) + \frac{\partial P}{dt} + \frac{1}{2}\frac{\partial^2 P}{\partial r^2}\sigma^2 = rP$$

The boundary condition for a zero-coupon bond is

$$P(r, T, T) = 1$$

Define $\tau \equiv T - t$. We conjecture a solution of the form

$$P(r, t, T) = A(\tau)\exp[-B(\tau)r]$$

in which case

$$\frac{\partial P}{dr} = -A(\tau)B(\tau)\exp[-B(\tau)r]$$

$$\frac{\partial P}{dt} = rA(\tau)B'(\tau)\exp[-B(\tau)r] - A'(\tau)\exp[-B(\tau)r]$$

$$\frac{\partial^2 P}{\partial r^2} = A(\tau)B^2(\tau)\exp[-B(\tau)r]$$

Replacing these expressions in the partial differential equation and using the short form, we get

$$-AB[\mu - \lambda\sigma] - A' + \frac{1}{2}AB^2\sigma^2 = rA(1 - B')$$

Because this equation must hold for all values of r, both sides of the equation are equal to zero. This yields two ordinary differential equations:

$$-AB(\mu - \lambda\sigma) - A' + \frac{1}{2}AB^2\sigma^2 = 0$$

and

$$A(1 - B') = 0$$

So $B' = 1$. In addition, from $P(r, T, T) = 1$, we infer that $A(0)\exp[-B(0)r] = 1$, for all r. Therefore, $A(0) = 1$ and $B(0) = 0$.

Hence $B' = 1$ and $B(0) = 0$ mean that

$$B = \tau$$

And we know that:

$$\frac{A'}{A} = -\tau(\mu - \lambda\sigma) + \frac{\sigma^2\tau^2}{2}$$

subject to $A(0) = 1$. Thus we can infer the expression for A:

$$A = \exp\left[-\frac{\tau^2}{2}(\mu - \lambda\sigma) + \frac{\sigma^2\tau^3}{6}\right]$$

We finally get the solution for the zero-coupon price at time t across all maturities r:

$$P(r,t,T) = \exp\left[-r\tau - \frac{\tau^2}{2}(\mu - \lambda\sigma) + \frac{\sigma^2\tau^3}{6}\right]$$

The term structure of zero-coupon yields is given by

$$R(t,T) = \frac{-\ln P(r,t,T)}{\tau} = r + \frac{\tau}{2}(\mu - \lambda\sigma) - \frac{\sigma^2\tau^2}{6}$$

The main issue with the Merton model is that yields always become negative for long enough maturities, as can be seen from this equation.

Solution of the Merton Model: The Martingale Method
We now want to find an expression for

$$P(t,T) = E_t^Q\left\{\exp\left[-\int_t^T r(s)ds\right]\right\}$$

to find a solution for bond prices in the Merton model. First note that $Y \equiv -\int_t^T r(s)ds$ is a sum of normal variables and is therefore a normal variable. We know that for a normal variable Y with mean m and variance v,

$$E(e^Y) = e^{m+\frac{v}{2}}$$

We need to find the mean m and variance v of $-\int_t^T r(s)ds$.

Under the Q probability measure, the short rate follows an arithmetic Brownian motion of the form

$$dr = (\mu - \lambda\sigma)dt + \sigma dB^Q$$

Integrating between t and s gives

$$r(s) = r(t) + (\mu - \lambda\sigma)(s - t) + \sigma[B(s) - B(t)]$$

We are interested in $-\int_t^T r(s)ds$. Thus

$$Y = \int_t^T -\{r(t) + (\mu - \lambda\sigma)(s - t) + \sigma[B(s) - B(t)]\}ds$$

$$= -r(t)(T - t) - \frac{\mu - \lambda\sigma}{2}(T - t)^2 - \sigma\int_t^T B(s)ds + \sigma(T - t)B(t)$$

Use the product differentiation rule to get

$$d[(T - s)B(s)] = -B(s)ds + (T - s)dB(s)$$

Then it follows that

$$Y = -r(t)(T - t) - \frac{\mu - \lambda\sigma}{2}(T - t)^2 - \sigma\int_t^T (T - s)dB(s)$$

Because $E_t^Q\left[\int_t^T (T - s)dB(s)\right] = 0$, then

$$m = -r(t)(T - t) - \frac{\mu - \lambda\sigma}{2}(T - t)^2$$

and, by Itô isometry, we have

$$v = \sigma^2\left[\int_t^T (T - s)dB(s)\right]^2 = \sigma^2\int_t^T (T - s)^2 ds = \frac{\sigma^2(T - t)^3}{3}$$

The solution immediately follows:

$$P(t,T) = E_t^Q(e^Y) = e^{m+\frac{v}{2}} = \exp\left[-r(t)(T - t) - \frac{\mu - \lambda\sigma}{2}(T - t)^2 + \frac{\sigma^2(T - t)^3}{6}\right]$$

13.3.2 The Vasicek Model

The premise of the Vasicek model is mean reversion in short rates:

$$dr = k(\theta - r)dt + \sigma dB$$

As long as the short rate r is below its unconditional mean θ, the drift term will be positive, and the short rate will, all else equal, get closer to θ as a result. The higher the speed of mean reversion k (k is assumed to be positive), the more positive the drift will be. A drawback of this equation is that the short rate can be negative for negative realizations of dB.

The partial differential pricing equation now becomes

$$\frac{\partial P}{dr}[k(\theta - r) - \lambda\sigma] + \frac{\partial P}{dt} + \frac{1}{2}\frac{\partial^2 P}{\partial r^2}\sigma^2 = rP$$

and the boundary condition for a zero-coupon bond paying $1 is

$$P(r, T, T) = 1$$

As with the Merton model, we conjecture that

$$P(r, t, T) = A(\tau)\exp[-B(\tau)r]$$

And there again, the partial derivatives will be

$$\frac{\partial P}{dr} = -A(\tau)B(\tau)\exp[-B(\tau)r]$$

$$\frac{\partial P}{dt} = rA(\tau)B'(\tau)\exp[-B(\tau)r] - A'(\tau)\exp[-B(\tau)r]$$

$$\frac{\partial^2 P}{\partial r^2} = A(\tau)B^2(\tau)\exp[-B(\tau)r]$$

Replacing these expressions in the partial differential equation gives

$$-AB(k\theta - \lambda\sigma) - A' + \frac{1}{2}AB^2\sigma^2 = rA(1 - kB - B')$$

This gives two separable ordinary differential equations:

$$kB + B' = 1$$

with boundary condition $B(0) = 0$ and

$$-AB(k\theta - \lambda\sigma) + \frac{1}{2}AB^2\sigma^2 = A'$$

with boundary condition $A(0) = 1$.

The solutions for A and B follow immediately:

$$A = \exp\left[B\left(\theta - \frac{\lambda\sigma}{k} - \frac{\sigma^2}{k^2}\right) - \left(\theta - \frac{\lambda\sigma}{k} - \frac{\sigma^2}{2k^2}\right)\tau + \left((1 - e^{-2k\tau})\frac{\sigma^2}{4k^3}\right)\right]$$

and

$$B = \frac{1 - e^{-k\tau}}{k}$$

Replacing A and B by their values in $P(r, t, T) = A(\tau)\exp[-B(\tau)r]$ and rearranging terms, we obtain the zero-coupon bond prices:

$$P(r,t,T) = \exp\left\{-R(t,\infty)\tau + [R(t,\infty) - r]\left(\frac{1 - e^{-k\tau}}{k}\right) - \frac{\sigma^2}{4k}\left(\frac{1 - e^{-k\tau}}{k}\right)^2\right\}$$

where $R(t,\infty) \equiv \theta - \frac{\lambda\sigma}{k} - \frac{\sigma^2}{2k^2}$.

Why is this term called $R(t,\infty)$? Calculate the zero-coupon yields:

$$R(t,T) = \frac{-\ln P(r,t,T)}{\tau} = R(t,\infty) - [R(t,\infty) - r]b(\tau) + \frac{\sigma^2\tau}{4k}b^2(\tau)$$

with $b(\tau) = \frac{1 - e^{-k\tau}}{k\tau}$. Then

$$R(t,\infty) = \lim_{\tau \to \infty} R(t,T)$$

13.3.3 The Cox–Ingersoll–Ross Model

The stochastic differential equation for the short rate is now

$$dr = k(\theta - r)dt + \sigma\sqrt{r}dB$$

allowing mean reversion while precluding negative rates. Indeed, when the interest rate is close to zero, the dB term goes to zero, and the rate goes higher.

Generally, for ease of calculation, the market price of risk is expressed as

$$\lambda(r,t) = \frac{\lambda\sqrt{r}}{\sigma}$$

Then the pricing partial differential equation becomes

$$\frac{\partial P}{\partial r}[k\theta - (k + \lambda)r] + \frac{\partial P}{\partial t} + \frac{1}{2}\sigma^2 r\frac{\partial^2 P}{\partial r^2} = rP$$

As in the Merton and Vasicek models, we conjecture that

$$P(r,t,T) = A(\tau)\exp[-B(\tau)r]$$

The partial derivatives are

$$\frac{\partial P}{dr} = -A(\tau)B(\tau)\exp[-B(\tau)r]$$

$$\frac{\partial P}{dt} = rA(\tau)B'(\tau)\exp[-B(\tau)r] - A'(\tau)\exp[-B(\tau)r]$$

$$\frac{\partial^2 P}{\partial r^2} = A(\tau)B^2(\tau)\exp[-B(\tau)r]$$

Replacing these expressions in the partial differential equation gives

$$-ABk\theta - A' + r\left[AB(k+\lambda) + B'A + \frac{1}{2}\sigma^2 AB^2 - A\right] = 0$$

This gives two ordinary differential equations:

$$-ABk\theta - A' = 0$$

and

$$\frac{1}{2}\sigma^2 B^2 + B(k+\lambda) + B' - 1 = 0$$

subject to $A(0) = 1$ and $B(0) = 0$.

The reader can check the following solution:

$$P(r,t,T) = A(\tau)\exp[-B(\tau)r]$$

with

$$A = \left\{\frac{\alpha\exp\left[\left(\dfrac{k+\lambda+\alpha}{2}\right)\tau\right]}{\left(\dfrac{k+\lambda+\alpha}{2}\right)[\exp(\alpha\tau)-1]+\alpha}\right\}^{\beta}$$

$$B = \frac{\exp(\alpha\tau)-1}{\left(\dfrac{k+\lambda+\alpha}{2}\right)[\exp(\alpha\tau)-1]+\alpha}$$

$$\alpha = \sqrt{2\sigma^2 + (k+\lambda)^2}$$

and

$$\beta \equiv \frac{2k\theta}{\sigma^2}$$

The term structure of zero-coupon yields is given by

$$R(t,T) = \frac{-\ln A(\tau) + rB(\tau)}{\tau}$$

13.4 Term-Structure-Consistent Models

13.4.1 The Heath–Jarrow–Morton (HJM) Model

Bond Prices and Forward Rates

A forward rate $f(t, T_1, T_2)$ is the rate agreed on at time t that applies to a loan or a bond starting at T_1 and maturing at T_2. It is easy to see that for $t < T_1 < T_2$,

$$P(t,T_2) = P(t,T_1)e^{-f(t,T_1,T_2)(T_2-T_1)}$$

This is equivalent to

$$f(t,T_1,T_2) = \frac{-1}{T_2 - T_1} \ln \frac{P(t,T_2)}{P(t,T_1)}$$

We now define the instantaneous short forward $f(t, T)$ as the forward rate at time t that applies to a loan starting at T and maturing at $T + dt$. In other words,

$$f(t,T) = \lim_{T_1 \to T_2} \frac{-\ln \dfrac{P(t,T_2)}{P(t,T_1)}}{T_2 - T_1} = -\frac{\partial \ln P}{\partial T}$$

We integrate between t and T to get

$$-\int_t^T f(t,s)ds = \int_t^T -d \ln P(t,s) = \ln P(t,T) - \ln P(t,t)$$

Noting that $\ln P(t, t) = 1$ and taking exponentials, we obtain

$$P(t,T) = \exp\left[-\int_t^T f(t,s)ds\right]$$

This simple relationship expresses the bond price in terms of observable short forwards. It bypasses the difficulties encountered in factor models, where the market risk is hard to estimate.

HJM Derivation

We assume that the forward rate follows an Itô process:

$$df(t,T) = \mu(t,T)dt + \sigma(t,T)dB(t)$$

Using Leibniz rule and because $f(t, t) = r(t)$, we can calculate

$$d\int_t^T -f(t,s)ds = f(t,t)dt - \int_t^T df(t,s)ds$$
$$= r(t)dt - \left[\int_t^T \mu(t,s)ds\right]dt - \left[\int_t^T \sigma(t,s)ds\right]dB(t)$$

From $P(t,T) = \exp\left[-\int_t^T f(t,s)ds\right]$, a simple application of Itô's lemma gives

$$\frac{dP(t,T)}{P(t,T)} = \left\{r(t)dt - \left[\int_t^T \mu(t,s)ds\right]dt + \frac{1}{2}\left[\int_t^T \sigma(t,s)ds\right]^2 dt\right\}$$
$$- \left[\int_t^T \sigma(t,s)ds\right]dB(t)$$

But we know from our analysis of equilibrium models that

$$E_t^Q\left[\frac{dP(t,T)}{P(t,T)}\right] = r(t)dt$$

Hence the drift adjustment for bond price returns is

$$\int_t^T \mu(t,s)ds = \frac{1}{2}\left[\int_t^T \sigma(t,s)ds\right]^2$$

Differentiating both sides with respect to T, we get

$$\mu(t,T) = \sigma(t,T)\int_t^T \sigma(t,s)ds$$

The conclusion is that to preclude arbitrage, we must have

$$df(t,T) = \left[\sigma(t,T)\int_t^T \sigma(t,s)ds\right]dt + \sigma(t,T)dB(t)$$

13.4.2 The Ho–Lee Model as a Special Case of HJM

In the case where $\sigma(t,T) = \sigma$, a scalar, then

$$df(t,T) = \sigma^2(T-t)dt + \sigma dB(t)$$

Integrating between 0 and t, we get

$$\int_0^t df(s,T) = \int_0^t \sigma^2(T-s)ds + \int_0^t \sigma dB(s)$$

The expression for the short forward thus is

$$f(t,T) = f(0,T)\sigma^2 t\left(T - \frac{t}{2}\right) + \sigma B(t)$$

The instantaneous short rate $r(t)$ being equal to $f(t, t)$, it follows that

$$r(t) = f(0,t) + \frac{\sigma^2 t^2}{2} + \sigma B(t)$$

and

$$dr(t) = a(t)dt + \sigma dB(t)$$

with

$$a(t) \equiv f'(0,t) + \frac{\sigma^2 t}{2}$$

Because the drift term involves the derivative of the short forward with respect to time, it can be messy to obtain. It is generally more convenient to obtain the drift term $a(t)$ numerically from a binomial model, as shown next.

13.4.3 Binomial Ho-Lee Model

Equation $dr(t) = a(t)dt + \sigma dB(t)$ can be discretized as

$$r^u = r(0) + a(1)\Delta t + \sigma\sqrt{\Delta t}$$

and

$$r^d = r(0) + a(1)\Delta t - \sigma\sqrt{\Delta t}$$

where r^u and r^d are, respectively, the short rate in the upstate and the short rate in the downstate. For example, a two-period tree would look as follows:

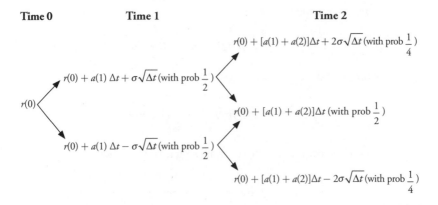

The drift term $a(t)$ is designed to fit the existing term structure. It is in this sense that the Ho-Lee model is term-structure consistent. The following example should clarify the use of this model.

Example: Consider a yield curve with one- and two-year maturities. The zero-coupon yields and prices are as follows:

TABLE 13.2

Maturity (years)	Zero-Coupon Yield (%)	Zero-Coupon Price
1	1	$1/1.01 \approx 0.99$
2	1.5	$1/(1.015)^2 \approx 0.97$

The volatility of the one-year rate is 1%. Find the price of a one-year European call on the two-year zero-coupon bond with a strike of 98.

With $\sigma = 1\%$ and $\Delta t = 1$, the two-period tree for short (one-year) rates is

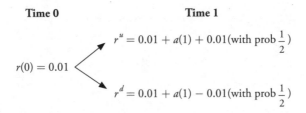

The aim of the exercise is to find $a(1)$. This should enable us to complete the tree and price the European call.

First note that

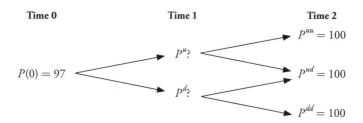

To find P^u and P^d, the upstate and downstate prices of the zero-coupon bond in one year (remember that the two-year bond becomes a one-year bond in one year), note that

$$P^u = \frac{\left(\frac{1}{2} \times 100\right) + \left(\frac{1}{2} \times 100\right)}{1 + r^u} = \frac{\left(\frac{1}{2} \times 100\right) + \left(\frac{1}{2} \times 100\right)}{1.02 + a(1)}$$

and

$$P^d = \frac{\left(\frac{1}{2} \times 100\right) + \left(\frac{1}{2} \times 100\right)}{1 + r^d} = \frac{\left(\frac{1}{2} \times 100\right) + \left(\frac{1}{2} \times 100\right)}{1 + a(1)}$$

One step further in the recursion, we have, in turn,

$$97 = \frac{\left(\frac{1}{2} \times P^u\right) + \left(\frac{1}{2} \times P^d\right)}{1.01} = \frac{\frac{1}{2}\left[\frac{\left(\frac{1}{2} \times 100\right) + \left(\frac{1}{2} \times 100\right)}{1.02 + a(1)}\right] + \frac{1}{2}\left[\frac{\left(\frac{1}{2} \times 100\right) + \left(\frac{1}{2} \times 100\right)}{1 + a(1)}\right]}{1.01}$$

Solve to get $a(1) \approx 0.0108$, $P^u = 97.01$, and $P^d = 98.93$. The price of the European call with strike 98 is then

$$C = \frac{\left(\frac{1}{2} \times C^u\right) + \left(\frac{1}{2} \times C^d\right)}{1.01} = \frac{\left[\frac{1}{2} \times \max(0, 97.01 - 98)\right] + \left[\frac{1}{2} \times \max(0, 98.93 - 98)\right]}{1.01} \approx 0.46$$

14
Risk Premia

Summary

A risk premium is defined as the expected return on an asset minus the expected return on the risk-free asset. Equivalently, it is the difference between the forward price and the expected value on the underlying asset.

Siegel's paradox ensures that as long as there is randomness, risk premia are prevalent in all asset classes.

Two famous risk premium puzzles, the equity risk premium puzzle and the risk-free rate puzzle, state that the observed equity risk premium is too high and the observed risk-free rate is too low compared with model predictions. These puzzles shed some light on the failings of standard models.

There are a number of risk premium narratives. They are largely compatible, if only because it is so unlikely that we will ever derive a unified theory of risk premia.

These risk premium narratives tackle the risk problem from various angles: the more procyclical an asset is, the higher is its risk premium; if its returns are negatively skewed, this also explains a higher premium; habit formation and disaster risk also can account for the discrepancies between observations and theory. We discuss a number of alternative explanations, including dubious statistical practices that find risk premia where there are none.

Another way of describing a risk premium is by gauging the difference between physical and martingale probabilities of return. In a simple binomial model, for example, the difference between the physical and the martingale probabilities of one-period return is about half a Sharpe ratio.

Taken to their logical extremes, risk premia can result into somewhat surprising paradoxes: long-dated puts can appear to be extremely "expensive" and long-dated calls extremely "cheap."

14.1 Basics of Risk Premia

We introduce the topic of risk premia by giving a motivating example and then showing that risk premia are ubiquitous across asset classes. We then discuss basic expressions of risk premia for stocks and bonds and review associated puzzles.

14.1.1 An Offer You Cannot Refuse

Loyal reader, we offer you a deal you cannot refuse. Every year for the next 10 years, we will give you the return on the Standard & Poor's 500 Index (S&P 500). And every year for the next 10 years, you give us the return on the 1-year T-bill. Suppose that the notional amount is $1 billion. Suppose in addition that you and we are solvent and that credit risk is no object. How much is this deal worth to you? Naturally, you would want to backtest this trade by looking at its historical profit and loss. It turns out, as many of our readers already know, that the S&P 500 has outperformed the 1-year T-bill by about 7% over the last century. If history is any guide, we are giving you the equivalent of $70 million a year, on average, for the next 10 years. If, as mentioned, you are not money constrained, how much is this deal worth to you? Most financially literate colleagues to whom this deal was offered said that they would be willing to offer north of $100 million to access this deal. And yet . . .

All this is a standard debt–equity swap. Its cash flows can be trivially replicated by entering a 1-year forward contract on the S&P 500 and rolling this contract over for another 9 years. The cost of manufacturing forward contracts is zero. So you should not be willing to pay anything for the deal we offered you. As a matter of fact, S&P 500 futures contracts can be entered for free by many qualified individual investors. So what's the catch? Why is a deal worth an average $70 million a year (based on history) for the next 10 years accessible for free? Do perpetual money machines really exist in finance?

The answer is evidently "No." A historical average is just an average. It is said that statistics is the only discipline that tells you that if your head is in the oven and your feet are in the freezer, you are doing well, on average. Of course, there is plenty of risk around that average. There are crashes and booms. And investors need to be paid a premium to compensate them for that risk. On a more technical level, under this swap you were just offered, the T-bill leg (meaning cash flows) should be discounted by the T-bill yield, whereas the S&P 500 equity leg should be discounted at the S&P 500 equity yield, typically higher than the T-bill yield. *The difference between the two yields is the so-called equity risk premium.* When cash flows are properly discounted, the value of the deal at inception is zero.

To give another example, buying a 2-year bond and financing it monthly is a trading strategy that has proven historically profitable. Like the equity–T-bill swap, this 2-year versus 1-month swap benefits from a risk premium: it is sometimes called the *front-end risk premium*, or *duration extension risk premium*. We will have more to say about duration extension later in this chapter. Here again, the net present value at inception is zero. The expected value under the physical measure is positive. And the trade is evidently risky: for example, aggressive sudden interest-rate hikes by the central bank may invert the curve and cause substantial losses.

14.1.2 Risk Premia Everywhere: Siegel's Paradox

Equivalently, one can define the risk premium as the difference between the forward price and the expected value of the underlying asset. To many practitioners, the forward price is the best predictor of price. For example, the so-called uncovered interest parity says that the forward price of a currency is the expected value of that currency or that it is an unbiased predictor of the currency value, meaning that the risk premium is zero. This is expressed as

$$F_{t,T} = E_t(S_T)$$

where $F_{t,T}$ is the forward price at time t of a currency contract expiring at time T, and $E_t(S_T)$ is the expected value at time t of the currency value at T. This is the same as saying that there is no risk premium in foreign exchange markets.

But it is straightforward to prove that this can never happen, except in the degenerate case of deterministic markets. Indeed, if $F_{t,T}$ is the forward price of a euro in dollars and S_T is the price at T of a euro in dollars, then for forwards to be unbiased predictors of future prices in all generality, this relationship also should hold for the price of a dollar in euros; that is,

$$\frac{1}{F_{t,T}} = E_t\left(\frac{1}{S_T}\right)$$

But $F_{t,T} = E_t(S_T)$ and $\dfrac{1}{F_{t,T}} = E_t\left(\dfrac{1}{S_T}\right)$ taken together imply that

$$\frac{1}{E_t(S_T)} = E_t\left(\frac{1}{S_T}\right)$$

But this can never happen by Jensen's inequality except if S is deterministic. Generally,

$$E_t(S_T) > \frac{1}{E_t\left(\dfrac{1}{S_T}\right)}$$

In short,

$$F_{t,T} \neq E_t(S_T)$$

More revealing, perhaps, is the fact that this example is not just about exchange rates: it is about any price. Replace euros by butter and dollars by guns and you realize that Siegel's paradox applies to any relative or absolute price. *Risk premia are the rule, not the exception, across all asset classes and all prices.*

Also note that the expected value of the dollar in euros can be equal to the expected value of the euro in dollars. Assume that the current dollar per euro exchange rate is one and can take two possible values (2 or ½) in 1 year with equal probabilities:

So the expected value of that exchange rate is $1.25 per euro. Looking at the value of a dollar in euros, the tree is therefore

And the expected value of that exchange rate is 1.25 euros per dollar! Assuming that the value X of a euro in dollars follows a geometric Brownian motion:

$$\frac{dX}{X} = \mu dt + \sigma dW$$

Then, by Itô's lemma, the value of a dollar in euros, $Y \equiv 1/X$, follows the process

$$\frac{dY}{Y} = (\sigma^2 - \mu)dt - \sigma dW$$

and

$$E\left(\frac{dX}{X}\right) = E\left(\frac{dY}{Y}\right)$$

When $\mu = \sigma^2/2$. It can be shown that in a wide variety of cases such as the one shown here, dollar-based investors and euro-based investors can both improve their expected returns by holding foreign currencies (meaning foreign to their domestic consumption basket).

Be that as it may, the main conclusion is that risk premia are prevalent across all asset classes. This conclusion is model free because we have not assumed much to obtain it. Siegel's paradox is also largely silent on the sign of risk premia. In what follows, we try to put a sign on these risk premia and motivate their existence.

14.1.3 Equity Premium, Risk-Free Rate, and Related Puzzles

The equity premium puzzle and, to a lesser extent, the risk-free rate puzzle are *causes célèbres* in the financial literature. We will discuss them briefly. But first, we remind our readers of standard expressions of the equity premium and the risk-free rate.

Recall from Chapter 10 that in a consumption capital assets pricing model (CAPM) world with constant relative risk-aversion (CRRA) utility, the risk-free rate is

$$r = \theta + \gamma g - \frac{\gamma^2 \sigma^2}{2}$$

with θ being the rate of time preference, γ the risk-aversion coefficient, and g and σ^2 the mean and variance of log consumption growth. We reformulate slightly the risky asset equation from Chapter 10 to get the expression for the expected *net* return of a risky asset r_i:

$$E(r_i) = r + \gamma \sigma \sigma_{r_i} \operatorname{corr}\left[\ln\frac{C_{t+1}}{C_t}, r_i \right]$$

because $\sigma \sigma_{r_i} \operatorname{corr}\left[\ln\frac{C_{t+1}}{C_t}, r_i \right] = \operatorname{cov}\left[\ln\frac{C_{t+1}}{C_t}, r_i \right]$. The equity risk premium is therefore

$$E(r_i) - r = \gamma \sigma \sigma_{r_i} \operatorname{corr}\left[\ln\frac{C_{t+1}}{C_t}, r_i \right]$$

Plausible historical values for the S&P 500 real return, the US real risk-free rate, and the US real consumption parameters are

$$E(r_i) = 8\%;\ r = 1\%;\ \sigma = 1.5\%;\ \sigma_{r_i} = 17\%;\ \text{and}\ \operatorname{corr}\left[\ln\frac{C_{t+1}}{C_t}, r_i \right] = 0.4$$

So the historical equity risk premium in the United States is close to 7%. The risk-aversion coefficient γ that solves for the equity risk premium is close to 68. This is a gross overestimation of the risk-aversion coefficient that, on the basis of surveys and plausible experience, is generally assumed to be between 2 and 5. This, in a nutshell, is the equity premium puzzle. Expressed differently, for reasonable values of covariance and risk-aversion parameters, the equity risk premium should have been lower than 1%, whereas it turned out to be close to 7%.

So either the United States got lucky, or the parameters are very wrong, or the model is misspecified (or, what is most likely, all of the above). Assume for a moment that we hang our hat on the luck factor: The US equity risk premium is the product of dumb luck. Then we are still left with another major puzzle: how do we explain the risk-free rate? As mentioned earlier, the US real risk-free rate has been close to a 1% historical average. With our set of plausible parameters and $\theta = 1\%$, $g = 1\%$, and $\gamma = 3$, we find that the real risk-free rate should be close to 4%, about four times higher than observed.

Or say that we want to do away with the equity risk premium by assuming a risk-aversion factor of 68 instead of 3. Then the real risk-free rate ought to be 17%, far too high. We are in a pickle: no matter the assumptions, the observed average risk-free rate appears to be far too low against the model. We will say more on this later.

14.1.4 Term Structure Premia

We now proceed to use the Merton toy model of the term structure to extract a few useful measures of term structure premia. Recall four equations of the Merton model from Chapter 13. The short rate follows a simple arithmetic Brownian motion:

$$dr = \mu dt + \sigma dB$$

Under the Q probability measure, the short rate follows an arithmetic Brownian motion of the form

$$dr = (\mu - \lambda \sigma)dt + \sigma dB^Q$$

where λ is defined as the market price of risk.

The solution for the zero-coupon price at time t across all maturities $\tau = T - t$ is

$$P(r, t, T) = \exp\left[-r\tau - \frac{\tau^2}{2}(\mu - \lambda\sigma) + \frac{\sigma^2 \tau^3}{6} \right]$$

And the term structure of zero-coupon yields is given by

$$R(t, T) = \frac{-\ln P(r, t, T)}{\tau} = r + \frac{\tau}{2}(\mu - \lambda\sigma) - \frac{\sigma^2 \tau^2}{6}$$

How do we represent interest-rate premia based on this equation?

The futures premium is the difference between the futures rate—that is, the expectation of the short rate under the martingale measure Q—and the expected short rate over the same maturity. The futures rate is

$$E_t^Q(r_T) = r + (\mu - \lambda\sigma)\tau$$

The expected short rate is

$$E_t(r_T) = r + \mu\tau$$

and the futures premium over a given maturity is

$$\text{Futures rate premium} = E_t^Q(r_T) - E_t(r_T) = -\lambda\sigma\tau$$

This is, more often than not, positive. Recall that $\lambda = (a - r)/b$ and is, on average, negative. Indeed, $a > r$ insofar as investors require compensation for holding a risky long bond versus an instantaneous money-market account. Also recall that

$$b \equiv \frac{\dfrac{\partial P}{\partial r}\sigma}{P}$$

is negative because $\partial P/\partial r < 0$ for standard zero-coupon bonds. This is a way of saying that buying interest-rate futures (i.e., betting on lower short rates) makes money on average.

How about the slope of the yield curve? Do bond yields increase with maturity? In fact,

$$\frac{\partial R}{\partial \tau} = \frac{\mu - \lambda\sigma}{2} - \frac{\sigma^2\tau}{3}$$

For $\mu \leq \lambda\sigma$, the slope is negative. For $\mu > \lambda\sigma$, the curve is humped. Lastly, remember from Chapter 13 that a short forward is given by

$$f(t, T) = -\frac{\partial \ln P}{\partial T}$$

In the Merton model, this is

$$f(t, T) = r + (\mu - \lambda\sigma)\tau - \frac{\sigma^2\tau^2}{2}$$

which shows that a forward rate is always lower than a future rate. The difference is called a *convexity adjustment* (for fixed-income geeks, this is because a forward promises to deliver a very short-maturity bond and therefore has a hyperbolic payoff, whereas a future contract has a linear payoff). Thus

$$\text{Convexity adjustment} = E_t^Q(r_T) - f(t,T) = \frac{\sigma^2 \tau^2}{2}$$

And the forward risk premium, defined as the difference between the short forward and the expected short rate, is

$$\text{Forward risk premium} = f(t,T) - E_t(r_T) = -\lambda \sigma \tau - \frac{\sigma^2 \tau^2}{2}$$

The forward risk premium is positive if the futures risk premium dominates the convexity adjustment. It is a decreasing function of τ.

All these results are, of course, extracted from an elementary model of the term structure. But there is virtue in simplicity because Merton's model highlights a number of intuitive properties of bond risk premia.

14.2 Ten Narratives of the Risk Premium

As discussed in Chapter 10, the intertemporal CAPM relates the risk premium on every asset i to the market and to a number of state variables. That is,

$$\mu_i - r = \beta_i (\mu_M - r) + \sum_{j=1}^{m} \beta_i^j (\mu_j - r)$$

where $\mu_i - r$ is the expected risk premium on asset i ($i = 1, ..., n$), β_i and the β_i^j's are multiple regression coefficients of asset i risk premium on the market risk premium ($\mu_M - r$) and m state variable risk premia ($\mu_j - r$) with $j = 1, ..., m$. In this context, there are ($m + 1$) stories of the risk premium. We will select ten appealing narratives below, bearing in mind that every trader and investor has his or her own narratives. You can, at a stretch, think of these narratives as different risk premia.

14.2.1 Covariance with Rainy Days

This is the dominant paradigm in academic asset pricing. Economic agents value insurance: an umbrella when it rains is more valuable than an umbrella when it is sunny. Insurance (countercyclical) assets attract more demand and therefore have higher prices and lower expected returns than anti-insurance (pro-cyclical) assets.

Example (Equity Risk Premium): The general equation for the equity risk premium is

$$E(R_i) - R_f = \frac{\text{cov}[-U'(C_{t+1}), R_i]}{E[U'(C_{t+1})]}$$

Here $-U'(C_{t+1})$ increases with consumption. As mentioned earlier, the equity risk premium is positive when the equity return covaries positively with consumption. This point has been made abundantly clear, and the reader can refer to Chapter 10 for details.

Example (Inflation Risk Premium): We define the inflation risk premium as the difference between breakeven inflation and expected inflation. Breakeven inflation is the difference between the nominal yield (the yield on a nominal bond) and the real yield (the yield on an inflation-indexed bond) of equal maturities. To calculate this risk premium, we use the standard consumption-based pricing model. Consider an agent choosing the amount of nominal bonds she purchases to optimize utility

$$\max_{C_t} u(C_t) + E_t \beta u(C_{t+1})$$

$$\text{subject to } C_t = W_t - B_t$$

$$\text{and } \Pi_{t+1} C_{t+1} = B_t I$$

where C_t is the real consumption at t, β is the time preference discount factor, W_t is the initial real endowment, B_t is the amount of nominal bonds purchased, Π_{t+1} is the (stochastic) gross rate of inflation between t and $t+1$, and I is the (known) gross nominal interest rate. Then the first-order condition implies that

$$u'(C_t) = E_t \left[\beta u'(C_{t+1}) \frac{I}{\Pi_{t+1}} \right]$$

or

$$E_t \left(\frac{M_{t+1}}{\Pi_{t+1}} \right) = \frac{1}{I} \tag{14.1}$$

with the stochastic discount factor

$$M_{t+1} \equiv \frac{\beta u'(C_{t+1})}{u'(C_t)}$$

Consider the case of log utility

$$u(C) = \ln(C)$$

In this case,

$$M_{t+1} = \beta \left(\frac{C_{t+1}}{C_t} \right)^{-1}$$

Now define log consumption growth $\ln C_{t+1}/C_t = g_{t+1}$ and log inflation $\ln \Pi_{t+1}$ $= \pi_{t+1}$, and assume that log consumption growth and log inflation are jointly normally distributed. That is,

$$\begin{bmatrix} g_{t+1} \\ \pi_{t+1} \end{bmatrix} \sim N\left(\begin{bmatrix} \mu_c \\ \mu_\pi \end{bmatrix}, \begin{bmatrix} \sigma_c^2 & \sigma_{c\pi} \\ \sigma_{c\pi} & \sigma_\pi^2 \end{bmatrix} \right)$$

Thus Equation (14.1) can be rewritten as

$$\ln \frac{1}{I} = -i = \ln E_t \left(M_{t+1} \frac{1}{\Pi_{t+1}} \right) = \ln \beta E_t [\exp(-g_{t+1} - \pi_{t+1})]$$

With the log-normal assumption, we arrive at the following equation for the log nominal interest rate:

$$i = -\ln \beta + \mu_c - \frac{1}{2}\sigma_c^2 + \mu_\pi - \frac{1}{2}\sigma_\pi^2 - \sigma_{c\pi}$$

Recall that the real interest rate $r = -\ln E(M_{t+1})$. Because breakeven inflation is the difference between nominal and real rates, we obtain

$$\text{Inflation risk premium} = i - r - E(\pi) = -\frac{1}{2}(\sigma_\pi^2 + 2\sigma_{c\pi})$$

How do we interpret this result? If the covariance between inflation and consumption growth is positive (what one might call a "normal" Phillips curve), then a nominal bond will appreciate in times of negative growth (because inflation decreases). This means that a nominal bond will be sought after: its price is high and its expected return low relative to an inflation-indexed bond. Under these circumstances, the inflation risk premium is negative.

To give further intuition, note that $-\frac{1}{2}(\sigma_\pi^2 + 2\sigma_{c\pi}) = -\frac{1}{2}(\sigma_\pi^2 + 2\sigma_{c\pi}$ $+\sigma_c^2 - \sigma_c^2)$ and $\sigma_\pi^2 + 2\sigma_{c\pi} + \sigma_c^2 = \text{var}(\pi + c)$, or the variance of nominal consumption growth. It follows that

$$\text{Inflation risk premium} = -\frac{\text{var(nominal growth)} - \text{var(real growth)}}{2}$$

The higher the covariance between inflation and consumption growth and the higher the difference between nominal and real growth volatility, the more investors will want inflation-linked bonds and the lower will be the inflation risk premium.

14.2.2 Habit Formation

Among the many valiant attempts to resolve the equity premium puzzle, a plausible solution is given by the so-called habit-formation hypothesis. Agents maximize

$$E \sum_{t=0}^{\infty} \beta^t u(C_t)$$

where

$$u(C_t) \equiv \frac{(C_t - X_t)^{1-\gamma} - 1}{1 - \gamma}$$

The game changer in this habit equation is X_t. Think about X_t as a minimum consumption level that agents cling to or as a psychological subsistence level. Then the relative risk-aversion curvature (RRAC) is

$$\text{RRAC} = \frac{-C_t u_{CC}}{u_C} = \gamma \frac{C_t}{C_t - X_t}$$

As consumption C_t converges toward the subsistence level X_t, the RRAC goes to infinity, so a given change in consumption generates a large change in the RRAC and a time-varying equity risk premium. Because consumption is far above the minimum level, the RRAC is low, and the market does well, and vice versa. Small changes in consumption can result in large variations in $1/(C_t - X_t)$ and can explain high levels of equity returns for reasonable levels of the risk-aversion curvature. There is no need to tweak γ to explain the risk premium puzzle and market cycles: a small γ is compatible with a large curvature.[1]

14.2.3 Survivorship Bias and Disaster Risk

Financial data are a luxury good and are found mostly in rich countries. Often, poor countries are too busy surviving and cannot always afford data analysts and statisticians. In extreme cases, in markets that disappear because of crises, wars, institutional failures, or political regime changes, market data disappear or are hard to find.

---

1 For details, please see Campbell and Cochrane (1999).

It is fair to say that most stock data analyzed are US data. Yet the United States is first in its class, an order statistic. If this is true, then data analysis may lead to some unwarranted optimism about economic and financial performance. For example, if US equity performance is due to good luck, then maybe there is no equity premium puzzle, and US equity return forecasts that extrapolate from past performance should be more restrained.

The impact of survivorship bias is substantial. For example, Jorion and Goetzmann (1999) analyzed a sample of 39 markets from 1921 to 1996, including markets subject to temporary and permanent interruptions. Their conclusion was that US equities had a real return of appreciation of 4.3% versus a median of 0.8% for the remaining countries. This would point to the fact that equity returns are way lower than what is commonly believed.

Another implication of survivorship bias in the data is skepticism toward mean reversion: if you analyze survivors' data, then your research will be biased toward mean reversion in returns. Why? Because an index that disappears is an example of mean aversion—a low price going to zero. Jorion (2003) analyzed 30 equity markets from 1921 to 1996 and found no evidence in favor of mean reversion. Because mean reversion implies lower long-term volatility and therefore a higher allocation to equity, Jorion's findings argue for a lower equity allocation.

A related narrative explains the equity premium puzzle by evaluating disaster risk. For example, Barro (2006) suggests a disaster probability of 1.5%–2.5% per year across countries with per capita gross domestic product (GDP) declines between 15% and 64%. He builds a model of the equity premium that accounts for those jumps and finds ex ante estimates that appear to explain both the equity premium puzzle and the real rate puzzle.

14.2.4 Skewness

Because the basic asset pricing model assumes normality of returns, there is little room for higher-order moments on the standard finance menu. Higher-order moments can be accommodated by assuming nonnormality or by adding a jump to the stochastic process.

We will focus on the third moment of returns, also called *skewness*. If an asset return X has mean μ and volatility σ, then skewness s is defined as

$$s \equiv E\left[\left(\frac{X - \mu}{\sigma}\right)^3\right]$$

Skewness measures the asymmetry of the return distribution. For example, broad stock indices tend to be negatively skewed, whereas single stocks display positive skewness. For a normal distribution, for $n \geq 0$, we have

$$E\left[\left(\frac{X-\mu}{\sigma}\right)^n\right] = \begin{cases} 0 & \text{for odd } n \\ (n-1)!! & \text{for even } n \end{cases}$$

where $(n-1)!!$ is the product of all the integers from 1 to $(n-1)$ that have the same parity. For $n \geq 4$, $(n-1)!! \equiv (n-1)(n-3)\cdots$.

The skewness of a normal distribution is zero. Positive (negative) skewness means that the distribution has a longer right (left) tail. It stands to reason that investors dislike negative skewness. Why? For evolutionary reasons, some may claim. Because left-tail events can be life terminating, strong risk aversion is the price to pay for survival and for mitigating extreme risk events. We may, as a result, overstate the probability of adverse events. Under these preferences and biases, negatively skewed assets will be "offered"; their price will be low and their expected return high. As an example of negative skew leading to positive expecting returns, we discuss volatility selling and seek to explain the volatility risk premium.

Example (Volatility Risk Premium): The volatility implied by option prices tends to be higher than the volatility realized by the underlying asset returns. The difference between implied and expected realized volatility is called the *volatility risk premium*. We discuss this premium by detailing the economics of a volatility-selling trade.

Volatility selling (buying) consists of selling (buying) an option and delta hedging it so as to avoid first-order directional risk on the underlying asset. A non-dividend-paying asset's price S follows $dS/S = \mu dt + \sigma dW$. An investor sells a call with value C_0 at time zero

$$C_0 = C(\sigma_I, S_0, K, 0, T)$$

where σ_I is the implied volatility (i.e., the volatility that, when input into the BMS option-pricing formula, returns the call value), S_0 is the underlying value at time zero, K is the strike price, current time is 0, and T is the time to expiration of the call. The investor is short a call while continuously delta hedging it. Continuous delta hedging involves holding at each instant t a number $\Delta_t = \partial C(\sigma_I, S_0, K, t, T)/\partial S$ of units of the underlying asset and holding $C(\sigma_I, S_0, K, t, T) - \Delta_t S_t$

(which is negative) in the risk-free asset. The risk-free rate r is constant. The total net profits from this strategy have three components: the premium received at time 0, the liability on the short option equal to $-\max[S(T) - K, 0]$, and the profits from the delta hedge.

The profits from the delta hedge are

$$\int_0^T \Delta_t \, dS_t + r \int_0^T [C(\sigma_I, S_0, K, t, T) - \Delta_t S_t] \, dt$$

The total net profits from this strategy thus are

$$-\max[S(T) - K, 0] + C_0 + \int_0^T \Delta_t \, dS_t + r \int_0^T [C(\sigma_I, S_0, K, t, T) - \Delta_t S_t] \, dt$$

Note that $\max[S(T) - K, 0] = C(\sigma_I, S_T, K, T, T)$. Dropping the time indices where not needed, we get, by Itô's lemma,

$$C(\sigma_I, S_T, K, T, T) = C_0 + \int_0^T \frac{\partial C}{\partial S} \, dS + \int_0^T \frac{1}{2} \frac{\partial^2 C}{\partial S^2} \sigma^2 S^2 \, dt + \int_0^T \frac{\partial C}{\partial t} \, dt$$

Note that the call pricing dynamics use the realized (not the implied) volatility σ. Using the BMS partial differential equation $rS \frac{\partial C}{\partial S} + \frac{1}{2} \frac{\partial^2 C}{\partial S^2} \sigma_I^2 S^2 + \frac{\partial C}{\partial t} = rC$ to substitute for the last term of the preceding equation, we get

$$C(\sigma_I, S_T, K, T, T) = C_0 + \int_0^T \frac{\partial C}{\partial S} \, dS + \int_0^T \frac{1}{2} \frac{\partial^2 C}{\partial S^2} \sigma^2 S^2 \, dt + \int_0^T r \left[C - S \frac{\partial C}{\partial S} \right] dt$$
$$- \int_0^T \frac{1}{2} \frac{\partial^2 C}{\partial S^2} \sigma_I^2 S^2 \, dt$$

This allows us to recover a simple expression for the total net profits:

$$-\max[S(T) - K, 0] + C_0 + \int_0^T \Delta_t S_t \, dt + r \int_0^T [C(\sigma_I, S_0, K, t, T) - \Delta_t S_t] \, dt$$
$$= \int_0^T \frac{1}{2} \frac{\partial^2 C}{\partial S^2} (\sigma_I^2 - \sigma_t^2) S^2 \, dt$$

So the upshot is that

Net profits from a delta-hedged volatility sale $= \int_0^T \frac{1}{2} \frac{\partial^2 C}{\partial S^2} (\sigma_I^2 - \sigma_t^2) S^2 \, dt$

One can see why the short volatility trade is skewed: all else equal, an increase in realized volatility increases the loss parabolically. Because investors are averse to negative skewness, they will buy volatility (bid up implied volatility) until the wedge between implied and expected volatility—also called the *volatility risk premium*—is high enough to make up for their aversion to the risks embedded in that trade.

There are other candidate explanations for the volatility risk premium. For example, we know that leverage and consumption growth are highly correlated. In recessions, balance-sheet leverage increases because equity values fall more than debt values on balance sheets, and so does equity volatility. Volatility is therefore anticyclic: its price, implied volatility, is high relative to realized volatility.

Example (Momentum Trading): Momentum trading is a strategy that consists of buying recent winners and selling recent losers. *Recent* has conventionally meant 200 or 300 trading days: So, to take a naïve example, if an asset is trading above its 200-day moving average, you buy it. In the alternative, you sell it. Momentum is a factor that has done consistently well across long data samples. The question is, why? We argue that as in short-volatility trades, negative skewness may explain the positive performance.

Let us illustrate this point by showing a simple model by Dao et al. (2016): a security priced at S_t at time t is bought (sold) if $S_t - S_0$ is positive (negative). The number of securities bought or sold is $S_t - S_0$. In other words, it is proportional to the size of the signal. Then the daily profit from day $t - 1$ to day t is

$$P_t = (\Delta S_t)(S_{t-1} - S_0) = \Delta S_t \sum_{i=1}^{t-1} \Delta S_i$$

The cumulative profit up to some time τ is

$$\sum_{t=2}^{\tau} P_t = \sum_{t=2}^{\tau} \Delta S_t \sum_{i=1}^{t-1} \Delta S_i = \sum_{\substack{2 \leq t \leq \tau \\ i < t}} \Delta S_t \Delta S_i$$

Note that $P_1 = 0$. But we know that

$$2 \sum_{\substack{1 \leq t \leq \tau \\ i < t}} \Delta S_t \Delta S_i = \left(\sum_{t=1}^{\tau} \Delta S_t \right)^2 - \sum_{t=1}^{\tau} \Delta S_t^2$$

It follows that

$$2 \sum_{t=1}^{\tau} P_t = (S_t - S_0)^2 - \sum_{t=1}^{\tau} \Delta S_t^2$$

And therefore, the expected profits are

$$\text{Expected profits} = \frac{1}{2}\left[E(S_t - S_0)^2 - E\left(\sum_{t=1}^{\tau}\Delta S_t^2\right)\right]$$

This expression shows that the momentum strategy is long long-dated variance and short short-dated variance. Evidently, the more positively autocorrelated the returns, the greater is the difference between long- and short-dated realized variances and the higher are the profits.

This expression also shows that a momentum buyer is exposed to crash risk to the extent that a crash is generally associated with a spike in short-dated variance. This is why the momentum risk premium is sometimes interpreted as compensation for crash risk.

Both the short-volatility and momentum-trading stories are explained at least in part by aversion to negative skewness. But this skewness narrative is not always valid. One can even conjecture that much as in the case of volatility trading, some investors may relish left tails and avoid positive skewness for reasons discussed below.

14.2.5 Method in the Madness: Bubbles and the Value Factor

Not all money dislikes negative skewness. We now show a counterexample arising in asset management that may go a long way toward explaining bubbles and the failure of value investing. Picture an "expensive" asset priced at 100 with a fundamental value of 50. Assume that its expected (continuously compounded) return is −3%. Over the next period, it can take one of two values: it can either become even more expensive at 115 with probability p or come back to its fundamental value of 50 with probability $1 - p$. This asset therefore has less upside than downside and has a negative expected return, two typical characteristics of expensive assets.

The first question is, what is p? In other words, what is the probability that expensive gets even more expensive? The answer is given by

$$100 = [115p + 50(1 - p)]e^{-(-0.03)}$$

Hence $p = 0.72$. This tells you that for a bubble to be sustainable at equilibrium, the probability of a continued bull market must be high.

So far so good. But a more consequential question is, will investors sell this asset? Because, after all, one should expect informed investors to sell, not buy, an expensive asset. Yet, consider the following situation: a risk-neutral asset manager is paid a fixed fee of one per period and wants to maximize his expected lifetime gains. Assume further that he receives his fixed fee as long as he makes money. If he ever loses money, he is fired at year end. Should he buy or sell?

If he buys the asset, his life expectancy or, equivalently, his net expected lifetime income is

$$\frac{1}{1-p} = 3.57$$

If he sells the asset, his net expected lifetime income is

$$\frac{1}{p} = 1.39$$

In this simple example, you buy the expensive asset and keep chasing the trend. Clearly, the asset manager's (or delegated money's) incentive is to buy high and sell low because the upside probability (or, equivalently, lifetime income, which is higher when you buy than when you sell) matters more than the expected return (which is negative when you buy).

Note that even under less stringent work conditions, the incentive can still be lopsided: say that if he is long and loses money, the asset manager is fired that same year as before. If he is short and loses money, he gets only fired after n years (if only because losses are less substantial than in the long case). In this case, one can prove that the net expected lifetime income of the short is

$$\frac{p^{-n} - 1}{1-p}$$

whereas the net expected lifetime income of the long is still $1/(1-p)$. As long as $n < -\ln 2/\ln p$, delegated money will still want to buy high and sell low.

Unlike in previous examples, investors (in this case delegated money) may be willing to pay for negative skewness because it increases their expected lifetime incomes. This example may explain why expensive assets are bought and cheap assets are sold. There is method in the madness. Buying high and selling low may be perfectly rational in the presence of wrong incentives, in this case a combination of fixed fees and payoff asymmetries. This can lead to return chasing, excessive reliance on momentum, and failure of value investing. All these themes have been known to endure in periods of market exuberance.[2]

---

2 For details, see Baz et al. (2020).

14.2.6 Clientele Effects

Preferred habitats express the idea that investors or investor groups favor specific market segments and, by influencing net demand, end up driving risk premia in these markets. Two examples come to mind: the term structures of both interest rates and commodity futures curves are influenced by investor clienteles with idiosyncratic preferences.

Example (Preferred Habitats and the Duration Risk Premium): Culbertson (1957) and Modigliani and Sutch (1966) discussed the role of preferred habitats in the term structure of interest rates. Investors—bank depositors or buyers of short fixed-income paper—tend to prefer the short end to the longer end of the curve. The reason may be preference for liquidity or aversion to interest-rate risk. This results in excess demand for short bonds, making them expensive versus long bonds. Prices on the long end of the term structure become lower and yields become higher than on the short end. Under these conditions, interest-rate futures levels are, more often than not, higher than expected rates. Investors with no marked preferences such as mutual funds or arbitrageurs will then favor duration-extension trades, meaning long maturities. Leveraged arbitrageurs typically will take advantage of preferred habitats by buying the long end and financing their purchases in short maturities. This is also known as the *carry and roll-down trade*, as arbitrageurs take advantage of both the difference between the rates on the long and short positions and the long yield rolling down the curve as the trade ages.

Example (Backwardation and Commodity Risk Premium): A similar idea applies to the commodity futures curve. Both Keynes and Hicks stated that commodity producers went normally short commodity futures to hedge their physical inventories.[3] This means excess supply in futures contracts, resulting in lower prices. This, it is claimed, is why commodity futures curves are often downward sloping. This is also called *normal backwardation*.

In a backwardation, a futures price tends to be lower than the expected commodity spot price. In similar fashion to the carry, roll-down trade in fixed income, arbitrageurs buy the short-maturity futures in the hope that they will appreciate by rolling up to the spot commodity price. A trade similar in spirit is the so-called calendar spread trade, where investors tend to

---

3 See Keynes (1930) and Hicks (1946).

buy futures contracts with different expiration months (in a backwardation, traders generally buy a liquid contract further down the commodity futures curve against the front-month contract) to take advantage of the curve shape.

14.2.7 Leverage Aversion

All else being equal, investors tend to dislike leverage. Yet there is no room for leverage aversion in conventional portfolio theory. Leverage aversion may arise from investment guideline constraints, rules, and procedures or from the (largely justified) belief that volatility is not sufficient to capture the risk in a leveraged trade: After all, lenders may decide to discontinue the liquidity they offer to leveraged investors in a financial crisis while simultaneously the long end of the leveraged trade sells off. Many hedge funds incurred substantial losses or went bankrupt under these circumstances.

Leverage aversion means that an investor is willing to trade beta against leverage. If this is true, then there is excess demand for high-beta assets. This makes them expensive versus low-beta assets. A competing explanation for expensive high-beta assets is that investors like positive skewness and will pay high prices for high-risk assets with lottery-like payoffs.

We give two examples of risk premia that leverage aversion may explain: the low-beta premium and the yield-curve-steepness premium.

Example (The Low-Beta Premium): Leverage-constrained investors managing equity portfolios against an S&P 500 benchmark may want to buy high-beta equity to maximize their expected return and their probability of outperformance against their benchmark. The price of high-beta equity increases, and its expected return drops as a result. This helps explain the so-called low-beta anomaly: the security market line is flatter than predicted by the CAPM. Asset managers exploit this so-called low-beta defensive premium by forming long low-beta, short high-beta equity portfolios.

Example (The Yield-Curve-Steepness Premium): As in the preceding example, leverage-constrained investors managing a bond portfolio against a bond index will want to buy the highest-yielding bonds. In a "normal" upward-sloping yield curve, this means buying long-maturity bonds. Excess demand on long-maturity bonds makes them expensive versus short-maturity bonds. This steepness premium can be exploited by entering a so-called steepener trade, that is, a short position in long-maturity bonds versus a long position in short-maturity bonds, duration weighted.

14.2.8 Patience

It is said that patience is bitter but its fruit is sweet. Amihud and Mendelson (1986a, 1986b) show that patient investors end up collecting a liquidity premium over and above the returns received by less patient investors. We illustrate this intuition with a simple numerical example.

Example (Liquidity Risk Premium and Investor Patience): Assume an economy with a risk-free rate of 1.5% and with two types of assets and two types of investors: there is a liquid security trading at a bid–ask spread of 0.5% and an illiquid security trading at a bid–ask spread of 5%, and there is a short-term investor with an average holding horizon of 3 months and a long-term investor with a holding horizon of 10 years. If investors are risk neutral, then the expected return of the liquid security net of transaction costs should be the risk-free rate of 1.5%. The expected gross return therefore will be 1.5% + (0.5% × 4) = 3.5% because the investor makes four round trips a year. Of course, the long-term investor also can buy the liquid security at 3.5%. So the expected net return to the long-term investor is 3.5% – (0.5%/10) = 3.45%. This is 1.95% more than the expected return of the short-term investor after transaction costs. At a minimum, therefore, the illiquid security needs to yield 3.45% net to the long-term investor, who would otherwise prefer the liquid security. Thus, in equilibrium, the gross yield of the illiquid security should be 3.45% + (5%/10) = 3.95%. The long-term investor ends up owning the illiquid security with net expected return of 3.45% and the short-term investor the liquid security with net expected return of 1.5%. The difference is called the *liquidity premium*. Note that the liquidity premium LP is

$$LP = (f_{ST} - f_{LT})B_L$$

where f_{ST} and f_{LT} are the frequencies of trading of the short- and long-term investors, respectively, and B_L is the bid–ask spread on the liquid security. In this example, $f_{ST} = 4$ and $f_{LT} = 0.1$. The difference of 3.9 can be interpreted as the differential of impatience, with the liquidity premium being the product of this differential and the bid–ask spread on the liquid security, in this case, 3.9 × 0.5% = 1.95%. The shorter the short-term investor's horizon and the longer the long-term investor's horizon, the higher is the liquidity premium. Also, note that the liquidity risk premium moves with the bid–ask spread of the liquid security but does not depend on the bid–ask spread of the illiquid security.

14.2.9 Opportunity Cost: Liquidity Risk Revisited

An alternative way of thinking about liquidity premia is to account for illiquidity as an opportunity cost. Indeed, it is felt by many investors holding illiquid securities that they should be compensated for the opportunity cost of being precluded from using the funds that went into the illiquid investments to exploit alpha opportunities in liquid markets instead. One can assume, contrary to conventional finance canons, that alpha opportunities do exist for investors willing to exploit dynamic asset-allocation rules or market dislocations. We may think of the forgone alpha as coming from two possible sources: a continuous alpha and a jump process. The continuous alpha corresponds to "normal" market opportunities linked to market timing and asset selection. The jump alpha is used to mimic a "dry powder" strategy that buys cheap assets when markets experience significant sell-offs.

The continuous alpha α_t is modeled as a mean-reverting Ornstein–Uhlenbeck process:

$$d\alpha_t = k(\mu - \alpha_t)dt + \sigma dW_t$$

where $k > 0$ is the speed of mean reversion, μ is the long-term average available alpha, and σ is the volatility of the continuous alpha. The solution to this equation is

$$\alpha_t = e^{-kt}\alpha_0 + \mu(1 - e^{-kt}) + \sigma e^{-kt}\int_0^t e^{ks}dW_s$$

Note that α_t is normally distributed with

$$E(\alpha_t) = e^{-kt}\alpha_0 + \mu(1 - e^{-kt})$$

and

$$\text{var}(\alpha_t) = \frac{\sigma^2(1 - e^{-2kt})}{2k}$$

The jump component is modeled as a Poisson counting process q_t. Given its intensity λ, the probability of an instantaneous jump is $P(dq_t \geq 1) = \lambda dt$. The expected return on the dry-powder strategy is

$$E(Jdq_t) = \lambda J dt$$

where J is the alpha an investor earns when a jump occurs. The liquidity premium is the expected total alpha opportunity, meaning the sum of the discounted continuous alpha and jump alpha:

$$V = E\left[\int_0^T e^{-rt}(\alpha_t dt + J dq_t)\right]$$

where the cash flows are discounted at the risk-free rate r because they are coming from alpha as opposed to beta trades. Integrating this expression gives a closed-form solution for the value of illiquidity:

$$V = \frac{\mu}{r}(1 - e^{-rT}) + \frac{\lambda J}{r}(1 - e^{-rT}) + \frac{\alpha_0 - \mu}{r + k}[1 - e^{-(r+k)T}]$$

14.2.10 P-Hacking and Lucky Factors

Have you ever heard of the skirt-length theory? It originated at the Wharton School of Business in the 1920s and argued that shorter skirts were a great predictor of stock market rallies, whereas longer hemlines predicted sell-offs. A more modern, politically correct "risk factor" holds that a win by the National Football Conference in the Super Bowl predicts a market rally.

Some risk factors are the result of P-hacking, which is the (often unintended) misuse of statistics to find significant patterns in data. With enough imagination, perseverance, and incompetence, one can always reach seemingly valid statistical conclusions when none of these conclusions is warranted.

So it goes for trading strategies. Because investors have been known to invest in a strategy on the basis of naïve backtests, this has fostered an aggressive search for factors. Several hundred factors have been discussed in finance papers, with a substantial proportion of these factors underperforming out of sample. The suspicion is that during a "fishing" expedition, so many regressions are performed that some, however unfounded, will be found to be significant by sheer luck. Why all the statistical arm twisting? Of course, there is a strong incentive to publish about factors that appear to work and little incentive to discuss factors that do not. This imparts a double bias: every effort will be made to find significant factors in a trading strategy, and papers that have nothing impressive to show end up in filing cabinets.

The data-mining process is often a tradeoff between type I and type II errors. Overinvesting in data mining or lowering the burden of proof may increase (reduce) the probability of type I (type II) error. False discoveries (type I error or false-positive results) and missed opportunities (type II error or false-negative results) carry different penalty functions depending on the context: telling a patient that she has no cancer when she does in reality (type II error) can be more serious than misdiagnosing a healthy person (type I error). In trading, a false discovery may have a zero expected return, whereas a missed opportunity may be costly. This may be another reason why the financial industry is tilted toward risking false rather than missed discoveries. We illustrate spurious statistical inference with two examples: unit roots and data snooping.

Example (Stationarity and Spurious Regressions): Suppose that we run an ordinary least-squares regression of a variable y on a variable x and a constant. That is,

$$y_t = \hat{\alpha} + \hat{\beta} x_t + \hat{e}_t$$

with $t = 1, \ldots, T$. And suppose that y_t and x_t follow independent random walks. That is,

$$y_t = y_{t-1} + v_t \text{ and } x_t = x_{t-1} + w_t$$

where v_t and w_t are independent and identically distributed (iid) normal variables with mean zero and variances σ_v^2 and σ_w^2, respectively.

Then, using the functional central limit theorem, it can be shown that as $T \to \infty$ (see Phillips [1986] for details),

$$\hat{\beta} = \frac{\sigma_v}{\sigma_W} \delta$$

with

$$\delta \equiv \frac{\int_0^1 V(t)W(t)dt - \int_0^1 V(t)dt \int_0^1 W(t)dt}{\int_0^1 W(t)^2 dt - \left[\int_0^1 W(t)dt\right]^2}$$

where $V(t)$ and $W(t)$ are independent Wiener processes.

The R^2 is in turn given by

$$R^2 = \delta^2 \frac{\int_0^1 W(t)^2 dt - \left[\int_0^1 W(t)dt\right]^2}{\int_0^1 V(t)^2 dt - \left[\int_0^1 V(t)dt\right]^2}$$

Because y_t and x_t follow independent random walks, the theoretical β and R^2 should both be zero. Yet, as can be seen from the preceding equations, none of β or R^2 converge asymptotically in probability to zero. Even worse, it can be shown that the absolute value of the t-statistics for β is

$$|t_\beta| \to \infty \text{ in probability}$$

indicating that the null hypothesis of a zero regression coefficient—which we know is true by construction—will be rejected almost always in large samples.

We can infer a couple of conclusions from these results. First, never regress a price level against another price level because both are presumed to follow, at least to first order, a random walk unless you hold a priori that a linear combination of these prices is stationary. Second, financial variables often can be near-random walks. Unfortunately, in typical samples, estimates for regressions between near-random walks are not well behaved. See Phillips (2001) for further details on this topic.

Example (Data Snooping): Data snooping may be roughly defined as the practice of whipping data until they confess. In this example, we try to size the impact of adding regressors on the R^2 statistic. From basic econometrics, we know that

$$F = \frac{R^2 / k}{(1 - R^2) / (T - k - 1)} \sim F(k, T - k - 1)$$

where T is the number of observations, k is the number of regressors including the constant, and $F(\cdot, \cdot)$ refers to the F (Fisher–Snedecor) distribution. Solving for R^2 gives

$$R^2 = \frac{kF}{(T - k - 1) + kF}$$

From standard statistics, we know that R^2 therefore follows a beta distribution:

$$R^2 = \frac{kF}{(T - k - 1) + kF} \sim Beta\left(\frac{k}{2}, \frac{T - k - 1}{2}\right)$$

under the hypothesis that the ($k \times 1$) vector of regression coefficients is zero.

The distribution function of the R^2 of a multiple regression with k regressors will therefore be

$$P(R^2 \leq r) = \beta(r)$$

where $\beta(r)$ is the cumulative distribution function of *Beta* $\left(\dfrac{k}{2}, \dfrac{T-k-1}{2}\right)$.

Now assume that we are considering $m > k$ possible regressors but decide to select the best k out of m so as to maximize R^2. This boils down to trying $\dbinom{m}{k} = \dfrac{m!}{k!(n-k)!}$ regressions. Then, assuming independent regressions, this "fishing expedition" will have the following distribution function for the maximum R^2:

$$P\left(R_1^2 \leq r, R_2^2 \leq r, ..., R_{\binom{m}{k}}^2 \leq r\right) = [\beta(r)]^{\binom{m}{k}}$$

To discuss a simple numerical application, if $T = 100$, $m = 10$, and $k = 3$, the likelihood of an R^2 above 10% is 88%, whereas the likelihood of an R^2 above 10% for one regression with $T = 100$, $k = 3$, is 1.7%.

In a more striking case with $T = 100$, $m = 100$, and $k = 8$, the likelihood of an R^2 above 50% is more than 99%, whereas the likelihood of an R^2 above 50% for one regression with $T = 100$, $k = 8$, is zero (of order 10^{-11}). As you increase the number of regressors and widen the universe of potential regressors to choose from, there is little that one is not able to (spuriously) explain. See Douglas Foster, Smith, and Whaley (1997) for details.

14.3 Risk-Neutral Probabilities and Physical Probabilities

We now compare risk-neutral probabilities to physical probabilities and infer the risk premium attached to derivatives. From Chapter 10, we know that the value of an asset π is the expectation under the physical probability P of the stochastic discount factor multiplied by the asset payoff:

$$\pi = E^P(MX)$$

where the stochastic discount factor

$$M \equiv \delta \frac{U'[C_{t+1}(\omega)]}{U'(C_t)}$$

and X is the asset payoff (see Chapter 10 for notation).

With the Radon–Nikodym derivative

$$\frac{dQ}{dP} = \frac{\delta\dfrac{U'[C_{t+1}(\omega)]}{U'(C_t)}}{\displaystyle\sum_{\omega=1}^{n} P(\omega)\delta\dfrac{U'[C_{t+1}(\omega)]}{U'(C_t)}} = M(1+r)$$

we showed that π also could be expressed as

$$\pi = E^P(MX) = E^P\left(\frac{dQ}{dP}\frac{X}{1+r}\right) = E^Q\left(\frac{X}{1+r}\right)$$

While we have established the formal expression of the ratio of probabilities, we will try below to make it more concrete. Is it typically bigger or smaller than 1? Can it be expressed more intuitively? We will compare the physical and risk-neutral probability in a simple binomial model.

14.3.1 Simple Binomial Model

A few reminders from Chapter 12 are in order. For a standard derivative tree:

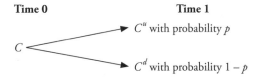

There are two ways to find C.

Under the physical probability measure,

$$C = \frac{pC^u + (1-p)C^d}{1+r+\rho_c}$$

where ρ_c is the risk premium applicable to this derivative.

Or we can price the derivative under the standard martingale measure:

$$C = \frac{qC^u + (1-q)C^d}{1+r}$$

with q defined as

$$q \equiv \frac{1+r-d}{u-d}$$

Equating the pricing expressions

$$\frac{pC^u + (1-p)C^d}{1+r+\rho_C} = \frac{qC^u + (1-q)C^d}{1+r}$$

we obtain

$$p - q = \frac{C\rho_C}{C^u - C^d}$$

But we know from Chapter 12 that the elasticity of a derivative is $\beta_{CS} = \frac{\beta_C}{\beta_S} = \frac{\Delta C}{\Delta S}\frac{S}{C} = \frac{C^u - C^d}{C(u-d)}$. We also know from the basic CAPM that $\rho_C = \beta_{CS}[E(R_S) - r]$, where R_S is the return on the underlying asset. Finally, to go from the binomial model to the Black–Merton–Scholes model, we can use the approximation $u, d \approx e^{\pm\sigma} \approx 1 \pm \sigma$ for small σ, where σ is the one-period volatility of the underlying asset returns. With these equations in mind, we obtain

$$p - q \approx \frac{[E(R_S) - r]}{2\sigma} = \frac{s}{2}$$

So the difference between the physical and risk-neutral probability can be approximated by the expected risk premium of the underlying asset divided by twice the volatility. This is also half the expected Sharpe ratio of the underlying asset. If the expected Sharpe ratio for a typical equity market is 0.2, then the physical probability is 10% higher than the risk-neutral probability. This relationship also shows that the difference in probabilities is simply about the volatility-scaled risk premium.

14.3.2 An Option-Pricing Puzzle: Something for Nothing?

Physical and Martingale Probabilities of Stocks Outperforming Bonds

What is the probability of \$1 invested in stocks outperforming \$1 invested in bonds? For stocks following a geometric Brownian motion, we have

$$S_T = \exp\left[\left(\mu - \frac{\sigma^2}{2}\right)T + \sigma W(T)\right]$$

whereas a risk-free bond price is

$$B_T = \exp(rT)$$

So the physical probability of a stock outperforming a bond at horizon T is

$$P = \Pr(S_T > B_T) = \Phi\left[\left(\frac{\mu - r}{\sigma} - \frac{\sigma}{2}\right)\sqrt{T}\right]$$

where $\Phi(\cdot)$ is the cumulative normal operator. The corresponding martingale probability assumes a stock drift equal to the risk-free rate and is therefore

$$Q = \Phi\left(-\frac{\sigma}{2}\sqrt{T}\right)$$

Note that if $\frac{\mu - r}{\sigma} > \frac{\sigma}{2}$, P goes to 1, whereas Q goes to zero for large horizon T.

The difference between P and Q is:

$$P - Q = \int_{-\frac{\sigma}{2}\sqrt{T}}^{\left(\frac{\mu-r}{\sigma} - \frac{\sigma}{2}\right)\sqrt{T}} \frac{1}{\sqrt{2\pi}} e^{-\frac{u^2}{2}} du$$

We use a Taylor expansion of $e^{-\frac{u^2}{2}}$:

$$e^{-\frac{u^2}{2}} = 1 - \frac{u^2}{2} + \frac{u^4}{4} + \ldots$$

and limit ourselves to the first term of the expansion to obtain:

$$P - Q \approx \frac{1}{\sqrt{2\pi}} \frac{\mu - r}{\sigma}\sqrt{T}$$

For a one-year horizon,

$$P - Q \approx 0.4s$$

where s is the one-year Sharpe ratio.

Something for Nothing? An Option Pricing Paradox

As mentioned above, if $\frac{\mu - r}{\sigma} > \frac{\sigma}{2}$, P goes to one while Q goes to zero for large horizon T.

Picture a binary call that pays Fe^{rT} if $S_T > B_T$ and zero otherwise. This call will be valued as the product of the martingale probability of exercise Q and the payoff

$$C_B = e^{-rT}\Phi\left(-\frac{\sigma}{2}\sqrt{T}\right)Fe^{rT} = F\Phi\left(-\frac{\sigma}{2}\sqrt{T}\right)$$

Now pick an asset with $\frac{\mu-r}{\sigma} > \frac{\sigma}{2}$. For large expiration T, the price of the binary call on this asset goes to zero, whereas the probability of exercise goes to one. The market is pricing at zero an asset that pays the future value of F with probability (almost) one. This is as close as it gets to a "something for nothing" deal in finance. The leverage implicit in a binary call compounds the risk premium to produce what certainly may look like a puzzling result.

Note that the case of a corresponding binary put (that pays Fe^{rT} if $S_T < B_T$ and zero otherwise) leads to the opposite scenario. The binary put value is $F\Phi\left(\frac{\sigma}{2}\sqrt{T}\right)$ and therefore goes to F for large expirations. Yet the probability of exercise of the put is $1 - P$ and goes to zero with $\frac{\mu-r}{\sigma} > \frac{\sigma}{2}$. So the market is pricing at F a put that is exercised with probability (almost) zero.

14.3.3 Beta of an Option and Risk Premium

To give some intuition about option risk premia, we approximate the beta of a plain-vanilla European put or call. From Chapter 12, we know that the beta of a derivative is

$$\beta_C = \frac{\partial C}{\partial S}\frac{S}{C}\beta_S$$

Consider the case of a 1-year at-the-money forward (ATMF) European option. Then we know from Chapter 12 that

$$\frac{C}{S} \approx 0.4\sigma$$

To calculate the beta of an ATMF call, note that

$$\frac{\partial C}{\partial S} = \Phi\left(\frac{\sigma}{2}\right) = \frac{1}{2} + \int_0^{\frac{\sigma}{2}}\frac{1}{\sqrt{2\pi}}e^{-\frac{u^2}{2}}\,du \approx \frac{1}{2} + \int_0^{\frac{\sigma}{2}}\frac{1}{\sqrt{2\pi}}\,du = 0.2\sigma + \frac{1}{2}$$

It follows that

$$\beta_{call} \approx \frac{1.25}{\sigma} + \frac{1}{2}$$

14.3.4 Economics of the Short Put

Similarly, one can find

$$\beta_{put} \approx -\frac{1.25}{\sigma} + \frac{1}{2}$$

For $\sigma = 0.2$, $\beta_{call} \approx 6.75$, and $\beta_{put} \approx -5.75$, to calculate the expected return on a 1-year at-the-money forward (ATMF) European option (call or put) on the S&P 500, assume that $r = 0$ and that the equity risk premium is 3%. Then, by the standard CAPM, the expected return on the call is $6.75 \times 3\% = 20.25\%$, and the expected return on the put is $-5.75 \times 3\% = -17.25\%$. The expected return on the call is substantially higher than the expected return on the put. All else equal, a risk-neutral investor generally will prefer to buy calls than to buy puts on a positive risk premium asset. But, buying calls, the investor will need to "pay up" for the volatility risk premium. By selling puts, the investor would be leveraging the equity risk premium and the volatility risk premium at the same time.

It is no coincidence that all major market actors are short puts: governments are short guarantees, commercial banks are short puts on underlying assets through their loan portfolios, and insurance companies are in the business of selling puts. The buy-the-dip trade, so popular among investors, is implicitly short a put. Unwittingly, everyone appears to converge toward the high-expected-return trade. Yet it is also the trade with the highest probability of ruin.

PART IV

Asset Allocation in Practice

15

Motivations for Robust Asset Allocation

Summary

The mean variance optimization (MVO) framework introduced by Harry Markowitz in 1952 is the foundation of modern portfolio theory, for which he won the 1990 Nobel Prize in Economic Sciences. It revolutionized the investment management world by providing a mathematical framework that formalizes the diversification benefits of combining risky assets and quantifies the maximum expected return attainable at any given level of risk (measured by variance or standard deviation) at the portfolio level.

Despite the theoretical importance and intuitive appeal of this quantitative model, many portfolio managers today are still reluctant to apply it to portfolio construction in practice. One major issue with the traditional MVO framework is that it assumes that the inputs are known with certainty; that is, there are no estimation errors in the model inputs. In reality, investors have to estimate both expected returns and covariance matrices.

We show the difficulty of estimating expected returns from historical realized return data with a simple yet common example, as in Merton (1980).

Then we move on to the empirical issues with naive MVO and illustrate them with a real-world asset-allocation problem. Finally, we outline the popular solutions to these issues in the literature, which can serve as an introduction to the next few chapters.

15.1 Estimation Errors: An Example

Merton (1980), among others, argues that estimating expected returns from historical realized return data is very difficult. Even if the expected return is constant over time, it would still take a very long history of realized returns to obtain an accurate estimate. Compared with return estimates, variance or covariance estimates from historical returns tend to be more accurate.

Suppose that the logarithmic return on an asset for each (nonoverlapping) period of length Δ over a sample period of T is independent and identically distributed as

$$Y_k \sim N(\mu\Delta, \sigma^2\Delta), \ k = 1, \ldots, n$$

where $n = T/\Delta$. For example, if T is 3 years and Δ is 1 month, the number of observations n is 36.

Consider the following usual estimator for μ:

$$\hat{\mu} \equiv \frac{1}{T}\sum_{k=1}^{n}Y_k$$

The expectation and the variance of $\hat{\mu}$ are

$$E(\hat{\mu}) = \mu, \ \text{var}(\hat{\mu}) = \frac{\sigma^2}{T}$$

Note that the variance of the unbiased estimator $\hat{\mu}$ depends only on the length of the sample period but not on the frequency of the realized returns. Suppose that we want to estimate the expected annual logarithmic return of an asset with an annual volatility of 20% using 10-year realized (daily/weekly/monthly) returns; that is, $\sigma = 20\%$, and $T = 10$ years. Then the standard error of the sample mean $\text{SE}(\hat{\mu}) \approx 6.3\%$, which makes the estimate almost useless. In addition, the assumption that the expected logarithmic return is constant over the 10-year sample period is a very strong one, which means that the estimate in reality can be even more unreliable.

Now consider the following estimator for σ^2:

$$\widehat{\sigma^2} \equiv \frac{1}{T}\sum_{k=1}^{n}(Y_k - \hat{\mu})^2$$

The expectation and the variance of $\widehat{\sigma^2}$ are

$$E\left(\widehat{\sigma^2}\right) = \frac{n-1}{n}\sigma^2, \; \mathrm{var}\left(\widehat{\sigma^2}\right) = \frac{2(n-1)}{n^2}\sigma^4$$

Unlike $\hat{\mu}$, the variance of $\widehat{\sigma^2}$ depends on the number of observations. For a fixed length of sample period T, the availability of higher-frequency realized returns can improve the precision of this estimator. For the preceding example, where $\sigma = 20\%$ and $T = 10$ years, the standard error of the variance estimate $SE(\widehat{\sigma^2}) \approx 0.5\%$ for monthly data and 0.2% for weekly data.

The presence of estimation errors makes the estimated optimal portfolio suboptimal and can completely alter the theoretical recommendation of the traditional Markowitz model (see, e.g., Kan and Zhou [2007]). Furthermore, the optimal solution is very sensitive to the inputs, especially to the means. As a result, traditional MVO often leads to highly concentrated and unintuitive allocations that are "estimation error maximizing" (see Michaud [1989]) with poor out-of-sample performance (see Jobson and Korkie [1980] and Michaud [1998]). The sensitivity of the optimization to small estimation errors in the inputs also results in unnecessary turnover and increased transaction costs.

15.2 Empirical Issues with Naive MVO

Consider the following simple MVO with only the constraint that the sum of asset weights equals one:

$$\max_{x} x^T\mu - \frac{\lambda}{2}x^T\Sigma x$$

$$\text{subject to } x^T 1 = 1$$

Assume that $\lambda = 3$. The hypothetical expected return and risk assumptions for the six assets are shown in Table 15.1. The solution to this simple optimization problem is shown in Figure 15.1.

TABLE 15.1 Hypothetical Return and Risk Parameter Estimates

Expected Return	Volatility	Correlation	US Equity	DM ex-US Equity	EM Equity	US IG	US HY	Non-US Gov
5.5%	16.9%	US Equity	1.00	0.83	0.65	−0.16	0.69	0.01
5.0%	17.2%	DM ex-US Equity	0.83	1.00	0.79	−0.09	0.73	0.31
8.0%	23.6%	EM Equity	0.65	0.79	1.00	−0.11	0.65	0.20
3.0%	3.5%	US IG	−0.16	−0.09	−0.11	1.00	0.18	0.50
4.0%	6.5%	US HY	0.69	0.73	0.65	0.18	1.00	0.22
2.0%	8.4%	Non-US Gov	0.01	0.31	0.20	0.50	0.22	1.00

DM: developed markets. EM: emerging markets. IG: investment grade. HY: high yield.

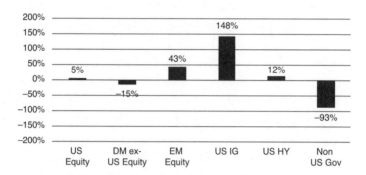

FIGURE 15.1 Naive MVO (total weight = 1)

As expected for MVO with minimum constraint, we observe large long and short positions in the solution, which is not investable for most institutional investors.

Next, we introduce the popular no-short-sale constraint $x_i \geq 0, \forall i$. The new solution is shown in Figure 15.2.

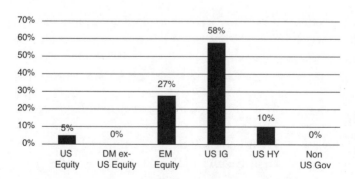

FIGURE 15.2 Naive MVO (total weight = 1, no short sale)

The no-short-sale constraint is binding for the two assets with negative optimal weights in the preceding MVO, so their new optimal weights are truncated at zero. We call them *corner solutions*. The weights to the remaining assets are concentrated in one single asset, US IG. This solution is still hardly investable for most investors in reality.

Moreover, suppose that the expected return for US equity is 1% higher (which is probably well within its estimation error); then the optimal allocation will change drastically, as shown in Figure 15.3. This indicates that the highly concentrated optimal allocation is also highly sensitive to small changes in the input.

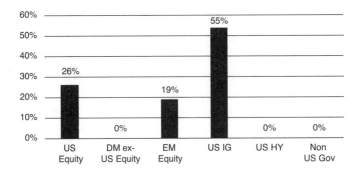

FIGURE 15.3 Naive MVO (total weight = 1, no short sale) with 1% higher US equity expected return

15.3 Solutions

Many practitioners deal with these problems by imposing constraints on asset weights directly to ensure diversification and stability of the optimal portfolio. There is some research showing that constraints could potentially improve out-of-sample performance of the optimal portfolio (see, e.g., Frost and Savarino [1988]). However, in reality, many of these constraints are arbitrary and will lead to largely corner solutions, which defeats the purpose of a quantitative optimization model.

Others try to impose more subtle constraints on portfolio weights. For example, some may specify ranges for the relative weight between one asset or asset group and another. Compared with direct constraints on asset weights, these constraints allow more flexibility for the optimizer. However, the ranges are still arbitrary and often lead to corner solutions, just in a less obvious fashion. In addition, some practitioners may specify a maximum tracking error of the optimal portfolio relative to a benchmark portfolio that is well diversified. This usually is not as effective as constraining absolute or relative weights for diversification purposes because tracking error is measured by the same covariance matrix used for calculating portfolio variance and shares similar issues. Unless the investor truly cares about the tracking error, it is not a recommended approach for diversification and stability of MVO.

Some investors turn to simple portfolio construction heuristics such as risk parity and equally weighted portfolios and avoid estimating some or even all of the return parameters.

In this final part of this book, we discuss a few methodologies that explicitly address estimation errors as opposed to ignoring the potentially useful but noisy estimates or abandoning a quantitative optimization framework completely. There are generally two directions of efforts to achieve more robust asset allocations. Models of the first type attempt to construct more robust estimators of expected returns and covariance matrices that are less sensitive to outliers and other sampling errors. Examples include various shrinkage estimators. Models of the second type incorporate the uncertainty on the input estimates explicitly in the optimization process, such as penalized optimization, robust optimization (see Tütüncü and Koenig [2004], for example) and portfolio resampling (see Michaud [1998]). The two types of models are not mutually exclusive, and in many cases they are complements rather than substitutes.

In selecting the models to discuss in the following chapters, our goal is not to be exhaustive. We pick a few representative approaches in the literature and focus our discussion on *when* and *why* each of them helps mitigate the issues of extreme and unstable allocations for naive MVO. After describing and contrasting the individual approaches, we explore the connections between them and identify conditions under which one model is equivalent to another. Although some topics are inevitably technical, our emphasis is on the intuition rather than the technical details.

16

Risk Budgeting Approach to Asset Allocation

Summary

To construct a portfolio based on a given risk budget to its different components, one needs to understand how to decompose portfolio risk into these components, which can be defined based on asset classes, securities, or risk factors that are the underlying drivers of risk.

Consider a portfolio whose return is given by

$$r = \sum_{j=1}^{n} w_j r_j$$

where w_j is the portfolio's exposure to the jth component, and r_j is the return of the jth component.

Under this assumption, most common portfolio risk measures such as volatility, value at risk, and conditional value at risk are homogeneous functions of degree one with respect to the portfolio's risk factor exposures or asset weights. Based on Euler's homogeneous function theorem, we have

$$f(w) = \sum_{j=1}^{n} w_j \frac{\partial f(w)}{\partial w_j}$$

where $f(w)$ is the function mapping the vector of risk factor exposures or asset weights w to the risk measure.

Risk parity is a special case of risk budgeting where risk is allocated equally across portfolio components. It often uses volatility as the portfolio risk measure and can be implemented in various ways.

There is no consensus on the exact definition of a risk parity portfolio. The general philosophy is to equalize risk from different portfolio components. The risk can be the stand-alone volatilities of the components, ignoring correlations between them.

First Definition

An equal stand-alone risk (ESR) portfolio equalizes the products of the portfolio weights in the components and the volatilities of those components. If the portfolio weight of asset i is x_i and the portfolio comprises N assets, then

$$x_i = \frac{\dfrac{1}{\sigma_i}}{\sum_{j=1}^{N} \dfrac{1}{\sigma_j}}, \text{ for all } i = 1, \dots, N$$

where σ_i is the standard deviation of asset i's return.

Second Definition

An equal risk contribution (ERC) portfolio equalizes the portfolio volatility contribution from each component. In other words,

$$RC_i = x_i \frac{\partial \sigma_p}{\partial x_i} = x_j \frac{\partial \sigma_p}{\partial x_j} = RC_j, \text{ for all } i\text{'s and } j\text{'s}$$

Identical Sharpe ratios are the only condition needed for the mean-variance optimal portfolio to be a risk parity portfolio when $N = 2$. When $N > 2$, we need both identical Sharpe ratios and constant pairwise correlations.

16.1 Portfolio Risk Decomposition

To construct a portfolio based on a given risk budget to its different components, one needs to understand how to decompose portfolio risk into these components, which can be defined based on asset classes, securities, or risk factors[1] that are the underlying drivers of risk.

Euler's homogeneous function theorem provides a natural decomposition of some of the most popular portfolio risk measures with desirable properties. This section discusses this methodology for the most commonly used portfolio risk measures and describes both the parametric and nonparametric methodologies to estimate their contributions to portfolio risk.

16.1.1 General Methodology: Euler's Homogeneous Function Theorem

Consider a portfolio whose return is given by

$$r = \sum_{j=1}^{n} w_j r_j$$

where w_j is the portfolio's exposure to the jth risk factor, and r_j is the return of the jth risk factor. Under the preceding assumption, most common portfolio risk measures such as volatility, value at risk, and conditional value at risk are homogeneous functions of degree one with respect to the portfolio's risk factor exposures. Based on Euler's homogeneous function theorem, we have

$$f(w) = \sum_{j=1}^{n} w_j \frac{\partial f(w)}{\partial w_j} \qquad (16.1)$$

where $f(w)$ is the function mapping the vector of risk factor exposures w to the risk measure.

Equation (16.1) allows us to decompose the portfolio risk measure into risk factor exposures: the contribution of each risk factor to a risk measure is the product of the portfolio's exposure to the risk factor and the marginal risk contribution of the risk factor. We will show below how to compute the marginal contributions either parametrically under a normality assumption when possible or nonparametrically such as using bootstrap for individual risk measures.

---

1 Roncalli (2014) showed that risk parity for factors is equivalent to risk budgeting for asset classes with a specific risk budget profile.

16.1.2 Volatility

The volatility of a portfolio's return is a function of the portfolio's risk factor exposures and the covariance matrix of the risk factors:

$$\text{vol} = \sqrt{\sum_{i=1}^{n}\sum_{j=1}^{n} w_i w_j \sigma_{ij}}$$

where σ_{ij} is the covariance between risk factor i and risk factor j when $i \neq j$ and the variance of risk factor j when $i = j$.

It is easy to verify by differentiation that the marginal contribution to volatility from risk factor j is given by

$$\frac{\partial \text{vol}}{\partial w_j} = \sum_{i=1}^{n} w_i \sigma_{ij} / \text{vol} \qquad (16.2)$$

Therefore, contribution to volatility from risk factor j based on Euler's theorem is given by

$$\text{vol}_j = \sum_{i=1}^{n} w_i w_j \sigma_{ij} / \text{vol}$$

16.1.3 Value at Risk

Unlike volatility, value at risk is a tail risk measure. It is the threshold of loss that a portfolio will not exceed at a certain confidence level. Mathematically, we define value at risk for a portfolio at a confidence level $\alpha \in (0, 1)$, VaR(α), as

$$\Pr(\sum_{j=1}^{n} w_j r_j \leq -\text{VaR}(\alpha)) = 1 - \alpha \qquad (16.3)$$

If the r_j's are jointly normally distributed, that is, $(r_1, \ldots, r_n)' \sim N(\mu, \Sigma)$, then the portfolio return is also normally distributed with $\sum_{j=1}^{n} w_j r_j \sim N(\sum_{j=1}^{n} w_j \mu_j, \sum_{i=1}^{n}\sum_{j=1}^{n} w_i w_j \sigma_{ij})$. This allows us to write VaR(α) as a function of μ and Σ:

$$\text{VaR}(\alpha) = -\sum_{j=1}^{n} w_j \mu_j - z_{1-\alpha}\sqrt{\sum_{i=1}^{n}\sum_{j=1}^{n} w_i w_j \sigma_{ij}}$$

where $z_{1-\alpha}$ is the critical value for a standard normal distribution with a left tail probability of $1-\alpha$.

Therefore,

$$\frac{\partial \text{VaR}}{\partial w_j} = -\mu_j - z_{1-\alpha} \sum_{i=1}^{n} w_i \sigma_{ij} \, / \, \text{vol}$$

Thus the contribution to value at risk from risk factor j based on Euler's theorem is given by

$$\text{VaR}_j = w_j \frac{\partial \text{VaR}}{\partial w_j} = -w_j \mu_j - z_{1-\alpha} \sum_{i=1}^{n} w_i w_j \sigma_{ij} \, / \, \text{vol}$$

Without the normality assumption, one can use the sample equivalent of the following expression for marginal contributions to value at risk from component j to estimate it nonparametrically using historical or simulated data:

$$\frac{\partial \text{VaR}}{\partial w_j} = -E[r_j \,|\, r = -\text{VaR}] \tag{16.4}$$

For example, one can select a small positive real number ε and define a subset of the set of all simulated paths B as follows:

$$A(\varepsilon,\alpha) = \{b \in B : |\, r^b + \text{VaR}(\alpha)\,| < \varepsilon\}$$

where r^b is the simulated portfolio return for path b. In other words, we select the paths with portfolio returns falling into a small neighborhood of loss $\text{VaR}(\alpha)$.

The marginal contribution to value at risk from each risk factor can be estimated by averaging the component returns along these paths:

$$\widehat{\frac{\partial \text{VaR}}{\partial w_j}} = -\frac{1}{N(\varepsilon,\alpha)} \sum_{b \in A(\varepsilon,\alpha)} r_j^b$$

where $N(\varepsilon, \alpha)$ is the number of paths in $A(\varepsilon, \alpha)$, and r_j^b is the return of the jth component for path b. We can improve the accuracy of the estimates by increasing the number of simulations or reducing the value of ε while maintaining a reasonably large value for $N(\varepsilon, \alpha)$.

Contribution to value at risk from component j then can be estimated by

$$\text{VaR}_j = w_j \frac{\partial \text{VaR}}{\partial w_j}$$

16.1.4 Conditional Value at Risk

Like value at risk, conditional value at risk (CVaR, also known as *expected shortfall*) is also a tail risk measure. Compared with value at risk, conditional value at risk has some desirable properties as a risk measure, such as coherence. Conditional value at risk at a given confidence level α is the expected loss of a portfolio conditional on the loss being greater than or equal to VaR(α):

$$\text{CVaR}(\alpha) = -E[r \mid r \le -\text{VaR}(\alpha)] = -\sum_{j=1}^{n} w_j E[r_j \mid r \le -\text{VaR}(\alpha)]$$

If the r_j's are jointly normally distributed, that is, $(r_1, \ldots, r_n)' \sim N(\mu, \Sigma)$, then the portfolio return is also normally distributed with $\sum_{j=1}^{n} w_j r_j \sim N(\sum_{j=1}^{n} w_j \mu_j, \sum_{i=1}^{n} \sum_{j=1}^{n} w_i w_j \sigma_{ij})$. Thus we have

$$\text{CVaR}(\alpha) = -\sum_{j=1}^{n} w_j \mu_j + \frac{1}{1-\alpha} \varphi(z_{1-\alpha}) \sqrt{\sum_{i=1}^{n} \sum_{j=1}^{n} w_i w_j \sigma_{ij}}$$

where $z_{1-\alpha}$ is the critical value for a standard normal distribution with a left tail probability of $1-\alpha$, and φ is the probability density function of a standard normal distribution. Therefore,

$$\frac{\partial \text{CVaR}}{\partial w_j} = -\mu_j + \frac{1}{1-\alpha} \varphi(z_{1-\alpha}) \sum_{i=1}^{n} w_i \sigma_{ij} / \text{vol}$$

The contribution to conditional value at risk from component j based on Euler's theorem is given by

$$\text{CVaR}_j = w_j \frac{\partial \text{CVaR}}{\partial w_j} = -w_j \mu_j + \frac{1}{1-\alpha} \varphi(z_{1-\alpha}) \sum_{i=1}^{n} w_i w_j \sigma_{ij} / \text{vol}$$

Without the normality assumption, one can use the sample equivalent of the following expression for marginal contributions to conditional value at risk from component j to estimate it nonparametrically using historical or simulated data:[2]

$$\frac{\partial \text{CVaR}}{\partial w_j} = -E[r_j \mid r \le -\text{VaR}]$$

---

2 Alternatively, some researchers proposed estimating and decomposing non-normal CVaR (VaR) using modified CVaR (VaR) which corrects normal CVaR (VaR) for skewness and kurtosis based on the Cornish-Fisher expansion (see, for example, Boudt, Peterson, and Croux [2008]). Scaillet (2004) proposed kernel estimators of conditional value at risk and its first-order derivatives with respect to portfolio allocation under strong regularity conditions.

Similar to the case of value at risk, one can estimate the marginal contribution to conditional value at risk from component j by

$$\frac{\partial \widehat{\mathrm{CVaR}}(\alpha)}{\partial w_j} = -\frac{1}{N(\alpha)} \sum_{b \in A(\alpha)} r_j^b$$

where $A(\alpha) = \{b \in B\colon r^b \le -\mathrm{VaR}(\alpha)\}$, B is the set of all simulated paths, and $N(\alpha)$ is the number of paths in $A(\alpha)$.

The contribution to conditional value at risk from component j then can be estimated as

$$\mathrm{CVaR}_j = w_j \frac{\partial \mathrm{CVaR}}{\partial w_j}$$

16.2 Risk Parity

Risk parity is a special case of risk budgeting where risk is allocated equally across portfolio components. It often uses volatility as the portfolio risk measure and can be implemented in various ways. We discuss risk parity in this section as an example. The risk budgeting approach is simply an extension of the risk parity approach with alternative risk measures or risk budgets (other than equal weights).

16.2.1 Definitions

There is no consensus on the exact definition of a risk parity portfolio. The general philosophy is to equalize risk from different portfolio components. The risk can be the components' stand-alone volatilities, ignoring correlations between returns.

First Definition

An equal stand-alone risk (ESR) portfolio equalizes the products of the portfolio weights in the components and the volatilities of those components. If the portfolio weight of asset i is x_i and the portfolio comprises N assets, then

$$x_i = \frac{\dfrac{1}{\sigma_i}}{\displaystyle\sum_{j=1}^{n} \dfrac{1}{\sigma_j}}, \text{ for all } i = 1,\dots,N$$

where σ_i is the standard deviation of asset i's return. Equivalently,

$$x_i\sigma_i = \frac{1}{\sum_{j=1}^{n}\frac{1}{\sigma_j}}, \text{ for all } i = 1,\dots,N$$

Second Definition

An equal risk contribution (ERC) portfolio equalizes the portfolio volatility contribution from each component. In other words,

$$RC_i = x_i\frac{\partial\sigma_p}{\partial x_i} = x_j\frac{\partial\sigma_p}{\partial x_j} = RC_j, \text{ for all } i\text{'s and } j\text{'s}$$

If $N = 2$, then ESR implies that

$$x_1 = \frac{\frac{1}{\sigma_1}}{\frac{1}{\sigma_1}+\frac{1}{\sigma_2}} \text{ or } x_1\sigma_1 = \frac{1}{\frac{1}{\sigma_1}+\frac{1}{\sigma_2}}$$

and

$$x_2 = \frac{\frac{1}{\sigma_2}}{\frac{1}{\sigma_1}+\frac{1}{\sigma_2}} \text{ or } x_2\sigma_2 = \frac{1}{\frac{1}{\sigma_1}+\frac{1}{\sigma_2}}$$

In the ERC case, recall that

$$\sigma_p = \sqrt{x_1^2\sigma_1^2 + x_2^2\sigma_2^2 + 2x_1x_2\rho\sigma_1\sigma_2}$$

and

$$x_1\frac{\partial\sigma_p}{\partial x_1} = \frac{x_1(2x_1\sigma_1^2 + 2x_2\rho\sigma_1\sigma_2)}{2\sigma_p} = \frac{x_1^2\sigma_1^2 + x_1x_2\rho\sigma_1\sigma_2}{\sigma_p}$$

and

$$x_2\frac{\partial\sigma_p}{\partial x_2} = \frac{x_2^2\sigma_2^2 + x_1x_2\rho\sigma_1\sigma_2}{\sigma_p}$$

Note that in the two-asset case, ESR implies ERC because when $x_1 \sigma_1 = x_2 \sigma_2$, $x_1^2 \sigma_1^2 = x_2^2 \sigma_2^2$, and therefore,

$$x_1 \frac{\partial \sigma_p}{\partial x_1} = x_2 \frac{\partial \sigma_p}{\partial x_2}$$

Example: Consider a stock-bond portfolio where the volatilities for stocks and bonds are 16% and 4% respectively. A risk parity portfolio with these two assets would invest $(1/16\%)/(1/16\% + 1/4\%) = 20\%$ in stocks and 80% in bonds, regardless of the correlation between stocks and bonds.

16.2.2 Mean Variance and Risk Parity

Risk parity and risk budgeting in general have gained a lot of popularity since the 2008 global financial crisis. Part of this popularity stems from the lack of robustness of the traditional MVO technique because of its sensitivity to estimation errors in the inputs, especially in expected returns. Risk budgeting and other risk-based approaches, such as minimum variance portfolios, usually require only a risk model, which is often believed to be more reliable than expected-return estimates.

Under what conditions will an MVO portfolio also be a risk parity portfolio? Recall that $x_{MV} = \Sigma^{-1} \frac{\mu - r}{\gamma}$, and start from the simple case where $N = 2$. Then we can write the optimal weights of the two risky assets as functions of their volatilities, Sharpe ratios, and correlation ρ:

$$\begin{bmatrix} x_1^* \\ x_2^* \end{bmatrix} = \frac{1}{\gamma(1-\rho^2)} \begin{bmatrix} \dfrac{S_1 - \rho S_2}{\sigma_1} \\ \dfrac{S_2 - \rho S_1}{\sigma_2} \end{bmatrix}$$

If the two risky assets have the same Sharpe ratios, the MVO portfolio is also a risk-parity portfolio in the sense of both equal stand-alone risk ($x_1 \sigma_1 = x_2 \sigma_2$) and equal risk contributions ($x_1^2 \sigma_1^2 + x_1 x_2 \rho \sigma_1 \sigma_2 = x_2^2 \sigma_2^2 + x_1 x_2 \rho \sigma_1 \sigma_2$). Therefore, identical Sharpe ratios are the only condition needed when $N = 2$.

How about the $N > 2$ case? Define the following notations:

$$\sigma_{(N\times1)} = \begin{bmatrix} \sigma_1 \\ \sigma_2 \\ \vdots \\ \sigma_N \end{bmatrix}$$

$$D_{(N\times N)} = \begin{bmatrix} \sigma_1 & & \\ & \ddots & \\ & & \sigma_N \end{bmatrix}$$

$$\mathbf{1}_{(N\times1)} = \begin{bmatrix} 1 \\ 1 \\ \vdots \\ 1 \end{bmatrix}$$

$C_{(N\times N)}$ is the correlation matrix of the risky assets:

$$\begin{bmatrix} 1 & \rho_{12} & \cdots & \rho_{1N} \\ \rho_{21} & 1 & \cdots & \rho_{2N} \\ \vdots & & \ddots & \vdots \\ \rho_{N1} & \rho_{N2} & \cdots & 1 \end{bmatrix}$$

We have $\Sigma = DCD$.

Assume further that

1. All risky assets have the same Sharpe ratio $\mu - r = k\sigma$ with k a constant.
2. All pairwise correlations are the same $\rho_{ij} = \rho,\ \forall i \neq j$

Then

$$C \times \mathbf{1} = \begin{bmatrix} 1+(N-1)\rho \\ \vdots \\ 1+(N-1)\rho \end{bmatrix} = [1+(N-1)\rho]\mathbf{1}$$

Hence

$$C^{-1}C\mathbf{1} = [1+(N-1)\rho]C^{-1}\mathbf{1}$$

$$\Rightarrow C^{-1}\mathbf{1} = \frac{1}{1+(N-1)\rho}\mathbf{1}$$

Thus

$$Dx^* = D\left[\frac{1}{\gamma}\Sigma^{-1}(\mu - r)\right] = \frac{1}{\gamma}DD^{-1}C^{-1}D^{-1}k\sigma = \frac{kC^{-1}1}{\gamma} = \frac{k}{\gamma[1+(N-1)\rho]}1$$

where we used $\Sigma^{-1} = D^{-1}C^{-1}D^{-1}$ and $\mu - r = k\sigma$.

This means that $x_i^* \sigma_i = \dfrac{k}{\gamma[1+(N-1)\rho]}$, $\forall i$. In other words, the mean variance portfolio is a risk parity portfolio in the sense of both equal stand-alone risks and equal risk contributions (the two coincide under the assumption of identical pairwise correlations).

17

Black–Litterman Model

Summary

The Black–Litterman (BL) model is a widely used quasi-Bayesian model that blends market-implied expected returns (the prior) with investors' private information (the views) to overcome the practical issues with the conventional mean-variance optimization (MVO), including highly concentrated and unstable asset allocations. Although commonly represented as an asset allocation model, the model is essentially a model to estimate future expected returns. The resulting return estimates can be used as input for any portfolio optimization, not just MVO.

The BL model starts with implied equilibrium expected excess returns derived using a reverse optimization process for an unconstrained MVO:

$$\pi = \lambda_{mkt} \Sigma x_{mkt}$$

where π is the implied equilibrium excess return vector, Σ is the covariance matrix of excess returns, x_{mkt} is the vector of market capitalization weights, and λ_{mkt} is the market risk aversion coefficient that characterizes the risk-return tradeoff at the market level.

To form the prior, the BL model assumes further that the true expected excess return vector μ follows a (multivariate) normal distribution

$$\mu \sim N(\pi, \Phi)$$

where Φ is the covariance matrix of the prior distribution of μ representing uncertainty in the prior expected returns. The BL model also makes the following assumption:

$$\Phi = \tau\Sigma$$

where τ is a positive number.

The second step of the BL model is to construct views on returns. Assume that there are k views on the n assets. Let $P(k \times n)$ be the matrix that identifies the assets involved in the views, $q(k \times 1)$ be the view vector, and $\Omega(k \times k)$ be the covariance matrix of the error terms from the expressed views representing the uncertainty of the views. Similarly, assume that the errors of the views are normally distributed:

$$P\mu - q \sim N(0, \Omega)$$

Once we have the prior and the views, we can combine the prior and the views to obtain blended (posterior) expected excess returns under Bayes' theorem, assuming that the estimation errors for the prior and for the views are independent. The blended (posterior) expected returns and uncertainty covariance are given by

$$\mu_p = (\Phi^{-1} + P'\Omega^{-1}P)^{-1}(\Phi^{-1}\pi + P'\Omega^{-1}q)$$
$$\Sigma_p = (\Phi^{-1} + P'\Omega^{-1}P)^{-1}$$

17.1 The Model

Developed by Fischer Black and Robert Litterman in the 1990s (Black and Litterman 1990, 1991, 1992), the BL model allows investors to combine their views on asset performance along with the market-implied priors to generate more diversified and stable portfolios. We will start with a description of the model in a general setup and then provide a simple example with a single asset for the intuitions.

17.1.1 The Prior

Consider a market of n risky assets. Let R be the excess return vector of the assets with mean $\mu(n \times 1)$ and covariance $\Sigma(n \times n)$:

$$R|\mu \sim (\mu, \Sigma)$$

Traditional MVO assumes that μ and Σ are known or can be estimated without errors. The BL model acknowledges that μ is usually estimated with errors. The Bayesian interpretation of the model therefore assumes that μ is a random vector whose prior distribution can be drawn from the market portfolio based on the capital asset pricing model (CAPM) and combined with investors' views to achieve a more precise posterior distribution.

The BL model starts with implied equilibrium expected excess returns derived using a reverse optimization process for an unconstrained MVO with $x^* = \lambda^{-1} \Sigma^{-1} \mu$:

$$\pi = \lambda_{mkt} \Sigma x_{mkt} \tag{17.1}$$

where π is the implied equilibrium excess return vector, Σ is the covariance matrix of excess returns, x_{mkt} is the vector of market capitalization weights, and λ_{mkt} is the market risk aversion coefficient that characterizes the risk-return tradeoff at the market level.

Premultiplying both sides of Equation (17.1) by x'_{mkt}, we have

$$x'_{mkt} \pi = \lambda_{mkt} x'_{mkt} \Sigma x_{mkt}$$

Therefore,

$$\lambda_{mkt} = \frac{x'_{mkt} \pi}{x'_{mkt} \Sigma x_{mkt}} = \frac{\pi_{mkt}}{\sigma^2_{mkt}} \tag{17.2}$$

This means that if the market portfolio is the solution to the unconstrained MVO, the market risk-aversion coefficient λ_{mkt} is equal to the ratio between the risk premium and the variance of the market portfolio.

Also note that $cov(R_i, R_m) = \Sigma^n_{j=1} x_{mkt,j} \sigma_{ij}$, therefore

$$\Sigma x_{mkt} = \begin{pmatrix} \sigma_{1,m} \\ \vdots \\ \sigma_{n,m} \end{pmatrix} \tag{17.3}$$

where $\sigma_{i,m}$ is the covariance between asset i and the market portfolio.

Combining Equations (17.1)–(17.3), we have

$$\pi_i = \frac{\sigma_{i,m}}{\sigma^2_{mkt}} \pi_{mkt}, i = 1,\ldots,n$$

This is the well-known CAPM formula. It allows us to estimate the implied equilibrium excess return for any single asset without knowing its market capitalization weight.

To form the prior, the BL model assumes further that the true expected excess return vector μ follows a (multivariate) normal distribution

$$\mu \sim N(\pi, \Phi)$$

where Φ is the covariance matrix of the prior distribution of μ representing uncertainty in the prior expected returns. The BL model also makes the following assumption:

$$\Phi = \tau \Sigma$$

where τ is a positive number. This effectively assumes that the volatilities of estimation errors for the expected returns in the prior are proportional to the volatilities of asset returns and that the correlations between the errors are the same as those between asset returns.

The scalar τ is presumably small, reflecting the belief that the uncertainty in the expected returns is usually much smaller than the uncertainty in the returns. To better understand this parameter, we can draw an analogy between $\tau \Sigma$ and the variance of the sample mean of T random draws of a multivariate normal distribution $N(\mu, \Sigma)$, $\bar{R} \sim N(\mu, \frac{\Sigma}{T})$. A popular value of τ used in the literature is 0.05. It indicates a confidence level in the prior expected returns similar to that in the sample mean estimated based on a sample of 20 observations.

The set of market-implied equilibrium returns provides a neutral reference point in the BL model. In the absence of additional views on the expected returns, the solution of the unconstrained MVO under the prior will be the same as the market portfolio when $\tau = 0$ or very close when τ is a small positive number.

17.1.2 The Views

The second step of the BL model is to construct views on returns. The views in the BL model do not have to be complete, involving all the assets. A view can be absolute such as "asset A is expected to return 5%" or relative such as "asset B is expected to outperform asset C by 2%." More generally, let us assume that there are k views on the n assets. Let $P(k \times n)$ be the matrix that identifies the assets involved in the views, $q(k \times 1)$ be the view vector, and $\Omega(k \times k)$ be the covariance matrix of the error terms from the expressed views representing the uncertainty of the views. Similarly, assume that the errors of the views are normally distributed:

$$P\mu - q \sim N(0, \Omega)$$

For example,

$$
\begin{array}{c}
\begin{array}{ccccc}
\text{Asset A} & \text{Asset B} & \text{Asset C} & \text{Asset D} & \text{Asset E}
\end{array} \\
\begin{array}{c}
\text{View 1} \\ \text{View 2} \\ \text{View 3}
\end{array}
\begin{pmatrix}
1 & 0 & 0 & 0 & 0 \\
0 & 1 & -1 & 0 & 0 \\
0.6 & 0.4 & 0 & -1 & 0
\end{pmatrix}
\end{array}
\times
\begin{pmatrix}
\mu_1 \\ \mu_2 \\ \mu_3 \\ \mu_4 \\ \mu_5
\end{pmatrix}
=
\begin{pmatrix}
5\% \\ 2\% \\ 1\%
\end{pmatrix}
+
\begin{pmatrix}
\varepsilon_1 \\ \varepsilon_2 \\ \varepsilon_3
\end{pmatrix}
$$

$$\underbrace{}_{P} \quad \underbrace{}_{\mu} \quad \underbrace{}_{q}$$

Alternatively, we can interpret each view on absolute or relative returns as a view on the expected return of a portfolio. For example, the second view above is equivalent to saying that a portfolio that is 100% long in asset B and 100% short in asset C has a 2% expected return.

The original BL model assumes that Ω is diagonal, meaning that the errors for different views are independent of each other. The diagonal elements in the Ω matrix represent the uncertainty around the views (larger value implies more uncertainty). The canonical model suggests setting the variance of each view at $c p_k \Sigma p_k'$, where pk is the $1 \times n$ row vector from matrix P corresponding to the kth view, and c is a positive scalar similar to τ for the prior. In other words, Ω is assumed to be a diagonal matrix with diagonal elements taken from $cP\Sigma P'$. Note that the assumption of independent views is not essential for deriving the BL model and therefore can be relaxed (see Meucci [2010]).

17.1.3 Blending the Prior and the Views

Once we have the prior and the views, we can combine the prior and the views to obtain blended (posterior) expected excess returns under Bayes' theorem, assuming that the estimation errors for the prior and for the views are independent. The blended (posterior) expected returns and the uncertainty covariance are given by

$$\mu_P = (\Phi^{-1} + P'\Omega^{-1}P)^{-1}(\Phi^{-1}\pi + P'\Omega^{-1}q) \tag{17.4}$$

$$\Sigma_P = (\Phi^{-1} + P'\Omega^{-1}P)^{-1} \tag{17.5}$$

Equation (17.4) and (17.5) show that the blended expected excess returns are simply the weighted average of π (the prior) and q (the views). The posterior uncertainty for μ_p is smaller than both the uncertainty for the prior and that for the views because μ_p contains information from both the prior and the views and is supposed to be more precise.

Alternatively, we can rewrite the formulas as

$$\mu_p = \pi + \Phi P'(P\Phi P' + \Omega)^{-1}(q - P\pi) \tag{17.6}$$

$$\Sigma_p = \Phi - \Phi P'(P\Phi^{-1}P' + \Omega)^{-1}P\Phi \tag{17.7}$$

Equations (17.6) and (17.7) provide alternative and numerically equivalent formulas with different insights.

Example (BL with One Asset): Suppose that the implied equilibrium excess return for the asset $\pi = 3\%$. The variance of its estimation error Φ is assumed to be $\dfrac{1}{100} \times 10\%^2$. Then the prior distribution for the true expected excess return μ is

$$\mu \sim N(3\%, 1\%^2)$$

Now the investor has a view that the expected excess return is 5% instead. And the variance of the estimation error for this view Ω is believed to be $\dfrac{1}{25} \times 10\%^2$. Here $P = 1$, $q = 5\%$, and the distribution for the estimation error of the view is

$$P\mu - q \sim N(0, 2\%^2)$$

Equation (17.4) allows us to combine the information from the prior and the view. Thus

$$\mu_p = (\Phi^{-1} + P'\Omega^{-1}P)^{-1}(\Phi^{-1}\pi + P'\Omega^{-1}q)$$

$$= (1\%^{-2} + 2\%^{-2})^{-1}(1\%^{-2} \times 3\% + 2\%^{-2} \times 5\%)$$

$$= 0.8 \times 3\% + 0.2 \times 5\% = 3.4\%$$

Notice that the prior received a higher weight than the view in the blending (0.8 versus 0.2). This is because the uncertainty for the prior is assumed to be much smaller than that for the view ($1\%^2$ versus $2\%^2$). As a result, the posterior mean 3.4% is closer to the prior than to the view.

Based on Equation (17.5), the posterior uncertainty is

$$\Sigma_p = (\Phi^{-1} + P'\Omega^{-1}P)^{-1} = (1\%^{-2} + 2\%^{-2})^{-1} \approx 0.9\%^2$$

As expected, the posterior mean has an uncertainty that is lower than both the prior and the view.

Example (BL with Six Assets): Let's reuse the six-asset mix example. Suppose that the market or reference portfolio is given as in Table 17.1. Assume that $\lambda = 3$ and covariance Σ is given by Table 15.1. Then we can estimate the implied excess returns π based on Equation (17.1). The estimates are shown in Table 17.1.

TABLE 17.1 Illustration of the BL Model with Six Assets

Asset Class	Market Portfolio	Implied Excess Returns	Blend V1	Blend V2
US Equity	35%	5.2%	4.2%	4.8%
DM ex-US Equity	15%	5.4%	4.6%	6.0%
EM Equity	14%	6.7%	5.8%	7.3%
US IG	21%	0.0%	0.0%	0.0%
US HY	2%	1.7%	1.4%	1.7%
Non US Gov	13%	0.7%	0.7%	1.2%

Assume that $\tau = 0.05$. Then the uncertainty in the prior expected excess returns is $\Phi = \tau\Sigma = 0.05 \times \Sigma$. This completes modeling of the prior distribution for μ:

$$\mu \sim N(\pi, 0.05 \times \Sigma)$$

Now suppose that the investor has a view that the expected risk premium for US equity is 3%, with the error in the view assumed to have a variance of $4\%^2$. This is an absolute view. Under the BL notation, we have $P = (1, 0, 0, 0, 0, 0)$, $q = 3\%$. Then we have the distribution of the view:

$$P\mu - 3\% \sim N(0, 4\%^2)$$

Next, we apply the BL formula for combining the prior and the view. The blended expected excess returns are reported in column "Blend V1" in Table 17.1. The blended return for US equity is between the prior and the view, which is intuitive. What might be interesting is the blended returns for the other assets for which the investor did not express a view also changed from the prior. This is because by setting $\Phi = \tau\Sigma$, we assume that the estimation errors for different assets in the prior are correlated, just like the returns. Therefore, when the view indicates that the US equity return is overestimated in the prior, those assets that are positively correlated with US equity also have lower returns after blending.

Next, let's consider an alternative view that is relative. Assume that the investor has a view that US equity will underperform developed markets (DM) ex-US equity by 2% in expectation with an uncertainty variance of $2\%^2$. Under the BL notation, we have $P = (1, -1, 0, 0, 0, 0)$, $q = -2\%$. Then we have the distribution of the view:

$$P\mu - (-2\%) \sim N(0, 2\%^2)$$

The blended expected excess returns are reported in column "Blend V2" in Table 17.1. Because in the prior US equity is expected to underperform DM ex-US equity only by 0.2%, the view predicts a bigger gap and therefore is relatively bearish on US equity and bullish on DM ex-US equity. The blended returns confirm this intuition. After blending, US equity expected return decreases, and DM ex-US equity's expected return increases. With a relative view involving more than one asset, it is more difficult to predict its impact on other expected returns. Generally speaking, the expected returns of those assets tend to move in the same direction as the asset with which they are more positively correlated. For example, non-US gov has zero correlation with U.S. equity but positive correlation with DM ex-US equity (possibly due to similar currency exposures), and its expected return ends up increasing after blending.

Figure 17.1 plots the market portfolio against the new optimal allocations under blended returns V1 and V2, respectively. Here we fix λ at 3 and do not impose any constraint, including the constraint on total weight. By construction, when we apply the estimated implied returns, we recover the market portfolio as the optimal solution.[1] After we combine the implied returns with a view that US equity risk premium is 3% as opposed to the implied return of 5.2%, the new optimal portfolio only has a reduced allocation to US equity, and all the other assets have the same optimal weights as before. If we combine the implied returns with the relative view that US equity will underperform DM ex-US equity by 2%, the resulting optimal allocation has 33% less allocation for US equity and 33% more allocation for DM ex-US equity.

---

1 For simplicity, we do not adjust the covariance for asset returns based on the uncertainty around the mean returns and therefore implicitly take a frequentist's view (see Section 17.3 for details).

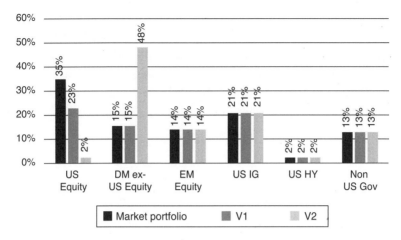

FIGURE 17.1 Unconstrained optimal allocations

Under unconstrained optimization, we can think of each view (each row in matrix P) as a portfolio, which is an overlay on top of the original market or reference portfolio from which the implied returns are estimated. An absolute view will only affect the weight of the asset involved in the view. A relative view will create long-short overlay portfolios.

In both cases, using the market portfolio that is diversified by construction as an anchor, the new optimal portfolios are also relatively diversified, except for those assets involved in the views. The deviation from the market portfolio depends on the degree to which the views deviate from the prior and the confidence level on the views. This indicates that one may face a tradeoff between expressing views effectively versus maintaining diversification and stability of the optimal portfolios.

Example (Special Cases for the BL Model): A few special cases follow directly from Equations (17.4)–(17.7):

- When the views are completely consistent with the prior, that is, $q = P\pi$, the posterior mean returns μ_p will be the same as the prior mean returns π, but the posterior uncertainty on μ, Σ_p, will be reduced because the additional information from the views confirms the prior mean returns.

- With 100% confidence in the views, $\Omega = 0$. Therefore, $\mu_p = \pi + \Phi P' (P\Phi P')^{-1} (q - P\pi)$, and we can verify that in this case $P\mu_p = P\pi + P\Phi P' (P\Phi P')^{-1} (q - P\pi) = q$; that is, the views are completely maintained in the posterior mean.

- With completely uninformative views with 0% confidence, the diagonal elements of Ω go to infinity. In this case, $\mu_p = \pi$ and $\Sigma_p = \Phi$; that is, there is no update on the prior.

In more general cases, the BL posterior expected return vector is a complex, weighted average of the prior and the view expected return vectors. The posterior distribution for the expected returns has reduced uncertainty or improved confidence compared with the prior as long as the views are informative.

Consider a special but common case in practice where investors have views on every single asset. Let's assume further that $\Phi = \tau\Sigma$, $P = I_n$, and $\Omega = c\Sigma$. The posterior distribution is then characterized by

$$\mu_P = \frac{c}{\tau+c}\pi + \frac{\tau}{\tau+c}q \tag{17.8}$$

$$\Sigma_P = \frac{1}{\frac{1}{\tau}+\frac{1}{c}}\Sigma \tag{17.9}$$

The simplified formulas shed light on the roles of the parameters τ and c in the BL model. Because they represent the level of uncertainties on the prior and the views, respectively, the blended return vector is simply a weighted average of the prior and the views with the weights inversely proportional to their uncertainty levels. The higher the uncertainty, the lower is the impact of that distribution on the posterior means. The posterior uncertainty will be lower than the uncertainty on the prior or the views. Again, using the analogy between BL blending and uncertainty in the sample mean of independent and identically distributed (iid) historical observations, if $\tau = 1/N_1$ and $c = 1/N_2$, then $\Sigma_P = \frac{1}{N_1+N_2}\Sigma$; that is, it combines information from the prior and the views that is equivalent to having $N_1 + N_2$ iid historical observations.

Another observation from the preceding formulas is that although the posterior uncertainty depends on the absolute values of τ and c, the posterior mean depends only on the ratio between them. This motivates some non-Bayesian applications of the BL model where the parameter τ is omitted completely (see Meucci [2010] for example).

17.2 Asset Allocation Implications

Given the posterior distribution described by Equations (17.4) and (17.5), the new unconstrained MVO becomes

$$\max_x x'\mu_P - \frac{\lambda}{2}x'(\Sigma+\Sigma_P)x \tag{17.10}$$

Note that under the Bayesian interpretation of the BL model, μ is a random vector. Therefore, the unconditional variance of asset returns has to take into account the uncertainty of μ, which is Σ_p after BL blending.

Assuming that $\Phi = \tau\Sigma$, the new unconstrained optimal portfolio is

$$x_{\mathrm{BL}} = \lambda^{-1}(\Sigma + \Sigma_p)^{-1}\mu_p$$

$$= \lambda^{-1}[(I_n + \Sigma^{-1}\Sigma_p)^{-1}\Sigma^{-1}][\pi + \tau\Sigma P'(P\tau\Sigma P' + \Omega)^{-1}(q - P\pi)]$$

$$= (I_n + \Sigma^{-1}\Sigma_p)^{-1}[(\lambda^{-1}\Sigma^{-1}\pi) + \tau P'\lambda^{-1}(P\tau\Sigma P' + \Omega)^{-1}(q - P\pi)] \quad (17.11)$$

Note that $\lambda^{-1}\Sigma^{-1}\pi = x_{\mathrm{mkt}}$ if we assume that $\lambda = \lambda_{\mathrm{mkt}}$ and that $q - P\pi$ represents the deviations of the views from the prior. Intuitively, we can think of the unconstrained BL optimal portfolio as the market portfolio plus deviations from the market portfolio in the direction of the portfolios about which the views are expressed (see He and Litterman [1999]). The first term $(I_n + \Sigma^{-1}\Sigma_p)^{-1}$ simply reflects the adjustment to the unconstrained optimal weights to the posterior total variance of asset returns. It increases as additional information from the views is blended with the prior to reduce the uncertainty around the means and therefore the total variance of returns.

To see this point more clearly, assume further that $P = I_n$ and $\Omega = c\Sigma$. Then we have

$$x_{\mathrm{BL}} = \frac{\tau + c}{\tau + c + \tau c}\left(\frac{c}{\tau + c}\lambda^{-1}\Sigma^{-1}\pi + \frac{\tau}{\tau + c}\lambda^{-1}\Sigma^{-1}q\right)$$

$$= \frac{\tau + c}{\tau + c + \tau c}\left(\frac{c}{\tau + c}w_{\mathrm{mkt}} + \frac{\tau}{\tau + c}w_{\mathrm{view}}\right) \quad (17.12)$$

In this special case, the unconstrained BL optimal portfolio is simply the weighted average of the market equilibrium portfolio and the optimal view portfolio with weights inversely proportional to the relative uncertainty in the prior and the views, respectively.

Unconstrained portfolio optimizations are rare in practice. However, the preceding example provides insights into why the BL model tends to generate more diversified and stable allocations than traditional MVO. The capitalization-weighted market portfolio is naturally a diversified portfolio, and the BL model shrinks the optimal portfolio toward the market portfolio, the extent to which depends on how confident the investor is in his or her prior versus the views. Equation (17.12) also demonstrates how the BL model can reduce the sensitivity of optimal weights to changes in the views. The higher the uncertainty on the views relative to that on the prior, the lower is the weight given to the optimal view portfolio. This improves the stability of the optimal portfolio.

Another potential source of diversification or stability effect of the BL model lies in the assumption of independent estimation errors across views in the original BL model. It is not conceptually more appealing than the assumption of correlated errors in the views. However, this assumption effectively shrinks the covariance matrix for the optimal deviation portfolio. To see this, let's assume that $\Phi = \tau\Sigma$, $P = I_n$, and $\Omega = \mathrm{diag}(c\Sigma)$. Equation (17.11) then becomes

$$x_{\mathrm{BL}} = (I_n + \Sigma^{-1}\Sigma_p)^{-1}\left\{(\lambda^{-1}\Sigma^{-1}\pi) + \lambda^{-1}\left[\Sigma + \frac{c}{\tau}\mathrm{diag}(\Sigma)\right]^{-1}(q - \pi)\right\} \quad (17.13)$$

The weighting matrix for the deviation portfolio, $\Sigma + \frac{c}{\tau}\mathrm{diag}(\Sigma)$, resembles one special case of covariance shrinkage that we will discuss in Chapter 18 as another potential solution to achieve more robust asset allocation than traditional MVO.

Equation (17.12), however, also explains why the BL model may not be adequate for solving the problems of traditional MVO. The optimal view portfolio w_{view} suffers from all the issues traditional MVO has. To alleviate these issues with the BL approach, we need to specify a lower confidence level for the views relative to the prior. However, this effort will at the same time reduce the usefulness of expert views in the posterior expected returns. Therefore, in practice, there is often a tradeoff between expressing views effectively versus maintaining diversification and stability of the optimal portfolios.

In the BL model, the CAPM equilibrium provides a neutral reference point for expected returns. The model assumes that expected returns might fluctuate from their equilibrium values but that they will not deviate too much. This provides an elegant theoretical foundation motivating the prior. However, there are two potential issues using the market capitalization–weighted portfolio as the reference portfolio in practice.

First, the market portfolio is unobservable (see Roll [1977]). Theoretically, it should include every single possible available asset with any worth, including real estate and collectibles. The returns for many of these investments are not observable. In practice, people use broad market indexes to proxy the market portfolio.

Second, and more importantly, for BL models, the reference portfolio is the unconstrained optimal portfolio without views. In reality, however, the market portfolio is not necessarily a desirable portfolio that an investor wants to hold in the absence of views. In some cases, the asset space for optimization may not even remotely resemble that of the market portfolio. For example, an investor may want to optimize a portfolio of fixed income assets only. In this case, if we stick with the market portfolio to derive equilibrium expected returns using the CAPM, the resulting equilibrium expected returns would not guarantee a well-diversified optimal portfolio even without views. This defeats the purpose of using the BL model to achieve more robust asset allocations. As a result, some practitioners choose to define alternative reference portfolios that match the asset space for the specific optimizations and are desirable to hold in the absence of views. This is often done at the cost of losing the nice theoretical justification for using equilibrium expected return as the prior by the BL models.

Another challenge for nonquantitative asset managers to implement the BL model is that it involves many statistical assumptions and exogenously specified parameters without clear theoretical guidance or consensus on the values of these parameters. The most challenging and abstract parameters in the model are probably τ and Ω. The literature diverges widely from defining τ as 1 to between 0.01 and 0.05 to 1/number of observations.[2] He and Litterman (1999) assumed a value of τ and calibrated values of Ω such that $\frac{\omega_k}{\tau} = p_k \Sigma p'_k$, which is effectively assuming $c = \tau$ in our previous examples. Thus, changing the value of τ will change Ω, but the blended expected return vector will remain the same. Idzorek (2007) reparameterized the original BL model using an implied confidence framework. The user-defined confidence levels can control the magnitude of the portfolio tilts and are more intuitive to specify than τ and Ω for investors with a less quantitative background. Meucci (2010) relaxed the assumption of independent errors in the views and allowed even more flexible specification of the view uncertainty matrix Ω by introducing view-specific multipliers: $\Omega = \text{diag}(u) P c \Sigma P' \text{diag}(u)$, where u is a $k \times 1$ vector of positive numbers to adjust the relative uncertainty across views. Allaj (2013) attempted to estimate τ from historical data using complex econometric models. The magnitude of the departure of a BL optimal portfolio from the reference portfolio depends on the ratio of the scalar τ to the variance in the error term of the view (elements in matrix Ω).

---

2 See Walters (2013) for a comprehensive summary.

17.3 Bayesian Versus Frequentist Interpretations

One attractive feature of the BL model is its quasi-Bayesian interpretation that provides a nice theoretical foundation for the model. However, in addition to popular Bayesian interpretation, the BL model also can be motivated from a frequentist's perspective. However, most papers in the literature do not make an effort to distinguish the two interpretations and sometimes use both implicitly within the same paper.

In fact, early papers such as Black and Litterman (1991) referred to Theil's mixed estimator, which is a generalized least-squares estimator for linear regressions mixing sample and nonsample information and does not require Bayes' theorem.[3] One key difference between the Bayesian and frequentist approaches is that a Bayesian statistician tends to model any uncertainty using a probability distribution, whereas a frequentist may assume that the true parameter is fixed but unknown and try to come up with the best point estimate and statistical inference. For BL models, this means whether the true expected return vector μ is random or fixed but unknown.

The two approaches produce the same formula for the expected returns after BL blending but slightly different covariance matrices for asset returns. The Bayesian approach assumes that μ is random, and therefore, the posterior covariance matrix for asset returns has this additional randomness: $\Sigma + \Sigma_p$, where Σ is the covariance for asset returns conditional on the value of μ. In contrast, the frequentist approach focuses on obtaining the best possible point estimate for μ and does not have to adjust the total covariance since μ is assumed to be fixed.

The need to adjust the posterior covariance matrix for returns under the Bayesian interpretation for the BL model is a nuance often ignored in the literature. A paper that ignores this adjustment or normalizes the value of τ to 1 is effectively using the frequentist interpretation regardless of what the paper states explicitly.

---

3 The Appendix provides the derivations of the same formula for the BL expected return vector using two estimation methods from a frequentist perspective.

18

Shrinkage

Summary

Shrinkage is a statistical concept introduced by Stein (1956) and used in many quantitative techniques nowadays, either implicitly or explicitly. A shrinkage estimator typically takes the following form:

$$\hat{\theta}_{shrink} = (1 - \delta)\hat{\theta} + \delta\hat{\theta}_{target}$$

where $\hat{\theta}$ is an estimator with little structure, such as the sample mean or sample covariance matrix, $\hat{\theta}_{target}$ is an estimator with more structure and a smaller number of free parameters (*shrinkage target*), and the weight given to the shrinkage target δ is called the *shrinkage factor* or *shrinkage intensity*.

The optimal shrinkage factor minimizes the expected distance between the shrinkage estimator and the true value of the parameter based on a certain loss function. There are different types of loss functions. Below are some examples:

The squared error loss: $L(\hat{\theta}, \theta) = (\hat{\theta} - \theta)^2$

The absolute error loss: $L(\hat{\theta}, \theta) = |\hat{\theta} - \theta|$

The Huber loss: $L_\delta(\hat{\theta}, \theta) = \begin{cases} \dfrac{1}{2}(\hat{\theta} - \theta)^2 & \text{if } |\hat{\theta} - \theta| \le \delta \\ \delta|\hat{\theta} - \theta| - \dfrac{1}{2}\delta^2 & \text{otherwise} \end{cases}$

The expected value of the loss function is called the *risk function*. The most common and simplest risk function is perhaps the mean squared error (MSE): $E(\hat{\theta} - \theta)^2$. The MSE is the expected squared error between the estimator and the true value of the parameter. It can be written as the sum of the variance and the squared bias of the estimator:

$$\text{MSE}(\hat{\theta}) \equiv E(\hat{\theta} - \theta)^2 = \text{var}\,(\hat{\theta}) + \text{bias}(\hat{\theta})^2$$

A popular group of statistically efficient and computationally fast covariance shrinkage estimators is represented by Ledoit–Wolf shrinkage estimators and their extensions. Each of the shrinkage estimators is a convex combination of the sample covariance matrix with a specific shrinkage target. Thus

$$\hat{\Sigma}_{\text{shrink}} = (1 - \delta)S + \delta\hat{\Sigma}_{\text{target}}$$

We list below a few covariance shrinkage targets in the literature that have been shown empirically to be helpful to improve diversification and stability of the MVO:

1. A single-index covariance matrix (see Ledoit and Wolf [2003])
2. The identity matrix (see Ledoit and Wolf [2004a])
3. Constant correlation matrix with all the pairwise correlations identical (see Ledoit and Wolf [2004b])
4. The diagonal of the sample covariance matrix (see Schafer and Strimmer [2005])

We conclude this chapter by an illustrative example showing how covariance shrinkage can help mitigate the empirical issues of naive MVO.

18.1 Basic Concepts

Shrinkage is a statistical concept introduced by Stein (1956) and used in many quantitative techniques nowadays, either implicitly or explicitly. A shrinkage estimator is the weighted average of different estimators. The basic idea behind it is that shrinking an unbiased estimator toward a lower-variance target can reduce the variance of the resulting estimator in finite samples at the cost of potentially introducing bias into it.

A shrinkage estimator typically takes the following form:

$$\hat{\theta}_{\text{shrink}} = (1 - \delta)\hat{\theta} + \delta\hat{\theta}_{\text{target}}$$

where $\hat{\theta}$ is an estimator with little structure such as the sample mean or sample covariance matrix, $\hat{\theta}_{\text{target}}$ is an estimator with more structure and a smaller number of free parameters (*shrinkage target*), and the weight given to the shrinkage target δ is called the *shrinkage factor* or *shrinkage intensity*. The optimal shrinkage factor minimizes the expected distance between the shrinkage estimator and the true value of the parameter based on a certain loss function.

Example (Intuitions on Shrinkage): With the following simple example, we will explain the basic concepts involved in shrinkage and illustrate how a shrinkage estimator can potentially outperform both the original estimator and the shrinkage target.

Suppose that there is a series of independently and identically distributed (iid) normal random variables $y_t \sim NID(\mu, \sigma^2)$, for $t = 1, \ldots, T$. Assume that σ^2 is known. The standard estimator for μ is the sample mean $\bar{y} = \frac{1}{T}\Sigma_{t=1}^{T} y_t$, with mean μ and variance $\frac{\sigma^2}{T}$. To evaluate or rank estimators, we have to first define a loss function that measures the distance between the estimator and the true value of the parameter. There are different types of loss functions. Below are some examples:

- The squared error loss: $L(\hat{\theta}, \theta) = (\hat{\theta} - \theta)^2$
- The absolute error loss: $L(\hat{\theta}, \theta) = |\hat{\theta} - \theta|$

- The Huber loss: $L_\delta(\hat{\theta}, \theta) = \begin{cases} \dfrac{1}{2}(\hat{\theta} - \theta)^2 & \text{if } |\hat{\theta} - \theta| \le \delta \\ \delta|\hat{\theta} - \theta| - \dfrac{1}{2}\delta^2 & \text{otherwise} \end{cases}$

The expected value of the loss function is called the *risk function*. The quality of an estimator is measured by its risk function. The most common and simplest risk function is perhaps the mean squared error (MSE): $E(\hat{\theta} - \theta)^2$. MSE is the expected squared error between the estimator and the true value of the parameter. It can be written as the sum of the variance and the squared bias of the estimator:

$$\text{MSE}(\hat{\theta}) \equiv E(\hat{\theta} - \theta)^2 = \text{var}(\hat{\theta}) + [E(\hat{\theta}) - \theta]^2 = \text{var}(\hat{\theta}) + \text{bias}(\hat{\theta})^2$$

Variance and bias are both undesirable for an estimator. The sample mean $\bar{y}$ is the best linear unbiased estimator (BLUE), which means that it has the lowest variance and therefore the lowest MSE among all linear unbiased estimators. However, it is not necessarily always the best estimator measured by MSE if we allow biased or nonlinear estimators.

Consider an alternative estimator that is always equal to zero regardless of the realized data:

$$\hat{\mu}_C \equiv 0$$

It may seem absurd to suggest that this could be a better estimator than the sample mean, but let's compare their MSEs:

$$\text{MSE}(\bar{y}) = \frac{\sigma^2}{T} \quad \text{MSE}(\hat{\mu}_C) = \text{var}(\hat{\mu}_C) + \text{bias}(\hat{\mu}_C)^2 = \mu^2$$

Because this extreme estimator is a constant, its variance is zero, and its MSE is equal to its squared bias. Which estimator is better really depends on the values of σ^2/T and μ^2. When T is large enough, $\text{MSE}(\bar{y}) < \text{MSE}(\hat{\mu}_C)$, which means that the sample mean is a better estimator. For small samples, however, $\hat{\mu}_C$ may be a better estimator. For example, let $\mu = 5\%$ and $\sigma = 20\%$ (not too unrealistic for equity-type asset returns). Then any sample period less than 16 years would make $\hat{\mu}_C$ a better estimator than $\bar{y}$ for the asset's annualized expected return.

In this simple example, neither estimator dominates the other for all possible values of μ. The point is that there can be a tradeoff between the variance and bias of the estimator, and sometimes a biased estimator can achieve a lower MSE than a good unbiased estimator.

What happens if we combine the two estimators or shrink $\bar{y}$ toward $\hat{\mu}_C$? Define the new estimator as follows:

$$\hat{\mu}_{\text{shrink}} = (1-\delta)\bar{y} + \delta\hat{\mu}_C$$

The MSE of the shrinkage estimator is

$$\text{MSE}(\hat{\mu}_{\text{shrink}}) = \text{var}(\hat{\mu}_{\text{shrink}}) + \text{bias}(\hat{\mu}_{\text{shrink}})^2 = (1-\delta)^2 \frac{\sigma^2}{T} + \delta^2 \mu^2 \qquad (18.1)$$

Note that $\text{MSE}(\hat{\mu}_{\text{shrink}})$ is a convex function of δ:

$$\frac{\partial^2 \text{MSE}(\hat{\mu}_{\text{shrink}})}{\partial \delta^2} = 2\left(\frac{\sigma^2}{T} + \mu^2\right) > 0$$

Given σ^2/T and μ^2, we can solve for the optimal shrinkage factor δ^* that minimizes $\mathrm{MSE}(\hat{\mu}_{\mathrm{shrink}})$ based on the first-order condition:

$$\frac{\partial \mathrm{MSE}(\hat{\mu}_{\mathrm{shrink}})}{\partial \delta} = -2(1-\delta)\frac{\sigma^2}{T} + 2\delta\mu^2 = 0$$

$$\Rightarrow \delta^* = \frac{\dfrac{\sigma^2}{T}}{\dfrac{\sigma^2}{T} + \mu^2} \in (0,1]$$

If $\sigma^2/T = \mu^2$, then $\delta^* = \dfrac{1}{2}$; that is, the optimal shrinkage estimator is equally weighted between $\bar{y}$ and $\hat{\mu}_C$. If $\sigma^2/T < \mu^2$, then $\delta^* < \dfrac{1}{2}$, and vice versa. When T goes to infinity and $\mu \neq 0$, δ^* goes to zero, and the shrinkage estimator converges to $\bar{y}$.

Plugging it back into Equation (18.1), we have

$$\mathrm{MSE}[\hat{\mu}_{\mathrm{shrink}}(\delta^*)] = \frac{\dfrac{\sigma^2}{T} \times \mu^2}{\dfrac{\sigma^2}{T} + \mu^2} \leq \min\left(\frac{\sigma^2}{T}, \mu^2\right)$$

By combining $\bar{y}$ and $\hat{\mu}_C$, the shrinkage estimator can have an MSE that is lower than both $\mathrm{MSE}(\bar{y})$ and $\mathrm{MSE}(\hat{\mu}_C)$. Given σ^2/T, the improvement of MSE from $\mathrm{MSE}(\bar{y})$ is larger when the optimal shrinkage factor δ^* is larger.

We have so far assumed that $\hat{\mu}_C \equiv 0$ for simplicity. In fact, we can set the shrinking target to any constant and most of the results would still follow. Suppose that $\hat{\mu}_C \equiv c$, where c can be any real number. We have the following slightly modified results:

$$\mathrm{MSE}(\hat{\mu}_C) = (c - \mu)^2$$

$$\mathrm{MSE}(\hat{\mu}_{\mathrm{shrink}}) = \mathrm{var}(\hat{\mu}_{\mathrm{shrink}}) + \mathrm{bias}(\hat{\mu}_{\mathrm{shrink}})^2 = (1-\delta)^2 \frac{\sigma^2}{T} + \delta^2(c-\mu)^2$$

$$\frac{\partial \mathrm{MSE}(\hat{\mu}_{\mathrm{shrink}})}{\partial \delta} = -2(1-\delta)\frac{\sigma^2}{T} + 2\delta(c-\mu)^2 = 0$$

$$\Rightarrow \delta^* = \frac{\dfrac{\sigma^2}{T}}{\dfrac{\sigma^2}{T} + (c-\mu)^2} \in (0,1]$$

$$\text{MSE}[\hat{\mu}_{\text{shrink}}(\delta^*)] = \frac{\dfrac{\sigma^2}{T} \times (c - \mu)^2}{\dfrac{\sigma^2}{T} + (c - \mu)^2} \leq \min\left[\frac{\sigma^2}{T}, (c - \mu)^2\right]$$

Therefore, there is nothing magical about setting c to zero. In fact, c can be any constant. However, if c is closer to μ, both $\text{MSE}(\hat{\mu}_C)$ and $\text{MSE}[\hat{\mu}_{\text{shrink}}(\delta^*)]$ will improve. Therefore, even though we do not know the true value of μ, we should still set c closer to μ based on our prior knowledge about μ in practice.

In this simple example with only one expected return to estimate, the shrinkage estimator does not always have a lower MSE than $\bar{y}$ for any possible value of μ. In fact, it can be shown that such an estimator does not exist when there are only one or two expected returns to estimate, that is, when the dimension of $\bar{y}(n \times 1)$ is less than or equal to 2.

Stein (1956) discovered a phenomenon that when there are three or more parameters to estimate simultaneously, there exist combined estimators with lower MSEs than any estimators that handle each parameter separately for any true values of the parameters. This means that there exist other estimators with lower MSEs than the sample mean $\bar{y}(n \times 1)$ when $n \geq 3$ for any value of μ. This phenomenon is often referred to as *Stein's paradox*. The finding was striking at the time because apart from being intuitive and commonly used, the sample mean is also the best linear unbiased estimator, the maximum-likelihood estimator under normality, and the least-squares estimator. Yet Stein's paradox claims that some combined estimators dominate the sample mean even if the underlying parameter estimates are independent. The Bayes–Stein estimator we discuss in the next section is one of these estimators proposed in the literature that dominates the sample mean.

18.2 Bayes–Stein Estimator for Expected Returns for $n \geq 3$

A popular shrinkage estimator for expected returns is the Bayes–Stein estimator proposed by Jorion (1986). The name came from the fact that it is based on the James–Stein estimator with a Bayesian interpretation.

Consider the problem of estimating the vector of means μ for n normally distributed random variables with a known covariance matrix Σ from T random observations:

$$y_t \sim NID(\mu, \Sigma), \text{ for } t = 1, ..., T$$

Consider the popular quadratic loss function associated with mean variance optimizations (MVOs):

$$L[\mu, \hat{\mu}(y)] = [\mu - \hat{\mu}(y)]' \Sigma^{-1} [\mu - \hat{\mu}(y)]$$

For $n \geq 3$, Efron and Morris (1976) generalized Stein (1956) and showed that the maximum-likelihood estimator of μ (which is also the sample mean), $\hat{\mu}_{ML}$, is inadmissible under the quadratic loss function. *Inadmissible* here means that there exists some alternative estimator with equal or lower loss than $\hat{\mu}_{ML}$ for any true value of μ. The James–Stein estimator is one of such alternative estimators proposed in the literature and probably the most popular one.

The James–Stein estimator for μ has the following form:

$$\hat{\mu}_{JS}(y) = (1 - \hat{\delta})\hat{\mu}_{ML}(y) + \hat{\delta}\mu_0 \mathbf{1}$$

where μ_0 is an arbitrary constant, and $\mathbf{1}$ is the column vector of ones.

The shrinkage factor $\hat{\delta}$ itself is a function of data:

$$\hat{\delta} = \min\left[1, \frac{\dfrac{n-2}{T}}{(\hat{\mu}_{ML} - \mu_0 \mathbf{1})' \Sigma^{-1} (\hat{\mu}_{ML} - \mu_0 \mathbf{1})} \right], \text{ for } n \geq 3$$

By construction, the James–Stein estimator is biased and nonlinear because $\hat{\delta}$ is a function of data. However, it has uniformly lower MSEs than the sample mean. This is true for any arbitrary value of μ_0, and the assumptions of known Σ and normality are not critical. The improvement is most significant in *symmetric* situations, where the assets have similar variances that are large relative to the sample means, such as the example of optimal allocation to stock markets in major developed countries in Jorion (1986).

Despite the convincing statistical advantage of the Bayes–Stein estimator over the sample mean, it is not implemented by practitioners as widely as one might expect. One possible reason is that asset returns in reality are not independent and identically distributed, and asset allocators do not typically use sample means as forward-looking expected returns. In fact, lower historical returns may indicate higher expected returns in the future due to mean reversions in the long run.

In addition, because the Bayes–Stein estimator is a linear transformation of the sample mean vector, it will not change the optimal portfolio in a mean variance optimization with only the budget constraint. To see this, consider the following problem:

$$\max_{x} x'\mu - \frac{1}{2}\lambda_1 x'\Sigma x$$
$$\text{subject to } x'1 = 1$$

The Lagrangian function is

$$L(x,\lambda_1,\lambda_2) = x'\mu - \frac{1}{2}\lambda_1 x'\Sigma x + \lambda_2(1 - x'1)$$

From the first-order conditions, we have

$$\frac{\partial L}{\partial x} = \mu - \lambda_1 \Sigma x - \lambda_2 1 = 0$$

$$\Rightarrow \mu = \lambda_1 \Sigma x + \lambda_2 1$$

This is the formula for implied returns given an optimal allocation x for MVO with only a budget constraint. It is unique up to a linear transformation. Therefore, the Bayes–Stein estimator does not necessarily lead to more diversified and stable portfolios.

In contrast, it is much more common among practitioners to estimate the covariance matrix with sample covariances of historical returns. Some covariance shrinkage estimators also can effectively mitigate the issues of highly concentrated and unstable allocations in traditional MVO.

18.2.1 Shrinkage and Bayesian Inference

Shrinkage is generally implicit in Bayesian inference. In loose terms, shrinkage means improving a naive estimator by combining it with another that contains additional information or beliefs about the true characteristics of the unknown quantity to be estimated. In this sense, shrinkage is often used to regularize ill-posed problems, such as a singular and therefore noninvertible sample covariance matrix.

The Bayesian framework treats true model parameters as random variables and shrinks their posterior distribution toward the prior distribution. The Black–Litterman model under the Bayesian interpretation is a special case of this approach with the prior distribution for expected returns coming from the capital asset pricing model (CAPM) equilibrium-implied returns. As a result, it shrinks the mean return estimator toward the theoretical expectations implied by market equilibrium.

Conversely, for an explicit shrinkage estimator, it is possible to find a natural Bayesian interpretation. A case in point is the James–Stein estimator we just discussed.

Consider an informative prior that the true mean return μ follows a normal distribution

$$p(\mu|\eta, \tau, \Sigma) \sim N(\eta\mathbf{1}, \tau\Sigma)$$

where τ is a constant representing uncertainty in the prior. An empirical Bayes approach allows the parameters η and τ to be estimated from data.

Jorion (1986) showed that given the preceding prior and $\{y_t\}_{t=1,\ldots,T}$, the posterior distribution of μ is still a multivariate normal distribution with mean

$$E(\mu \mid y, \tau, \Sigma) = (1 - \delta)\hat{\mu}_{\mathrm{ML}}(y) + \delta\mu_0\mathbf{1}$$

where

$$\delta = \frac{\tau}{T + \tau} \text{ and } \mu_0 = \left(\frac{\Sigma^{-1}\mathbf{1}}{\mathbf{1}'\Sigma^{-1}\mathbf{1}}\right)' \hat{\mu}_{\mathrm{ML}}(y)$$

Here μ_0 happens to be the return of the minimum-variance portfolio (with a constraint that total weights sum up to 1) evaluated at the sample mean.

18.3 Covariance Shrinkage

Compared with the estimation of expected returns, the estimation of covariance matrices usually relies more heavily on historical data. There are a few practical and intuitive approaches to improve the precision of these historical covariance estimates. For example, Section 15.1 shows that the variance of the sample covariance matrix $\widehat{\sigma^2}$ depends on the number of observations for any given length of sample period. Therefore, using higher-frequency realized returns can improve the precision of this estimator. For 10-year historical data where $\sigma = 20\%$, the standard error of the variance estimate $\mathrm{SE}(\widehat{\sigma^2}) \approx 1.7\%$ for annual data, 0.5% for monthly data, and 0.2% for weekly data. This approach, however, depends on the availability of high-frequency return data.

Another popular approach to reduce the estimation error in covariance matrix estimates is to impose a factor structure to reduce the dimension of the covariance matrix and the number of parameters to estimate. The design of the factor structure can be subjective to some extent, influenced by one's belief on what the right factor structure should look like. The cost of this approach is to potentially introduce bias into the estimate with poorly designed factor structure.

In addition to these two approaches, shrinkage can help further reduce the estimation error for covariance matrix. With properly selected shrinkage targets, covariance shrinkage also can be effective in improving the diversification and stability of MVO portfolios. The next section provides some intuitions.

18.3.1 Why Does Covariance Matter?

Conventional wisdom suggests that estimation errors in expected returns have a much bigger impact on the traditional MVO portfolio than errors in covariance matrix estimates. For example, Chopra and Ziemba (1993) estimated that the impact was 10 times larger. We have also shown previously that the estimation errors for covariance matrixes can be reduced relatively more easily than those for expected returns. These were at least partially the reason why many early models of robust asset allocation focused on expected returns and ignored the uncertainty in the covariance matrix estimate. One such example is the original Black–Litterman model.

Example (Covariance Matters): Let's take a closer look at the traditional unconstrained MVO problem:

$$\max_{x} x'\mu - \frac{\lambda}{2} x'\Sigma x$$

Based on the first-order condition, the solution is

$$x^* = \lambda^{-1}\Sigma^{-1}\mu$$

To evaluate the sensitivity of optimal weights to changes in expected returns, we take the first-order derivative of x^* with respect to μ. Thus

$$\frac{\partial x^*}{\partial \mu} = \lambda^{-1}\Sigma^{-1} \tag{18.2}$$

Here λ is the risk-aversion parameter for the investor. Investors with higher risk aversion tend to have optimal portfolios with lower sensitivity to changes in expected returns. If we construct an efficient frontier, each allocation on that frontier corresponds to a specific λ, with less risky portfolios associated with higher λ and therefore lower sensitivity to changes in expected returns.

It is clear from Equation (18.2) that the inverse of the covariance matrix (a.k.a. the *precision matrix*) also can play an important role in determining the sensitivity of optimal weights to expected returns. To get the intuition, let's look at the following simple example of two risky assets:

$$\Sigma^{-1} = \begin{pmatrix} \sigma_{11} & \sigma_{12} \\ \sigma_{12} & \sigma_{22} \end{pmatrix}^{-1} = \frac{1}{\sigma_{11}\sigma_{22} - \sigma_{12}^2} \begin{pmatrix} \sigma_{22} & -\sigma_{12} \\ -\sigma_{12} & \sigma_{11} \end{pmatrix}$$

$$= \frac{1}{\sigma_{11}\sigma_{22}(1-\rho^2)} \begin{pmatrix} \sigma_{22} & -\sigma_{12} \\ -\sigma_{12} & \sigma_{11} \end{pmatrix}$$

Now we have the 2×2 matrix to represent the sensitivity of each asset's optimal weight to its own expected return and to the other asset's expected return. For example,

$$\frac{\partial x_1^*}{\partial \mu_1} = \lambda^{-1} \frac{1}{\sigma_{11}(1-\rho^2)}$$

If $\lambda = 2.5$ (moderate risk aversion), $\rho = 0$, and $\sigma_{11} = 0.15^2$, then $\partial x_1^*/\partial \mu_1 = 18$. This means that a 1% increase in the expected return in asset 1 will lead to an 18% increase in its optimal weight. If we increase the correlation to 0.8, then $\partial x_1^*/\partial \mu_1 = 49$, which means that simply increasing the expected return of asset 1 by 1% can lead to 49% increase in the optimal weight in this asset. Other things being equal, all the (own or cross) sensitivities are minimized when $\rho = 0$.

This simple example indicates that estimation errors in the covariance matrix can potentially compound with the estimation errors in the expected returns to cause the solution to deviate substantially from the true optimal solution and become very unstable. The estimation errors for the optimal portfolio weights can come from the uncertainty in the expected returns, the uncertainty in the covariance matrix, and the superposition of the two. It is not sufficient to reduce the estimation errors in the expected returns only while ignoring the errors in the covariance matrix estimate.

18.3.2 Ledoit–Wolf Covariance Shrinkage Estimators

If the sample size is small relative to the number of parameters to be estimated for a covariance matrix, the sample covariance can become very unstable. In the extreme case where the number of observations is less than the number of parameters, the sample covariance matrix would be singular and cannot even be inverted to perform the MVO. Covariance shrinkage is potentially very helpful in this situation to improve on the sample covariance to make it better conditioned.

A popular group of statistically efficient and computationally fast covariance shrinkage estimators is represented by Ledoit–Wolf shrinkage estimators and their extensions (see, e.g., Ledoit and Wolf [2003, 2004a, 2004b]). Each of the shrinkage estimators is a convex combination of the sample covariance matrix with a specific shrinkage target:

$$\hat{\Sigma}_{\text{shrink}} = (1 - \delta)S + \delta\hat{\Sigma}_{\text{target}}$$

The shrinkage target should fulfill two requirements at the same time: (1) it should involve only a small number of free parameters (i.e., a lot of structure), but (2) it should also reflect important characteristics of the unknown quantity to be estimated (see Ledoit and Wolf [2004b]). The first requirement ensures that the target covariance matrix is well conditioned, and the second reduces the possibility of large biases due to misspecification errors.

The optimal shrinkage factor (or intensity) δ is derived for each shrinkage target to minimize a specific loss function for the shrinkage estimator. The resulting shrinkage covariance estimator can be shown to outperform the sample covariance matrix for finite samples. For very large samples, the optimal shrinkage factor (or intensity) will reduce to zero because the sample covariance matrix is consistent and converges to the true covariance matrix when the sample size goes to infinity.

We list below a few covariance shrinkage targets in the literature that have been shown empirically to be helpful in improving diversification and stability of the MVO:

A. A single-index covariance matrix (Ledoit and Wolf [2003])[1]
B. The identity matrix (Ledoit and Wolf [2004a])
C. A constant correlation matrix with all the pairwise correlations identical (Ledoit and Wolf [2004b])
D. The diagonal of the sample covariance matrix (Schafer and Strimmer [2005])

---

1 The covariance matrix implied by the single-index model (Sharpe [1963]) is $\sigma_m^2 \beta\beta' + D$, where σ_m^2 is the variance of the market returns, β is the vector of market betas for the assets, and D is the diagonal matrix containing idiosyncratic or residual variances.

Target B and target D can be applied to optimization of multiasset portfolios, whereas target A and target C are only suitable for highly homogeneous sets of assets such as pure equity portfolio selections.

Example (Covariance Shrinkage for Multiasset Portfolio Optimizations):
Let's reuse the six-asset mix example. Because this is a multiasset portfolio optimization problem, the covariance shrinkage targets A and C would not be appropriate. We will only consider targets B (identity matrix) and D (diagonal of the sample covariance matrix). To make the results more comparable between the two shrinkage targets, we scale the identity matrix with the average variance across assets.

Mathematically, $\widehat{\Sigma}_B = \overline{\sigma^2} I_n$, where $\overline{\sigma^2}$ is the average estimated variance across assets, and $\widehat{\Sigma}_D = diag(\widehat{\Sigma})$. Because the optimal shrinkage factor is provided for the sample covariance matrix and requires additional data to calibrate, we create grids for the shrinkage factor instead to explore its impact on the optimal portfolio.

Figure 18.1 shows graphically how covariance shrinkage using target $\widehat{\Sigma}_B$ improves the diversification of the optimal portfolio of MVO with minimum constraint (weight sum = 1). The higher the shrinkage factor we choose, the more significant the effect is. The shrinkage is especially helpful to mitigate the extreme allocations in naive MVO for US IG and non-US gov.

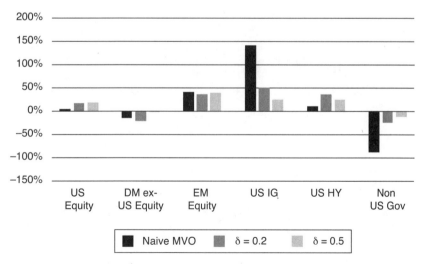

FIGURE 18.1 Naive MVO versus covariance shrinkage
(weight sum = 1, target $\widehat{\Sigma}_B$)

Similarly, Figure 18.2 shows the effect of shrinkage on the optimal portfolio when we use the alternative covariance shrinkage target $\widehat{\Sigma}_D$. The pattern of improvement in diversification is again evident with this shrinkage target. Because $\widehat{\Sigma}_D$ allows the diagonal elements (i.e., the estimates for individual assets' variances) in the covariance shrinkage target to differ, it penalizes lower-risk assets less harshly than higher-risk assets than the scaled identity matrix target. This may explain why the reduction in extreme allocations (that happen to be in US IG and non-US gov with lower risk) is less dramatic than using shrinkage target $\widehat{\Sigma}_B$.

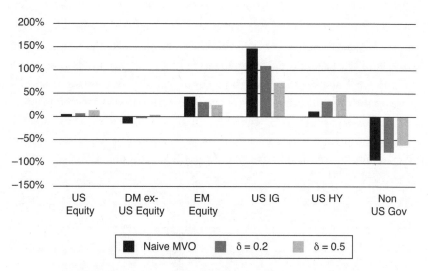

FIGURE 18.2 Naive MVO versus covariance shrinkage (weight sum = 1, target $\widehat{\Sigma}_D$)

As we introduce additional constraints in the optimization, the diversifying benefit of covariance shrinkage can be less predictable or discernible because of its interaction with any constraints that are binding. For example, if an asset's weight is floored at zero due to a binding no-short-sale constraint, covariance shrinkage may help reduce the tightness of the constraint but not push the weight above zero. Figures 18.3 and 18.4 show the impact of covariance shrinkage on asset allocation with targets B and D, respectively, when we add the no-short-sale constraint.

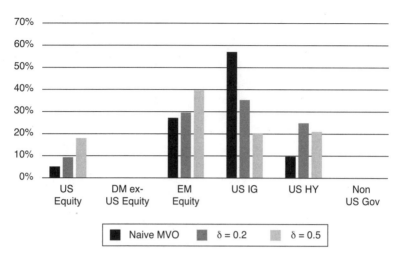

FIGURE 18.3 Naive MVO versus covariance shrinkage (weight sum = 1, no short sales, target $\hat{\Sigma}_B$)

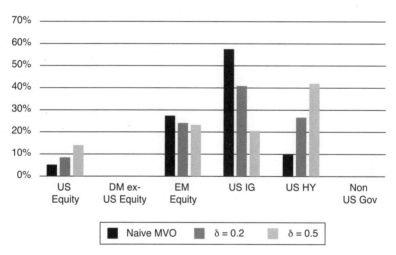

FIGURE 18.4 Naive MVO versus covariance shrinkage (weight sum = 1, no short sales, target $\hat{\Sigma}_D$)

In addition to the simple linear covariance shrinkage estimators, some more sophisticated estimators also have been proposed in the literature. For example, Lancewicki and Aladjem (2014) generalized the model to a multitarget shrinkage estimator that used several targets simultaneously. Ledoit and Wolf (2017) proposed a nonlinear shrinkage estimator that is more flexible than previous linear shrinkage estimators and has just the same number of free parameters as the number of assets.

19

Robust Optimizers

Summary

Apart from constructing robust estimators of optimization inputs that are less sensitive to outliers and other estimation errors, one also could incorporate the uncertainty on the input estimates explicitly in the optimization process. Popular examples of these solutions include penalized optimization, max-min robust optimization, and portfolio resampling, which we will review in this chapter.

One approach to overcome the issues of naive mean variance optimization (MVO) is to introduce a penalty term or a regularizer on the portfolio weight vector into the traditional optimization problem. The penalty is often in the form of a norm, which is a convex function from a vector space to the nonnegative real numbers that satisfies certain properties pertaining to scalability and additivity and takes the value zero if only the input vector is zero. Just as we can formulate the traditional MVO in different ways, this penalty term can be introduced by adding a weighted norm in the objective function or by adding a constraint explicitly.

In finance, the idea of a robust optimization (RO) is to choose the allocation that will perform well even in the worst-case model misspecification due to uncertainty on the input parameters. It generally solves the following maximin problem:

$$\max_{x \in X} \min_{(\mu, \Sigma) \in U} x'\mu - \frac{\lambda}{2} x'\Sigma x$$

where U is the uncertainty set for the unknown parameters (μ, Σ).

Under this optimization, the portfolio choice is guaranteed to perform adequately for all the markets or scenarios within the given uncertainty set. However, to receive this "insurance," the investor has to give up some market upside, regardless of its probability. Therefore, this strategy tends to be very pessimistic. In addition, there is no consensus on the choice of the uncertainty set or theoretical guidance on how to calibrate the parameters, which may seem arbitrary. We will discuss three popular types of uncertainty sets for RO in the literature: box, ellipsoid, and norm bounded.

Portfolio resampling is one of the better-known approaches to take into account parameter uncertainty explicitly in the optimization process, and it was invented by Richard and Robert Michaud. This approach generally involves the following steps:

1. Generate N random samples of history by resampling from an actual history of returns or simulating from an estimated distribution $N(\hat{\mu}, \hat{\Sigma})$. Estimate sample mean and sample covariance matrix $(\hat{\mu}_i, \hat{\Sigma}_i)$ for each simulated history.
2. Construct an efficient frontier with each $(\hat{\mu}_i, \hat{\Sigma}_i)$.
3. Average the N resampled efficient frontiers.

19.1 Penalized Optimization

One approach to overcome the issues of naive MVO is to introduce a penalty term or a regularizer on the portfolio weight vector into the traditional optimization problem. The penalty is often in the form of a norm, which is a convex function from a vector space to the nonnegative real numbers that satisfies certain properties pertaining to scalability and additivity and takes the value zero if only the input vector is zero. Just as we can formulate the traditional MVO in different ways, this penalty term can be introduced by adding a weighted norm in the objective function or by adding a constraint explicitly.

19.1.1 L_1 and L_2 Penalties

L_1 norm (also known as *Manhattan norm* or *taxicab norm*[1]) is simply the sum of absolute values of the elements of the vector. It is the most natural way of measuring distance between vectors. In this norm, all the individual components are weighted equally.

$$\|x\|_1 \equiv \sum_{i=1}^{n} |x_i|$$

L_2 norm (also known as *Euclidean norm* and *square norm*) is the square root of the inner product of a vector with itself. It is the most popular norm.

$$\|x\|_2 \equiv \sqrt{\sum_{i=1}^{n} x_i^2}$$

Or in matrix notation

$$\|x\|_2 \equiv \sqrt{x'x}$$

More generally, we can define the *p*-norm or L_p norm ($p \geq 1$) of vector $x = (x_1, \ldots, x_n)'$ as

$$\|x\|_p \equiv \left(\sum_{i=1}^{n} |x_i|^p \right)^{1/p}$$

The partial derivative of the *p*-norm is given by

$$\frac{\partial \|x\|_p}{\partial x_i} \equiv \frac{x_i |x_i|^{p-2}}{\|x\|_p^{p-1}}$$

For $p = 1$,

$$\frac{\partial \|x\|_1}{\partial x_i} \equiv \frac{x_i}{|x_i|}$$

For $p = 2$,

$$\frac{\partial \|x\|_2}{\partial x_i} \equiv \frac{x_i}{\|x\|_2}$$

---

1 The name relates to the distance a taxi has to drive in a rectangular street grid, $|x_1| + |x_2|$, to get from the origin to the point $x = (x_1, x_2)$.

Different norm penalties have different effects on the MVO. Recall the following formulation of the traditional mean variance problem with only the constraint that total weight equals one:

$$\min_{x} \frac{1}{2} x' \Sigma x$$

subject to $x'\mu = \mu_p$ and $x'1 = 1$

The Lagrangian function is

$$L(x, \lambda_1, \lambda_2) = \frac{1}{2} x' \Sigma x + \lambda_1 (\mu_p - x'\mu) + \lambda_2 (1 - x'1)$$

The first-order conditions are

$$\frac{\partial L}{\partial x} = \Sigma x - \lambda_1 \mu - \lambda_2 1 = 0$$

$$\frac{\partial L}{\partial \lambda_1} = \mu_p - x'\mu = 0$$

$$\frac{\partial L}{\partial \lambda_2} = 1 - x'1 = 0$$

Therefore,

$$x = \lambda_1 \Sigma^{-1} \mu + \lambda_2 \Sigma^{-1} 1$$

L_1 Norm Penalty

Now add an additional constraint on the L_1 norm of portfolio weight x:

$$\| x \|_1 \leq a$$

Because $x^T 1 = 1$, we can rewrite the L_1 norm constraint in a more intuitive way:

$$\sum_{j \in \{i | x_i < 0\}} | x_j | \leq \frac{a-1}{2}$$

That is, it restricts the total negative weight across assets to be less than or equal to $(a - 1)/2$, which is effectively a short-sale budget for the portfolio optimization.

- If $a < 1$, there is no feasible solution for the optimization problem.
- If $a = 1$, the L_1 norm constraint is equivalent to the no-short-sale constraints on all the assets.
- If $a > 1$, a short-sale budget of $(a - 1)/2$ can be distributed across all assets.

The new Lagrangian after we introduce the L_1 constraint is

$$L(x, \lambda_1, \lambda_2) = \frac{1}{2} x' \Sigma x + \lambda_1 (\mu_p - x'\mu) + \lambda_2 (1 - x'1) + \lambda_3 (\| x \|_1 - a)$$

The new necessary first-order condition becomes

$$\frac{\partial L}{\partial x} = \Sigma x - \lambda_1 \mu - \lambda_2 1 + \lambda_3 x \oslash |x| = 0$$

where $x \oslash |x|$ is the element-wise division with its ith element given by $x_i / |x_i|$, which is also the sign of x_i (for example, for $x = (2, -3)$, $x \oslash |x| = (1, -1)$).

Note that if the L_1 norm constraint is binding (and therefore $\lambda_3 > 0$), it will exert a pressure to push portfolio weights toward zero because reducing positive weights or increasing negative weights will help relax the L_1 norm constraint:

$$x^* = \lambda_1 \Sigma^{-1} \mu + \lambda_2 \Sigma^{-1} 1 - \lambda_3 \Sigma^{-1} x \oslash |x|$$

$$\frac{x_i}{|x_i|} = \begin{cases} 1 & \text{if } x_i > 0 \\ -1 & \text{if } x_i < 0 \end{cases}$$

Therefore, the L_1 norm penalty is most helpful for mitigating extreme long/short positions due to high correlations between assets in the absence of any short sale constraint. An analogy for this is the effect of adding the absolute value of the magnitude of coefficient as a penalty term to the loss function in least absolute shrinkage and selection operator (LASSO) regression. LASSO shrinks the less important explanatory variables' coefficients to zero and therefore works well for variable selection when there are many candidate variables. Similarly, MVO with an L_1 norm penalty term or regularizer tends to generate sparser portfolios than without and therefore usually does not help with diversification.

As discussed earlier, in the presence of a no-short-sale constraint, the L_1 norm penalty no longer works because the L_1 norm for the weight vector will always be equal to the total weight budget.

L_2 Norm Penalty

Now let's add a constraint on the L_2 norm of portfolio weight x to the original MVO:

$$\|x\|_2 \equiv \sqrt{\sum_{i=1}^{n} x_i^2} \leq b$$

or, equivalently, on the squared L_2 norm of the weight vector:

$$\|x\|_2^2 \equiv \sum_{i=1}^{n} x_i^2 \leq b^2$$

Given the budget constraint $x^T \mathbf{1} = 1$, we can rewrite the (squared) L_2 norm constraint in a more intuitive way:

$$\sum_{i=1}^{n}\left(x_i - \frac{1}{n}\right)^2 \leq b^2 - \frac{1}{n}$$

That is, it restricts the Euclidean distance between the portfolio weight vector and the equally weighted portfolio.

- If $b < \dfrac{1}{\sqrt{n}}$, there is no feasible solution for the optimization problem.

- If $b = \dfrac{1}{\sqrt{n}}$, the only feasible solution is the equally weighted portfolio, and the optimization problem becomes trivial.

- If $b > \dfrac{1}{\sqrt{n}}$, the optimal portfolio will be chosen within a neighborhood of the equally weighted portfolio with a maximum distance of $\sqrt{b^2 - (1/n)}$ in the Euclidean space.

Alternatively, we can look at the new Lagrangian function:

$$L(x, \lambda_1, \lambda_2, \lambda_3) = \frac{1}{2}x'\Sigma x + \lambda_1(\mu_p - x'\mu) + \lambda_2(1 - x'\mathbf{1}) + \lambda_3(x'x - b^2)$$

The new first-order conditions include

$$\frac{\partial L}{\partial x} = \Sigma x - \lambda_1 \mu - \lambda_2 \mathbf{1} + 2\lambda_3 x = 0$$

This is another way to see that if the L_2 norm constraint is binding (and therefore $\lambda_3 > 0$), it will exert a pressure to push portfolio weights toward the equally weighted portfolio because the marginal contribution to the penalty term, $\lambda_3(x'x - b^2)$, for each asset is proportional to its weight.

Because the L_2 norm penalty pushes the optimal portfolio toward the equally weighted portfolio, it tends to lead to more diversified optimal allocations. The extent to which it helps with diversification depends on how tight the constraint is (the Lagrange multiplier λ_3) or the weight assigned to the penalty term if we were to add it in the objective function directly.

The analogy for the L_2 norm penalty for MVO is the *ridge regression*, which is particularly useful to mitigate the problem of multicollinearity in linear regression.

Example (Six-Asset MVO with L_2 Norm Penalty): Consider the following formulation of a penalized MVO:

$$\max_x x'\hat{\mu} - \frac{\lambda}{2} x'\Sigma x - \lambda_p x'x$$

$$\text{subject to} \quad x'\mathbf{1} = 1$$

where λ_p is the weight given to the penalty term $x'x = \|x\|_2^2$. If $\lambda_p = 0$, this would be a traditional MVO.

Note that this problem is equivalent to

$$\max_x x'\hat{\mu} - \frac{\lambda}{2} x'\Sigma x$$

$$\text{subject to } x'\mathbf{1} = 1 \text{ and } \|x\|_2 \equiv \sqrt{\sum_{i=1}^{n} x_i^2} \leq b$$

for a certain value of $b = b(\lambda_p)$. Let's reuse the same six-asset mix. Assume that the risk-aversion parameter $\lambda = 3$ as usual. For comparability, we use two values for λ_p, 0.008 and 0.03, corresponding roughly to the covariance shrinkage examples and shrinkage factors of 0.2 and 0.5, respectively.

Figure 19.1 shows the naive MVO and the penalized optimizations with two values for λ_p under only the constraint that asset weights sum up to one. Figure 19.2 shows the optimization results with one additional constraint that there are no short sales. You may find that the two charts look familiar. In fact, they also look like the figures for covariance shrinkage with identity matrix target with the same parameters and constraints. This is actually expected. The next section explores the connections between penalized optimization and covariance shrinkage in more details.

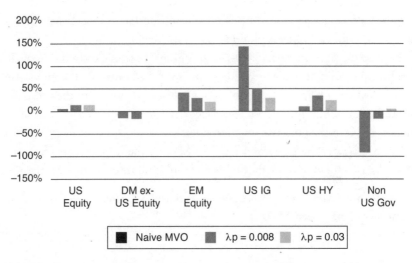

FIGURE 19.1 Naive MVO versus L_2 penalized optimization (weight sum = 1)

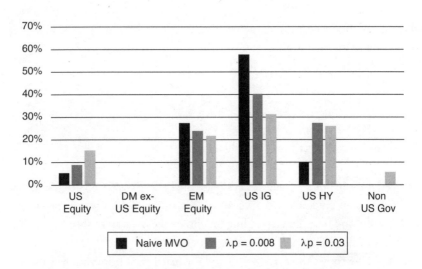

FIGURE 19.2 Naive MVO versus L_2 penalized optimization
(weight sum = 1, no short sale)

19.1.2 Penalized Optimization and Covariance Shrinkage

Consider the following penalized MVO with a generalized quadratic penalty $x'\Omega x$:

$$\max_{x \in X} x'\mu - \frac{\lambda}{2}x'\Sigma x - \frac{\lambda_p}{2}x'\Omega x$$

where Ω is an $n \times n$ matrix, and $\dfrac{\lambda_p}{2}$ is the weight given to the quadratic penalty. When $\Omega = I_n$, $x'\Omega x = x'x = \|x\|_2^2$, so the (squared) L_2 norm penalty is a special case of it.

Note that we can rewrite the problem above as

$$\max_{x \in X} x'\mu - \frac{\tilde{\lambda}}{2} x'\tilde{\Sigma}x$$

where $\tilde{\lambda} = \lambda + \lambda_p$ and $\tilde{\Sigma} = \dfrac{\lambda}{\lambda + \lambda_p}\Sigma + \dfrac{\lambda_p}{\lambda + \lambda_p}\Omega$. It is easy to see that $\tilde{\Sigma}$ is effectively a shrunk covariance matrix with a shrinkage target Ω and a shrinkage factor $\dfrac{\lambda_p}{\lambda + \lambda_p}$. This means that any shrinkage target in the literature that is approximate for a specific situation can potentially motivate a corresponding functional form for Ω. These include but are not limited to

1. A single-index covariance matrix
2. The identity matrix
3. A constant-correlation matrix with all the pairwise correlations identical
4. The diagonal of the sample covariance matrix

The empirical success of covariance shrinkage in generating more diversified and stable optimal portfolios will likely carry over to these penalized MVOs as well. In addition, $\tilde{\lambda} = \lambda + \lambda_p$ also indicates the quadratic penalty term and also increases the effective relative risk aversion parameter for the optimization. Based on our discussion in preceding sections, higher risk aversion also helps mitigate extreme and unstable allocations.

Penalized optimization also enjoys a higher level of flexibility than covariance shrinkage. For example, it is much more straightforward to extend penalized optimization to other types of optimizations such as the mean CVaR optimization than to extend covariance shrinkage.

19.2 Robust Optimization

Robust optimization (RO) is a relatively young and active research area. Its application in finance started in the 2000s. Unlike stochastic optimization (SO), which is the other approach to deal with input uncertainty in optimization, RO does not assume that the probability distribution of the uncertain input is known. Instead, it assumes that the values of inputs reside in a so-called uncertainty set. RO's computational tractability for many classes of uncertainty and problem types makes it popular among practitioners with quantitative backgrounds.

In finance, the idea of a robust optimization is to choose the allocation that will perform well even in the worst-case model misspecification due to uncertainty on the input parameters. It generally solves the following maximin problem:

$$\max_{x \in X} \min_{(\mu, \Sigma) \in U} x'\mu - \frac{\lambda}{2} x'\Sigma x$$

where U is the uncertainty set for the unknown parameters (μ, Σ).

Under this optimization, the portfolio choice is guaranteed to perform adequately for all the markets or scenarios within the given uncertainty set. However, to receive this "insurance," the investor has to give up some of the upside regardless of its probability. Therefore, this strategy tends to be very pessimistic. In addition, there is no consensus on the choice of the uncertainty set or theoretical guidance on how to calibrate the parameters, which may seem arbitrary.

Example (Intuitions for Maximin RO): Consider a simple decision problem: Given the uncertainty on the weather (sun versus rain) today, I need to decide whether to bring an umbrella. My happiness (or utility) for the day is measured on a scale of 1 to 10. If it rains and I did not bring an umbrella, I will feel unhappy. If I brought my umbrella and it does rain, I will feel somewhat better. If it is sunny and I brought my umbrella, I will be happy, but not as happy as if I did not bring my umbrella because of the small inconvenience. My utility contingent on my decision and the realization of nature can be summarized in the following table:

	Sun	Rain
No umbrella	10	1
Umbrella	6	3

Now suppose that I follow a maximin decision rule: for each decision, I find the worst outcome with respect to the uncertainty set (sun or rain); then I pick the decision that provides the best worst outcome. In this example, I will always bring my umbrella to avoid the worst-case scenario (rain, no umbrella). In addition, I will make the same decision even if there is only a very small chance of rain, which makes the expected utility much higher if I do not bring my umbrella because the maximin rule does not take into account probability distribution of the uncertainty set.

	Sun	Rain	Worst Utility	Expected Utility
No umbrella	10	1	1	9.1
Umbrella	6	3	3	5.7
Probability	90%	10%	Best Worst Utility	Best Expected Utility
			3	9.1

To solve the RO problem, the uncertainty set has to be explicitly specified. Tütüncü and Koenig (2004) proposed robust MVO with box uncertainty on return estimates. Garlappi et al. (2007) discussed ellipsoid uncertainty as part of the multiprior approach. El Ghaoui et al. (2003) proposed norm-bounded uncertainties. Examples of more recent development include Zhu and Fukushima (2009) on worst-case CVaR and Ben-Tal et al. (2010) on soft robustness.

The way one chooses to define the uncertainty set usually depends on the parameter estimation method. For instance, Meucci (2011) proposed a Bayesian estimator of the model parameters that naturally defines the location-dispersion ellipsoid of their posterior distributions.

We will discuss three popular types of uncertainty sets for RO in the literature.

19.2.1 Box Uncertainty

As the name indicates, box uncertainty defines lower and upper bounds for each input parameter independently. The uncertainty about expected returns and covariance matrix in general can be represented as

$$U_\mu = \{\mu : \mu^L \le \mu \le \mu^U\}$$

$$U_\Sigma = \{\Sigma : \Sigma^L \le \Sigma \le \Sigma^U, \Sigma \text{ is symmetric and positive semidefinite}\}$$

$$U_{\mu,\Sigma} = \{\mu, \Sigma : \mu \in U_\mu, \Sigma \in U_\Sigma\}$$

Example (Box Uncertainty with Two Assets): In the case of two assets with uncertainty about the expected returns,

$$U_\mu = \{\mu_1, \mu_2 : \mu_{1,L} \le \mu_1 \le \mu_{1,U}, \mu_{2,L} \le \mu_2 \le \mu_{2,U}\}$$

Expected returns for the two assets have independent upper and lower bounds (see Figure 19.3).

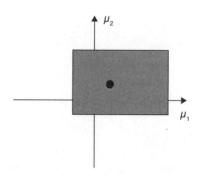

FIGURE 19.3 Box uncertainty

Example (A Special Case for RO with Box Uncertainty): If there are long-only constraints on asset weights, we can solve the following maximin problem sequentially:

$$\max_{x \in \mathbb{R}^n} \min_{(\mu, \Sigma) \in U} x'\mu - \frac{\lambda}{2} x'\Sigma x$$
$$\text{subject to } x'\mathbf{1} = 1$$
$$x \ge 0$$

Consider the interior minimization problem first:

$$\min_{(\mu, \Sigma) \in U} x'\mu - \frac{\lambda}{2} x'\Sigma x$$

Because μ and Σ are separable in both the objective function and the uncertainty set, it is equivalent to solving two separate minimization problems:

$$\min_{\mu \in U_\mu} x'\mu \text{ and } \min_{\Sigma \in U_\Sigma} -\frac{\lambda}{2} x'\Sigma x$$

Because $x \ge 0$, the solution to the first problem is

$$\mu^* = \mu^L$$

For example, if we assume that the expected stock return varies from 4% to 10% and that expected bond return varies from 2% to 6%, then in the RO we are actually working on an MVO with expected stock return of 4% and expected bond return of 2%. This is the worst case in terms of input uncertainty for all the long-only fully invested portfolios.

Similarly, because $x \geq 0$ and $x'\Sigma x = \sum_{i=1}^{n} \sum_{j=1}^{n} x_i x_j \sigma_{ij}$, if Σ^U is symmetric and positive semidefinite, the solution to the second problem is

$$\Sigma^* = \Sigma^U$$

We can then solve the exterior maximization problem after plugging in the solution to the interior problem:

$$\max_{x \in \mathbb{R}^n} x'\mu^L - \frac{\lambda}{2} x'\Sigma^U x$$

$$\text{subject to } x' \mathbf{1} = 1$$

$$x \geq 0$$

This is a simple MVO with which we are familiar. Therefore, in this special case, although the portfolio choice is guaranteed to perform adequately for all the markets or scenarios within the given uncertainty set, it is not necessarily more diversified or stable than their counterpart in a naive MVO.

In more general cases, the solution for the interior minimization problem is not necessarily the same for all possible portfolios, so we cannot solve the maximin problem sequentially. Fortunately, special algorithms have been developed to solve this type of problem. For example, Tütüncü and Koenig (2004) formulated the problem as a saddle-point problem and applied an interior-point algorithm to solve it. They proposed two techniques for generating uncertainty sets from historical data—bootstrapping and moving averages—and eliminated some of the lowest and highest quantiles of the processed data to minimize outlier effects. Their numerical experiments indicated that RO is more stable over time but can be even more concentrated than naive MVO.

In general, box uncertainty tends to lead to overly conservative solutions because all parameters are allowed to take their worst values simultaneously. The ellipsoid uncertainty to be discussed next can alleviate this problem to some extent.

19.2.2 Ellipsoid Uncertainty

Because asset returns often correlate with each other, it may be natural to expect estimation errors for expected asset returns to be correlated as well. Ellipsoid uncertainty on mean returns is of the form

$$U = \{\mu : (\mu - \hat{\mu})'\Sigma^{-1}(\mu - \hat{\mu}) \leq \delta^2\}$$

where δ is a nonnegative number that controls the size the uncertainty set. When $\delta = 0$, there is no uncertainty around the mean returns, and we are back to the traditional MVO.

If we assume that asset returns follow a multivariate normal distribution with a known covariance matrix Σ and that $\hat{\mu}$ is the sample mean based on T observations, we have $\hat{\mu} \sim N(\mu, \frac{1}{T}\Sigma)$. Then $T(\mu - \hat{\mu})'\Sigma^{-1}(\mu - \hat{\mu})$ follows a chi-squared distribution with degree of freedom equal to the number of assets. Empirically, we can set the value of δ^2 to the critical value of the chi-squared distribution corresponding to a chosen confidence level divided by T.

Example (Ellipsoid Uncertainty with One or Two Assets): In the extreme case with only one asset,

$$U = \{\mu : |\mu - \hat{\mu}| \leq \delta\sqrt{\Sigma}\}$$

In the case with two assets, the ellipsoid uncertainty becomes

$$U = \{\mu_1, \mu_2 : \omega_{11}(\mu_1 - \hat{\mu}_1)^2 + 2\omega_{12}(\mu_1 - \hat{\mu}_1)(\mu_2 - \hat{\mu}_2) + \omega_{22}(\mu_2 - \hat{\mu}_2)^2 \leq \delta^2\}$$

where the ω_{ij}'s are elements in the inverse matrix $\Omega = \Sigma^{-1}$ (see Figure 19.4).

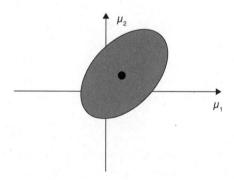

FIGURE 19.4 Ellipsoid uncertainty

In order to solve the maximin problem under ellipsoid uncertainty, consider the interior minimization problem first:

$$\min_{\mu} x'\mu - \frac{\lambda}{2} x'\Sigma x$$

$$\text{subject to } (\mu - \hat{\mu})'\Sigma^{-1}(\mu - \hat{\mu}) \le \delta^2$$

This minimization problem has a linear objective and a quadratic inequality constraint in the control variable μ. Therefore, we can solve it with the Kuhn–Tucker condition:

$$\mu^* = \hat{\mu} - \frac{\delta\Sigma x}{\sqrt{x'\Sigma x}}$$

We can then solve the exterior maximization problem after plugging in this solution into the interior problem:

$$\max_{x \in X} x'\hat{\mu} - \delta\sqrt{x'\Sigma x} - \frac{\lambda}{2} x'\Sigma x$$

This can be cast as a second-order cone program (SOCP), which is a convex optimization problem. There exists a $\tilde{\lambda} = \tilde{\lambda}(\lambda,\delta) > \lambda$ such that the solution to the preceding optimization problem is the same as the following problem (Fabozzi et al. 2010):

$$\max_{x \in X} x'\hat{\mu} - \frac{\tilde{\lambda}}{2} x'\Sigma x$$

Therefore, the RO with ellipsoid uncertainty effectively increased the risk-aversion parameter in the mean variance objective function. This is consistent with the notion that RO is more conservative than traditional MVO. This increase in risk aversion will push the MVO solution toward the minimum variance portfolio, which generally improves diversification and stability of the optimal portfolio.

19.2.3 Norm-Bounded Uncertainty

Norm-bounded uncertainty for expected returns is in the following form:

$$U_\mu = \{\mu : \mu - \hat{\mu} = E\delta, \forall \|\delta\|_2 \le 1\}$$

where E is an $n \times n$ invertible matrix that controls the size, shape, and rotation of the uncertainty set, and δ is an $n \times 1$ vector with its L_2 norm bounded by 1.

Norm-bounded uncertainty for covariance is as follows:

$$U_\Sigma = \{\Sigma : \Sigma = \hat{\Sigma} + \rho\Delta, \forall \|\Delta\|_2 \le 1\}$$

where ρ is a positive scalar that controls the size of the uncertainty set for covariance, and Δ is a symmetric positive semidefinite $n \times n$ matrix with its 2-norm bounded by 1. The combined uncertainty set is

$$U_{\mu,\Sigma} = \{\mu, \Sigma : \mu \in U_\mu, \Sigma \in U_\Sigma\}$$

Example (Norm-Bounded Uncertainty for Expected Returns with One or Two Assets): In the extreme case where $n = 1$, $\|\delta\|_2 \le 1$ implies $-1 \le \delta \le 1$; therefore,

$$U_\mu = \{\mu \in \mathbb{R} : |\mu - \hat{\mu}| \le E\}$$

More generally, we can rewrite the uncertainty set

$$\mu - \hat{\mu} = E\delta \Rightarrow E^{-1}(\mu - \hat{\mu}) = \delta$$

$$\Rightarrow (\mu - \hat{\mu})'(E^{-1})'E^{-1}(\mu - \hat{\mu}) = (\mu - \hat{\mu})'(EE')^{-1}(\mu - \hat{\mu}) = \delta'\delta = \|\delta\|_2^2 \le 1$$

When $n = 2$, assume that $E = \begin{pmatrix} \sigma & 0 \\ 0 & \sigma \end{pmatrix}$, that is, an identity matrix scaled by σ. Then

$$U_\mu = \{\mu_1, \mu_2 : (\mu_1 - \hat{\mu}_1)^2 + (\mu_2 - \hat{\mu}_2)^2 \le \sigma^2\}$$

The uncertainty set is the area within a circle centered at $(\hat{\mu}_1, \hat{\mu}_2)$ with radius σ (see Figure 19.5).

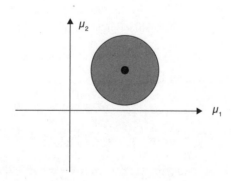

FIGURE 19.5 Norm-bounded uncertainty (first example)

If $E = \begin{pmatrix} \sigma_1 & 0 \\ 0 & \sigma_2 \end{pmatrix}$, where $\sigma_1 > \sigma_2$, we have

$$U_\mu = \{\mu_1, \mu_2 : \frac{(\mu_1 - \hat{\mu}_1)^2}{\sigma_1^2} + \frac{(\mu_2 - \hat{\mu}_2)^2}{\sigma_2^2} \leq 1\}$$

In this case, the uncertainty set is the area within an ellipse centered at $(\hat{\mu}_1, \hat{\mu}_2)$ with semimajor axis σ_1 and semiminor axis σ_2 (see Figure 19.6).

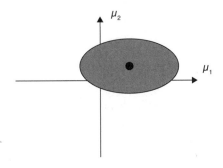

FIGURE 19.6 Norm-bounded uncertainty (second example)

For RO with norm-bounded uncertainty, we can solve the maximin problem sequentially. First, let's look at the interior minimization problem:

$$\min_{(\mu, \Sigma) \in U} x'\mu - \frac{\lambda}{2} x'\Sigma x$$

Because μ and Σ are separable in both the objective function and the uncertainty set, it is equivalent to solving two separate minimization problems:

$$\min_{\mu \in U_\mu} x'\mu \quad \text{and} \quad \min_{\Sigma \in U_\Sigma} -\frac{\lambda}{2} x'\Sigma x$$

Solve the first minimization problem:

$$\min_{\mu \in U_\mu} x'\mu, \quad \text{where } U_\mu = \{\mu : \mu - \hat{\mu} = E\delta, \forall \|\delta\|_2 \leq 1\}$$

$$\Leftrightarrow \min_{\|\delta\|_2 \leq 1} x'E\delta$$

$$\Rightarrow \mu^* = \hat{\mu} + E\delta^* = \hat{\mu} - \frac{EE'x}{\|E'x\|_2} \Rightarrow x'\mu^* = x'\hat{\mu} - \frac{x'EE'x}{\|E'x\|_2} = x'\hat{\mu} - \|E'x\|_2$$

Solve the second minimization problem:

$$\min_{\Sigma \in U_\Sigma} -\frac{\lambda}{2} x'\Sigma x, \text{ where } U_\Sigma = \{\Sigma : \Sigma = \hat{\Sigma} + \rho\Delta, \forall \, \|\Delta\|_2 \leq 1\}$$

$$\Leftrightarrow \max_{\|\Delta\|_2 \leq 1} x'\Delta x$$

$$\Rightarrow \Delta^* = I_n \Rightarrow \Sigma^* = \hat{\Sigma} + \rho I_n \Rightarrow -\frac{\lambda}{2} x'\Sigma^* x = -\frac{\lambda}{2} x'(\hat{\Sigma} + \rho I_n)x$$

Note that we used the Cauchy–Schwarz inequality to solve for Δ^*.

Therefore, the original RO problem is simplified to

$$\max_{x \in X} x'\hat{\mu} - \|E'x\|_2 - \frac{\lambda}{2} x'(\hat{\Sigma} + \rho I_n)x$$

Compared with the naive MVO, there are two main changes in the new objective function. First, there is an additional term, $-\|E'x\|_2$. Note that $\|E'x\|_2 = \sqrt{x'EE'x}$. If E is chosen such that EE' resembles the covariance matrix Σ, $\|E'x\|_2$ will resemble the volatility of the portfolio, with an effect on the optimal portfolio similar to ellipsoid uncertainty. In other words, it effectively increases the risk-aversion parameter of the objective function.

Second, the norm-bounded uncertainty on covariance replaces the covariance matrix estimate $\hat{\Sigma}$ in the mean variance model with $(\hat{\Sigma} + \rho I_n)$. This is similar to shrinking the covariance matrix toward a scaled identity matrix, which is known to improve the diversification and stability of the optimal portfolio.

Example (Norm-Bounded RO with Six Assets): Consider the naive MVO with six assets again. By changing the value of the risk-aversion parameter λ from 10 to 1, we can construct part of the efficient frontier for MVO2 (with only two constraints: sum of weights equals one and there is no short sale). Figure 19.7 shows the optimal allocations along the efficient frontier.

Now define a norm-bounded uncertainty set where $E = 0.01 \times I_n$ and $\rho = 0.01$. All the other parameters and constraints remain the same. The new optimal allocations are shown in Figure 19.8. In this example, the robust optimization leads to a much more diversified portfolio than the naive MVO at any given level of risk aversion.

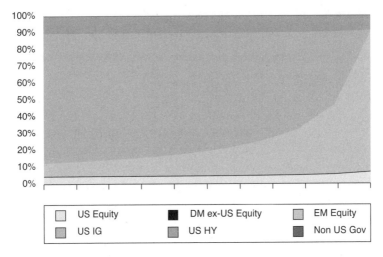

FIGURE 19.7 Optimal allocations for naive MVOs ($\lambda = 10, ..., 1$)

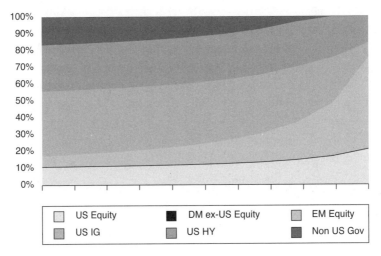

FIGURE 19.8 Optimal allocations for norm-bounded RO ($\lambda = 10, ...,1$)

19.3 Portfolio Resampling

Portfolio resampling is one of the better-known approaches to take into account parameter uncertainty explicitly in the optimization process, and it was invented by Richard and Robert Michaud. This approach generally involves the following steps:

1. Generate N random samples of history by resampling from an actual history of returns or simulating from an estimated distribution $N(\hat{\mu}, \hat{\Sigma})$. Estimate sample mean and sample covariance matrix $(\hat{\mu}_i, \hat{\hat{\Sigma}}_i)$ for each simulated history.

2. Construct an efficient frontier with each $(\hat{\mu}_i, \hat{\hat{\Sigma}}_i)$.

3. Average the N resampled efficient frontiers.

There are different ways to average the resampled frontiers. The rank-association algorithm proposed by Michaud (1998) creates a fixed number of grids between the minimum variance and the maximum return portfolios for each frontier and averages the allocations corresponding to the same grid across frontiers. Another algorithm proposed by Michaud is the λ-association method, which groups allocations by their associated risk-aversion parameters, but Michaud pointed out that it is less statistically stable and requires a larger number of simulated paths. Morningstar introduced a risk-binning method for its optimization software that groups allocations on the frontiers based on their standard deviations.

With long-only constraints, most assets will likely have some nonzero weights in the average portfolio. In this sense, portfolio resampling is effective at generating more diversified long-only portfolios. However, the long-only constraints may create *optionality* for high-volatility assets because favorable return draws lead to higher allocations, but unfavorable ones do not lead to negative allocations. The average frontier may exhibit turning points changing from concave to convex (Scherer 2002). Because of the averaging, constraints that hold for all frontiers may no longer hold for the average portfolio, except for those convex (including linear) ones. For example, if there is a constraint on the maximum number of assets for the optimization, the average portfolio most likely will violate this constraint, even though it is satisfied by all the resampled portfolios. Another critique of this methodology is that any bias in the initial estimates will be carried over to the resampled estimators, and averaging the resulting optimal allocations will not remove it.

Example (Portfolio Resampling with and without a Short-Sale Constraint): Let's start with the naive MVO with six assets described previously:

$$\max_x x'\mu - \frac{\lambda}{2} x'\Sigma x$$

$$\text{subject to} \quad x'\mathbf{1} = 1$$

where $\lambda = 3$.

Now, assume that $\hat{\mu} \sim N(\mu, c\Sigma)$, where $\hat{\mu}$ is given as in previous sections, and c is a positive number controlling assumed uncertainty around the return estimate. We then simulate the true expected return vector from the assumed distribution for given values of c and run the MVO above for each simulated expected return vector. Figure 19.9 shows the average allocations of the resampled optimal portfolios without any constraint on short sales for two values of c, respectively. Similarly, Figure 19.10 shows the version with the short-sale constraint.

When there is no short-sale constraint, the over- and underweights on assets tend to offset each other on average. Therefore, the resampled optimal portfolio resembles the naive MVO portfolio in this case. Once we add the no-short-sale constraint, the average portfolio is significantly more diversified because the negative weights are truncated, and every asset ends up with some positive allocation in the average portfolio.

Markowitz and Usmen (2003) compared the out-of-sample performance of Michaud's resampled frontier with an MVO using a Bayesian estimator with diffuse prior and found (surprisingly) that the Michaud player won. Several similar studies have been conducted since then with mixed results.[2] Portfolio resampling remains an interesting heuristic to deal with estimation errors in the traditional MVO framework.

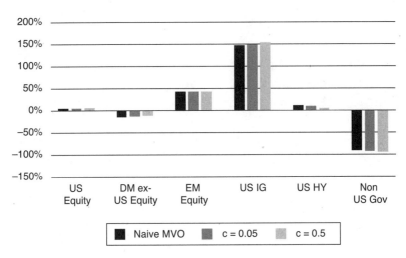

FIGURE 19.9 Average resampled optimal portfolios without a constraint on short sales

2 See, for example, Harvey et al. (2008) and Becker et al. (2013).

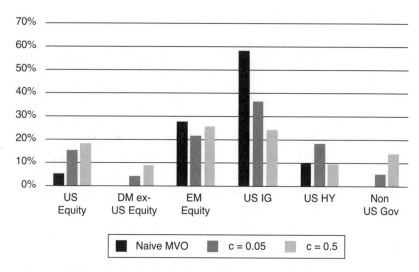

FIGURE 19.10 Average resampled optimal portfolios with a short-sale constraint

19.4 Final Remarks

The models discussed earlier in this part are not mutually exclusive. In fact, some are closely and interestingly connected to others under seemingly unrelated model setups. We have shown some examples such as the connections between penalized MVOs and covariance shrinkage and between shrinkage and Bayesian inference (e.g., BL estimator, James–Stein estimator).

The models aiming for more robust portfolio construction can be potentially combined to achieve better outcomes. It obviously does not hurt to obtain robust estimators for both expected returns and the covariance matrix. In addition, portfolio construction can benefit from combining improved inputs with better optimizers. For example, the posterior mean of expected returns from the BL model can be used not only by a naive mean variance optimizer but also by a robust optimizer. In fact, the posterior distribution obtained from the BL model also provides a natural starting point to define the uncertainty set of expected returns for portfolio resampling. Lastly, even different robust optimizers can be combined in some cases. For instance, Li and Kwon (2013) introduced a penalty term into an RO framework to provide flexibility to define prior reference models using the distributional information of the first two moments and account for model ambiguity in terms of extreme moment uncertainty.

Appendix

Some Useful Results from Linear Algebra

We assume that our readers are familiar with basic matrix algebra, such as matrix addition and multiplication, determinants, and matrix inversion. Below is a reminder of some useful results.

Transposed Matrices

$$(A^T)^T = A$$
$$(A + B)^T = A^T + B^T$$
$$(AB)^T = B^T A^T$$
$$(ABC)^T = C^T B^T A^T$$

Quadratic Form

x is an $N \times 1$ vector of portfolio weights, and Ω is an $N \times N$ covariance matrix; then $x^T \Omega x$ is the variance of the portfolio. When $N = 2$,

$$x^T \Omega x = [x_1 \; x_2] \begin{bmatrix} \sigma_1^2 & \rho\sigma_1\sigma_2 \\ \rho\sigma_1\sigma_2 & \sigma_2^2 \end{bmatrix} \begin{bmatrix} x_1 \\ x_2 \end{bmatrix} = x_1^2\sigma_1^2 + 2x_1 x_2 \rho\sigma_1\sigma_2 + x_2^2\sigma_2^2$$

Inverse Matrices

$$(AB)^{-1} = B^{-1}A^{-1}$$
$$(ABC)^{-1} = C^{-1}B^{-1}A^{-1}$$
$$(A^{T})^{-1} = (A^{-1})^{T}$$
$$(A^{-1})^{T} = A^{-1}, \text{ for symmetric } A$$

Matrix Differentiation

$$\frac{\partial x_1^T x_2}{\partial x_2} = x_1 \text{ for } x_1 \text{ and } x_2 \ (N \times 1) \text{ vectors}$$

$$\frac{\partial x^T \Omega x}{\partial x} = 2\Omega x \text{ for } x \text{ an } (N \times 1) \text{ vector and } \Omega \text{ an } (N \times N) \text{ matrix}$$

The two results above are a matter of perspective. For example, for $N = 2$, one can view $\dfrac{\partial x^T \Omega x}{\partial x}$ as

$$\begin{bmatrix} \dfrac{\partial x^T \Omega x}{\partial x_1} \\ \dfrac{\partial x^T \Omega x}{\partial x_2} \end{bmatrix} = \begin{bmatrix} 2(x_1 \sigma_1^2 + x_2 \rho \sigma_1 \sigma_2) \\ 2(x_2 \sigma_2^2 + x_1 \rho \sigma_1 \sigma_2) \end{bmatrix} = 2\Omega x$$

or as

$$\begin{bmatrix} \dfrac{\partial x^T \Omega x}{\partial x_1} & \dfrac{\partial x^T \Omega x}{\partial x_2} \end{bmatrix} = [2(x_1 \sigma_1^2 + x_2 \rho \sigma_1 \sigma_2) \ 2(x_2 \sigma_2^2 + x_1 \rho \sigma_1 \sigma_2)] = 2x^T \Omega$$

Vector Differentiation

Let $f(x)$ be a function of the vector x. The *gradient* of the function is given by

$$\nabla f(x) = \frac{\partial f}{\partial x} = \left(\frac{\partial f}{\partial x_1}, \frac{\partial f}{\partial x_2}, \ldots, \frac{\partial f}{\partial x_n} \right)$$

The *Hessian* of the function is given by

$$H_f = \frac{\partial^2 f}{\partial x \partial x^T} = \begin{pmatrix} \dfrac{\partial^2 f}{\partial x_1^2} & \dfrac{\partial^2 f}{\partial x_1 \partial x_2} & \cdots & \dfrac{\partial^2 f}{\partial x_1 \partial x_n} \\[2mm] \dfrac{\partial^2 f}{\partial x_2 \partial x_1} & \dfrac{\partial^2 f}{\partial x_2^2} & \cdots & \dfrac{\partial^2 f}{\partial x_2 \partial x_n} \\[2mm] \vdots & \vdots & & \vdots \\[2mm] \dfrac{\partial^2 f}{\partial x_n \partial x_1} & \dfrac{\partial^2 f}{\partial x_n \partial x_2} & \cdots & \dfrac{\partial^2 f}{\partial x_n^2} \end{pmatrix}$$

where x^T is the transpose of vector x.

Taylor Series

If f and all its derivatives exist up to order n in a region $[x, x + \Delta x]$, then

$$f(x + \Delta x) = f(x) + f'(x)\Delta x + \frac{1}{2} f''(x)\Delta x^2 + \cdots \cdots$$

$$+ \frac{1}{(n-1)!} f^{(n-1)}(x)\Delta x^{(n-1)} + \frac{1}{n!} f^{(n)}(x)\Delta x^n + \cdots$$

where the superscript n of f refers to the nth derivative.

For a function of two arguments, the extension is

$$F(x + \Delta x, y + \Delta y) = F(x, y) + \frac{\partial F(x, y)}{\partial x}\Delta x + \frac{\partial F(x, y)}{\partial y}\Delta y$$

$$+ \frac{1}{2}\frac{\partial^2 F(x, y)}{\partial x^2}\Delta x^2 + \frac{1}{2}\frac{\partial^2 F(x, y)}{\partial y^2}\Delta y^2 +$$

$$\frac{\partial^2 F(x, y)}{\partial x \partial y}\Delta x \Delta y + \cdots + \frac{1}{n!}(\Delta x^n \frac{\partial^n F(x, y)}{\partial x^n} + n\Delta x^{n-1}\Delta y \frac{\partial^n F(x, y)}{\partial x^{n-1}\partial y} + \cdots$$

$$+ \frac{n!}{(n-1)!1!}\Delta x \Delta y^{n-1} \frac{\partial^n F(x, y)}{\partial x \partial y^{n-1}} + \Delta y^n \frac{\partial^n F(x, y)}{\partial y^n}) + \cdots$$

Properties of the Normal and Log-Normal Distributions

If a random variable x is distributed normally with a mean μ and a variance σ^2, its density function is written as

$$f(x) = (2\pi\sigma^2)^{-\frac{1}{2}} e^{-\frac{(x-\mu)^2}{2\sigma^2}}$$

If x_1 and x_2 are bivariate normal variables with means μ_1 and μ_2, variances σ_1^2 and σ_2^2, and covariance σ_{12}, the weighted sum of $\alpha_1 x_1 + \alpha_2 x_2$ is normally distributed with mean and variance

$$\mu = \alpha_1\mu_1 + \alpha_2\mu_2$$
$$\sigma^2 = \alpha_1^2\sigma_1^2 + 2\alpha_1\alpha_2\sigma_{12} + \alpha_2^2\sigma_2^2$$

If random variable x is normally distributed, then $y \equiv e^x$ is said to be log-normal with a density function

$$f(y) = (\sqrt{2\pi}\sigma y)^{-1} e^{-\frac{(\log(y)-\mu)^2}{2\sigma^2}}$$

Mean of $y = e^{(\mu+\frac{\sigma^2}{2})}$. Variance of $y = e^{(2\mu+\sigma^2)}(e^{\sigma^2} - 1)$.

Probability That the Kelly Strategy Will Outperform Another Fixed-Mix Strategy

Consider the following simple example with one risky asset. The price of the risky asset follows a geometric Brownian motion with parameters (μ, σ^2):

$$\frac{dP_t}{P_t} = \mu dt + \sigma dB_t$$

The risk-free asset follows a geometric growth rate of r. Thus

$$\frac{dM_t}{M_t} = rdt$$

Denote by x_t the portfolio weight in the risky asset at time t. Then $1 - x_t$ is the portfolio weight in the risk-free asset. For a given strategy, the dynamics of wealth is given by the following budget constraint:

$$\frac{dW_t}{W_t} = [r + x_t(\mu - r)]dt + x_t\sigma dB_t$$

By Itô's lemma and the budget constraint, we have

$$d \ln W_t = \left[r + x_t(\mu - r) - \frac{1}{2}\sigma^2 x_t^2 \right] dt + x_t \sigma dB_t$$

$$\Rightarrow \ln W_T = \ln W_0 + \int_0^T \left[r + x_t(\mu - r) - \frac{1}{2}\sigma^2 x_t^2 \right] dt + \int_0^T x_t \sigma dB_t$$

$$\Rightarrow E[\ln W_T] = \ln W_0 + \int_0^T \left[r + x_t(\mu - r) - \frac{1}{2}\sigma^2 x_t^2 \right] dt.$$

To maximize $E[\ln W_T]$, the Kelly strategy selects $x_t^K = x^K = \dfrac{\mu - r}{\sigma^2}$, which maximizes

$$f(x) \equiv r + x(\mu - r) - \frac{1}{2}\sigma^2 x^2$$

Now suppose that there is an alternative fixed-mix strategy. We can state the wealth under the two strategies at time T as

$$W_T^K = W_0 \exp\left\{ \left[r + x^K(\mu - r) - \frac{1}{2}x^{K^2}\sigma^2 \right] T + x^K \sigma \sqrt{T}Z \right\}$$

$$W_T^A = W_0 \exp\left\{ \left[r + x^A(\mu - r) - \frac{1}{2}x^{A^2}\sigma^2 \right] T + x^A \sigma \sqrt{T}Z \right\}$$

where $Z \sim N(0,1)$.

The probability that the Kelly strategy will outperform the alternative strategy at time T is

$$P(W_T^K > W_T^A)$$

$$= P\left(\left[r + x^K(\mu - r) - \frac{1}{2}x^{K^2}\sigma^2 \right] T + x^K \sigma \sqrt{T}Z > \left[r + x^A(\mu - r) - \frac{1}{2}x^{A^2}\sigma^2 \right] T + x^A \sigma \sqrt{T}Z \right)$$

$$= \begin{cases} P\left(Z > \dfrac{f(x^A) - f(x^K)}{(x^K - x^A)\sigma}\sqrt{T} \right) = \Phi\left(\dfrac{f(x^K) - f(x^A)}{(x^K - x^A)\sigma}\sqrt{T} \right), & \text{if } x^K > x^A \\[3mm] P\left(Z < \dfrac{f(x^A) - f(x^K)}{(x^K - x^A)\sigma}\sqrt{T} \right) = \Phi\left(\dfrac{f(x^A) - f(x^K)}{(x^K - x^A)\sigma}\sqrt{T} \right), & \text{if } x^K < x^A \end{cases}$$

where Φ is the cumulative distribution function (CDF) of a standard normal random variable.

Because x^K is the unique solution to $\max\limits_{x} f(x)$, we have $f(x^K) > f(x^A)$, $\forall x^A \neq x^K$. Therefore, $P(W_T^K > W_T^A) > 0.5, \forall T > 0$, and $\lim\limits_{T \to \infty} P(W_T^K > W_T^A) = 1$.

Derivation of the Martingale Probability Measure for a Contingent Claim

We know from derivative pricing theory that for the purpose of pricing or "cooking" a contingent claim, the relevant probability q to be used, also called the *martingale probability measure*, is

$$q = \frac{1 + r - d}{u - d}$$

where r is the risk-free rate, and u and d are the upside and downside multipliers on the risky-asset price. The cost of a contingent claim is then the expectation under q of the payoff, discounted at the risk-free rate.

The proof of these claims is straightforward. If

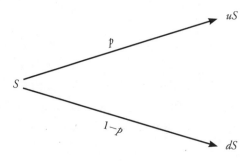

and the bond M follows

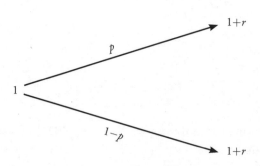

Then a contingent claim with payoff C^u and C^d can be priced by noting that a combination of Δ units of stocks and of an amount M of bonds will have payoffs.

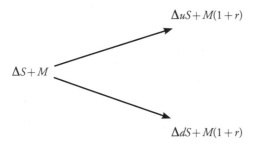

$$\Delta u S + M(1+r)$$

$$\Delta S + M$$

$$\Delta d S + M(1+r)$$

Setting the payoff of the combination equal to the contingent claim payoffs, we get

$$\Delta u S + (1 + r)M = C^u$$
$$\Delta d S + (1 + r)M = C^d$$

And solving for Δ and M, we get

$$\Delta^* = \frac{C^u - C^d}{(u - d)S}$$

$$M^* = \frac{1}{1+r}(C^u - \Delta^* u S)$$

Then the cost of the contingent claim is $\Delta^* S + M^*$ because the payoff of $\Delta^* S + M^*$ is C^u and C^d by construction. Simple algebra shows that

$$C = \Delta^* S + M^* = \frac{qC^u + (1-q)C^d}{1+r}$$

with $q \equiv \dfrac{1+r-d}{u-d}$ being a probability measure. Why? For bonds and stocks not to be dominant, then $u \geq 1 + r \geq d$ and $0 \leq q \leq 1$. Moreover, q is called a *risk-neutral probability* because

$$C_0 = \frac{E^q(C_1)}{1+r}$$

The contingent claim cost is computed as if investors were risk neutral. To check further that q is a risk-neutral probability, note that in a risk-neutral world,

$$S = \frac{p_{RN}uS + (1 - p_{RN})dS}{1 + r}$$

where p_{RN} is the risk-neutral probability. And it turns out that

$$p_{RN} = \frac{1 + r - d}{u - d} = q$$

where q is also called a *martingale probability* because if $m_t \equiv \dfrac{C_t}{(1+r)^t}$, then it can be easily shown that $m_0 = E^q(m_1)$, this being the definition of a martingale.

Proof of the Black–Litterman Formulas Based on Bayes' Theorem

To derive a closed-form expression for the posterior distribution, we assume a Gaussian prior distribution and a Gaussian likelihood function to ensure that the posterior distribution is also Gaussian. This is because the Gaussian distribution is a conjugate prior for a Gaussian likelihood function.

Assume that the prior distribution for the expected return M is

$$M \sim N(\pi, \Phi), \text{with} f_M(\mu) = (2\pi)^{-\frac{n}{2}} |\Phi|^{-\frac{1}{2}} \exp\left[-\frac{1}{2}(\mu - \pi)'\Phi^{-1}(\mu - \pi)\right]$$

Also assume that the conditional distribution of the expected returns of the view portfolios is

$$Q|\mu \sim N(P\mu, \Omega), \text{with} f_{Q|M=\mu}(q) = (2\pi)^{-\frac{m}{2}} |\Omega|^{-\frac{1}{2}} \exp\left[-\frac{1}{2}(q - P\mu)'\Omega^{-1}(q - P\mu)\right]$$

Then Bayesian inference derives the posterior distribution of M according to Bayes' theorem:

$$f_{M|Q=q}(\mu) = \frac{f_{Q|M=\mu}(q)f_M(\mu)}{f_Q(q)}$$

And the unconditional probability density function of Q in the denominator can be eliminated based on the law of total probability, so the only terms containing μ are in the numerator.

The numerator is

$$f_{Q|M=\mu}(q)f_M(\mu) = C \times \exp\left\{-\frac{1}{2}[(\mu-\pi)'\Phi^{-1}(\mu-\pi)+(q-P\mu)'\Omega^{-1}(q-P\mu)]\right\}$$

where C is a constant.

Given that the posterior distribution $f_{M|Q=q}(\mu)$ is the probability density function of a Gaussian distribution, we only need to rewrite the numerator in the form of constant $\times \exp\left[-\frac{1}{2}(\mu-\mu_p)'\Sigma_p^{-1}(\mu-\mu_p)\right]$ for some μ_p and Σ_p not dependent on μ to find the posterior mean and variance.

Note that

$$(\mu-\pi)'\Phi^{-1}(\mu-\pi)+(q-P\mu)'\Omega^{-1}(q-P\mu)$$

$$= \mu'\Phi^{-1}\mu - 2\mu'\Phi^{-1}\pi + \mu'P'\Omega^{-1}P\mu - 2\mu'P'\Omega^{-1}q + \text{constant}$$

Also note that

$$[\mu-(\Phi^{-1}+P'\Omega^{-1}P)^{-1}(\Phi^{-1}\pi+P'\Omega^{-1}q)]'(\Phi^{-1}+P'\Omega^{-1}P)[\mu-(\Phi^{-1}+$$

$$P'\Omega^{-1}P)^{-1}(\Phi^{-1}\pi+P'\Omega^{-1}q)] = \mu'\Phi^{-1}\mu + \mu'P'\Omega^{-1}P\mu - 2\mu'\Phi^{-1}\pi - 2\mu'P'\Omega^{-1}q +$$

constant

By comparing the terms containing μ in these two equations, we have shown that

$$f_{M|Q=q}(\mu) = \text{constant} \times \exp\left[-\frac{1}{2}(\mu-\mu_p)'\Sigma_p^{-1}(\mu-\mu_p)\right]$$

where $\mu_p = (\Phi^{-1}+P'\Omega^{-1}P)^{-1}(\Phi^{-1}\pi+P'\Omega^{-1}q)$ and $\Sigma_p = (\Phi^{-1}+P'\Omega^{-1}P)^{-1}$

Proofs of the Black–Litterman Formulas from a Frequentist Perspective

We provide two proofs for the Black–Litterman formulas based on the following methods, respectively:

1. Theil's mixed estimation
2. Maximum-likelihood estimation (MLE)

Proof of the Black–Litterman Formulas Based on Theil's Mixed Estimation

A linear model for the prior distribution of expected returns is

$$\pi = I_n \mu + u, \text{ for } u \sim (0, \Phi)$$

where μ is the vector of n (unknown) expected returns, and π is the mean of the prior distribution for expected returns.

Next, consider additional information expressed as a set of linear views:

$$q = P\mu + v, \text{ for } v \sim (0, \Omega)$$

where P is the $m \times n$ matrix representing m view portfolios, and q is the expected returns of the view portfolios.

Assume that Φ and Ω are positive definite and that the error terms u and v are independent. Stack the preceding two linear models as follows:

$$\begin{pmatrix} \pi \\ q \end{pmatrix} = \begin{pmatrix} I_n \\ P \end{pmatrix} \mu + \begin{pmatrix} u \\ v \end{pmatrix}$$

Define

$$y = \begin{pmatrix} \pi \\ q \end{pmatrix}, X = \begin{pmatrix} I_n \\ P \end{pmatrix}, \beta = \mu, \varepsilon = \begin{pmatrix} u \\ v \end{pmatrix}, \text{ and } \Sigma = \begin{pmatrix} \Phi & 0 \\ 0 & \Omega \end{pmatrix}$$

Then we have a linear regression model

$$y = X\beta + \varepsilon, \text{ for } \varepsilon \sim (0, \Sigma)$$

Given the heteroscedasticity and correlations between the error terms, the generalized-least-squares (GLS) estimator is the best linear unbiased estimator (BLUE) for β, with

$$\hat{\beta}_{\text{GLS}} = (X'\Sigma^{-1}X)^{-1}X'\Sigma^{-1}y = \left[(I_n \ P') \begin{pmatrix} \Phi & 0 \\ 0 & \Omega \end{pmatrix}^{-1} \begin{pmatrix} I_n \\ P \end{pmatrix} \right]^{-1} (I_n \ P') \begin{pmatrix} \Phi & 0 \\ 0 & \Omega \end{pmatrix}^{-1} \begin{pmatrix} \pi \\ q \end{pmatrix}$$

$$= (\Phi^{-1} + P'\Omega^{-1}P)^{-1}(\Phi^{-1}\pi + P'\Omega^{-1}q)$$

$$\text{var}\left(\hat{\beta}_{\text{GLS}}\right) = (X'^{\Sigma^{-1}}X)^{-1} = \left[(I_n \ P') \begin{pmatrix} \Phi & 0 \\ 0 & \Omega \end{pmatrix}^{-1} \begin{pmatrix} I_n \\ P \end{pmatrix} \right]^{-1} = (\Phi^{-1} + P'\Omega^{-1}P)^{-1}$$

Proof of the Black–Litterman Formulas Based on Maximum-Likelihood Estimation

Assume that Π and Q are two normally distributed estimators for μ and $P\mu$, respectively, with independent estimation errors:

$$\Pi \sim N(\mu, \Phi)$$
$$Q \sim N(P\mu, \Omega)$$

The two likelihood functions are

$$f_\Pi(\pi \mid \mu) = (2\pi)^{-\frac{n}{2}} |\Phi|^{-\frac{1}{2}} \exp\left[-\frac{1}{2}(\pi - \mu)'\Phi^{-1}(\pi - \mu)\right] f_Q(q \mid \mu)$$

$$= (2\pi)^{-\frac{m}{2}} |\Omega|^{-\frac{1}{2}} \exp\left[-\frac{1}{2}(q - P\mu)'\Omega^{-1}(q - P\mu)\right]$$

Then the log-likelihood function is

$$\log \mathcal{L}(\Pi = \pi, Q = q \mid \mu) = \log[f_\Pi(\pi \mid \mu)] + \log[f_Q(q \mid \mu)]$$

$$= -\frac{1}{2}[(\pi - \mu)'\Phi^{-1}(\pi - \mu) + (q - P\mu)'\Omega^{-1}(q - P\mu)] + \text{constant}$$

The MLE is obtained by maximizing the log-likelihood function, which is equivalent to

$$\min_\mu (\pi - \mu)'\Phi^{-1}(\pi - \mu) + (q - P\mu)'\Omega^{-1}(q - P\mu)$$

The solution satisfies the first-order condition (it can be shown that the Hessian is negative definite; i.e., the second-order condition holds)

$$\Phi^{-1}(\pi - \mu) + P'\Omega^{-1}(q - P\mu) = 0$$

$$\Rightarrow (\Phi^{-1} + P'\Omega^{-1}P)\mu = \Phi^{-1}\pi + P'\Omega^{-1}q$$

Therefore,

$$\hat{\mu}_{\text{MLE}} = (\Phi^{-1} + P'\Omega^{-1}P)^{-1}(\Phi^{-1}\pi + P'\Omega^{-1}q)$$

$$\text{var}(\hat{\mu}_{\text{MLE}}) = (\Phi^{-1} + P'\Omega^{-1}P)^{-1}(\Phi^{-1}\Phi\Phi^{-1} + P'\Omega^{-1}\Omega\Omega^{-1}P)(\Phi^{-1} + P'\Omega^{-1}P)^{-1}$$

$$= (\Phi^{-1} + P'\Omega^{-1}P)^{-1}(\Phi^{-1} + P'\Omega^{-1}P)(\Phi^{-1} + P'\Omega^{-1}P)^{-1}$$

$$= (\Phi^{-1} + P'\Omega^{-1}P)^{-1}$$

Bibliography

Aït-Sahalia, Y., and Hansen, L. P. (2010). *Handbook of Financial Econometrics Tools and Techniques*, Vol. 1. Amsterdam: North Holland–Elsevier.

Allaj, E. (2013). "The Black–Litterman model: a consistent estimation of the parameter tau." *Financial Markets and Portfolio Management* 27(2):217–51.

Ambarish, R., and Seigel, L. (1996). "Time is the essence." *Risk Magazine* 9(8):41–2.

Amihud, Y., and Mendelson, H. (1986a). "Asset pricing and the bid-ask spread." *Journal of Financial Economics* 17:223–49.

Amihud, Y., and Mendelson, H. (1986b). "Liquidity and stock returns." *Financial Analysts Journal* 42(3):43–8.

Anderson, R., Bianchi, S., and Goldberg, L. (2012). "Will my risk parity strategy outperform?" *Financial Analysts Journal* 68:75–93.

Arnott, R. D., and Hsu, J. C. (2008). "Noise, CAPM, and the size and value effects." *Journal of Investment Management* 6(1):1–11.

Arnott, R. D., Harvey, C. R., Kalesnik, V., and Linnainmaa, J. T. (2021). "Reports of Value's death may be greatly exaggerated." *Financial Analysts Journal* 77(1):44–67.

Arrow, K. J. (1971). *Essays in the Theory of Risk-Bearing*. Devon, UK: Markham Publishing.

Arrow, K. J., and Hurwicz, L. (1960). "Decentralization and computation in resource allocation," in R. W. Pfouts (ed.), *Essays in Economics and Econometrics*. Durham: University of North Carolina Press.

Asness, C., Frazzini, A, and Pedersen, L. H. (2012). "Leverage aversion and risk parity." *Financial Analysts Journal* 68(1):47–59.

Athans, M., and Falb, P. L. (1966). *Optimal Control.* New York: McGraw-Hill.

Ball, C. A., and Torous, W. N. (1983). "Bond price dynamics and options." *Journal of Financial and Quantitative Analysis* 18(4):517–31.

Barberis, N., Shleifer, A., and Vishny, R. (1998). "A model of investor sentiment." *Journal of Financial Economics* 49(3):307–43.

Barro, R. J. (2006). "Rare disasters and asset markets in the twentieth century." *The Quarterly Journal of Economics* 121(3):823–66.

Bartle, R. G. (1966). *The Elements of Integration.* New York: John Wiley & Sons.

Bartle, R. G., and Sherbert, D. R. (2010). *Introduction to Real Analysis*, 4th ed. Hoboken, NJ: John Wiley & Sons.

Baz, J., and Chacko, G. (2004). *Financial Derivatives.* New York: Cambridge University Press.

Baz, J., Davis, J., Fuenzalida, C., and Hakanoglu, E. (2020a). "Sovereign wealth fund management with commodity extraction." Newport Beach, CA: PIMCO Quantitative Research and Analytics Publication.

Baz, J., Davis, J., Fuenzalida, C., and Hakanoglu, E. (2020b). "Sovereign assets, optimal growth and volatility pumping." Newport Beach, CA: PIMCO Quantitative Research and Analytics Publication.

Baz, J., Davis, J., Fuenzalida, C., and Tsai, J. (2020). "Method in the madness: bubbles, trading, and incentives." *Journal of Portfolio Management* 46(8):27–33.

Baz, J., Davis, J., Tsai, J., and Zhang, Z. (in press). "Inflation risk premia." *Journal of Portfolio Management.*

Baz, J., Feuillet, L., and Le Roux, N. (2015). "Something for nothing: Probability measures, expected returns and a pricing puzzle." Available at SSRN: https://ssrn.com/abstract=2695812 or http://dx.doi.org/10.2139/ssrn.2695812.

Baz, J., Granger, N., Harvey, C. R., Le Roux, N., and Rattray, S. (2015). "Dissecting investment strategies in the cross section and time series." Available at SSRN: https://ssrn.com/abstract=2695101 or http://dx.doi.org/10.2139/ssrn.2695101.

Baz, J., and Guo, H. (2017). "An asset allocation primer: connecting Markowitz, Kelly and Risk Parity." Newport Beach, CA: PIMCO Quantitative Research and Analytics Publication.

Baz, J., Naik, V., Prieul, D., Putyatin, V., and Yared, F. (2000). "Option strategies: selling risk at a premium." *Risk Magazine* 13(12):135–8.

Baz, J., Sapra, S., Stracke, C., and Zhao, W. (2021). "Valuing a lost opportunity: an alternative perspective on the illiquidity discount." *Journal of Portfolio Management* 47(3):112–21.

Becker, F., Gürtler, M., and Hibbeln, M. (2013). "Markowitz versus Michaud: portfolio optimization strategies reconsidered." *European Journal of Finance* 21(4):269–91.

Bellman, R. (1959). *Dynamic Programming.* Princeton, NJ: Princeton University Press.

Bellone, B., Declerck, P., Nordine, M., and Vy, T. (2019). "Multi-asset style factors have their shining moments." Available at SSRN: https://ssrn.com/ abstract=3444208 or http://dx.doi.org/10.2139/ssrn.3444208.

Ben-Tal, A., Bertsimas, D., and Brown, D. (2010). "A soft robust model for optimization under ambiguity." *Operations Research* 58(4):1220–34.

Billingsley, P. (1968). *Convergence of Probability Measures.* New York: John Wiley & Sons.

Black, F. (1972). "Capital market equilibrium with restricted borrowing." *Journal of Business* 45(3):444–55.

Black, F., and Hakanoglu, E. (1988). "Simplifying portfolio insurance for the seller," in F. J. Fabozzi (ed.), *The Institutional Investor Focus on Investment Management.* Philadelphia: Ballinger.

Black, F., and Jones, R. (1987). "Simplifying portfolio insurance." *Journal of Portfolio Management* 14(1):48–51.

Black, F., and Jones, R. (1988). "Simplifying portfolio insurance for corporate pension plans." *Journal of Portfolio Management* 14(4):33–7.

Black, F., and Litterman, R. (1990). "Asset allocation: combining investor views with market equilibrium." Fixed Income Research, Goldman Sachs & Co, New York.

Black, F., and Litterman R. (1991). "Asset allocation combining investor views with market equilibrium." *Journal of Fixed Income* 1(2):7–18.

Black, F., and Litterman R. (1992). "Global portfolio optimization." *Financial Analysts Journal* 48(5):28–43.

Black, F., and Perold, A. F. (1992). "Theory of constant proportion portfolio insurance." *Journal of Economic Dynamics and Control* 16:403–26.

Black, F., and Rouhani, R. (1988a). "Constant proportion portfolio insurance and synthetic put options: a comparison," in F. J. Fabozzi (ed.), *The Institutional Investor Focus on Investment Management.* Philadelphia: Ballinger.

Black, F., and Rouhani, R. (1988b). "Constant proportion portfolio insurance: volatility and the soft-floor strategy." Portfolio Strategy, Goldman, Sachs & Co., New York.

Black, F., and Scholes, M. (1973). "The pricing of options and corporate liabilities." *Journal of Political Economy* 81:637–59.

Borges, J. L. (1975). "On exactitude in science," in *A Universal History of Infamy.* New York: Penguin.

Boudt, K., Peterson, B. G., and Croux, C. (2008). "Estimation and decomposition of downside risk for portfolios with non-normal returns." *Journal of Risk* 11(2):79–103.

Boyd, S., and Vandenberghe, L. (2004) *Convex Optimization.* New York: Cambridge University Press.

Breeden, D. T., and Litzenberger, R. H. (1978). "Prices of state-contingent claims implicit in option prices." *Journal of Business* 51(4):621–51.

Breiman, L. (1961). "Optimal gambling system for favorable games," in *Proceedings of the 4th Berkeley Symposium on Mathematical Statistics and Probability*, Berkeley and Los Angeles: University of California Press, Vol. 1, pp. 63–8.

Brennan, M. J., and Solanki, R. (1981). "Optimal portfolio insurance." *Journal of Financial and Quantitative Analysis* 16:279–300.

Brennan, T. J., Lo, A. W., and Nguyen, T.-D. (2015). "Portfolio theory," in N. J. Higham (ed.), *The Princeton Companion to Applied Mathematics.* Princeton, NJ: Princeton University Press, pp. 648–58.

Brenner, M., and Subrahmanyam, M. G. (1994). "A simple approach to option valuation and hedging in the Black-Scholes model." *Financial Analysts Journal* 50(2):25–8.

Brezhneva, O., Tretyakov, A. A., and Wright, S. E. (2012). "A short elementary proof of the Lagrange multiplier theorem." *Optimization Letters* 6:1597–601.

Bryson, A. E., and Ho, Y.-C. (1975). *Applied Optimal Control: Optimization, Estimation and Control.* New York: John Wiley & Sons.

Calvino, I. (1988). *Six Memos for the Next Millennium.* Cambridge, MA: Harvard University Press.

Campbell, J. Y., and Cochrane, J. H. (1999). "By force or habit: a consumption-based explanation of aggregate stock market behavior." *Journal of Political Economy* 107(2):205–51.

Campbell, J. Y., Lo, A. W., and MacKinlay A. C. (1997). *The Econometrics of Financial Markets.* Princeton, NJ: Princeton University Press.

Capinski, M. J., and Kopp, E. (2014). *Portfolio Theory and Risk Management.* Cambridge, UK: Cambridge University Press.

Chaves, D. J., Hsu, F. L., and Shakernia, O. (2011). "Risk parity portfolio vs. other asset allocation heuristic portfolios." *Journal of Investing* 20(1):108–18.

Chopra, V. K., and Ziemba, W. T. (1993). "The effect of errors in means, variances, and covariances on optimal portfolio choice." *Journal of Portfolio Management* 19(2):6–11.

Cochrane, J. H. (2005). *Asset Pricing*. Princeton, NJ: Princeton University Press.

Cox, J. C., Ingersoll, J. E., Jr., and Ross, S. A. (1985a). "An intertemporal general equilibrium model of asset prices." *Econometrica* 53:363–84.

Cox, J. C., Ingersoll, J. E., Jr., and Ross, S. A. (1985b). "A theory of the term structure of interest rates." *Econometrica* 53:385–408.

Culbertson, J. M. (1957). "The term structure of interest rates." *Quarterly Journal of Economics* 71(4):485–517.

Dao, T. L., Nguyen, T. T., Deremble, C., Lemperiere, Y., Bouchaud, J. P., and Potters, M. (2016). "Tail protection for long investors: Trend convexity at work." Available at SSRN: https://ssrn.com/abstract=2777657 or http://dx.doi.org/10.2139/ssrn.2777657.

DeGroot, M. H. (1986). *Probability and Statistics*, 2d ed. Reading, MA: Addison-Wesley.

DeGroot, M. H. (2004). *Optimal Statistical Decisions*. Hoboken, NJ: John Wiley & Sons.

DeMiguel, V., Garlappi, L., and Uppal, R. (2009a). "Optimal versus naive diversification: how inefficient is the 1/N portfolio strategy?" *Review of Financial Studies* 22:1915–53.

DeMiguel, V., Garlappi, L., Nogales, F. J., and Uppal, R. (2009b). "A generalized approach to portfolio optimization: improving performance by constraining portfolio norms." *Management Science* 55(5):798–812.

Diris, B., Palm, F., and Schotman P. (2014). "Long-term strategic asset allocation: an out-of-sample evaluation." *Management Science* 61(9):2185–202.

Dixit, A. K., and Pindyck, R. S. (1994), *Investment Under Uncertainty*. Princeton, NJ: Princeton University Press.

Donsker, M. D. (1951). "An invariance principle for certain probability limit theorems," in *Four Papers on Probability (Memoirs of the American Mathematical Society)*, Vol. 6. Providence, RI: American Mathematical Society.

Dreyfus, S. E. (1965). *Dynamic Programming and Calculus of Variations*. New York: Academic Press.

Duffie, D. (1988). *Security Markets*. New York: Academic Press.

Duffie, D. (1996). *Dynamic Asset Pricing Theory*, 2d ed. Princeton, NJ: Princeton University Press.

Efron, B., and Morris, C. (1976). "Families of minimax estimators of the mean of a multivariate normal distribution." *Annals of Statistics* 4:11–21.

El Ghaoui, L., Oks, M., and Oustry, F. (2003). "Worst-case value-at-risk and robust portfolio optimization: a conic programming approach." *Operations Research* 51(4):543–56.

Engle, R. F., Lilien, D. M., and Robins, R. P. (1987). "Estimating time varying risk premia in the term structure: the ARCH-M model." *Econometrica* 55:391–407.

Erindi, A. (2013). "The Black–Litterman model: a consistent estimation of the parameter tau." *Financial Markets and Portfolio Management* 27(2):217–51.

Fabozzi, F. J., Huang, D, and Guofu, Z. (2010). "Robust portfolios: contributions from operations research and finance." *Annals of Operations Research* 176(1):191–220.

Fama, E. F., and French, K. R. (1993). "Common risk factors in the returns on stocks and bonds." *Journal of Financial Economics* 33:55–84.

Fama, E. F., and French, K. R. (1996). "Multifactor explanations of asset pricing anomalies." *Journal of Finance* 33:3–56.

Fama, E. F., and French, K. R. (2015). "A five-factor asset pricing model." *Journal of Financial Economics* 116:1–22.

Feller, W. (1957). *Introduction to Probability Theory and Its Applications*, Vols. 1 and 2. New York: John Wiley & Sons.

Fernandes, J. L. B., Ornelas, J. R. H., and Cusicanqui, O. A. M. (2012). "Combining equilibrium, resampling, and analyst's views in portfolio optimization." *Journal of Banking and Finance* 36:1354–61.

Foster, F. D., Smith, T., and Whaley, R. E. (1997). "Assessing goodness-of-fit of asset pricing models: the distribution of the maximal $R2$." *Journal of Finance* 52(2):591–607.

Frazzini, A., and Pedersen, L. H. (2012). "Betting against beta." *Journal of Financial Economics* 111:1–25.

Frost, P. A., and Savarino, J. E. (1988). "For better performance: constrain portfolio weights." *Journal of Portfolio Management* 15(1):29–34.

Garlappi, L., Uppal, R., and Wang, T. (2007). "Portfolio selection with parameter and model uncertainty: a multi-prior approach." *The Review of Financial Studies* 20 (1):41–81.

Girsanov, I. V. (1960). "On the transforming a certain class of stochastic processes by absolutely continuous substitution of measures." *Theory of Probability and Its Applications* 5(3):285–301.

Griffin, J. M. (2002). "Are the Fama and French factors global or country specific?" *Review of Financial Studies* 15(3):783–803.

Groth, C. (2017). *Lectures in Macroeconomics*. Copenhagen: University of Copenhagen.

Hakanoglu, E. (1982). "Construction of dual resource allocation algorithms using duality properties of electrical networks," in *Proceedings of the International Conference on Cybernetics and Society*, New York: IEEE, pp. 281–4.

Hakanoglu, E., Kopprasch, R., and Roman, E. (1989a). "Portfolio insurance in the fixed income market," in F. Fabozzi (ed.), *Fixed Income Portfolio Strategies*. London: Probus.

Hakanoglu, E., Kopprasch, R., and Roman, E. (1989b). "Constant proportion portfolio insurance for fixed-income investment." *Journal of Portfolio Management* 15(4):58–66.

Hakanoglu, E., Shung, E., Miljkovic, N, and Jones, E. P. (2002). "The capital structure efficient frontier." Issuer Perspectives, Capital Markets Strategies, Goldman, Sachs & Company, New York.

Hakanoglu, E., Shung, E., and Miljkovic, N. (2003). "Corporate pension management within the capital structure," Issuer Perspectives, Capital Markets Strategies, Goldman, Sachs & Co., New York.

Hansen, L. P., and Jagannathan, R. (1991). "Implications of market security data for models of dynamic economies." *Journal of Political Economy* 99(2):225–62.

Hardy, G. H., Littlewood, J. E., and Polya, G. (1952). *Inequalities*, 2d ed. Cambridge, UK: Cambridge University Press.

Harrison, J. M. (1985). *Brownian Motion and Stochastic Flow Systems*. New York: John Wiley & Sons.

Harvey, C. R., Liechty, J. C., and Liechty, M. W. (2008). "Bayes vs. resampling: a rematch." *Journal of Investment Management* 6:1–17.

Harvey, C. R., Liechty, J. C., Liechty, M. W., and Müller, P. (2010). "Portfolio selection with higher moments." *Quantitative Finance* 10(5):469–85.

Harvey, C. R., and Liu, Y. (2021). "Lucky factors." *Journal of Financial Economics* 141(2):413–35.

Harvey, C. R., Liu, Y., and Zhu, H. (2016). "… and the cross-section of expected returns." *Review of Financial Studies* 29(1):5–68.

Haugh, M., and Lo, A. W. (2001). "Asset allocation and derivatives." *Quantitative Finance* 1:45–72.

He, G., and Litterman, R. (1999). "The intuition behind Black-Litterman model portfolios." Investment Management Research, Goldman, Sachs & Co., New York.

Heal, G. M. (1973). *The Theory of Economic Planning.* Amsterdam: North Holland.

Heath, D., Jarrow, R., and Morton, A. (1992). "Bond pricing and the term structure of interest rates: a new methodology for contingent claims valuation." *Econometrica* 60(1):77–105.

Hicks, J. R. (1946). *Value and Capital,* 2d ed. New York: Clarendon Press, pp 136–9.

Ho, T. S. Y., and Lee, S. B. (1986). "Term structure movements and pricing interest rate contingent claims." *Journal of Finance* 41:1011–29.

Hoel, P. G., Port, S. C., and Stone, C. J. (1972). *Introduction to Stochastic Processes.* Boston: Houghton-Mifflin.

Huberman, G. (1982). "A simple approach to arbitrage pricing." *Journal of Economic Theory* 28:183–91.

Huberman, G., and Wang, Z. (2008) "Arbitrage pricing theory" in *The New Palgrave Dictionary of Economics.* London: Palgrave Macmillan.

Idzorek, T. (2007). "A step-by-step guide to the Black–Litterman model: incorporating user-specified confidence levels," in S. Satchell (ed.), *Forecasting Expected Returns in the Financial Markets.* New York: Academic Press, pp.17–38.

Ingersoll, J. E., Jr. (1984). "Some results in the theory of arbitrage pricing." *Journal of Finance* 39:1021–39.

Ingersoll, J. E., Jr. (1987). *Theory of Financial Decision Making.* Lanham, MD: Rowman & Littlefield.

Intrilligator, M. (1971). *Mathematical Optimization and Economic Theory.* Englewood Cliffs, NJ: Prentice-Hall.

Ito, K., and McLean, H. P., Jr. (1964). *Diffusion Processes and Their Sample Paths.* New York: Academic Press.

Jagannathan, R., and Ma, T. (2003). "Risk reduction in large portfolios: why imposing the wrong constraints helps." *Journal of Finance* 58(4):1651–83.

Jobson, D., and Korkie, B. (1980). "Estimation for Markowitz efficient portfolios." *Journal of the American Statistical Association* 75(371):544–54.

Jorion, P. (1986). "Bayes–Stein estimation for portfolio analysis." *Journal of Financial and Quantitative Analysis* 21(3):279–92.

Jorion, P. (2003). "The long-term risks of global stock markets." *Financial Management* 32 (4):5–26.

Jorion, P., and Goetzmann, W. N. (1999). "Global stock markets in the twentieth century." *Journal of Finance* 54(3):953–80.

Kan, R., and Zhou, G. (2007). "Optimal portfolio choice with parameter uncertainty." *Journal of Financial and Quantitative Analysis* 42(3):621–56.

Kahneman, D. (2011). *Thinking, Fast and Slow*. New York: Farrar Straus and Giroux.

Karlin, S., and Taylor, H. (1981). *A Second Course in Stochastic Processes*. New York: Academic Press.

Kennedy, D. (2018). *Stochastic Financial Models*. London: Chapman and Hall.

Keynes, J. M. (1930). *A Treatise on Money*, Vol. 2: *The Applied Theory of Money*. London: Macmillan, pp. 142–7.

Korn, R. (1997). "Optimal portfolios: stochastic models for optimal investment and risk management in continuous time." *World Scientific*.

Kreuser, J., and Seigel, L. (1995). "Derivative securities: The atomic structure," World Bank Working Papers.

Kushner, H. J. (1967). *Stochastic Stability and Control*. New York: Academic Press.

Lancaster, K. (1968). *Mathematical Economics*. London: Macmillan.

Lancewicki, T., and Aladjem, M. (2014). "Multi-target shrinkage estimation for covariance matrices." *IEEE Transactions on Signal Processing* 62(24):6380–90.

Lang, S. (1969). *Analysis*. Reading, MA: Addison-Wesley.

Lasdon, L. S., (1970). *Optimization Theory for Large Systems*. London: Macmillan.

Ledoit, O., and Wolf, M. (2003). "Improved estimation of the covariance matrix of stock returns with an application to portfolio selection." *Journal of Empirical Finance* 10(5):603–21.

Ledoit, O., and Wolf, M. (2004a). "A well-conditioned estimator for large-dimensional covariance matrices." *Journal of Multivariate Analysis* 88:365–411.

Ledoit, O., and Wolf, M. (2004b). "Honey, I shrunk the sample covariance matrix." *Journal of Portfolio Management* 30(4):110–18.

Ledoit, O., and Wolf, M. (2017). "Nonlinear shrinkage of the covariance matrix for portfolio selection: Markowitz meets Goldilocks." *Review of Financial Studies* 30(12):4349–88.

Lee, W. (2011). "Risk-based asset allocation: a new answer to an old question?" *Journal of Portfolio Management* 37(4):11–28.

Leland, H. E., and Rubinstein, M. (1988). "The evolution of portfolio insurance," in D. L. Luskin (ed.), *Dynamic Hedging: A Guide to Portfolio Insurance*. New York: John Wiley & Sons.

Levy, H., and Markowitz, H. M. (1979). "Approximating expected utility by a function of mean and variance." *The American Economic Review* 69(3), 308–317.

Li, J. Y., and Kwon, R. H. (2013). "Portfolio selection under model uncertainty: a penalized moment-based optimization approach." *Journal of Global Optimization* 56:131–64.

Lintner, J. (1965). "The valuation of risk assets and the selection of risky investments in stock portfolios and capital budgets." *Review of Economics and Statistics* 47(1):13–37.

Lipster, R. S., and Shirayev, A. N. (1977). *Statistics of Random Processes*, Vol. 1. New York: Springer.

Liu, X., and Zhang, L. (2008). "Momentum profits, factor pricing, and macroeconomic risk." *Review of Financial Studies* 21(6):2417–48.

Lo, A. W. (2019). "The statistics of Sharpe ratios." *Financial Analysts Journal* 58(4).

Lo, A. W., and MacKinlay, A. C. (1990). "Data-snooping biases in tests of financial asset pricing models." *Review of Financial Studies* 3(3):431–67.

Lobo, M. S., Vandenberghe, L., Boyd, S., and Lebret, H. (1998). "Applications of second-order cone programming." *Linear Algebra and Its Applications*, 284(1–3):193–228.

Luenberger, D. G. (1969). *Optimization by Vector Space Methods*. New York: John Wiley & Sons.

Luenberger, D. G. (1973). *Introduction to Linear and Nonlinear Programming*. Reading, MA: Addison-Wesley.

Luenberger, D. G. (1979). *Dynamic Systems*. New York: John Wiley & Sons.

Luenberger, D. G. (1993). "A preference foundation for log mean-variance criteria in portfolio choice problems." *Journal of Economic Dynamics and Control* 17:887–906.

Luenberger, D. G. (1998). *Investment Science*. Oxford, UK: Oxford University Press.

Luenberger, D. G. (2001). "Projection pricing." *Journal of Optimization and Applications* 109(1):1–25.

Maalej, H., and Prigent, J.-L. (2016). "On the stochastic dominance of portfolio insurance strategies." *Journal of Mathematical Finance* 6:14–27.

Maillard, S., Roncalli, T., and Teiletche, J. (2010). "The properties of equally weighted risk contribution portfolios." *Journal of Portfolio Management* 36(4):60–70.

Marglin, S. A. (1969). "Information in price and command systems of planning," in J. Margolis and H. Guitton (eds.), *Public Economics*. London: Macmillan.

Markowitz, H. M. (1952). "Portfolio selection." *Journal of Finance* 7(1):77–91.

Markowitz, H., and Usmen, N. (2003). "Resampled frontiers versus diffuse Bayes: an experiment." *Journal of Investment Management* 1(4):9–25.

Merton, R. C. (1969). "Lifetime portfolio selection under uncertainty: the continuous-time case." *Review of Economics and Statistics* 51(3):247–57.

Merton, R. C. (1971a). "Optimum consumption and portfolio rules in a continuous time model." *Journal of Economic Theory* 3:373–413.

Merton, R. C. (1971b). "An analytic derivation of the efficient portfolio frontier." *Journal of Financial and Quantitative Analysis* 7(4):1851–72.

Merton, R. C. (1973a). "The theory of rational option pricing." *Bell Journal of Economics and Management Science* 4(1):141–83.

Merton, R. C. (1973b). "An intertemporal capital pricing model." *Econometrica* 41(5):867–87.

Merton, R. C. (1980). "On estimating the expected return on the market: an exploratory investigation." *Journal of Financial Economics* 8:1–39.

Merton, R. C. (1990). *Continuous-Time Finance*. Hoboken, NJ: Basil Blackwell.

Meucci, A. (2011). "Robust Bayesian allocation." https://ssrn.com/abstract =681553.

Michaud, R. O. (1989). "The Markowitz optimization enigma: is optimized optimal?" *Financial Analysts Journal* 45:31–42.

Michaud, R. O. (1998). *Efficient Asset Management: A Practical Guide to Stock Portfolio Optimization and Asset Allocation*. Boston: Harvard Business School Press.

Modigliani, F., and Sutch, R. (1966). "Innovations in interest rates policy." *American Economic Review* 56(1–2):178–97.

Mossin, J. (1966). "Equilibrium in a capital asset market." *Econometrica* 34(4):768–83.

Perold, A. F. (1986). "Constant proportion portfolio insurance." Unpublished manuscript, Harvard Business School, Boston.

Perold, A. F., and Sharpe, W. F. (1995). "Dynamic asset allocation strategies." *Financial Analysts Journal* 51(1):149–60.

Phillips, P. C. B. (1986). "Understanding spurious regressions in econometrics." *Journal of Econometrics* 33(3):311–40.

Phillips, P. C. B. (2001). "Bootstrapping spurious regressions," Cowles Foundation Discussion Paper No. 1330, Yale University, New Haven.

Qian, Edward E. (2005). "On the financial interpretation of risk contribution: Risk budgets do add up." https://ssrn.com/abstract=684221 or http://dx .doi.org/10.2139/ssrn.684221.

Roll, R. (1977). "A critique of the asset pricing theory's tests, Part I: On past and potential testability of the theory." *Journal of Financial Economics* 4(2):129–76.

Roncalli, T. (2014). *Introduction to Risk Parity and Risk Budgeting.* London: Chapman & Hall.

Ross, S. A. (1976). "The arbitrage theory of capital asset pricing." *Journal of Economic Theory* 13:341–60.

Rubinstein, M. (1984). "A simple formula for the expected rate of return of an option over a finite holding period." *The Journal of Finance* 39(5):1503–1509.

Rudin, W. (1976). *Principles of Mathematical Analysis*, 3rd ed. New York: McGraw-Hill.

Rudin, W. (1987). *Real and Complex Analysis*, 3rd ed. New York: McGraw-Hill.

Rudin, W. (1991). *Functional Analysis*, 2nd ed. New York: McGraw-Hill.

Scaillet, O. (2004). Nonparametric estimation and sensitivity analysis of expected shortfall. *Mathematical Finance* 14(1):115–129.

Schafer, J., and Strimmer, K. (2005). "A shrinkage approach to large-scale covariance matrix estimation and implications for functional genomics." *Statistical Applications in Genetics and Molecular Biology* 4(1).

Scherer, B. (2002). "Portfolio resampling: review and critique." *Financial Analysts Journal* 58(6):98–109.

Scherer, B. (2007). "Can robust portfolio optimisation help to build better portfolios?" *Journal of Asset Management* 7(6):374–87.

Scherer, B., and Martin, R. D. (2005). *Introduction to Modern Portfolio Optimization with NUOPT and SPLUS*, New York: Springer.

Schondorf, E. (2019). "The Wiener process and Donsker's invariance principle." Unpublished paper, Department of Mathematics, University of Chicago.

Sharpe, W. F. (1963). "A simplified model for portfolio analysis." *Management Science* 9(2):277–293.

Sharpe, W. F. (1964). "Capital asset prices: a theory of market equilibrium under conditions of risk." *Journal of Finance* 19(3):425–42

Sherman J., and Morrison, W. J. (1950). "Adjustment of an inverse matrix corresponding to a change in one element of a given matrix." *Annals of Mathematical Statistics* 21(1):124–7.

Shreve, S. E. (2004). *Stochastic Calculus for Finance II: Continuous-Time Models.* New York: Springer.

Simonian, J., and Davis, J. (2011). "Incorporating uncertainty into the Black–Litterman portfolio selection model." *Applied Economics Letters* 18(17):1719–22.

Solow, R. M. (1956). "A contribution to the theory of growth." *Quarterly Journal of Economics* 70(1):165–94.

Stein, C. (1956). "Inadmissibility of the usual estimator for the mean of multivariate normal distribution," in J. Neyman (ed.), *Proceedings of the Third Berkeley Symposium on Mathematical Statistics and Probability.* Berkeley and Los Angeles: University of California Press, Volume 1, pp. 197–206.

Swan, T. W. (1956). "Economic growth and capital accumulation." *Economic Record* 32(2):334–61.

Theil, H. (1971). *Principles of Econometrics.* New York: John Wiley & Sons.

Thorp, E. O. (1971). "Portfolio choice and the Kelly criterion," in *Proceedings of the American Statistical Association.* Alexandria, VA: ASA, pp. 215–24.

Tütüncü, R. H., and Koenig, M. (2004). "Robust asset allocation." *Annals of Operations Research* 132:132–57.

van Binsbergen, J. H., and Brandt, M. W. (2016). "Optimal Asset Allocation in Asset Liability Management," Veronesi, P. (ed.), in *Handbook of Fixed-Income Securities.* Hoboken, NJ: John Wiley & Sons.

van den Bremer, T., van der Ploeg, F., and Wills, S. (2016). "The elephant in the ground: managing oil and sovereign wealth." *European Economic Review* 82:113.

von Neumann, J., and Morgenstern, O. (1944). *Theory of Games and Economic Behavior.* Princeton, NJ: Princeton University Press.

Walters, J. (2013). "The factor tau in the Black-Litterman model," SSRN: https://ssrn.com/abstract=1701467 or http://dx.doi.org/10.2139/ssrn.1701467.

Wilmott, P. (2006). *Paul Wilmott on Quantitative Finance,* Vols. 1 and 3. Hoboken, NJ: John Wiley & Sons.

Yaari, M. (1965). "Uncertain lifetime, life insurance, and the theory of the consumer." *Review of Economic Studies* 32(2):137–50.

Zagst, R., and Kraus, J. (2011). "Stochastic dominance of portfolio insurance strategies: OBPI versus CPPI." *Annals of Operations Research* 185:75–103.

Zhu, S., and Fukushima, M. (2009). "Worst-case conditional value-at-risk with application to robust portfolio management." *Operations Research* 57(5):1155–1168.

Ziemba, W. T. (2015). "Response to Paul A. Samuelson letters and papers on the Kelly capital growth investment strategy." *Journal of Portfolio Management* 41(1):153–67.

Ziemba, R. E. S., and Ziemba, W. T. (2007). *Scenarios for Risk Management and Global Investment Strategies.* Hoboken, NJ: John Wiley & Sons.

Index

About the Authors

Jamil Baz is a managing director at PIMCO. Prior to that, he was a senior managing director and chief investment strategist of the Man Group. Previously, he was a managing director in macro proprietary trading at Goldman Sachs in London and global chief investment strategist at Deutsche Bank. Earlier in his career, he was a managing director at Lehman Brothers and worked in derivatives and liability management at the World Bank. He holds an AM and a PhD from Harvard University, an SM degree from the MIT Sloan School of Management and a master's degree from the London School of Economics. He has taught mathematical finance at Oxford University for 20 years.

Helen Guo is an executive vice president at PIMCO, specializing in research and modeling to provide customized solutions to clients on asset allocation and risk management. She is a member of the Research Committee of the Institute for Quantitative Research in Finance (Q Group). She holds a PhD in economics and a master's degree in statistics from Stanford University.

Erol Hakanoglu is a senior advisor at PIMCO. He is managing partner of Hakanoglu Quantitative Strategies LLC, an analytic advisory firm he founded. Previously, he was at Goldman Sachs for 22 years where he was a managing director and global head of capital markets strategies, and later at Lehman Brothers and Barclays as a managing director and global head of enterprise risk management. He is a member of the steering committee of the financial engineering program of the University of California Berkeley's Haas Business School and has been a guest lecturer at Harvard, Columbia, and Berkeley. Dr. Hakanoglu holds a PhD and a master's degree from Harvard University and an undergraduate degree from Columbia University.